THE ECONOMICS OF CONSERVING WILDLIFE AND NATURAL AREAS

The Economics of Conserving Wildlife and Natural Areas

Clem Tisdell

Professor of Economics, School of Economics, University of Queensland, Australia

Edward Elgar

Cheltenham, UK • Northampton, MA, USA

Published by
Edward Elgar Publishing Limited
Glensanda House
Montpellier Parade
Cheltenham
Glos GL50 1UA
UK

Edward Elgar Publishing, Inc.
136 West Street
Suite 202
Northampton
Massachusetts 01060
USA

A catalogue record for this book
is available from the British Library

Library of Congress Cataloguing in Publication Data
Tisdell, C. A. (Clement Allan)
The economics of conserving wildlife and natural areas / Clem Tisdell.
p. cm.
Includes bibliographical references.
1. Wildlife conservation—Economic aspects. 2. Natural areas—Economic aspects. I. Title.

QL82 .T57 2002
333.95'16—dc21 200202367

ISBN 1 84064 811 2

Printed and bound in Great Britain by Biddles Ltd, *www.biddles.co.uk*

Contents

Preface

The economics of conserving, using and managing wildlife and natural areas is a fascinating area of ecological economics. Given increasing threats to the maintenance of biodiversity globally and changing human values, the practical importance of the subject has grown. It is becoming more widely accepted that the interaction of humans with nature needs to be sustainable because nature conservation is essential to the maintenance of human welfare, and that humankind has a moral obligation to care for nature. Many believe that humankind's duty of care to conserve or steward nature should not be just passive but ought to be proactive.

In any case, for many reasons significant interactions between the human economy and nature are unavoidable. Nevertheless, these interactions are often not clearcut. Even if one wishes to manage nature beneficially, the appropriate economic and institutional means for doing so can be uncertain and subject to controversy. The main purpose of this book is to clarify, outline and analyse economic policies and institutional arrangements designed to improve the conservation, management and use of nature by humans. I attach great importance to this subject since I have been writing and researching regularly about it for over thirty years. I was, therefore, delighted when Edward Elgar expressed an interest in publishing a collection of my essays dealing with the economics of conserving nature. The result is this volume.

While some of the essays in this volume are being published for the first time, most have been previously published. However, those published are in scattered and sometimes relatively inaccessible outlets. This book, as an integrated volume, increases the accessibility of these essays and provides a relatively comprehensive account of my approach to the economics of nature conservation. One trusts that on this occasion the value of the whole exceeds that of the sum of the individual parts. Many of the essays included in this volume have in fact been used by myself and others in teaching ecological and environmental economics. For this purpose, it is convenient to have them available as here.

Nonetheless, this collection does not include all my publications on the conservation, management and use of nature. More on this subject will be found, for instance, in the following list of relevant books:

- *Tourism Economics, the Environment and Development: Analysis and Policy*, Edward Elgar, Cheltenham, 2001.
- (with J. Wen) *Tourism and China's Development: Policies, Regional Economic Growth and Ecotourism*, World Scientific, Singapore, 2001.
- *Biodiversity, Conservation and Sustainable Development*, Edward Elgar, Cheltenham, 1999.
- *Environmental Economics*, Edward Elgar, Cheltenham, 1993.
- *Giant Clams in the Sustainable Development of the South Pacific*, Australian Centre for International Agricultural Research, Canberra, 1992.
- *Economics of Environmental Conservation*, Elsevier Science, Amsterdam, 1991.

- *Natural Resources, Growth and Development*, Praeger, New York, 1990.
- *Wild Pigs: Environmental Pest or Economic Resource?*, Pergamon Press, Sydney, 1982.

My research and publishing in this area also continues.

Some of the essays in this collection have been jointly written and I thank my co-authors for their contribution and for shared endeavours. So, thanks to Ranjith Bandara, James Broadus, Ray Byron, Ananda Ghose, Andreas Hohl, Yoshihiro Kuronuma, Zhuge Ren, Kartik Roy and Dradjad Wibowo for shared efforts that have enhanced this volume.

I am grateful to Alison Mohr and Genevieve Larsen for secretarial assistance in finalising material for this book, and to Alexandra Minton and others at Edward Elgar Publishing for bringing it to fruition, as well as the School of Economics at The University of Queensland for institutional support. Finally, but not least, I thank my wife, Mariel, for her support and appreciation of the importance of nature conservation. All of the essays in this volume have been written during our married life.

Clem Tisdell
Brisbane

Acknowledgements

Most of the articles/contributions in this book have been previously published. Unless otherwise stated, I am the sole author. I am grateful to the appropriate editors and/or publishers for permission to reproduce articles or material, as specified below.

Clem Tisdell

2. 'World conservation strategy, economic policies and sustainable resource-use in developing countries', *The Environmental Professional*, **7**(2), 1985, pp. 102–7. Reprinted with permission of the Editor.
3. 'Economics and the debate about preservation of species, crop varieties and genetic diversity', *Ecological Economics*, **2**, 1990, pp. 77–90. Reprinted with permission of Elsevier Science.
4. Andreas Hohl and Clement A. Tisdell, 'How useful are environmental safety standards in economics? – The example of safe minimum standards for protection of species', *Biodiversity and Conservation*, **2**, 1993, pp. 168–81, copyright 1993 Chapman & Hall. With kind permission from Kluwer Academic Publishers.
5. 'Keynote address: Does the economic use of wildlife favour conservation and sustainability?', in G. Grigg, P. Hale and D. Lunney (eds), 1995, *Conservation Through Sustainable Use of Wildlife*, Centre for Conservation Biology, The University of Queensland, pp. 86–91. Reprinted with permission of the Director, Centre for Conservation Biology, The University of Queensland.
6. 'Combining biological conservation, sustainability and economic growth: can we overcome potential conflict?', in D. Gladman, D. Mowbray and J. Duguman (eds), 1996, *From Rio to Rai: Environment and Development in Papua New Guinea*. Papers from the 20th Waigani Seminar (Vol. 6), University of Papua New Guinea. Reprinted with permission of the University of Papua New Guinea Press.
7. 'Issues in biodiversity conservation including the role of local communities', *Environmental Conservation*, **22**(3), Autumn 1995, pp. 216–22, 228, copyright 1995 The Foundation for Environmental Conservation. Reprinted with permission of Cambridge University Press.
8. 'The economic conservation and utilisation of wildlife species', *The South African Journal of Economics*, **40**(3), 1972, pp. 235–48. Reprinted with permission of the Managing Editor.
9. 'Kangaroos as an economic resource', *Economic Activity*, **16**(4), 1973, pp. 32–6. Reprinted with permission of The University of Western Australia.
10. 'Kangaroos: the economic management of a common-property resource involving interdependence of production', *Economic Analysis and Policy*, **4**(2), 1973, pp. 59–75. Reprinted with permission of the Editor.
11. 'On population effects, wildlife and the management of kangaroos', *Economic Analysis and Policy*, **5**(2), 1974, pp. 8–11. Reprinted with permission of the Editor.

12. 'Wildlife: a national asset or pest to be managed?', in Department of Science and the Environment, *Environmental Economics*, Australian Government Publishing Service, Canberra, 1979, pp. 79–87. Commonwealth of Australia copyright, reproduced with permission.
13. 'Conflicts about living marine resources in Southeast Asian and Australian waters: turtles and dugong as cases', *Marine Resource Economics*, **3**(1), 1986, pp. 89–109. Reprinted with permission of the Editor.
14. Yoshihiro Kuronuma and Clement A. Tisdell, 'Institutional management of an international mixed good: the IWC and socially optimal whale harvests', *Marine Policy*, **17**(3), 1993, pp. 235–50. Reprinted with permission of Elsevier Science.
15. Yoshihiro Kuronuma and Clement A. Tisdell, 'Economics of Antarctic minke whale catches: sustainability and welfare considerations', *Marine Resource Economics*, **9**, 1994, pp. 141–58. Reprinted with permission of the Editor.
16. 'Optimal Australian dugong populations and conservation plans: an economic perspective', *Economic Analysis and Policy*, **29**(1), March 1999, pp. 59–69. Reprinted with permission of the Editor.
18. 'Provision of parks and the preservation of nature – some economic factors', *Australian Economic Papers*, **11**(19), 1972, pp. 154–62, copyright 1972 by Clem Tisdell. Reprinted with permission of Blackwell Publishers Ltd.
19. 'Economics of wilderness', in R.W. Robertson, P. Helman and A. Davey, *Wilderness Management in Australia*, Department of Natural Resources, Canberra College of Advanced Education, Belconnen, 1980, pp. 131–49. Reprinted with permission of The University of Canberra.
20. 'The provision of wilderness by clubs', *Revista Internazionale di Scienze Economiche e Commerciali* (*International Review of Economics and Business*), **31**(8), 1984, pp. 758–61. Reprinted with permission of the Editor.
21. Clem Tisdell and James M. Broadus, 'Policy issues related to the establishment and management of marine reserves', *Coastal Management*, **17**, 1989, pp. 37–53. Reprinted with permission of the Editor-in-Chief.
22. Dradjad H. Wibowo, Clement A. Tisdell and R. Neil Byron, 'Deforestation and capital accumulation: lessons from the Kerinci-Seblat National Park, Indonesia', *Asia Pacific Journal on Environment and Development*, **4**(1), June 1997, pp. 11–28. Reprinted with permission of the Editor.
23. Zhuge Ren and Clem Tisdell, 'Community-based forestry in Yunnan: dictates of environment and socio-economics', in C.A. Tisdell and J.C.H. Chai (eds), *China's Economic Growth and Transition: Macroeconomic, Environmental and Social/Regional Dimensions*, Nova Science Publishers, New York, 1997, pp. 333–54. Reprinted with permission of Nova Science Publishers.

PART I

AN OVERVIEW

[1]

Economics of conserving wildlife and natural areas: topics and issues

Introduction

The economics of conserving, using and managing nature is an extensive field in ecological economics. This is so even when the discussion is confined to wildlife and natural areas, as is mainly the case in this book. Furthermore, the in-depth consideration of the conservation of nature, its use and management requires an interdisciplinary approach. Reliance in this field solely on knowledge of economics is usually unsatisfactory. While economics and ecology are often both relevant, contributions from disciplines such as philosophy, sociology, political science and geography must also be considered when addressing many problems.

The importance of the economics of conserving nature has grown in recent decades. This reflects growing concern about the continuing loss of biodiversity worldwide, strengthening support for sustainable development as an ideal, and the spreading conviction that humankind has a moral responsibility to care for nature. To some extent, this care is needed to promote human benefit but many believe that care of nature is required for intrinsic reasons.

The intrinsic view is that individuals have a moral responsibility to conserve nature independently of their own utilitarian benefits or its benefits to humankind (cf. Tacconi, 2000, Ch.3; Sagoff, 1988, 1994). However, the strength of this 'moral imperative' varies with individuals. Some individuals believe that humankind should be prepared to make considerable sacrifice, if required, for that end, whereas others consider human interest to be paramount and support little sacrifice for nature conservation *per se*.

Human motives, reflecting underlying values, for wanting to conserve nature usually vary amongst members of a population, and their distribution is likely to alter historically (cf. Passmore, 1974). It is doubtful whether utilitarian approaches to social decision-making, even when bolstered to allow for subjectivism in the way pioneered by Lionel Robbins (1952), can do full justice to the diversity of current values relating to nature conservation. This implies that most economic policy prescriptions are based on a partial set of social values. This does not mean that they are of no practical use but it does imply, as Pigou (1932) emphasised, that care is required before policies based on 'economic' welfare are implemented. It is necessary to assess these policies in relation to wider sets of values. Indeed, we cannot ignore the possibility that some of these wider values will at least, on occasion, be in serious conflict with economic values.

In this context, it might be observed that even the concept of total economic value (see Turner et al., 1994) of a species, or of a natural area, does not necessarily represent total value nor allow completely (and sometimes not appropriately) for the diversity of societal values about nature conservation (cf. Tisdell and Wen, 1997). This is so even though the concept makes particular allowance for the type of subjective values championed by Robbins (1952) and for collective goods. Hence, one must be especially careful when using such concepts for policy purposes. This is so apart from the empirical difficulty of accurately estimating total economic values.

Usually economic approaches to policy-making are partial and reductionist even when they are based on economy-wide models. This partly reflects our bounded rationality. While such an approach can yield useful and useable results, one must also remain firmly aware of its possible limitations, especially in relation to policies involving nature conservation. The essays in this book all need to be assessed in this light.

The essays in this book span a period of thirty years. The first was published in 1972 and two were written in 2001 to round out this volume.

The stimulus to begin research on the subject matter of this book actually came from the late Professor Trevor Swan. He had been joint supervisor of my Ph.D. thesis at The Australian National University. My thesis dealt with the theory of price uncertainty, production and profit and was subsequently published by Princeton University Press (Tisdell, 1968). Following completion of this thesis, I wrote several journal articles elaborating on themes in this thesis. Trevor Swan saw one of these articles and telephoned me in 1971 to say that it was a good article but why don't you do something different.

Being already interested in nature and nature conservation, I decided to do something that seemed very different at the time. I began researching on the economics of national parks, on the economics of wildlife conservation and utilisation and also decided to consider kangaroos as a case study. I was so surprised when two academic journals accepted my first article on this subject. (I made the mistake of offering it to two journals simultaneously, a mistake that I did not repeat subsequently.) I accepted publication in the journal that first responded (*Australian Economic Papers*) and offered to write another article on a different conservation topic for the *South African Journal of Economics*, which was subsequently accepted. These are included as Chapters 18 and 8 respectively in this volume. So, in an indirect way, this volume owes its existence to Trevor Swan. I remain grateful for his timely advice that convinced me to embark on research into the economics of nature conservation.

The material in this book is organized in four parts. Part I (this part) provides a general overview of the topics and issues covered in this book. Part II deals with general issues involved in biological conservation, especially biodiversity loss. Part III concentrates on policies for the conservation, use and management of wildlife species, particularly animals. In this part, general issues involving open-access or common-property are given attention and the management of particular species such as kangaroos, whales, dugong and Asian elephants are given specific consideration. Part IV covers economic aspects of protected areas, the economics of wilderness preservation, the utilisation and management of marine reserves, economic processes involved in deforestation in a national park in Indonesia, and aspects of forest management in China and India.

Hence, a wide range of points in the broad spectrum of the economics of conservation are visited in this book, although naturally not all possible topics are covered. Several of these essays should be seen in their historical context. Empirical data relates to the time of their writing, and are not updated. However, this is not really a problem since the main purpose of all the essays is to illustrate general principles and, as far as is possible, to fathom the fundamental nature of the economic phenomenon involved in biological conservation. Allowance ought also to be made for the fact that ecological economics has evolved during the period in which these articles were written, and hopefully also my knowledge has expanded. Nevertheless, I still believe that there are important messages, even in the earliest of these essays, otherwise I would not have spent the time preparing this collection.

Now consider more specifically the topics covered in each of the other parts.

An overview of Part II: general issues in biological conservation

All chapters in this part are concerned with general features of economics of biological conservation. Chapter 2 outlines the priorities for environmental conservation set out in the World Conservation Strategy and discusses the prospects and obstacles to implementation of this strategy in developing countries. Developing countries contain the lion's share of the world's remaining biodiversity. Although the World Conservation Strategy was drawn up in 1980 and has been revised and extended since then, it remains an early pivotal document in the sustainability literature. Its purpose was to suggest guidelines to reconcile biological conservation and economic development with the goal in mind of achieving sustainable development.

Chapter 3 outlines and discusses criteria or priorities that have been suggested for conserving species. Given the impossibility of saving all species from extinction, the choice of such a criterion takes on special significance. The nature and performance of a variety of criteria are considered. These include those implicit in the World Conservation Strategy (IUCN, 1980), application of cost–benefit analysis, safe minimum standard approaches based on minimising loss and on minimising regret, and a compromise criterion suggested by Randall (1986), combining aspects of cost–benefit analysis and a safe-minimum standard. The situation is shown to be complex and uncertain. It is concluded that humankind is in a weak position to decide rationally what species and varieties of living things to save from extinction and those to permit to become extinct. It is also suggested that the burden of proof should be shifted from conservationists to those engaging in activities that are likely to result in the extinction of species.

Although sympathetic to the intent of the safe minimum standard rule, Chapter 3 finds that it has some serious limitations. These difficulties are compounded when it is realised, as is specified in Chapter 4, that there may be no standard that ensures the survival of any species. The best we can usually do is to choose between different standards that give differing probabilities of survival, all of which fall short of certain survival. Once again, a strong case exists for reversal of the burden of proof in relation to developments threatening the continued existence of species.

Nevertheless, despite all the difficulties noted, the safe minimum standard criterion may still have some scope for application, especially if a distinction is made between the biological safe minimum standard and the social or institutional safe minimum standard. Ciriacy-Wantrup (1968) does in fact make such a distinction, and greater scope may exist for applying a social or institutional safe minimum standard in relation to nature conservation than the biological safe minimum standard (see Seidl and Tisdell, 2001; Tisdell and Wilson, 2002).

Whether private farming and the commercial use of wildlife favours conservation of biodiversity is examined in Chapter 5, and there is further discussion of the conservation consequences of farming in Chapter 13. The general tendency of commercialisation is found to be one of reducing biodiversity. While commercialisation and farming may save some species from extinction, farmed species are likely to evolve by human selection to a stage where they have limited resemblance to their wild relatives or former wild relatives.

It is widely believed to be desirable to combine biological conservation and economic growth and achieve sustainable development. Is this goal likely to be achieved and are structural adjustment policies, as advocated by several international economic institutions, likely to be favourable to this result? How relevant is the Environmental Kuznets' Curve (EKC) to this debate when loss of biodiversity as a result of economic growth is taken into account? These issues are taken up in Chapter 6 that is comprised of an essay that appeared as a working paper in 1993 and then subsequently in the proceedings of the 20th Waigani Seminar published in 1996.

In this chapter, it is argued that the EKC has little relevance to the relationship between biodiversity loss and economic growth mainly because biodiversity loss is cumulative and irreversible. This is a problem apart from the serious limitations of EKC-analysis as, for example, highlighted in Tisdell (2001). In addition, considering the world as a whole, empirical evidence supports the view that cumulative human-induced biodiversity loss is positively associated with economic growth. Note that this result is even compatible with an EKC for species loss of the 'normal' shape.

It seems that the rate of human-induced elimination of species in a region at first rises with economic growth and with continuing economic growth, peaks and then declines. Probably the EKC-type curve in this biodiversity-loss case is typically bell-shaped. Consequently, the cumulative level of the number of extinctions of species in a region may be typically S-shaped or logistic as a function of its economic growth, when a long period of time is considered.

Even if the bell-shaped rate of extinction relationship holds, it would not be grounds for complacency. Since many of the less developed countries of the world have either not shown significant economic growth or have only recently embarked on this path, their economic growth has the potential to cause high levels of biodiversity loss. This is especially so because most are situated in regions with a relatively high abundance of biodiversity, for example in tropical areas. It is still possible for the rate of human-induced extinctions to rise globally as economic growth becomes more widespread. Furthermore, even if the rate of biodiversity loss declines in more developed countries, critical losses (or losses avoidable at small cost) may still occur in these. For those who want to conserve biodiversity, there are thus no grounds for complacency on the basis of the EKC.

It is hypothesized that those countries embarking on a high rate of economic growth commencing from a relatively low level of per capita income, will experience especially high rates of species loss. In modern times, there is a high risk of this in China, for example, and special effort (possibly involving international contributions) is needed to avert extraordinary biodiversity loss in such cases.

The prime focus in Chapter 7 is on the role of local communities in conserving biodiversity. Types of institutional measures and economic incentives, which might be provided to encourage biodiversity conservation at the local level, are outlined. Difficulties and potentialities are illustrated by a case study from China. In relation to conservation planning and implementation, it is suggested that neither a top-down nor a bottom-up approach is likely to be ideal. Side-by-side approaches are likely to prove more effective.

This chapter also suggests that some earlier discussions of biodiversity by economists do not deal with the conservation of biodiversity *per se* but rather with the conservation of particular species or protected ecosystems. Thus, they fail to come to grips with the essence of biodiversity. Furthermore, some criteria considered to be favourable to the conservation of biodiversity, such as the safe minimum standard criterion, have only been considered (in most cases) for application to individual species or single environments. When they are applied to a whole set of species or environments and subjected to constraints on resource-availability, they may be viewed differently. The economics of conserving biodiversity needs to be addressed more directly in economics by concentrating on diversity itself. Doubts are also expressed in this chapter about some ecological propositions, at least bland statements of these. For instance, despite contrary claims, greater biodiversity is not always associated with greater stability or sustainability of ecological systems. While conservation of biodiversity seems to be virtuous, care should be taken not to base claims for this virtuosity on faulty hypotheses.

Coverage of Part III: economics of conserving wildlife species

Part III is concerned with economic issues involved in conserving, and for the most part using, individual species of wildlife. While the first of these chapters concentrates on the analysis of the efficient utilisation and conservation of wildlife for the production of private goods, even the earliest specifically recognises that wildlife usually supplies mixed products, some of which cannot be marketed. As this part unfolds, the analysis increasingly concentrates on wildlife as a source of mixed economic goods. In this part, account is also taken of the interdependence of wildlife availability with various forms of economic activity, for example farming. Wildlife may be a pest from the point of view of some economic activities or in some cases, a complementary relationship may be present. Note that although several chapters in this part concentrate on specific wild animals, all illustrate or raise general principles. Consider the particular chapters.

Chapter 8 begins with the observation that it is uneconomic to create effective individual property rights in many wildlife species and that therefore there may be no alternative to their remaining common property. Applying and extending earlier theories, such as that outlined by H. Scott Gordon (1954) for open-access fisheries, various economic efficiency failures from open-access are identified and illustrated. These economic failures include (1) the allocation of an economically excessive amount of resources to harvesting the open-access resource taking into account the marginal value of these resources if used elsewhere in the economy; (2) economically inefficient concentration of harvesting effort on those areas giving highest harvest yields; (3) failure to take account of user costs of harvesting and to undertake investments and actions able to enhance future returns profitably; and (4) perverse consequences from market signals – the possibility that rising prices for the produce of a species will drive an open-access species to extinction rather than foster its conservation.

Various policy measures such as taxes on the catch, quotas on supply of the harvested product and prohibitions are discussed as alternatives to open-access. It is argued that taxation approaches (and this also applies to pricing solutions involving tradeable quotas, see Tisdell, 1998a, b) are not always practical and economic because of enforcement difficulties and costs. These problems may be more acute in developing countries and restrict their range of policy options compared to more developed countries. Problems of ensuring optimal wildlife conservation actions on private land are also raised. The importance is stressed of recognising that normally the economic value of a species does not depend solely on the market value of the physical goods yielded by it but also on the value of the various intangibles produced by it. Where wildlife does produce private goods but is also a mixed good, managing it as a private good will usually be socially suboptimal. Nevertheless, its effective management as a private commodity *may be* more favourable to its conservation than open-access.

Chapter 9 outlines the general status of kangaroo species and sketches policies for their management in Australia in the 1970s. The failure of these policies to maximise the total economic value of land use is noted. This failure partly arises because kangaroos remain Crown or state property and no property rights are granted to landowners. Yet the land use patterns adopted by landholders influence the population levels of kangaroos. Institutional failures in kangaroo management are shown to occur both for species harvested for commercial use value and for those species having no such value but possessing non-use value.

Chapter 10 provides more specific analysis of the issues raised in Chapter 9 and pays particular attention to the economic management of a common-property resource involving interdependence in production. In particular, attention is given to several alternative possible production relationships between domestic livestock and kangaroos. Similar types of interdependent production relationships probably exist for other species of wildlife. The implications of the analysis for kangaroo management policies adopted by the various Australian states are outlined.

Waugh and Calvo (1974), as a response to Tisdell (1973; reprinted as Chapter 10 in this book), claim that it is generally preferable to regulate the commercial exploitation of wildlife species, including kangaroos, by controlling hunting and harvesting effort rather than by placing limits (quotas) on the maximum allowable catch. In Chapter 10, it is argued that restrictions on harvesting effort are not necessarily superior to restrictions on total allowable catch as a regulatory policy. Nevertheless, it is true that regulation of effort is sometimes the best available policy, for example where catch cannot be easily inspected, as is pointed out in Chapter 8. In the Pacific, most small Pacific island nations do not have the capacity to monitor the catch of tuna in their exclusive economic zones by distant water fishing (DWF) nations, such as Japan and Taiwan. However, with assistance from their large neighbours, such as Australia, small Pacific island nations do have some capacity to police the presence of DWF vessels in their exclusive economic zones and to monitor the catch capacity of these vessels. They may, therefore, be able to control the capacity of DWF nations to catch tuna in their exclusive economic zones. In turn, Pacific island nations could link their required royalty payments to this capacity, as Indonesia has done. Clearly, the best available regulatory policy for a commercially exploited wildlife species will vary with a nation's monitoring, enforcement and other transaction costs. These vary with factors such as geographical conditions, the policing and enforcement capacity of the nation involved and its level of economic development.

The values associated with many wildlife species are varied. Some species are perceived by some individuals or groups as pests whereas others see the same species as assets, or individuals or groups vary their valuation according to circumstances, such as the population level of a species. Chapter 12 takes up several issues associated with this theme. Commencing from some observations about the control of wildlife considered to be a pest, it then examines the socially optimal population of wildlife species. Taking kangaroos as an example, it assumes that different groups in society have different and, at least to some extent, conflicting valuations. The Kaldor–Hicks criterion is applied in this case to yield a socially optimal solution. Of course, it is only a socially optimal solution within the confines of the Kaldor–Hicks criterion.

The analysis is then extended further to take account of the commercial harvesting of the wildlife species. Depending upon the circumstances, harvesting of a wildlife species may need to be restricted below the commercial social optimum to take account of valuation-externalities or, in some cases, subsidised if the wildlife species is a net pest given the commercial rate of its harvesting. The final section of this chapter explores the practical difficulties involved in subsidising or placing a bounty on the catch of wildlife when it is regarded as a net pest. Ideas in this chapter are further developed and applied in relation to the management of whales (Chapter 14), policies for the protection of dugong (Chapter 16) and the conservation of Asian elephants (Chapter 17).

In Chapter 13, attention is given to fugitive wildlife displaying transborder or transfrontier movements, and marine turtles and dugong are selected as examples. Socioeconomic problems involved in managing turtles and dugong in Australia, Southeast Asia and the South Pacific are given particular attention. Furthermore, analysis is presented about the possible impact of the farming of wildlife on wild stocks, taking the aquaculture of green turtles as an example. Depending on the circumstances, this type of farming may reduce pressures on populations of wild stocks or increase these. This analysis is further extended in Tisdell (1991, Ch.5). The role of zoning and establishment of marine parks for the conservation of wildlife is also given attention. Limitations of these measures in relation to the conservation of transfrontier fugitive wildlife are noted and consequently, the importance of obtaining international agreements for the conservation of such wildlife is stressed.

Whales are an internationally mobile form of wildlife and their economic management is the subject of Chapters 14 and 15. As stated in Chapter 14, the International Whaling Commission (IWC) was established in 1946 by nations engaging in whaling at the time in an attempt to control open-access to whale stocks. The objective of their agreement was to manage the harvesting of whales more efficiently as a private good than had previously been the case. For various reasons, the scheme proved to be a failure and several species of whales were brought to the brink of extinction. In 1982, the IWC imposed a moratorium on the harvesting of all species of whales. In part, this reflected growing emphasis globally on the non-consumptive values of whales, and the fact that many IWC members were no longer engaged in whaling because it had become unprofitable for most, due to dwindling whale stocks and the increasing availability of competitive substitutes for products derived from whales. Thus, the predominant political interest of many IWC members no longer engaged in whaling became one of supporting members of their electorate opposed to whaling, on ethical and other grounds. Chapter 14 demonstrates that the voting rules of the IWC do not result in a Kaldor–Hicks optimum harvest of whales, given that whales are a mixed good and that there are still demands from some nations, for instance, Japan and Norway, to engage in whaling for traditional dietary purposes. There may be an economic case for the limited harvesting of some species of whales, such as the minke whale. However, this case is unlikely to extend to all species of whales. Particular attention is given in Chapter 15 to the economics and sustainability of Antarctic minke whale catches and the welfare considerations involved.

Using a similar type of economic analysis to that applied in Chapter 14 (also used by Campbell et al., 1997) to determine the optimal harvest of whales, Chapter 16 examines policies to control the incidental catch of dugong in Australian waters. In addition, the optimal population of dugong from an economic point of view, namely a Kaldor–Hicks point of view, is investigated. While it is recognized that economics should not and cannot be the final arbiter in wildlife conservation decisions, it would be irrational to ignore economic considerations entirely in decisions about wildlife conservation.

Economic issues involved in conserving Asian elephants are discussed in Chapter 17. While considerable attention has been given to the economics of conserving the African elephant, comparatively little attention of a similar type has been given to the Asian elephant, even though its status seems the most perilous. This chapter helps to rectify this imbalance. General issues involved in conserving elephants are reviewed in this chapter and the Asian elephant is envisaged as a mixed good with positive and negative attributes.

Concentrating on Sri Lanka, protected areas are shown to be of insufficient size to ensure the survival of elephants in Sri Lanka, if elephants are confined to such areas. The same seems to be true throughout Asia, with the possible exception of the Nilgiri Biosphere Reserve in India. This implies that the survival of Asian elephants in virtually all countries in Asia requires elephants to use both private lands as well as protected areas. Therefore, if this species is to be saved from extinction in most countries, economic policies need to be found to encourage landholders to tolerate elephants on private land. This is likely to be true for many roaming animals requiring large territories for their survival. In many (probably most) cases, conservation efforts cannot stop at the borders of national parks if many species of wildlife are to have a reasonable chance of long-term survival.

An overview of Part IV: conservation and use of natural areas

The preservation of wildlife depends on the adequate availability of the habitat on which wildlife depends. Protected areas, such as national parks, help to conserve such habitat, but they are not the only means by which habitat may be conserved. Vegetation protection orders on private property constitute another possibility.

Nevertheless, it is argued in Chapter 18 that private initiatives can be expected to result in insufficient preservation of nature from a Kaldor-Hicks point of view due to various market failures. Furthermore, when unique natural features are made private property, monopoly-pricing of access to these is liable to occur, and supply of the facilities involved is also liable to be restricted. While government provision of protected areas and conservation of nature by the state are far from perfect (political and administrative failures do occur), exclusive private supply of nature conservation seems to be even more imperfect because of serious market failures. The article reproduced in this chapter was intended as a counterweight to Dolan's neo-liberal view that the government should get out of the business of *protecting* the wilderness (1971, p.97). It is argued here that a useful role exists for both government and private efforts in protecting wilderness and nature.

Chapter 19 discusses the concept of wilderness and outlines intangible benefits from its conservation. Also the economic nature of 'goods' provided by wilderness is examined. The ability of different institutional arrangements and property rights regimes to ensure an optimal level of conservation of wilderness is explored. It is argued that private institutional arrangements are likely to result in insufficient wilderness being conserved from a social economic viewpoint. Voluntary associations or clubs cannot adequately compensate for the absence of government involvement in the conservation of wilderness, according to the analysis presented.

Methods for estimating the demand for wilderness are discussed and policies for controlling or restricting use of wilderness areas are assessed. In conclusion, questions are raised about the type of values that it is appropriate for economists to adopt in relation to nature conservation.

Chapter 20 overlaps with Chapter 19. It was previously published to emphasise that private associations and clubs are not likely to be socially efficient protectors of wilderness. It was intended as a further counterweight to the view of neo-liberals, like Dolan (1971), that governments should get out of the business of wilderness conservation and leave wilderness conservation to private initiatives, including those of voluntary associations.

Policy issues related to the establishment and management of marine reserves are considered in Chapter 21. Issues covered include reasons for establishing marine reserves and objectives for their management, their optimal size and configuration, natural constraints on the management of marine reserves compared with land-based protected areas, the multiple use and zoning of marine reserves, and the role of natural science and social science in the management of marine reserves.

Illegal deforestation in the Kerinci-Seblat National Park, Indonesia, provides a case study outlined in Chapter 22. Deforestation in this park is found to occur mainly for the purpose of growing cinnamon trees. The investment in this deforestation is initially financed by the richer members of the community. Subsequently, successful cinnamon farmers often accumulate capital to continue this process of deforestation. In such cases, poverty does not seem to be the root cause of deforestation but rather the availability of those with capital willing and able to finance it. While this pattern of deforestation may not be universal, the important role of capital in financing various forms of deforestation should not be overlooked.

Chapter 23 also focuses on Asia, in this case on Yunnan in China. After providing geographical background on Yunnan Province, it outlines traditional practices involved in rural land use and forestry in Yunnan and considers whether community-based forestry might provide a remedy for the environmental problems of Yunnan and assist in alleviating poverty. It argues that community-based forestry can be more effective, environmentally and economically, than top-down forestation policies. For example, recent practice for establishing shelter-belt forests in Yunnan, for the protection of the Yangtze River, involve forcibly trying to prevent local people from cultivating steeplands and the mass planting of trees by a central agency. However, without decentralisation, community support and the provision of economic incentives to locals, this important shelter-belt reforestation project may fail, or be less economic and environmentally effective than a project involving community-based forestry.

While joint forest management can provide incentives to villagers to protect state forest, much depends upon the nature of the co-management involved. Chapter 24 examines this matter in relation to India and reports on field results from West Bengal. The development of the joint forest management (JFM) scheme in India is outlined and the results from the survey of household heads in three forest-dependent villages in West Bengal are reported. The survey results reported provide information about the economic dependence of the villagers on forest resources, their perceptions about the sustainability consequences of present forest practices (for instance, in relation to their livelihood and conservation of biodiversity), and their views about the adequacy of JFM.

JFM as practised in West Bengal is found to involve only partial (very incomplete) co-management of forests. The scheme performs in practice much less satisfactorily than claimed by several of its advocates, and its shortcomings are listed and analysed. Ideally ways should be sought to address these shortcomings. While the JFM scheme in India is superior to open-access to forests or their management solely by the state, scope exists to improve the operation of the scheme by taking greater account of the interest of villagers, if not of the wider community. This is so despite the present inadequacy of village-level institutional mechanisms for governing the communal use of forestland. The type of favourable local community governance envisaged by Ostrom (1990) has yet to emerge, or re-emerge.

Concluding comments

While the chapters in this book are basically arranged so that the reader progresses from the general to the particular, even those chapters with a specific focus have wider implications, as this overview indicates. Furthermore, while the coverage in this book highlights the breadth of this subject, there are many other topics that could be covered and are in need of further research. Fortunately, in the 30 years since the first of the essays in this book was written, others have contributed much to this field and the promise of ecological economics, as mentioned (and hoped for) in the final sentence of the second paragraph of this essay written in 1972 and reproduced here as Chapter 18, is being increasingly realised. Let us hope that these research endeavours will continue and that ecological economics will increasingly contribute to a better and more compassionate world.

References

Campbell, H.F., A. McIlgorm and B.M. Tsmenyi (1997), 'Fishing Management, Environmental Protection and Trade Liberalization', *International Journal of Social Economics* **24**, 128–38.

Ciriacy-Wantrup, S.V. (1968), *Resource Conservation: Economies and Policies*, 3rd edn, Division of Agricultural Sciences, Berkeley, CA: University of California Press.

Dolan, E.G. (1971), *TANSTAAFL: An Economic Strategy for Environmental Crisis*, New York: Holt, Rinehart and Winston.

Gordon, H. Scott (1954), 'The Economic Theory of a Common Property Resource: The Fishery', *Journal of Political Economy* **62**, 124–42.

IUCN (1980), *World Conservation Strategy*, IUCN, Switzerland: Glands.

Ostrom, O. (1990), *Governing the Commons: The Evolution of Institutions for Collective Action*, Cambridge: Cambridge University Press.

Passmore, J.A. (1974), *Man's Responsibility for Nature: Ecological Problems and Western Traditions*, London: Duckworth.

Pigou, A.C. (1932), *The Economics of Welfare*, 4th edn, London: Macmillan.

Randall, A. (1986), 'Human Preferences, Economics and the Preservation of Species', in B.G. Gordon (editor), *The Preservation of Species: The Value of Biological Diversity*, Princeton, NJ: Princeton University Press, pp. 79–109.

Robbins, L. (1952), *An Essay on the Nature and Significance of Economic Science*, 2nd edn, London: Macmillan.

Sagoff, M. (1988), *The Economy of the Earth*, Cambridge: Cambridge University Press.

Sagoff, M. (1994), 'Should Preferences Count?', *Land Economics* **70**, 127–44.

Seidl, I. and C.A. Tisdell (2001), 'Neglected Features of the Safe Minimum Standard: Socio-economics and Institutional Dimensions', *Review of Social Economy* **59**(4), 417–42.

Tacconi, L. (2000), *Biodiversity and Ecological Economies: Participation, Values and Resource Management*, London: Earthscan Publishing.

Tisdell, C.A. (1968), *The Theory of Price Uncertainty, Production and Profit*, Princeton, NJ: Princeton University Press.

Tisdell, C. (1973), 'Kangaroos: The Economic Management of a Common-Property Resource Involving Interdependence of Production', *Economic Analysis and Policy* **4**(2), 59–75.

Tisdell, C. (1991), *Economics of Environmental Conservation*, Amsterdam: Elsevier Science.

Tisdell, C.A. (1998a), 'Economic Policy Instruments and Environmental Sustainability: Another Look at Environmental-use Permits', *Sustainable Development* **6**(1), 18–22.

Tisdell, C.A. (1998b), 'Environmental Taxation versus Tradeable Permits: Public Finance, Accounting and Related Aspects', *Environmental Taxation and Accounting* **2**(2), 55–60.

Tisdell, C. (2001), 'Globalisation and Sustainability: Environmental Kuznets Curve and the WTO', *Ecological Economics* **39**, 185–96.

Tisdell, C. and Jie Wen (1997), 'Total Economic Valuation of Protected Areas', *Annals of Tourism Research* **24**(4), 992–94.

Tisdell, C. and C. Wilson (2002), 'Developing Ecotourism for the Survival of Sea Turtles: Social Thresholds and Conservation', *Biodiversity Conservation* (in press).

Turner, R.K., D. Pearce and I. Bateman (1994), *Environmental Economics: An Elementary Introduction*, London: Harvester Wheatsheaf.

Waugh, G. and P. Calvo (1974), 'Kangaroos: Population Effects and Management', *Economic Analysis and Policy* **5**(2), 31–7.

PART II

GENERAL ISSUES IN BIOLOGICAL CONSERVATION

WORLD CONSERVATION STRATEGY, ECONOMIC POLICIES AND SUSTAINABLE RESOURCE-USE IN DEVELOPING COUNTRIES

Clem Tisdell
University of Newcastle

ABSTRACT. The World Conservation Strategy (WCS) proposed by international bodies stems from the fear that world economic activity, growth and development may prove unsustainable because it is damaging the biosphere and decision-makers are not making adequate allowance for this. The biosphere provides ecosystems supporting all life, including human life, and damage to it, especially if permanent, can at the very least be expected to reduce economic productivity. Population growth, rising consumption levels, inadequate environmental planning and lack of forethought may be so damaging ecologically that economic growth cannot be sustained and, indeed, affluence may give way to poverty.

However, WCS claims that if basic ecological guidelines are followed sustainable economic development is possible and it points to particular measures that need to be taken in developing countries. The concept of sustainable resource-use and development is important but needs to be defined more carefully. Different types of sustainable resource-use are possible and these are discussed in this paper. It is argued that policies for sustained resource use may be of more importance to less developed countries (LDCs) than developed countries. Policies for promoting environmentally-sound use of resources are discussed together with obstacles to their implementation.

The World Conservation Strategy (WCS) was drawn up in 1980 by the International Union for the Conservation of Nature in consultation with such bodies as the United Nations Environment Programme (UNEP), the Food and Agriculture Organization, and UNESCO, and individuals throughout the world. Its preparation was jointly financed by UNEP and the World Wildlife Federation. Its framers hoped that the document would encourage individual countries to formulate National Conservation Strategies incorporating policies for sustainable development; some countries have embarked on the process of drawing up such strategies. The WCS arose from concern about the rapid and continuing deterioration of the biosphere as a result of the growing human population and the impact of its activities on the environment, especially on living resources.

The strategy is based on the view that unless proper attention is paid to conserving the biosphere and natural ecosystems within it, economic development will be unsustainable. Man depends on living resources for his survival and economic well-being and it is for this reason that serious attention must be given to the deteriorating state of the biosphere. The biosphere contains ecosystems supporting all life, including human life, and damage to it, especially if permanent, can at the very least be expected to reduce economic productivity. The WCS claims that ecological considerations are not a luxury but a necessity for sound and sustainable economic development.

Clem Tisdell is Professor of Economics and Head of the Department at The University of Newcastle, New South Wales, Australia.

Requests for reprints may be addressed to Clem Tisdell, Department of Economics, The University of Newcastle, New South Wales, 2308, Australia.

THE ENVIRONMENTAL PROFESSIONAL, Vol. 7 pp. 102-107, 1985. Printed in the USA.

0191-5398/85 $3.00 + .00

The view expressed in the WCS document is anthropocentric. Human beings need to manage, arrest or slow down the deterioration of the biosphere for their *own* benefit. While the framers of the strategy may have a reverence for all life (for all species) they believe that most human beings are swayed by their own self-interest and therefore conservation proposals need to appeal to self-interest in order to gain widespread support. Again, the framers of WCS believe that there is little point in campaigning for the utopian conservation goals which policy-makers have no leeway for adopting.

A more realistic approach to influencing policy-makers is required, namely, one which ensures that conservational aspects are taken into account in relation to the options realistically open to the policy-maker. For example, it may have to be accepted that various species and certain natural ecosystems will continue to disappear for some time yet. If this is so, conservationists should provide some guidelines on those species or ecosystems that should be given preference for preservation.

ECONOMIC GROWTH, ENVIRONMENT

WCS states that sustainable economic development requires:

- the maintenance of essential ecological processes and life support systems
- the preservation of genetic diversity
- measures to ensure the sustainable use of species and ecosystems

Agricultural systems, forests, and coastal and freshwater systems are claimed to be the most important life-support systems for human beings and to be under the greatest threat. Economic growth in less developed countries (LDCs) involving the unmitigated exploitation of these systems (such as felling of tropical forests, the removal of mangroves, the felling of forests on steep hill slopes, open-access fishing) may result only in a temporary economic improvement. The long-term economic productivity of the land and the sea may be reduced by such exploitation of nature and may result in an eventual economic and ecological crisis, especially if the country's population rises in the interim (Tisdell and Fairbairn, 1984).

The World Conservation Strategy sees *informed* self-interest as being a powerful force for conservation in LDCs as well as in more developed countries. One of the ways in which LDCs might benefit from conservation is, for instance, through tourism based on conserved natural resources. But unfortunately such tourism sometimes fails to benefit local people who are forced to make a sacrifice for nature conservation. For example, Mishra (1982) suggests that local people in Nepal have been impoverished as a result of the establishment of national parks (Tisdell, 1983).

The way in which any cost of or gains from conservation are distributed cannot be ignored. WCS points out that "local commitment to a protected area can only be assured through provision of local advantage such as increased opportunities for employment and commerce."

Poverty in LDCs

Nevertheless, LDCs may not appropriate all the benefits from their conservation efforts — many of the benefits may spill over to inhabitants of more developed countries without payment being made for them. Furthermore, poverty itself in LDCs is a substantial barrier to conservation. WCS states:

> Much habitat destruction and overexploitation of living resources by individuals, communities and nations in the developing world is a response to relative poverty, caused or exacerbated by a combination of human population growth and inequities within and among nations.... Every country should have a conscious policy to avoid as far as possible the spread of such situations, and eventually to achieve a balance between numbers and environment. At the same time it is essential that the affluent constrain their demands on resources, and preferably reduce them, shifting some of their wealth to assisting the deprived.

Changes in the world economic order such as the removal of trade barriers to goods from developing countries and great development assistance to LDCs may help to improve their economic lot and scope for conservation. Nevertheless, rapid economic transformation of most LDCs is unlikely in the near future, even assuming that widespread change in the world economic order occurs.

SUSTAINABLE RESOURCE-USE AND DEVELOPMENT

Sustainable development and resource-use are seen in the WCS as important and desirable goals. However, "sustainability" is not defined nor is the question debated of whether it is ever desirable to trade off sustainable development for other goals.

One view of sustainability is that the existence of the human race on Earth should be assured for as long as possible (Daly, 1980) and that the economic and other activities of human beings should be so regulated as to make this possible. Daly argues that this is most likely to be achieved if a policy of zero-population growth is combined with one of holding levels of consumption steady, that is, by achieving a steady state economy.

In Daly's view, consumption by those with high levels of income should be reduced. Consumption per capita should not be maximised but brought to a "satisfactory" level for all. Steps should, in his opinion, be taken to ensure greater equality of income and this is likely to require a transfer of purchasing power from more developed countries to less developed ones.

However, is a steady state economy needed to maximise the length of existence of the human race? Much depends on one's theory of what will determine or influence the length of continuing existence of *homo sapiens*. It may be that a variety of patterns of economic activity (not necessarily all steady-state ones) are compatible with maximising the length of existence of the human race but that there is also a set which will reduce its length of existence. In light of Daly's hypothesis, should a nation also attempt to maximise the possible length of its existence? If so, would steady and sustainable levels of economic activity be the optimal way to achieve this? There are certainly many unresolved issues to consider.

There may be circumstances in which it is worthwhile achieving temporary economic growth because no future income has to be sacrificed to obtain it or only a relatively small amount of future income has to be lost for a temporary economic gain. On the other hand, some economic development may be such that a substantial amount of future income has to be given up for a temporary economic gain now. WCS is correct in highlighting possible scenarios of this type. Developing countries may make economic gains now by felling their tropical forests and earning foreign exchange by exporting the products to developed countries, but this may be at the expense of a substantial reduction in the ruture economic productivity of the land involved in the future.

Sustainability: Another View

In relation to agricultural systems, Conway (1983) has defined sustainability as:

> the ability of a system to maintain productivity in spite of a major disturbance such as that caused by intensive (maintained) stresses or a large perturbation. ... Satisfactory methods of measuring sustainability have still to be found. Lack of sustainability may be indicated by declining productivity but, equally, collapse may come suddenly and without warning.

In his view, modern agricultural technologies may at first give high yields when introduced but the associated agricultural systems often prove to be unsustainable. The use of chemical pesticides such as DDT may for example lead to temporary gains, followed by lower yields as resistance builds up. Modern agricultural technologies also require a high degree of management to ensure their productivity. Traditional agricultural systems call for less intensive management and in Conway's view are more likely to be sustainable than "modern" ones. It has been observed for example that high yielding varieties of crops show less tolerance as a rule to extremes in environmental conditions than do traditional varieties, and that traditional systems of mixed cropping are often more resilient and productive than monocultures.

While sustainability may be a virtue, many economists do not consider it to be an overriding goal. Many believe that the optimal social strategy is one which maximizes net present social value. In some cases this can imply that it is optimal to extinguish a species (Clark, 1976) or allow it to become extinct. Furthermore, the optimal agricultural production system is not necessarily one that sustains production. In some cases too, it *may* be optimal to engage in agricultural practices which accelerate erosion or lead to salting of soils (Dumsday et al., 1983).

This is not to say that these practices are always justifiable from an economic point of view. Furthermore, in assessing them one must take account of various sources of "market failure" such as externalities or spillovers. For example, if the accelerated soil erosion reduces the useful life of dams due to more rapid siltation, this should be taken into account. Undoubtedly, there are many environmentally degrading activities that cannot be justified on the basis of economic calculations when interdependencies and social factors are taken into account.

The sustainable use of common-property resources in LDCs is a particular subject for concern. Common-property resources are resources that are shared in common and to which there is common access. The inhabitants of many LDCs have common access, for example, to fishing stocks in coastal waters. When there is common access to such resources, they are liable to be overexploited. The fishing stock may, for instance, be reduced below the level that gives the maximum sustainable yield (as well as below the level that gives the maximum economic yield). In some cases, as a result of common access, a species may be eliminated due to intensive harvesting even though it is economically optimal to retain the species. LDCs therefore face the problem of trying to regulate the economic exploitation of common-property resources.

Restraints in LDCs

Adverse environmental impacts of economic activity in LDCs can have more serious consequences for human welfare than in developed countries. When the adverse environmental effects of economic activity in an area reduce future productivity there, affected communities in more developed countries find it relatively easy for their members to move elsewhere to other economic opportunities. Most developed countries are characterised by a high degree of mobility of labour and capital, and considerable social homogeneity.

On the other hand, most LDCs have low mobility of labour and capital (Todaro, 1981; Gunatilleke, 1973) and considerable social heterogeneity. This means that when an environmental disaster or misfortune strikes a particular area and threatens the livelihood of local people in LDCs, they are less able to move and obtain equal or comparable economic opportunities and social satisfaction elsewhere to those previously enjoyed. Thus their income suffers and they may be thrown into extreme poverty.

A further reason why the assessment of the environmental impacts of projects is likely to be important in LDCs is that when a project has an adverse effect on income or human welfare in a locality, it can be expected that compensating relief from elsewhere in the economy will be limited. Social security systems are poorly developed in LDCs (Nugent and Gillaspy, 1983) and the scope for giving aid from intra-national sources is limited.

The inhabitants of less developed countries are much more dependent for their livelihood on living resources than those of developed countries. The bulk of the population of LDCs is typically employed in agriculture, fishing and forestry and other industries directly dependent on a living resource base (Todaro, 1981). Disturbances to the ecosystems on which these industries depend can have widespread economic consequences. This is an additional reason why any developments in LDCs giving rise to ecological effects need careful assessment.

RESOURCE-USE POLICIES

Given the importance of the environment (especially the biosphere) to economic activity and human welfare in LDCs, what policies can be adopted to ensure wise resource-use and development in LDCs? Policies can be improved in this regard but one must also remember that the putting into effect of government policies is itself not without cost. Policies have to be devised (this may involve costly research and bargaining) and implemented, and implementation can involve communication, regulation and enforcement costs which can weigh heavily on countries that are already poor.

The cost of policies must be weighed against their likely effectiveness and consequent benefits. A policy that cannot be carried out is of no benefit and indeed may involve considerable cost to the community if government administrators spend their time in devising and debating it. Difficulties, however, are not an adequate excuse for taking no action.

It is important that when public projects are evaluated in LDCs (and the same is also true of private projects that come under public scrutiny) that account is taken of their main environmental impacts. Social cost-benefit analysis should not ignore environmental impacts and ecological spillovers in the assessment of projects in LDCs. In the past, however, major public projects, such as the building of the Kariba Dam, have gone ahead without any prior ecological surveys (James, 1978).

Failure to take account of ecological factors has sometimes occurred for reasons of political expediency, at other times because of failure to realize the potential importance of such variables, and on other occasions because of lack of skilled persons able to carry out evaluation. Lack of skilled evaluators, especially in very small countries (microstates), can be a significant constraint in project evaluation; this, however, can be overcome to some extent and at a cost by drawing on the worldwide body of professionals in the field.

In foreign aid projects, it is important that environmental dimensions are kept in view. Increasingly, environmental assessments are being made of aid and related projects; for example, United States AID (Agency for International Development) is doing this and so is the World Bank. To the extent that the menu or list of available projects presented to such agencies for possible aid involves presorting by power groups in aid-receiving countries, there may already be some bias against projects that are environmentally sound but less beneficial to these power groups. Yet, it is very difficult to think of practical ways of avoiding such potential biases.

IMPORTED TECHNOLOGIES

Technologies introduced to LDCs from abroad need to be assessed carefully. While some may lead to improved socio-economic and environmental conditions, other technologies may have adverse consequences. Some of the technologies in developed countries (DCs) are inappropriate to the factor composition of LDCs and *may give only temporary (nonsustainable) benefits.*

For example, the use of chemical pesticides in some LDCs has brought a temporary increase in crop yields but has been followed in some cases by increased resistance of pests to the chemicals involved and an increase in the population of non-target pests. Users of a technology may become economically "trapped" into its continuing use even though it would have been best from a collective point of view never to have used the technology at all. This, however, is not to deny the occurrence of circumstances where enlightened use of pesticide technology is preferable to its non-use.

One can take as another example the mechanisation of the traditional fisheries (Yahaya and

Wells, 1983). The fishing stock exploited by fishermen in many parts of the world is already overfished both from the point of view of obtaining maximum sustainable yield and from the point of view of obtaining maximum economic yield. The mechanisation of fisheries initially increases the catch, and improved economic gains may be noted at first. However, it eventually leads to a reduction in the fishing stock and a decrease in the total catch if common access to the fisheries is the rule and overfishing is already occurring.

It is possible (indeed, certain, under plausible conditions) that the total catch will eventually be lower than prior to the introduction of the new technology and the cost per unit of the catch higher than before its use. Thus, in the common-access case or in cases where it is not really possible for the government to limit access and exploitation rates or resources, the introduction of new technology can, in the end, have adverse economic and environmental consequences.

In certain cases, introduction of new technology will speed up the rate of extinction of species. Both turtles and dugongs (sea cows), for example, have suffered as a result of the introduction of modern technology (Carr, 1968; Tisdell, 1983): outboard motors make it easier to pursue and capture these animals than was the case with nonmechanised boats. Also, in the case of turtles, mechanisation makes it easier to visit nesting grounds in remote areas and take eggs and adults.

Influencing Factors

Political and economic pressure exists for the introduction of modern technologies into industries harvesting natural resources to which there is common access, despite adverse long-term consequences. Those who obtain the technology first may gain substantially. If the technology is widely available, all will gain *at first*. Any group which does not have the technology may press to maintain its share in the catch or to restore it. Thus, politically, a government may support the introduction of the technology even though collectively its introduction is economically and environmentally damaging in the medium-to-long term. Furthermore, those firms and countries able to sell their technology or equipment embodying the technology have an interest in promoting its adoption. In cases such as this, expressions of individual self-interest may conflict with collective long-term interests in resource-use.

The economic and environmental desirability of introducing a new technology to an LDC often depends on whether use of the technology can be or will be regulated by the government of the LDC. The economic scope for regulating economic activity in LDCs is more limited than in DCs. Consequently technologies that prove to be desirable in DCs may turn out to be unsatisfactory in LDCs because little control over their use can be exercised in LDCs. LDCs need to be selective in their import of foreign technologies.

To the extent that regulation of resource-use in LDCs is possible and socially desirable, governments in LDCs should adopt appropriate regulatory policies. An example would be land-use zoning. Furthermore, educational programs and extension services can be employed to encourage environmentally-sound methods of production and make individuals aware of changing environmental conditions. Sometimes individuals are slow to perceive or to foresee fundamental changes in ecological and environmental conditions (Tisdell, 1983). Nevertheless, one cannot rely purely on education and communication as the means of encouraging the most socially beneficial use of resources.

CONCLUDING OBSERVATIONS

LDCs do have an interest in the conservation of living resources, at least from the point of view of maintaining production dependent on these resources. This is not to say that LDCs have an interest in conserving or maintaining all of their living resources. Sometimes they find it worthwhile to sacrifice some of these resources for short-term gains.

Again, the prime beneficiaries of nature conservation in LDCs are not always the local people but individuals in DCs and/or the wealthier members of the LDC. This has sometimes led to the view that conservational causes are those of a a "rich men's club," and that efforts to promote conservation in LDCs are a scheme primarily to benefit DCs. Nevertheless, all types of conservation in LDCs do not favour the rich nor do they benefit primarily DCs, even though some may. One's view about the desirability of any conservation scheme is liable to be influenced by the way in which its costs and benefits are distributed. Therefore, not only total benefits and costs but also distributional factors should form a part of the assessment of conservational strategies in LDCs.

REFERENCES

Carr, A. 1968. *The Turtle: A National History of Sea Turtles*. Cassell, London.

Clark, C.W. 1976. *Mathematically Bioeconomics*. John Wiley, New York.

Conway, G.R. 1983. Agroecosystem Analysis. ICCET Series E, No. 1. Imperial College, London.

Daly, H. 1980. *Economics, Ecology and Ethics*. Freeman, San Francisco.

Dumsday, R.G., Oram, D.A. and Lumley, S.E. 1983. Economic aspects of the control of dryland salinity. *Proceedings of the Royal Society of Victoria* 95(3):139-145.

Gunatilleke, G. 1973. The urban-rural balance and development: The experience of Sri Lanka. *Marga Quarterly Journal* 2(1):35-68.

James, J. 1978. Growth, technology and the environment in less developed countries: A survey. *World Development* 6:937-965.

Nugent, J.B. and Gillaspy, R.T. 1983. Old age pensions and fertility in rural areas of less developed countries: Some evidence from Mexico. *Economic and Cultural Change* 31(4):809-829.

Mishra, H.R., 1982. Balancing human needs and conservation in Nepal's Royal Chitwan National Park. *Ambio* 11(5):246-251.

Myers, N. 1979. *The Sinking Ark: A New Look at the Problem of Disappearing Species*. Pergamon Press, Oxford.

Tisdell, C.A. 1983. Conserving living resources in Third World countries: Economic and social issues. *International Journal of Environmental Studies* 22:11-24.

Tisdell, C. and Fairbairn, T.I. 1984. Subsistence economies and unsustainable development and trade: Some simple theory. *The Journal of Development Studies* 20(2):227-241.

Todaro, M.P. 1981. *Economic Development in the Third World.* 2nd ed. Longman, London.

World Conservation Strategy (WCS). 1980. The World Conservation Strategy: Living Resource Conservation for Sustainable Development. International Union for the Conservation of Nature. Glands, Switzerland.

Yahaya, J. and Wells, R.J.G. 1983. A case study of three gears in the Tregganu fishery, Malaysia. *The Developing Economies* 20(1):73-99.

[3]

Ecological Economics, 2 (1990) 77–90 77
Elsevier Science Publishers B.V., Amsterdam – Printed in The Netherlands

ECONOMICS AND THE DEBATE ABOUT PRESERVATION OF SPECIES, CROP VARIETIES AND GENETIC DIVERSITY

CLEM TISDELL
Department of Economics, University of Queensland, St Lucia, Qld. 4067 (Australia)

(Accepted 28 April 1989)

ABSTRACT

Tisdell, C., 1990. Economics and the debate about preservation of species, crop varieties and genetic diversity. *Ecol. Econ.*, 2: 77–90.

The paper reviews and outlines criteria that have been suggested for determining whether or not to save a species for extinction. Priorities as set out in the World Conservation Strategy, cost–benefit analysis, and the safe minimum standard approach are given particular consideration. The different criteria also are compared assuming that there is an absolute upper constraint on the amount of resources available for the conservation of species. There is some discussion of whether the reduction in available crop varieties is adding to or reducing the instability of crop yields. It is claimed that relative variability appears to be falling but there may be an increasing risk of non-sustainability. The importance of the burden of proof in the conservation versus non-conservation debate is stressed and it is suggested that recent economic thought has swung more towards the view that the burden of proof should rest on those seeking to carry out activities which may extinguish a species.

INTRODUCTION

That the number of species and variety of species is diminishing rapidly in the world and is likely to continue to do so with economic growth is well documented. This appears to be so for both wild species and for domesticated species with the consequence that the world is coming to rely on an ever narrowing genetic base for its biological production. This may make it increasingly difficult to maintain economic production from biological re-

This is a revised version of a paper presented at a seminar given at Lincoln College, Canterbury, New Zealand, while William Evans Visiting Professor at the University of Otago, Dunedin. I wish to thank seminar participants for their useful comments which helped my preparation for this version of the paper.

sources. Because of the smaller gene pool, it is harder to counteract a weakness such as reduced disease resistance by varieties of plants, animals and other species used for economic production. This will become increasingly so unless miraculous progress is made in genetic engineering. Even with considerable progress in genetic engineering, increasing obstacles can be expected due to lack of genetic building blocks. However, it is not only that maintenance of existing production is at risk but the scope for developing new types of biological production and commodities based on living organisms is being reduced. This being so, the maintenance or expansion of production of commodities may provide a *materialistic* economic argument in favour of conservation even given a man-centred approach.

But economists do recognize that species can have economic value for other than materialistic purposes, that is for other than the physical commodities producible from them. Provided individuals are willing to pay for preservation of a species, it has economic value. It may, for example, be a species with pure existence value and no commerical value. Nevertheless, until the 1970s almost exclusive attention was given in the economics of conservation of living organisms contributing to material production.

Not all arguments in favour of conservation are based on economics, or on an anthropocentric approach. Some would argue that man has a responsibility or a moral duty to preserve nature or other sentient beings irrespective of his own self-interest. Such views have for example been expressed by Aldo Leopold (1966) and appear to be increasingly accepted (Passmore, 1974). To the extent that individuals are willing to pay, they should be taken into account in the standard approach of welfare economics using, for example, the Kaldor–Hicks criterion.

But what if the willingness of people to pay (or to accept payment) to preserve a species is less than the cost of doing so after account is taken of all the aspects mentioned above, including whatever moral obligation individuals feel towards other species? Strictly there is no economic argument for preserving the species. Yet the matter should not necessarily rest there. We may wish to ask such questions as

(1) How well informed are individuals about the species?
(2) Are their preferences likely to change?
(3) To what extent is their valuation affected by the distribution of income, and is it 'reasonable' that it be affected in the way it is by this distribution?

Having considered all of these matters, it may still be that the argument for the preservation of a species is weak from society's point of view. However, there may still be a group strongly in favour of preserving a species and prepared to take political and direct action to foster their cause. All sources of social conflict about species preservation cannot be resolved by rational argument or debate. Nevertheless such argument can help to resolve some conflicts and specify our alternatives more precisely, thereby making for some progress.

This paper has as its main objective the critical consideration of criteria suggested by ecologists and by economists as bases for deciding whether or not to save a species or an array of species or varieties from extinction. It suggests that the safe standard approach is compatible with minimax regret as well as with minimax loss, that is, with minimising the maximum possible regret (regret being defined as benefit forgone) *minimising* the maximum possible loss (cf. Luce and Raiffa, 1957). At least this is so for payoff matrices of a nature considered to be typical. It also emphasizes the importance of applying the criteria in a trade-off or constrained resource-availability situation which means that greater attention is focused on opportunities forgone. Lastly, some observations are made about reduction in the available varieties of crops with the introduction of high-yielding varieties.

In considering criteria or priorities for preserving species, let us in turn examine: (1) the priorities suggested in the World Conservation Strategy (WCS) (IUCN, 1980); (2) Cost–Benefit Analysis (CBA) as for example, used by the Resources for the Future Group (RFF) group; (3) the Safe Minimum Standard (SMS) approach based on minimax loss, as for example suggested by Ciriacy-Wantrup (1968) and Bishop (1979); (4) the alternative of SMS based on minimax regret; (5) the implications of these criteria in a constrained resource-availability situation; and (6) the compromise criterion, between CBA and SMS, as suggested by Randall (1986).

1. PRIORITIES FOR SPECIES PRESERVATION IN THE WORLD CONSERVATION STRATEGY

One of the aims of the World Conservation Strategy is to "prevent the extinction of species and preserve as many varieties as possible of crop plants, forage plants, timber trees, livestock, animals for aquaculture, microbes, and other domesticated organisms and their wild relatives" (IUCN, 1980, section 6.4). This is seen as important for two reasons:

(1) To promote diversity of species to maintain biological stability (and presumably stability of economic production dependent on biological resources).

(2) To keep options for future possible use of species or varieties by Man open. The future value of many species and varieties is imperfectly known and surely future uses will be found that are as yet unknown. Because of this uncertainty and the likelihood that new uses of species will be discovered, it is rational to keep options open or retain flexibility even at a cost (Hart,

TABLE 1

Priorities suggested in the WCS document for conserving species

		Rare	Imminence of loss	
			Vulnerable	Endangered
Size of loss	Family	4**	2***	1***
	Genus	7*	5**	3***
	Species	9*	8*	6**

1–9, Suggested order of priority: *** top priority, ** intermediate priority, * lower priority.

1942; Tisdell, 1968, 1970). This requires us to err in favour of conserving species.

However, the WCS recognizes that varieties and species will continue to be lost, and suggests that priorities need to be drawn up to choose what species to preserve. WCS suggests that priority should be given to the species where the loss is *large* and *imminent*. Depending upon whether only a single species, a whole genus or a whole family is at stake, the size of loss is assumed to be higher. The imminence of the loss is said to depend on whether the species is rare, vulnerable or endangered. The suggested system of priorities is indicated in Table 1.

In this system of priorities, no specific account is taken of the benefits and costs of preservation of a species, but the net benefit is assumed to be greater the more unique is the species in relation to the biological classification system and the more imminent the loss (cf. Tisdell, 1983a). But can we always assume that the benefit of saving a species which is the single representative of a whole plant or animal family is greater than that of saving a species which is less unique biologically but of great economic value? Should the costs involved in the conservation strategy be ignored? Should more effort be given to conserving endangered species rather than rare ones? In the last respect, if the costs are high and probability low of saving endangered species in relation to rare ones, it could be wiser to place more emphasis on ensuring that rare species do not become endangered.

While the WCS recognizes the importance of the interdependence of species and points out that the removal of a species which forms part of the food chain may result in the loss of dependant species, allowance for this is not incorporated specifically in the priority schema as represented in Table 1. But as Randall (1986) argues, it is of fundamental importance to address the issue for it determines the scope of the debate. Randall (1986, p. 101) says:

> "The ultimate instrumentalist argument - that every life form must be preserved in order to ensure the survival of the things people do care about and ultimately, of humanity tends to deny, or at least sharply restrict, the possibility of setting priorities..."

Randall suggests that if the survival of all species depends on he survival of every single one and if the disappearance of some is inevitable, then priorities may have to be set about the *sequence* of disappearance of species on the way to the ultimate extinction of all. However, the extreme interdependence proposition is not universally accepted and indeed, may not be commonly accepted. Nevertheless, even without accepting the extreme proposition that the removal of any one species seals the fate of all, interdependence between species is an important factor to take into account in determining whether or not a species should be saved from extinction.

While WCS does point out the case for conservation on the basis of keeping options open, it is not explicitly introduced into the priority schema. In some approaches by economists to determining priorities for conserving species such as the SMS approach, uncertainty about benefits provides a major rationale for the approach taken. Let us therefore, consider the approaches adopted by economists.

2. COST–BENEFIT, NET PRESENT VALUE APPROACH

The approach most widely used by economists in evaluating projects is cost–benefit analysis based on calculations of net present values. This involves expressing as many benefits and costs in monetary terms as possible and quantifying wherever this can be achieved. The plan is adopted which maximizes the net present value of the resources used in its implementation.

Resources for the Future (RFF) has been very active in applying this approach, as reviewed by Chisholm (1988), to decisions about the preservation of species. RFF has extended "conventional criteria for optimal investment to take account of the irreversibilities associated with actions involving natural environments" (Smith and Krutilla, 1979). Nevertheless, a considerable amount of information or knowledge is assumed to exist about the payoffs from preserving species. Attempts when using CBA (cost–benefit analysis) are normally made to characterize uncertainty by probability distributions and to use expected gain or utility characteristics as a deciding factor. However, whether such precision is possible or desirable is debatable.

It is frequently uneconomic to specify a decision problem precisely because the collection, organising and processing of data involves a cost. Bounded rationality as compared to unbounded rationality may be optimal (Simon, 1957). Unbounded rationality implies that decisions are *absolutely* the best possible whereas bounded rationality implies that decisions are optimal *relative* to the extra costs and benefits of imposing the decision. Furthermore, it may be impossible, no matter how many resources are allocated to data collection, to obtain reasonable approximations to benefits from conserving a species. In this regard Randall (1986, p. 95) says:

"preservation of species problems are among those for which impediments to high-quality BCA (benefit–cost analysis) are greatest. The procedure for BCA, once the various alternative strategies have been defined, involves identifying the physical consequences of each strategy, evaluating the physical consequences economically (i.e. costs and benefits), and calculating the net present value of each strategy."

Other writers such as Ciriacy-Wantrup (1968) and Bishop (1978) argue strongly that the degree of social uncertainty and natural uncertainty about the future possible value of a species is so great that it is unwise to try to apply CBA to decision-making in this area.

3. SAFE MINIMUM STANDARD APPROACH – MINIMAX LOSS

Because Ciriacy-Wantrup (1968) and Bishop (1978) believe that CBA is likely to be largely irrelevant to decisions about species preservation because of the degree of uncertainty involved, they suggest a safety-first approach which favours the preservation of a species at a safe minimum standard (SMS), that is, its conservation under conditions sufficient to ensure its survival. This may for example, necessitate a minimum amount of habitat for the species and a minimum breeding population. Bishop (1978) suggests that in relation to species conservation, the strategy should be adopted which minimizes the maximum possible loss.

For expository purposes two alternative strategies and two possible alternative states of nature can be considered. The two alternative strategies may be (a) to permit the species to become extinct, E, or (b) to preserve it at a safe minimum level, SMS. Assume that the two possible alternative states of nature are: (a) s_1, the species will have no economic value in the future; and (b) s_2, species will have a very large economic value in the future.

The available strategies and alternative states of nature and associated payoffs can be represented by the game matrix shown in Table 2. This matrix is similar to that used by Bishop (1978) to illustrate the SMS approach. In it, Y represents the maximum possible benefit from preserving the species (expressed as the loss from not conserving it), and C indicates the cost of conserving it. If the cost of saving the species is less than the maximum possible benefit of doing so, if $C < Y$, the minimax strategy is to

TABLE 2

Bishop-type matrix

	s_1	s_2	Max loss
E	O	Y	Y
SMS	C	$C - Y$	C

adopt SMS, that is to save the species from extinction by ensuring a safe minimum standard of conservation.

Bishop (1978) and Ciriacy-Wantrup (1968) argue that since the cost of conserving a species is usually low and the possible or potential future benefits are extremely high, almost always the optimal minimax loss strategy will be SMS, to conserve the species at a safe minimum standard. One should therefore, proceed on the presumption that conservation of a species is socially optimal until this is proven otherwise. This shifts the burden of proof to the anticonservationists. This point has been commented on by Randall (1986) and I shall take it up in subsequent discussion.

Although I am sympathetic to the general view of Bishop (1978) about nature conservation, some reservations about the manner in which he presents the SMS approach using game theory are in order. This assumes that Nature is a rational maximising opponent and that Man's loss is Nature's gain. But neither of these assumptions appears reasonable.

Nature does not have 'a mind' and is not a rational opponent. Secondly, Man's loss is often not Nature's gain and vice versa. In particular, if a species becomes extinct Man may lose a benefit of Y, but does Nature gain this amount? Presumably not. To the extent that the paradigm makes sense, Nature too would seem to lose by extinction of a species.

4. SAFE MINIMUM STANDARD APPROACH – MINIMAX REGRET

Nevertheless minimax loss can be used as an extremely risk-averse strategy even if the fundamental conditions of a zero-sum game are not satisfied. Game theory has been successfully applied to the evolutionary problem (ESS). However, it might be argued that if opportunity costs are important, a minimax regret rather than a minimax loss strategy would be more appropriate. For the problem *as modelled* by Bishop (1978), the minimax regret strategy turns out to be the same as that for minimax loss.

To see this, form the gain matrix for Man shown in Table 3. This is the same as that for Table 2, except the values are multiplied by -1. From Table 3, the regret matrix shown in Table 4 can be formed.

From Table 4, it can be seen that SMS minimizes the maximum of regret that is the minimax regret strategy if $C < Y$. Both minimax loss (or maxi-

TABLE 3

Man's gain from survival of a species

	s_1	s_2	Min. Gain if Y > C
E	O	$-Y$	$-Y$
SMS	$-C$	$Y-C$	$-C$

TABLE 4

Regret matrix corresponding to Table 3

	s_1	s_2	Max. Regret
E	0	Y	Y
SMS	C	0	C

mum gain) and minimax regret point towards the same policy conclusion in this case, the case in which the costs of conservation are assumed to be low in relation to the possible benefits. Since the costs of conserving a species are assumed to be relatively low and the potential benefits high, conservation is to be favoured.

Randall (1986) points out that the SMS approach involves a more pro-conservation stance than BCA from a political viewpoint. This is because proponents of SMS suggest that conservation of a species should be accepted as optimal until it is shown to be otherwise. It assumes that in practice the costs of conservation of a species can be expected to be small in relation to potential gains. By contrast, benefit–cost analysts tend to suppose in practice that a conservation project is not worthwhile until the benefits are shown to exceed the costs of the project. In the first case the *burden of proof* is placed upon those opposing conservation whereas in the latter case it falls on those wishing to see a species conserved.

SMS as expounded does make it *more probable* than in the case of CBA that conservation will be favoured. But politically and logically it is possible to argue that even when CBA is used the onus of proof should be on the opponents of conservation given the presence of irreversibility, that is given that the loss of a species is irreversible. The issue here is to decide what should be done about preserving a species while benefit-cost ratios are being determined, if indeed they can be determined accurately at all. Logically using a perfectionist's CBA approach one should suspend judgment about whether it is worthwhile preserving the species. But the political process does not wait for perfect decisions, and therefore an interim stance is needed. Taking the irreversibility argument into account it would be logical for cost–benefit analysts to err in favour of conservation as an interim desirable policy.

5. CHOOSING WHICH SPECIES TO SAVE GIVEN AN OUTLAY – OR RESOURCE – CONSTRAINT

In a world in which available resources or outlays for saving species from extinction are limited, a critical question is how do the various criteria compare in selecting species for survival. In a situation of no such constraint, it is of course true that even in the absence of differences in direction of burden of proof, SMS will tend to lead to more species being saved than CBA and tends to support greater resource use for conservation. But what if the amount of resources for conservation are limited? Is the SMS approach equally desirable? Consider the various criteria in this context.

Suppose that K is the maximum outlay available for preserving all species. Where C_i is costs of ensuring survival of the ith species, choice is constrained by the requirement that $\Sigma C_i < K$. The various criteria discussed so far would result in the following choices of species for survival:

(1) CBA would select the array of species which would maximize net present expected value. K would be allocated to saving species so as to maximize its present expected value. Species will be favoured for preservation which have the highest expected discounted benefit in relation to costs when this criterion is applied. The net present value of a strategy or plan is equal to the discounted and future (plus current) net benefits from it. Net benefits are discounted using the rate of interest. Economists in using this approach argue that \$1 now is worth less than \$1 in the future because \$1 available now will earn interest if invested and the capital plus interest will exceed \$1 in the future.

(2) The Bishop minimax loss or maximum gain approach results in preference being given to species with the highest *possible* benefit to cost ratios, that is to those for which Y_i/C_i is highest. To do so is to minimize the maximum possible loss per unit of outlay.

(3) In order to minimize maximum possible regret, those species should be selected for which $(Y_i - C_i)/C_i$ is greatest. This will minimize maximum possible regret per unit of outlay. Note that because $(Y_i - C_i)/C_i = Y_i/C_i - 1$, this ordering will be the same as for the Bishop minimax loss ordering.

In the constrained situation both the minimax regret and minimax loss criteria select the same species for preservation and are heavily influenced by the *maximum* possible or potential benefit from the species whereas CBA selection is mainly determined by expected benefits which involve a weighting of possibilities.

However, Randall (1986) interprets the SMS approach differently from me in this context. He claims that SMS involves maximizing the number of species saved subject to the outlay constraint. He says for example in relation to his own criterion:

> "SMS logic would play the dominant role in establishing priorities. All species would be treated as having a positive but unknown expected value; implicitly all would be treated as equally valuable. priorities would be set on the basis of opportunity costs; preserve that package which includes the most species given the cost constraint" (Randall, 1986, p. 103).

This assumes that uncertainty is so great that an estimate of the maximum possible value of species cannot be made. It relies on the principle of insufficient reason in assuming that all species may be equally valuable.

Randall (1986) suggests a two-tiered approach to selecting species for preservation: (a) use CBA to the extent possible to make an initial selection; (b) for those species not selected because information is inadequate to apply CBA (or because of failure to meet the CBA test?), apply (his) SMS approach, that is maximize the number of species saved in this group.

However, information is not nearly as dichotomous as Randall's approach assumes. Cases may not neatly fall into two sets, namely one in which information is sufficient to apply traditional CBA and another where ignorance is so great that no discrimination is possible between the maximum possible value of species. Degrees of uncertainty about the value of different species are likely to vary along a spectrum.

While CBA has its limitations in this area, neither of the SMS approaches as interpreted by me above are without difficulty because species are ranked only by reference to extreme values. The following illustrates the difficulty: Suppose that the smallest possible value of a species, is not zero but a value, V_i, which may be greater than zero. In addition $V_i - C_i$ may be positive. So even given the worst possible state of nature there is a net benefit in saving the species. However, the SMS strategy is only influenced by Y_i/C_i and not at all by V_i/C_i. Thus if Y/C is the same for two species the SMS approach will rank them equally even though V/C may be very much higher than one of the species.

Where V represents the benefit from a species under the worst possible conditions and Y is its additional maximum potential value, Table 3 is modified in the way shown in Table 5.

It might also be observed that if the conservative view of a bird in the hand being worth two in the bush is adopted, a case might be made for ranking species on the basis of V_i/C_i values, or at least a weighting of these and Y_i/C_i values. But of course such a criterion as well as several others for choice under uncertainty, as for example reviewed by Chisholm (1988), have blemishes (cf. Tisdell, 1968). Furthermore, the degree and nature of knowledge about possible payoffs from saving or not saving different species can vary considerably. So one has to deal with a mixed system of decision

TABLE 5

Man's gain from survival of a species given that its minimum value is V

	s_1	s_2
E	$-V$	$-(V+Y)$
SMS	$V-C$	$V+Y-C$

problems and payoff matrices involving for some species certainty, in other cases probability and in still other cases pure uncertainty. Yet one has to make an 'efficient' or optimal decision in relation to this *whole* collection or array. This problem has not been satisfactorily solved even though Randall (1986) does at least implicitly deal with such a problem in his approach.

6. DISAPPEARANCE OF CROP VARIETIES AND STABILITY OF PRODUCTION

Not only are wild species rapidly disappearing but the number of varieties of domestic crops appears to be declining and this is of concern to ecologists (Plucknett et al., 1986). In developed countries, almost all the total production from major crops is typically supplied by three or four varieties of the crop, and primitive cultivars have largely disappeared (IUCN, 1980). As a country becomes more developed and high-yielding or improved varieties are introduced, traditional cultivars tend to disappear and the genetic reserves available to scientists for breeding purposes decline.

Indications are that this happened in Greece (IUCN, 1980) and appears to be happening in Bangladesh (Alauddin and Tisdell, 1988a) with the introduction of high-yielding varieties of rice. It is possible especially where technology is introduced from abroad, for the number of varieties to increase at the same time as the fundamental gene bank for a species or a crop declines. For example, some genetic characteristics may be lost as a result of the loss of primitive cultivars and new varieties may involve a smaller bundle of characteristics. So there is a difficult problem in measuring the extent of genetic adversity by a simple index.

This raises the question of whether there is a market failure in the preservation of possible breeding traits or characteristics for animals and crops. While a case exists for applying economic criteria to breeding and crop improvement (see McArthur, 1987), the economic system may fail to preserve sufficient genetic diversity in relation to animals and crops due to such factors as externalities, private attitudes to risks and transaction costs (cf. Tisdell, 1982). Thus a case might be made out for government intervention.

Scientists have suggested that reduced diversity of agricultural production and of varieties and species involved in this production will increase instability of production. While high-yielding varieties appear to be less tolerant to environmental stress than traditional varieties (cf. Tisdell, 1983b) and reductions in mixed cropping seems to have occurred with economic development, a reduction in the relative instability of crop production also seems to have occurred. Alauddin and Tisdell (1988b, 1988c) have shown that the relative instability of annual rice yields in Bangladesh have fallen with the introduction of high yielding varieties. They attribute this to the increase in the incidence of multiple cropping and to greater control of the growing environment made possible by modern techniques and inputs. Evidence from elsewhere is also pointing towards a similar result (Hazell, 1986).

Nevertheless despite an apparent reduction in the relative instability or variability of yields with the introduction of high yielding varieties, the long-term *sustainability* of agricultural production and yields may be increasingly at risk. For example, due to reduced genetic diversity with disappearance of species and varieties, past data on variability of production and yields may fail to alert us to a rising danger in this regard (cf. Alauddin and Tisdell, 1988b). Even though variability at annual yields of crops may be falling, agricultural systems may become less adaptable to changed environmental conditions in the long term, that is less able to cope with large or 'catastrophic' environmental shocks or continuing steady environmental stress. Increased variability of yields of a crop may but need not be a harbinger of impending production collapse nor is reduced variability a sure sign that collapse of production is becoming less likely.

CONCLUDING COMMENTS

Man's responsibility in relation to nature is a heavy one since he is increasingly in a position to determine which species will survive and in any case his activities are expected to lead to the further disappearance of species. This responsibility cannot be avoided. However, Man is in a weak position to decide rationally what species and varieties of living things to save from extinction and which to permit to become extinct. While advances, in part due to the effort of economists, have been made in understanding the issues involved in conservation of species and in seeing the complexity and economic importance of the problem, we are still a considerable way from resolving the issues, particularly given the degree of uncertainty inherent in evaluations. Nevertheless, the drift of economic thought over the last two decades or so has been increasingly in favour of conserving species. This is true not only of approaches based on the safe minimum standard but those relying on cost–benefit analysis. Thus the view (discussed in Section 5) is increasingly gaining support that conservation of species should be the general rule unless opponents can prove in a particular case that there is net advantage in developments at the expense of species conservation. By altering the parties primarily responsible for the burden of proof in the conservation versus development debate, the chances of conserving species and coming closer to an optimal social solution may be improved. Those upon whom the burden of proof is placed have the greatest economic cost or risk in proposing a change or defending the status quo as the case may be. The burden of proof also tends to define policies that will be permitted *unless* they are proved to be sub-optimal. Thus the nature of the burden of proof is politically very important in the conservation versus non-conservation debate.

REFERENCES

Alauddin, M. and Tisdell, C., 1988a. New agricultural technology and sustainable food production: Bangladesh's achievements, predicament and prospects. In: C. Tisdell and P. Maitra (Editors), Technological Change, Development and the Environment: Socio-Economic Perspectives. Routledge, London.

Alauddin, M. and Tisdell, C., 1988b. Has the 'green revolution' destabilized food production? Some evidence from Bangladesh. Dev. Econ., 24: 141–160.

Alauddin, M. and Tisdell, C., 1988c. Impact of new agricultural technology on the instability of foodgrain production and yield: data analysis for Bangladesh and its districts. J. Dev. Econ., 29: 199–227.

Bishop, R.C., 1978. Endangered species and uncertainty. The economics of a safe minimum standard Am. J. Agric. Econ., 60: 10–18.

Bishop, R.C., 1979. Endangered species, irreversibility and uncertainty: A reply. Am. J. Agric. Econ., 61: 376–379.

Chisholm, A.H., 1988. Sustainable resource use and development: uncertainty, irreversibility and rational choice. In: C. Tisdell and P. Maitra (Editors), Technological Change, Development and the Environment: Socio-Economics Perspectives. Routledge, London.

Ciriacy-Wantrup, S.V., 1968. Resource Conservation: Economics and Policies (3rd Edition). Division of Agricultural Science, University of California, Berkeley, CA, 342 pp.

Hart, A.G., 1942. Risk, uncertainty and the unprofitability of compounding probabilities. In: O. Lange, F. McIntyre and F. Yntema (Editors), Studies in Mathematical Economics and Econometrics. University of Chicago Press, Chicago, IL, pp. 110–118.

Hazell, B.R., 1986. Introduction. In: B. Hazell (Editor), Summary Proc. Workshop Cereal Yield Variability. International Food Policy Research Institute, Washington, DC.

IUCN, 1980. World Conservation Strategy. IUCN, Glands, Switzerland, 50 pp.

Leopold, A., 1966. A Sand Country Almanac: With Other Essays from Round River. Oxford University Press, New York, 269 pp.

Luce, R.D. and Raiffa, H., 1957. Games and Decisions: Introduction and Critical Survey. Wiley, New York, 509 pp.

McArthur, A.T.G., 1987. Economic weights for breeding objectives. A paper presented at the Australian Agricultural Economics Conference, Blenheim, New Zealand. Lincoln College, Canterbury.

Passmore, J.A., 1974. Man's Responsibility for Nature: Ecological Problems and Western Traditions. Duckworth, London, 213 pp.

Plucknett, D.L., Smith, N.J., Williams, J.T. and Anishetty, N.M., 1986. Gene Banks and the World's Food. Princeton University Press, Princeton, NJ, 248 pp.

Randall, A., 1986. Human preferences, economics and the preservation of species. In: B.G. Gordon (Editor), The Preservation of Species: The Value of Biological Diversity. Princeton University Press, Princeton, NJ, pp. 79–109.

Simon, H., 1957. Models of Man. Wiley, New York, 287 pp.

Smith, V.K. and Krutilla, J.V., 1979. Endangered species, irreversibilities, and uncertainty: A comment Am. J. Agric. Econ., 61: 371–375.

Tisdell, C.A., 1968. The Theory of Price Uncertainty, Production and Profit. Princeton University Press, Princeton, NJ, 197 pp.

Tisdell, C.A., 1970. Implications of learning for economic planning. Econ. Planning, 10: 172–192.

Tisdell, C.A., 1982. Microeconomics of Markets. Wiley, Brisbane, 626 pp.

Tisdell, C.A., 1983a. An economist's critique of the world conservation strategy with examples from Australian experience. Environ. Conserv., 10: 43–52.

Tisdell, C.A., 1983b. Optimal choice of a variety of a species for variable environmental conditions. J. Agric. Econ., 34: 175–185.

Tisdell, C.A. and Alauddin, M., 1988. Diversification and stability implications of new crop varieties: theoretical and empirical evidence. A paper presented at Australian Agricultural Economics Conference, La Trobe University, February 1988. University of Newcastle, N.S.W.

Biodiversity and Conservation **2**, 168–181 (1993)

How useful are environmental safety standards in economics? – The example of safe minimum standards for protection of species

ANDREAS HOHL[1]* and CLEMENT A. TISDELL[2]‡
[1]*Institut für Landwirtschaftliche Betriebslehre, University of Hohenheim, Postfach 700562, W-7000 Stuttgart 70, Germany*
[2]*Department of Economics, The University of Queensland, Brisbane 4072, Australia*

Received 10 September 1992; accepted 7 October 1992

The use of environmental safety standards is being increasingly advocated, and economists are being increasingly required to adapt their policy models to take account of such standards, e.g. by the use of transferable environmental damage quotas. The use of these standards may be a consequence of a greater desire to achieve more sustainable development and preserve the natural wealth available to future generations. An important means to this goal is to preserve biodiversity and genetic variability. Safe minimum standards for conservation of wildlife have been suggested as a way to achieve this. Sometimes safe minimum standards for conservation of species are defined in terms of their minimum viable populations and their minimum habitat requirements. However, as a review of recent scientific literature indicates, these safe minimum standards are very uncertain.

Environmental safety standards have been integrated into economics in a variety of ways, e.g. via constraints to ensure sustainability at the macro-level, via minimum safety standards necessary to ensure survival of species. Despite the commendable support which safe minimum standards appear to give for nature conservation, they involve conceptual problems and uncertainties as outlined in this paper. In fact, safe minimum standards for the conservation of species do not exist – no standard ensures the continued existence of any species. This is not to deny that an improvement in standards can up to a point increase the probability of survival of a species for a specified period of time. It implies that minimum standards need to be cast in terms of those required to achieve a particular probability of survival of the targeted species for a specified period. It may, however, be impossible to achieve the goal specified, e.g. the probability of survival of a species aimed for, may be greater than can be achieved for any attainable standard. In general, the paper makes it clear that standards suggested by natural scientists and others need to be subjected to careful scrutiny before they can be used as a reliable basis for economic policy.

Keywords: environmental safety standards; conservation of species; probability of survival; safe minimum standards; game theory; social choice

Introduction

Since the early 1970s economists have taken a broader interest in environmental issues than previously. This change was largely due to natural scientists like Forrester (1971) and Meadows *et al.* (1972), who for the first time after the era of Malthus (1798) and

*To whom correspondence should be addressed.
‡Department of Economics, University of Queensland, St Lucia, QLD 4072, Australia.

Ricardo (1817) argued that there were 'limits to growth'. Fortunately not all of the early pessimistic scenarios, designed by the 'Club of Rome' and others, came into reality. However, undoubtedly there has always been a widespread view that there are natural limits to human development.

Economists have reacted in different ways to the new challenge (Tisdell, 1990a). The neoclassical mainstreamers argued that the price mechanism will act in favour of conservation and that human innovativeness is likely to overcome all difficulties. Therefore, they did not see any reason to change the growth orientated economic system. Others were less optimistic. Neo-Malthusians opted for a steady state economy (Daly, 1980) or even called for a reduction of the human population to a level sustainable by using renewable resources alone (Georgescu-Roegen, 1976).

The decisive question raised by these debates is still unanswered: how large can the human population become and how long can it be sustained with the given available set of resources? If the variables population size, resource stocks and resource-use intensity could be determined, we could predict the fate of mankind.

The objectives of this paper are not quite as ambitious. However, much of the incentive for defining environmental safety standards can be interpreted as attempts to contain an apparently uncontrolled and self-destroying human race.

Over the last 20 years it became obvious that environmental problems had been neglected and environmental costs had been externalized. Economists had to extend their theoretical horizon and consider a fourth production factor: the environment. In principle the English classical economists might however, have included this under land but in practice they did not emphasize environmental aspects of the economic problem. Today writers such as Pearce *et al.* (1989) do treat the environment as if it is an extra factor of production. Whereas the factors land, labour and capital are relatively homogeneous and arguably easy to quantify, the environment can only be taken into account in form of highly complex constraints. The heterogeneity and complexity of environmental influences demands an interdisciplinary approach. Today the findings of the natural or medical sciences have direct influences on economic modelling, no matter whether this relies on extended cost–benefit analysis or on cost efficiency analysis (a fixed standard approach).

Political decisions like where and how to construct an industrial plant that were formerly based almost entirely on economic considerations are influenced by a whole range of expert opinions from those expressed by geologists to those of toxicologists. Farmers, car drivers or garden owners have to observe ambient environmental quality standards for water, soil and air. Environmental safety standards define the framework for almost all enterprises. However, in many, if not in most cases, the environmental interdependencies are so complex that the scientific base of the safety standards is still incomplete or unsatisfactory. How should economists deal with this situation when political decision-makers and the public are demanding clear answers where there often are not more than crude rules of thumb?

After surveying different categories of environmental safety standards used in economics, this paper presents some of the special problems involved in defining and using safe minimum standards. It considers how precise these standards, as recommended by non-economic sciences, are and how well they can be integrated into economic theory. Finally, possible ways of dealing with political demands in relation to standards are discussed.

The new multiplicity of goals

Human welfare and inter-generational equity

Looking at classical definitions of economics (Samuelson, 1981), there is one inherent goal in all of them: the maximization of human welfare. Growing environmental problems did not lead to the abandonment of this goal but deprived it of its exclusivity. Subgoals or – depending on the philosophical view of the world – equally important goals emerged at its side.

The strong consensus, that human welfare should be maximized, has always been complemented by an equally strong dissent on how earthly wealth, however defined, should be won and distributed. One can see history as an endless chain of distributional conflicts, wiping out entire populations and peoples. Aspects of the distribution of wealth have been debated for many centuries and some have gained new importance with issues like poverty-caused environmental degradation being considered. However, there is a relatively new aspect of distribution: the distribution of wealth over time. Until recently, the time vector was not considered important. Current generations acted along similar lines to individuals guided by Adam Smith's 'invisible hand': what was in their interests was supposed to be good for future generations as well. As resources are known to be finite, this cannot be taken for granted any more. Many people feel a moral obligation to guarantee inter-generational equity. This change is very well characterized by the European Green Movement's slogan: 'We do not own the earth, we only have leased it from our children'.

Inter-generational equity can only be achieved if all development is sustainable or, in other words, if the services and qualities of the natural resource stock are maintained over time (Pearce and Turner, 1989). This implies the acceptance of two basic safety rules: renewable resources should not be exploited at a rate faster than natural regeneration occurs, and exhaustible resources should not be depleted at a rate faster than human inventiveness provides alternative technologies with substitute materials.

This is easily said but difficult to realize. Even if we assume an economically, socially and politically perfectly rational world with absolute control over resource utilisation, there are still unanswered questions. How fast does natural regeneration occur? What are the long-term effects of human resource exploitation on ecosystems? Decisive variables like growth and recruitment rates are governed by complex biological and ecological relationships: extinction thresholds, sigmoid growth curves, carrying capacities, and the like (Randall 1987). Production cycles can span several human generations. Despite ample research there is no available sustained management system for tropical rainforests (Fearnside, 1986; Keto et al., 1990; Keto and Scott, 1991). The management of the Queensland rainforests was not long ago presented as a model of sustainability to the world. The sustainable achievable yearly cut was estimated at 220 000 m^3, then 160 000 m^3 in the 1970s, in the 1980s it was revised down to 80 000 m^3 and later to 60 000 m^3, until the Australian Government decided to ban commercial logging in the rainforest altogether (Stocker *et al.*, 1977, Keto and Scott, 1991).

Prevention of pollution and preservation of the assimilative capacity of the environment.

Human welfare was in the past closely linked to the quantity of (material) goods available. This still holds true in many of the poor countries of the world. In the developed world, where all basic needs are satisfied, the growing side-effects of development have led to demands to replace quantity (of goods) by quality (of life).

One of the most obvious measures to improve the quality of life is to stop or reduce the release of toxic, pathogenic or otherwise deleterious substances into the environment. Catastrophes like Minamata, Bhopal or Chernobyl showed only the peak of the iceberg. Long-term developments like the lingering pollution of entire ecosystems may produce even more serious consequences. If the assimilative capacity of the environment is exceeded, even the output of such presumed harmless substances like carbon dioxide or methane may lead to global disaster.

Threshold values for substances considered deleterious to human health are among the best-known environmental safety standards. However, even the medical data, that appear so well founded, have their shortcomings. Grossly simplified, the traditional way to get a threshold value for a suspectedly harmful substance is to treat laboratory

Table 1. Options for pursuing genetic diversity in wild species

ALIVE
In situ
1. Single use wildland management
– Scientific reserves, strict nature reserves
2. Multiple use wildland management
– National parks
– Natural monuments
– Managed natural resources
– Protected landscapes
– Resource reserves
– Anthropological reserves
– Multiple use management areas
3. Areas other than wildlands
– Converted land managed for greater diversity
Ex situ
1. Whole organism
– Botanical gardens
– Zoos
– Culture collections (microorganisms)
2. Organism parts
– Sperm, egg and embryo banks
– Organ banks
– Seed and pollen banks
– Gene banks
– Tissue culture
DEAD
– Museums
– Herbaria

animals, normally rats, with growing doses of it, until 50% of the animals die. This is called the 'lethal dose 50 (LD_{50})'. The LD_{50}-value for the animals is multiplied with an estimated safety factor to get the 'acceptable daily intake (ADI) for humans'. The procedure to convert animal standards into human standards is today sufficiently refined to produce safe threshold values with a very high probability for the tested substance. However, no substance can be produced 100% pure. As there is still considerable danger coming from impurities, the effects of which may not be detected during the tests. The same accounts for reciprocal influences between various agents. Our environment is overloaded with myriads of potentially interactive substances, whose combined effects are largely unknown. Therefore, over time the recommended safety standards may prove not to be safe at all. Additionally, it has to be considered, that the probability of inadequate standards rises when the scientific threshold values have to be adapted to real world situations. The classical process of threshold value 'dilution' involves four steps: the scientifically recommended standard turns into the technically feasible, which is transformed into the economically bearable, which finally ends up as the politically enforceable.

Preservation of biodiversity and genetic variability within species

One of the greatest concerns in recent decades has been the irreversible loss of species and genetic varieties. The genetic base for biological production is narrowing. This may affect agriculture, forestry and the possiblities for medical advances. Not only the maintenance of existing production is at risk but the scope for developing new types of biological production and commodities based on living organisms is being reduced (Tisdell, 1990b). There are various possibilities to slow down genetic erosion (Goodland and Ledec, 1988). These are summarised in Table 1.

In order to preserve a species the decisive questions are:

- How many individuals are enough?
- How much habitat is enough?

The respective safety standards are the minimum viable population size and the minimum habitat size.

Defining minimum viable populations and minimum habitat sizes

According to Soulé (1987) the simple question 'How much is enough?' might be the quintessential issue in population biology. What are the minimum conditions to ensure a species' or population's long-term persistence and adaptation with a high degree of security in a given place?

When conservation efforts are made there are four key variables to be looked at: the persistence time, the degree of security, the population size and the habitat (or reserve) size.

It is impossible to define persistence time and the degree of security scientifically (Shaffer, 1987). Persistence cannot be forever, because extinction is a natural and inevitable process. Depending on the ethical point of view persistence time is assumed in population models ranging from the time span necessary to enable the next human generation to reconsider the species' future to evolutionary time dimensions. Assumptions on the degree of security require a value judgement too. The question 'How secure should the persistence of a given species be?' can only be answered by society.

Shaffer (1981, 1987) has shown that in order to estimate minimum viable population sizes and their respective area requirements the effects of various chance events on population persistence have to be considered:

(a) genetic uncertainty or random changes in genetic make-up due to the founder effect, genetic drift, or inbreeding, which alter the survival and reproductive probabilities of individuals;
(b) demographic uncertainty resulting from random events in the survival and reproduction of individuals;
(c) environmental uncertainty due to random, or at least unpredictable, changes in climate, food supply, and the populations of competitors, predators, parasites or pathogenic agents;
(d) natural catastrophes such as floods, fires, droughts or volcanic eruptions, which may occur at random intervals.

The genetic variability within a population or a species is a measure of its chances to persist in time. Mutation and immigration improve the genetic variability, whereas inbreeding, genetic drift and founder effects affect it adversely. The main obstacle to the short term survival of a population is inbreeding, caused by combination of deleterious genes (Gottschalk, 1978). The most important process endangering medium term survival is genetic drift, a change in gene frequencies caused by random recombination in meiosis (Crow and Kimura, 1970). A combination of both processes causes bottleneck or founder effects. They occur when a population is temporarily reduced in number or when a new population is founded by only a few individuals (Harris, 1984). To secure long term survival the genetic variability has to be big enough to enable the species to adapt to environmental changes, take part in the evolutionary process and develop new life forms.

Human knowledge of evolution is far too restricted to allow for complete genetic modelling. However, geneticists can provide rules of thumb for different time spans of persistence. As only the number of genetically active individuals in a population is important, the concept of effective population size is used (Harris, 1984). The number of non-reproductive individuals is subtracted from the actual population size and corrections such as those for unequal sex ratios are made. Considering genetic chance processes the effective population size to secure short-time survival should be at least 50 (Frankel and Soulé, 1981). For medium term survival it is estimated at 500 (Franklin, 1980), which will translate in an actual population size several times this number. To estimate minimum populations sizes for long-term persistence the effects of other random events have to be taken into account.

Schaffer (1987) suggested functional relationships for demographic, environmental and catastrophic uncertainty of the type shown in Fig. 1. Several important conclusions emerge from a perusal of these idealized functional forms. Average persistence times increase geometrically with increasing population sizes due to the effects of demographic uncertainty (Goodman, 1987). Therefore, demographic uncertainty will only pose an important hazard to relatively small populations (in the order of tens of hundreds). More troublesome is the relationship of average persistence times under the effects of environmental uncertainty. Persistence times increase linearly with increases in population size, which means that there is no critical population size that, once reached, ensures a

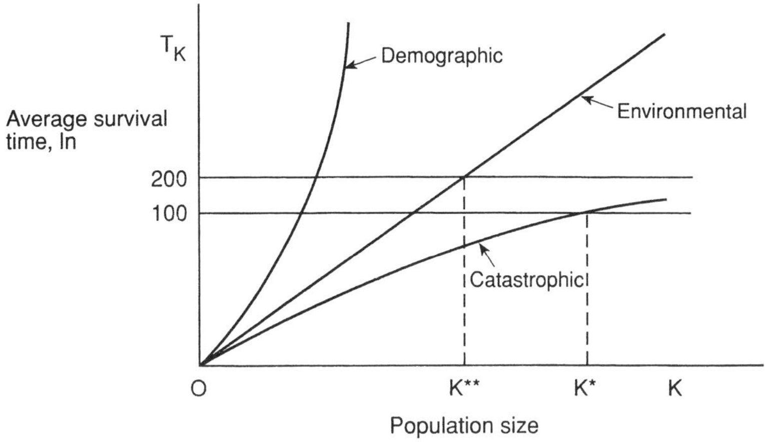

Figure 1. Functional forms of the relationship of the expected time to extinction, or average persistence time (T_k). To population size (K) for three classes of uncertainty. (Source: Shaffer, 1987)

high level of long term security. The most distressing function is the curve for catastrophic uncertainty. Here persistence times are believed to increase only with the natural logarithm of population size. Progressively increasing sizes of populations yield diminishing dividends in terms of increased persistence times. This curve is the theoretical confirmation of the inevitability of extinction (Shaffer, 1987). There is no curve for the relationship of persistence times to population size under the effects of genetic uncertainty because no clear relationship emerges from a consideration of genetic factors (Lande and Barrowclough, 1987). However, if environmental and catastrophic uncertainty effects are considered, genetic uncertainty will not always, perhaps not often, set the lower limit to acceptable population size.

Taking into account all the uncertainty effects it becomes obvious that there is no simple determination of minimum viable populations. Each case is different and requires a special viability analysis. For species with special social requirements, see e.g. Darling (1952). Therefore, Soulé (1987) only very reluctantly gives a rule of thumb: assuming 95% expectation of persistence, without loss of fitness, for several centuries, the minimum viable population of a vertebrate should be in the low thousands.

To calculate the minimum area requirements, the home ranges of the various species have to be known. A home range can be as little as 0.049 ha for the white footed vole or as much as 377 000 ha for the grizzly bear (Harris, 1984). The definition of home ranges is very time consuming, for this reason there are only data for a very limited number of species. It is assumed here that multiplication of the numbers for minimum viable populations and home ranges give the minimum area requirements. Edge and insularity effects, that are very important for the design of nature reserves (Harris, 1984; Soulé and Simberloff, 1986), are neglected. If the large predators, which can be considered as key species for entire biological communities, are looked at, the minimum area requirements are in the range of 1 000 000–100 000 000 ha (Shaffer, 1987; Soulé, 1987).

The safety standards suggested by scientists are highly inaccurate. The given numbers span a range of two or three orders of magnitude. The simple reason for this is the complexity of the biological world (Soulé, 1987).

Integrating environmental safety standards into economic theory

In traditional economics the state of the environment does not influence the calculation of economic optima. The Pareto optimality of allocation is independent of ecological states. Only since the beginning of the 1980s, with the publication of the World Conservation Strategy (IUCN, 1980) as a starting point, have sustainability aspects been considered. In order to achieve sustainability Pearce and Turner (1989) argue for an 'existence theorem': a guarantee that any economic optimum is associated with a stable ecological equilibrium.

There have been two alternative ways to approach this goal. Some analysts used an extended cost–benefit framework, utilising monetary valuations but also incorporating explicit recognition of uncertainty and irreversibilities. Others argued that there are principal limits to valuation and the assignment of probabilities. They adopted a fixed standard approach where macroenvironmental safety standards operate as binding constraints. A well known alternative concept of binding constraints is the safe minimum standard (SMS) that was first introduced by Ciriacy-Wantrup (1952) and later formalized by Bishop (1978). The SMS is a decision rule for problems involving irreversibility, very long time horizons and massive uncertainty like the extinction of plants and animals.

SMS has not been adequately tied to a theoretical model of social choice. Bishop's attempt to use game theory first seemed to prove successful. He used the Wald criteria (Wald, 1950) to minimise maximum losses (minimax) when making decisions under uncertainty. The minimax rule is an extremely pessimistic decision rule and is, therefore, biased towards conservation. The SMS approach makes preservation the preferred option unless it can be demonstrated that the social cost of preservation, i.e. the forgone development benefits, is unacceptably large (Pearce and Turner, 1989). In the game only two possible social states are assumed: in state 1, nothing unanticipated occurs in the future to create large social losses if the species ceases to exist (0); in state 2 the species turns out to be worth a large amount (Y) as, for example, a cure for cancer. The present value of net benefits from development is assumed to be x. The common base point is the intersection of 'Extinction' and 'State 1'. This leads to the loss matrix shown in Table 2.

Table 2. Bishop's original loss matrix

	State		
Strategy	1	2	Max loss
SMS	x	$x-Y$	x
Extinction	0	Y	Y

(Source: based on Bishop (1978), order of strategies exchanged)

Table 3. Revised loss matrix for the insurance game

	State		
Strategy	1	2	Max loss
SMS	0	0	0
Development	$L-B_d$	$-B_d$	$L-B_d$

(Source: based on Bishop and Ready (1990))

The original model contained a mistake. Bishop double counted the benefits from species preservation in state 2 of his loss matrix (it should be 'x' instead of '$x-Y$'). This has been criticized by Tisdell (1990b) and others and revised by Bishop himself (Bishop and Ready,1991). However, the double counting did not alter the original decision, as the revised matrix in Table 3 shows.

The situation in this so-called insurance game (because it insures against large future losses) is principally the same as in the first matrix. 'L' stands for 'large future losses', 'B_d' for 'development benefits'. Under the assumption that $L > B_d$, SMS is again chosen as the optimal strategy.

Bishop and Ready (1991) detected that only a slight change in the assumptions would reverse the conclusions. In a game called the lottery game, shown in Table 4, the disease is assumed to occur with certainty, but there is uncertainty about whether preservation of the species will lead to a cure. This game captures the argument that endangered species should be saved because they may lead to important new resources. Preserving the species is analogous to buying a lottery ticket. In state 1, the species does hold the cure, in state 2, it does not. The baseline for the game is no development and no cure.

The maximum possible loss under the SMS in the lottery game is 0, while under development it is $-B_d$, which is less than zero. The minimax strategy for the lottery game therefore is to choose development, and guarantee a gain of B_d, even if the extinction of the species and the losses to society associated with the disease are taken into account.

Bishop and Ready (1991) come to the conclusion that SMS cannot be motivated as the minimax loss solution to a two person game against nature. The situation is different when the Niehans–Savage rule of regret is considered for making decisions under uncertainty (Niehans, 1948; Savage, 1951). Using the minimax regret decision rule, the conslusion is that the SMS should be adopted for either kind of game. Individuals appear

Table 4. Loss matrix for the lottery game

	State		
Strategy	1	2	Max loss
SMS	$-L$	0	0
Development	$-B_d$	$-B_d$	$-B_d$

to consider regret in situations of massive uncertainty, rather than maximizing utility (Loomes and Sudgen, 1982). However, a general application is questionable. The Niehans–Savage rule is considered by decision theoreticians to be much weaker than the Wald criteria, because it does not fulfil the so-called 'mega-criteria' for decision rules (Borcherding, 1983), namely that the order, in which different alternatives are ranked by a decision rule should not be altered, if further alternatives are added or some of the existing alternatives are eliminated. This holds true for the minimax criteria but not for the minimax regret rule. There are still many open questions, and therefore it can be said, that currently no solid theoretical foundation exists for the use of SMS.

Additional limitations of the safe minimum standard as a guide to conservation of species

The safe minimum standard criterion as originally proposed by Ciriacy-Wantrup (1952) favours the conservation of species. However, closer examination of the requirements for applying the criterion reveal several considerable difficulties. While the criterion favours the conservation of as many species 'as possible', if available resources for the conservation of species are limited, it does not appear to provide a satisfactory guide to which species should be conserved (Tisdell, 1990b) given that some will be bound to disappear as a result of the economic choices made. It is unsatisfactory as a guide to determining which species should be conserved.

There is the further problem, as the above review indicates, that there appears to be no definite ecological–biological safe minimum standard for the conservation of any species either in terms of its population-size or its supply of habitat. The future survival of no species can be assured even though the probability of persistence of any species will rise as factors favourable to its survival are increased in availability.

As the standard of factors propitious to the survival of a species is increased, the probability of its survival for a specified period of time, say T_1, rises. Possibly the relationship tends to be of the logistic form shown in Fig. 2. There may be some standard below which the species will not survive (e.g. a standard of $S \leqslant S_0$) for a period T_1 but there may be no standard at which survival is assured. The probability of survival curve $P = F(S)$ is not asymptotic to $p = 1$ but to a value of $p < 1$, e.g. $p = a$.

From Fig. 2, there is no standard which ensures the survival of the species for a period, T_1, so there is no safe minimum standard. However, if one wants to have a probability of 0.5 of survival of the species for a period of T_1 then the minimum necessary environmental standard is S_1. Similarly for other probabilities of continued survival, other minimum standards can be determined.

However, this raises the question of what is the status of the probability function $p = f(S)$. In practice, the function may be uncertain or even unknown. If it is uncertain, and if there is a probability distribution of probabilities, are the probabilities in Fig. 2 to be average or expected probabilities or the most likely (modal) probabilities? How should choice be affected by changes in the characteristics of the probability distribution of possibilities, e.g. an increased variance of the distribition? These issues are as yet unresolved.

It might also be noted that a minimum standard might be achieved in a number of different ways. For example, a number of different environmental combinations (e.g. combinations of habitat and population size of a species) may yield an 0.5 probability of the survival of a species for a period of T_1 or longer. As May (1992) points out determining the relationship between habitat provision and survivability of a species is

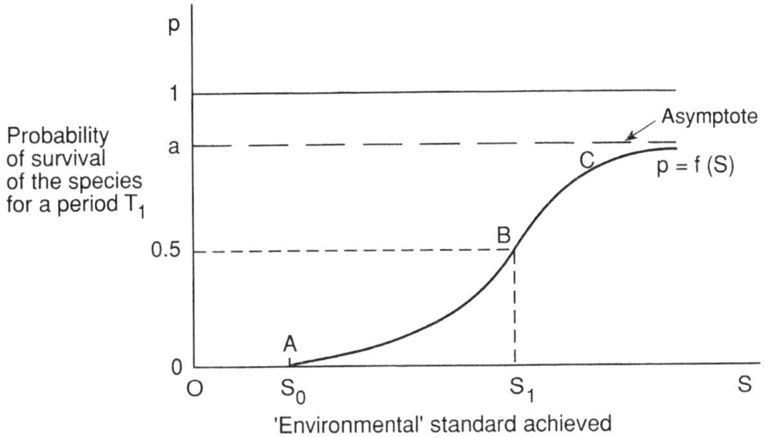

Figure 2. Relationship between (environmental) standard achieved and probability of survival of a species for a specific period of time (T_1).

extremely complicated. It does not depend merely on the size of habitat preserved. A common view expressed by ecologists is that the larger is a protected natural area the greater are the number of species likely to survive (MacArthur and Wilson, 1967). However, the relationship between the size of a protected area and the probability of survival of species is much more complicated than appears to be the case at first sight. Some of these limitations are reviewed by May (1992), e.g. complications raised by edge and patch effects.

In a world of climatic change, it also needs to be recognized that even very large protected areas may fail to save many species from extinction (see Goudie, 1990). Even large national parks and protected areas are like islands in a sea of human-dominated landscapes. Because human-dominated landscapes are an impediment to migration of many species, as climate changes, they may perish in their refuges because of their inability to migrate. The general problem has been discussed by Holdgate (1992). The drought during most of 1992 in Africa illustrates the problem. Hippopotami in the north-east of South Africa, in Kruger National Park, have been dying due to the drought. They are unable to move south. However, some have been captured and moved by humans to the south of South Africa in order to ensure their continued survival. Both natural corridors to facilitate movement of species and human assistance may become necessary for the survival of many species if global climate change occurs. Nevertheless despite such assistance, a number of species can be expected to disappear.

Conclusions

It has been shown that inaccuracies and uncertainties occur in the specification of minimum viable populations and minimum habitat sizes for survival of species. Also it was pointed out that the safe minimum standards have no sound theoretical foundation in game theory and further difficulties have been noted.

How should economists deal with the incompleteness of scientific knowledge? Should they ignore the limitations set by the environment on the grounds that much more research is needed and leave the blame to natural scientists? Or should they rather accept their part of responsibility to society and take a clear stand in the environmental debate? 'Administrators, policy makers, and managers have a right to ask for the bottom line . . . And biologists have the right and sometimes the obligation not to give an oversimplified, misleading answer to such a question' (Soulé, 1986).

A delicate balance has to be found between the obligation to consult decision makers and the obligation to disseminate only proved findings. However, decisions are necessary every day, and we have to keep in mind that in the political field non-action often only means that we approve the action of others. It may sound unsatisfactory but decisions on environmental issues still, for a considerable time to come, will have to be based on ethical considerations. As Bishop and Ready (1991) put it 'Society may choose to adopt the SMS not because it results from a rigorous model of social choice, but simply because individuals in the society feel that the SMS is "the right thing to do".' Without going any deeper into the value discussion it can be said that it does not necessarily take an ecocentric approach with sometimes quite cryptic intrinsic values to opt for the preservation of biodiversity. The anthropocentric, even the purely utilitarian approach should be enough to come to the same decision in a situation of irreversibility, very long time horizons and complete uncertainties (Tisdell, 1990b).

Scientists cannot wait for better safety values or better methods. The erosion of genetic variability, the degradation of the environment are taking place today. There are serious implications: if minimum viable population sizes of several thousands are accepted as necessary, and if long-term survival with a high degree of security is aspired to, it becomes quite obvious that in many countries there is already not enough space to preserve some of the bigger species in reserves alone. This means not only that international cooperation has to be enhanced, but also that other land uses, such as agriculture, have to be integrated into species conservation efforts. The latter should be easier in developed countries with their overproduction and their increasing demands for recreational areas. If inter-generational equity is thought to be a desirable goal, the dichotomy between developed and natural land has to be dissolved. In order to achieve sustainability we cannot restrict nature to parks, to natural monuments, and burn the earth or bury it under concrete elsewhere. Ecological interdependencies make interlinkages necessary: conservation networks must span from the most remote wildlands to the inner city parks. If the SMS, despite its theoretical shortcomings, is accepted as a model of social choice, it could alter the parties responsible for the burden of proof in the conservation versus development debate (Tisdell, 1990b). More generally, if the value of the 'precautionary principle' in relation to nature conservation is accepted whether on the basis of SMS or expected benefit, it suggests a change in the burden of proof as optimal. The developers would then have to prove in such a case that the preservation of species is the wrong choice because the forgone development benefits become unacceptably large.

More than ever policy makers ask for scientific advice and use scientific findings to achieve their goals. It is, therefore, of great political importance how environmental safety standards are defined and used.

References

Bishop, R.C. (1978) Economics of a safe minimum standard. *Amer. J. Agron. Econ.* **57**, 10–18.

Bishop, R.C. and Ready, R.C. (1991) Endangered species and the safe minimum standard. *Amer. J. Agron. Econ.* **73**, 309–12.

Borcherding, K. (1983) Entscheidungstheorie und Entscheidungs-hilfeverfahren für komplexe Entscheidungssituationen. In *Enzyklopädie per Psychologie – Methoden und Anwendungen in der Marktpsychologie* (M. Irle, ed.), Vol. 2, pp. 64–173. Göttingen: Holfgrefe.

Ciriacy-Wantrup, S.V. (1952) *Resource Conservation, Economics and Policies*. Berkeley: University of California Press.

Crow, J.F. and Kimura, M. (1970) *An Introduction to Population Genetics Theory*. New York: Harper and Row.

Daly, H. (1980) *Economics, Ecology and Ethics*. San Francisco: W.H. Freeman.

Darling, F.F. (1952) Social behaviour and survival. *Auk* **69**, 183–91.

Fearnside, P.M. (1986) *Human carrying capacity of the Brazilian rainforest*. New York: Columbia University Press.

Forrester, J.W. (1971) *World Dynamics*. Cambridge: Wright-Allen.

Frankel, O.H. and Soulé, M.E. (1981) *Conservation and Evolution*. Cambridge: Cambridge University Press.

Franklin, I.R. (1980) Evolutionary Change in small populations. In *Conservation Biology: an Evolutionary–Ecological Perspective* (M.E. Soulé and B.A. Wilcox, eds) pp. 135–50. Sunderland, MA: Sinauer Assoc.

Georgescue-Roegen, N. (1976) *Energy and Economic Myths, Institutional and Analytical Economic Essays*. New York: Pergamon Press.

Goodland R. and Ledec, G. (1988) *Wildlands, their Protection and Management in Economic Development*. Washington D.C.: The World Bank.

Gottschalk, W. (1978) *Allgemeine Genetik*. Stuttgart: Thieme.

Goudie, A. (1990) *The Human Impact on the Natural Environment*. Cambridge, MA: MIT Press.

Harris, L.D. (1984) *The Fragmented Forest – Island Biogeography Theory and the Preservation of Biotic Diversity*. Chicago: University of Chicago Press.

Holdgate, M. (1992) Protected areas and the future, The implications of change and the need for new policies. Paper presented to World Congress of National Parks and Protected Areas, Caracas, Venezuela, 10–21 February 1992.

IUCN (1980) *World Conservation Strategy*. Gland: IUCN, UNEP, WWF.

Keto, A.I. and Scott, K. (1991) Timber production from North Queensland rainforest. Paper presented at Colloquium, Sustainability in Natural Tropical Forest Management. Washington, D.C.: World Resources Institute.

Keto, A.I., Keto, A.I., Scott, K. and Olsen, M.F. (1990) *Sustainable Harvesting of tropical Rainforests, a Reassessment*. Brisbane: Rainforest Conservation Society.

Lande, R. and Barrowclough, G.F. (1987) Effective population size, genetic variation, and their use in population management. In *Viable Populations for Conservation* (M.E. Soulé, ed.) pp. 87–125. Cambridge: Cambridge University Press.

Loomes, G. and Sugden, R. (1982) Regret theory, an alternative theory of rational choice under uncertainty. *Econ. J.* **92**, 805–24.

MacArthur, R.H. and Wilson, E.O. (1967) *The Theory of Island Biogeography*. Princeton, New Jersey: Princeton University Press.

Malthus, T.R. (1798) *Essay on the Principle of Population*. London: MacMillan.

May, R.M. (1992) Ecological science and the management to protected areas. Paper presented in World Congress on National Parks and Protected Areas, Caracas, Venezuela, 10–21 February, 1992.

Meadows, D.L. (1972) *The Limits of Growth, a Report of the Club of Rome's Projection on the Predicament of Mankind*. New York: Universe Books.

Niehans, H. (1948) Zur Preisbildung bei ungewissen Erwartungen. *Schweizer Zeitschrift Volkswirtschaft Statistik* **84**, 433–56.

Pearce, D., Markandya, A. and Barbier, E.B. (1989) *Blueprint for a Green Economy*. London: Earthscan.

Pearce, D.W. and Turner, R.K. (1989) *Economics of Natural Resources and the Environment*. Baltimore: The John Hopkins University Press.

Randall, A. (1987) *Resource Economics*. New York: Wiley.

Ricardo, D. (1817) *On the Principles of Political Economy and Taxation*. London: John Murray.

Samuelson, P.A. (1980) *Economics*. New York: McGraw-Hill.

Savage, L.J. (1951) The theory of statistical decision. *J. Amer. Stat. Assoc.* **46**, 55–67.

Shaffer, M.L. (1981) Minimum population sizes for species conservation. *Bioscience* **31**, 131–4.

Shaffer, M.L. (1987) Minimum viable populations, coping with uncertainty. In *Viable Populations for Conservation* (M.E. Soulé, ed.) pp. 69–87. Cambridge: Cambridge University Press.

Soulé, M.E. (1986) Conservation biology and 'the real world'. In *Conservation Biology: Science of Scarcity and Diversity* (M.E. Soulé, ed.) pp. 1–12. Sunderland, MA: Sinauer Assoc.

Soulé, M.E. (1987) Where do we go from here? In *Viable Populations for Conservation* (Soulé, M.E. ed.) pp. 175–183. Cambridge: Cambridge University Press.

Soulé, M.E. and Simberloff, D. (1986) What do genetics and ecology tell us about the design of nature reserves? *Biol. Conserv.* **35**, 19–40.

Stocker, G.C., Gilmour, D.A. and Cassells, D.S. (1977) The future of our northern rain forests in the face of economic and political reality. Paper delivered at the Institute of Foresters of Australia Triennial Conference. Adelaide.

Tisdell, C. (1990a) The environment and economic welfare. *The University of Queensland Discussion Papers in Economics*, No. 42. Brisbane: University of Queensland.

Tisdell, C. (1990b) Economics and the debate about preservation of species, crop varieties and genetic diversity. *Ecol. Econ.* **2**, 77–90.

Wald, A. (1950) *Statistical Decision Functions*. New York: Wiley.

[5]

Keynote Address
Does the economic use of wildlife favour conservation and sustainability?

CLEMENT A. TISDELL[1]

Economic use of wildlife can be consumptive or non-consumptive, commercial or non-commercial. Given the preoccupation of virtually all modern societies with economics, conservation of wildlife of economic value or use appears to be favoured. However, does the commercial use of wildlife favour conservation? This depends largely on whether private property rights exist in it and are enforceable. If property rights can be economically established and commercial use of a species is profitable, a strong force exists for the preservation of the species. On the other hand, if private property rights do not exist and there is open-access to commercially valuable wildlife, the tragedy of the commons is liable to occur and species may be driven to extinction by commercialism. Farming of a wildlife species is one form of commercial use, but it does not necessarily favour conservation of biodiversity. Nevertheless commercial farming of some species may be environmentally more favourable than others, e.g., possibly the farming of kangaroos rather than sheep or cattle in parts of Australia. Commercialisation and choice based on economic value has selective impacts on the populations of living things. It changes the composition of species. It therefore alters the natural web of life and is bound to be unacceptable to followers of Aldo Leopold who see virtue in the land ethic. The general tendency of commercialisation is to reduce biodiversity and thereby, sustainability even though it may save some species from early extinction.

Keywords: commercial, wildlife, economics, property rights, wildlife farming, sustainable use

INTRODUCTION

Emphasis in policy formulation on using economic incentives and mechanisms to sustain biodiversity has increased. When the World Conservation Strategy (IUCN 1980) was drawn up in 1980, use of economic incentives as a means of conserving wildlife and biological diversity was not stressed, even though the importance of sustainable development for conservation was recognised. When the World Conservation Strategy was revised in 1991 much more emphasis was placed on the use of economic mechanisms and incentives (IUCN-UNEP-WWF 1991; Tisdell 1993, Ch.16). More recently the Convention on Biological Diversity (5 June 1992), agreed to at the United Nations' Conference on Environment and Development held in Rio de Janeiro, gave prominence to economic incentives for conservation. Article 11 states "Each Contracting Party shall, as far as is possible and as appropriate, adopt economically and socially sound measures that act as incentives for the sustainable use of components of biological diversity".

The purpose of this paper is to discuss the extent to which the greater economic use of wildlife favours nature conservation and sustainability. But before doing so, it may be useful to discuss the nature of the economic use of wildlife. Economists distinguish between consumptive and non-consumptive use of wildlife. The former involves the physical consumption of wildlife e.g. kangaroos for meat and hides whereas the latter involves non-physical use e.g. the use of wildlife for viewing or photography. The former normally involves the killing of wildlife and the latter does not. However, both types of economic use of wildlife can reduce wildlife populations e.g. tourists viewing wildlife or recreationists sometimes disturb wildlife and reduce their rate of reproduction or population levels. This is, for instance, well documented for a number of bird species such as the golden plover *Numenius aquata*, common sandpipers *Actitis hypoleucos* and a number of waterfowl (Yalden 1984, 1992; de Roos 1981; Yalden & Yalden 1990).

Economic use of wildlife may be for commercial market-related economic activities or for subsistence purposes. In the modern world, there is considerable emphasis on the commercial aspect of economic activity. Consequently, if economic use is to provide an incentive for the conservation of wildlife or nature, those responsible for its conservation must be able to make a profit or economic gain from it. Whether they can do so will be influenced by their property rights in wildlife. Let us consider this matter.

PROPERTY RIGHTS, ECONOMICS AND WILDLIFE CONSERVATION

The owner of private property has the right to exclude others from its use, to exclude others from using its product, its yield or output and to transfer its ownership to other persons. Thus exclusivity and transferability are features of private property (cf. Tietenberg 1992, Ch.3). Consequently any use of

---

[1] Professor of Economics, Department of Economics, The University of Queensland, Brisbane Qld 4072.

Pages 86-91 *in* CONSERVATION THROUGH SUSTAINABLE USE OF WILDLIFE, ed. by G.C. Grigg, P.T. Hale and D. Lunney. Centre for Conservation Biology, The University of Queensland. 1995.

such property by non-owners can be made subject to a payment and payment may be obtained for conservation, investment or improvement of property (an asset) when it is transferred. Thus private property provides a mechanism for economic reward.

However, the fact that private property legally exists does not make it possible or economic to enforce private property rights. The economic costs of exclusion may for example exceed the economic benefits from this. For instance, in a remote national park with several access routes, the cost of enforcing entrance fees may exceed the cost of employing rangers to enforce these. The creation of property rights is largely an economic question (Demsetz 1967; North 1981). As techniques or methods of exclusion improve or as the profitability of exclusion rises, economic incentives to create private property rights rise. The extension for example of the exclusive fishing zone from 3 miles to 200 kilometres is partly a consequence of improved methods for enforcing exclusion.

In relation to the conservation and utilisation of wildlife, although private property rights sometimes exist they are often too partial to encourage conservation. This is the case where there is open-access to harvesting of wildlife but the harvest becomes the private property of the harvester on capture. No individual has an incentive to conserve wildlife in this case because he/she cannot appropriate the benefit from it because all others are free as a result of open-access (common access) to reap the rewards of the individual's conservation effort (Tisdell 1991, Ch.6). Furthermore, under open-access, the rising economic value of a wildlife species results in its increased rate of exploitation and may result in its being extinguished. So, in this case, the market system with limited property rights results in a perverse economic reaction and does not favour conservation. This is an example of the tragedy of the commons.

This tragedy may, however, occur not only because of common (open) access to the 'output' of an ecological system but also if there is open-access to its 'inputs'. Open-access for example to habitat valuable for sustaining wildlife, may result in its destruction if components of the habitat have economic value or marketability.

The answer to the problem of nature conservation may appear to be one of extending private property rights. However, it is sometimes very costly to enforce such rights and the private property solution is then uneconomic. Thus control of resources as communal or state property may then be the most viable economic solution or sometimes there may be no viable economic alternative to tolerating open-access. This implies that no single type of property right (such as private property) is the best for all situations.

Even when a relatively comprehensive system of private property rights exists, there can still be difficulties in appropriating all benefits from conserving wildlife because of the existence of environmental externalities or spillovers (Tisdell 1991, Ch.3). Those for example conserving suitable habitats for migrating or mobile birds may confer benefits on bird-lovers beyond the confines of the habitats preserved. There may be no economic mechanisms for the conservationists of these birds to be fully compensated for their preservation of habitats and some political intervention may be necessary to support such conservation.

Furthermore, even when complete private property rights can be established in a species, they do not ensure its conservation. Even if the species has market value, it may pay to eliminate it, e.g., when the rate of growth of the biomass of a species is slow and its economic value is not expected to rise substantially. For instance, suppose that by the optimal conservation and utilisation of a species, a maximum return of 2 percent can be obtained but by replacing the species by another species, a maximum return of 8 percent can be achieved. The owner of the former species has an economic incentive to eliminate it and replace it by the latter species. For example, owners of properties containing slower growing species of trees often harvest these and replace them by faster growing species. Alternatively, if the going rate of interest on capital in excess of 2 percent, it may pay to harvest the stock of the slow growing species completely, sell the harvest and invest the capital sum obtained at the going rate of interest. In either case, one species is eliminated. Hence, full private property rights even in economically valuable species do not ensure their conservation or survival. They must be sufficiently valuable from a commercial viewpoint otherwise alternatives to their conservation will be chosen if commercial economics determines the decision.

This is not to say that private property rights and marketing of wildlife cannot assist conservation of particular species or natural areas. However, they are not a panacea for ensuring nature conservation.

African elephants (*Loxodonta africana*) in Hwange National Park, Zimbabwe, are protected but must be culled in order to conserve habitat. The ban on the trade in ivory was introduced to stop poaching but, as a result, avenues for sale of ivory obtained legally are no longer available. Elsewhere in Africa, villagers living close to parks where culls are carried out have been permitted to utilise the meat and skins and thus encouraged to report poachers. *Photo by S. Clegg.*

THE USER OR BENEFICIARY PAYS FOR WILDLIFE PRINCIPLE

In line with greater international emphasis on finding economic means to support wildlife conservation, the user pays or beneficiary pays principles have been promoted (McNeely 1988; Young 1992, Ch.3). It is possible for the user or beneficiary to be forced to pay for use of wildlife if exclusion is possible. Then use of the wildlife or access to wildlife resources can be made dependent on a payment. However, one needs to consider the economics of collecting the charge, that is the cost of policing and enforcing payment. If this is too costly, collection of fees will not be economic.

When resources are able to earn income, administrators and government officials generally take a more favourable view towards conserving these than when their management is a drain on the public purse. Thus if national parks and protected areas are able to earn income, this is likely to be considered a positive feature by governments. They may, for example, be able to earn income by entrance fees, camping fees and the sale of concessions to businesses such as shops and providers of accommodation within the park. However, to set user charges so as to maximise profit or net returns is not socially optimal as a rule. Because national parks or protected areas have some uniqueness, the demand curve for visits is likely to be downward sloping and a partial monopoly exists (Tisdell 1972). According to economists, the exploitation of a monopoly situation by 'charging what the traffic will bear' is usually not in the public or social interest. Sometimes, charges may be determined by conservational considerations – a high fee may be charged to reduce visitor numbers so as to reduce their load on the environment.

A modest fee has been introduced for visits to the Great Barrier Reef Marine Park (GBRMP) to defray some of the costs of operating the GBRMP Authority. The fee seems so low as not to be a significant deterrent to visits or to constitute a monopoly price.

EXAMPLES OF ECONOMIC USE ASSISTING CONSERVATION

In South Africa, national parks and protected areas are largely self-financing. For example, Kruger National Park obtains finances (1) from the culling of wildlife (mainly elephant and cape buffalo) and operates a processing plant for this purpose, (2) from entrance fees paid by visitors to the Park, and (3) from income from accommodation and shops within the Park. Culling of some species of large animals is considered necessary because their seasonal movement has been restricted by the Park and their numbers tend to increase beyond the carrying capacity of the Park unless they are culled.

It is interesting to note that both South Africa and Zimbabwe opposed the ban on international trade in ivory introduced in October 1989 under CITES (The Convention on International Trade in Endangered Species) (Barbier 1991, p.407). Both countries engage in harvesting of elephants within their national parks and sell the produce. Furthermore, elephant populations are not endangered in either country (Barbier 1991, p.407). There is, however, often debate about whether the elephant cull is too greatly influenced by commercial rather than biological considerations.

Selective culling of wildlife or habitat modification may be undertaken in protected areas to adjust the composition of species in the area so the composition is more suited to the demands of tourists for viewing different species. This increases tourist demand to visit such areas. Although this culling is economically motivated, one can debate whether the influence is positive from a conservation viewpoint.

An interesting case of nature conservation and economic use occurs in the Otago Peninsula, located near Dunedin in New Zealand. The royal albatross, *Diomedea epomophora* nests on Taiaroa Headland which is only accessible to humans by a narrow neck of land. In the past, this nesting ground was threatened by human disturbance and introduced pests. It is now under the protection of the Otago Peninsula Trust which earns income from visitors' fees paid for viewing the albatross colony from a viewing station. The colony is maintaining its own. Commercial conditions for conservation of the royal albatross colony are good for the following reasons which I have mentioned elsewhere:

"1. The amount of land that has had to be set aside for conservation is relatively small. The opportunity cost of keeping the colony is small.
2. Exclusion from the site is relatively easy, so the service of conserving species on the site for viewing can be sold to the public via entry fees. The service can be marketed, as is done with most private goods. Nevertheless, some individuals may see flying albatross from boats or from outside the enclosure without paying.
3. Since the Otago Peninsula Trust, as authorised by the Department of Conservation, has a monopoly (is the only operator able to sell rights to see royal albatross colonies in the area), it can charge a monopoly price for entry.
4. Because a high proportion of young albatrosses born in the colony return to the colony to breed on reaching adulthood, there is a close connection between attempts to conserve young in the colony and future populations of royal albatross at the colony.
5. The site is easily accessible in virtually all weather conditions.
6. Not only albatross but also breeding colonies of shags can be seen as a rule, and there is a magnificent view across the harbor, including Aramoana spit. So there is varied interest." (Tisdell 1990, p.89).

Another example, to consider is one of animal conservation ex situ. Lone Pine Koala Sanctuary in Brisbane claims to have the largest population of koalas in the world and operates as a commercial enterprise. It is reliant on income from visitors' fees and appears to be a profitable undertaking. Does it assist the conservation of koalas? By making the public more aware of koalas, it may make them more supportive of such conservation. Displays at the Sanctuary indicate that it has supported research into koalas and this may indirectly assist their conservation. Furthermore, eucalypt plantations have been commenced to provide food for the koalas in the Sanctuary rather than continuing to rely on collection of leaves from trees occurring naturally.

The keeping of wild animals in commercial zoos has often been controversial from a conservation point of view. One fear is that zoos may provide an economic incentive for the capture of rare animals from the wild and endanger their populations. On the other hand, zoos have occasionally been instrumental in saving species from extinction and sometimes zoos have been the source for the re-introduction of wildlife species to the wild.

FARMING AS A MEANS OF 'WILDLIFE' CONSERVATION

Biologists have sometimes seen farming of particular species as a practical way of saving them from extinction. This has been suggested for example for turtles, giant clams and crocodiles. In Africa, a number of private wildlife farms have been established to rear wildlife for sale for hunting and for the meat and for trade. For farming to be practical, it must be economical to confine the animals concerned (or to do so within reason) and for the owner to be able to exclude others from making use of them except on his/her terms.

When farming of a species is profitable, it will undoubtedly provide a strong incentive for conservation of this particular species. However, it does not necessarily follow that farming is favourable to the maintenance of biological diversity.

When the farming of a species is profitable, there is a tendency to select only the most economic varieties of it for farming. Varieties and breeds other than those found to be most economic are liable to be allowed to die out or are extinguished. Hence, natural genetic diversity is reduced. While this may be compensated for to some extent by artificial breeding programs, general evidence is that agriculture and the livestock industries are relying on an ever diminishing genetic base as a result of private economic selection.

There is a second way in which farming is liable to reduce genetic diversity. Where a species is farmed, habitat favoured by wild populations may be appropriated for farming and wild populations may be extinguished in this geographical range. This is also likely to lead to reduced genetic diversity.

Furthermore, farming generally leads to habitat modification and destruction of wild animals liable to compete with farmed animals. Farming, if widespread, results in greater uniformity of environments. Both of these elements can reduce genetic diversity. Sometimes it is even claimed that farming leads to greater demand for remaining wild members of a population or species and actually increases the harvesting of them (Tisdell 1991, Sec. 6.4).

Thus (even ignoring the last mentioned possibility) in the longer-term, farming is liable to lead to reduced genetic diversity. Indeed, it could reduce gene banks of significance for sustaining agricultural productivity to low levels which may make it difficult or impossible to sustain some types of farming in the long-term. Efforts to sustain genetic diversity outside the farming sector could therefore be important for the sustainability of farming.

The above does not imply that previously unfarmed species should not be farmed. Farming is bound to continue as an economic activity. It may well be that some existing wild species are environmentally more suitable for farming purposes than those animals currently farmed. For example, kangaroo farming in parts of Australia may be environmentally more suitable than sheep or cattle grazing. Currently one of the impediments to such farming is the difficulty of confining kangaroos to an individual property.

DISCUSSION AND CONCLUSION

Economic use of wildlife, particularly commercial use of a species, may be favourable to survival of wildlife but need not be. This depends upon the nature of property rights and the economic profit that can be obtained from using a species commercially. Under conditions of open-access, economic use of a species is unfavourable to its conservation and policy measures to control its utilisation are usually required. While the creation of private property rights in wildlife species may lead to their conservation, this is sometimes insufficient to ensure the survival of a commercially valuable species because alternatives to conserving the species are more profitable. Furthermore, it is not always economic to establish private property rights in wildlife species. So the creation of private property rights is not always a viable economic proposition.

Economic use of species, in a system designed to reflect economic values fully, is selective. It favours survival species and varieties of greatest economic value to the detriment of those of smaller or of no apparent economic value. Interference in natural systems is then designed solely with economic ends in mind. Such an approach to nature conservation is likely to be at odds with the land ethic, the ethical responsibility of humankind to conserve ecosystems as a whole (Leopold 1966). One would expect followers of Leopold (1966) to reject conservation intended solely to serve economic or utilitarian ends and to be increasingly alarmed by policy reforms which fostered this approach.

Even those taking a less ecocentric view may feel that the appropriate course of action is a middle course, namely that some but definitely not all wildlife conservation should be determined by economic use or values. They may do so because: (1) They are favourably disposed to the land ethic to some extent. They are neither completely anthropocentric or ecocentric in their value system. (2) Considerable uncertainty exists about future values, including economic values, of particular species and ecosystems and conservation of nature is a rational means of allowing for such uncertainties. This is an application of the precautionary principle (Young 1992, p.67). (3) The economic costs of conserving many remaining natural ecosystems may be low on average and the economic benefit of transforming them to their currently most economically valuable state may be slight. There may therefore be no case for the latter economic action when it is possible that such transformation could result in a significant economic loss in the more distant future e.g. due to extinction of species of possible future economic value (Ciriacy-Wantrup 1968; Bishop 1978). This view suggests that the only wise course of action is to allow current (or currently perceived) economic values to determine conservation of wildlife in a restricted spatial area reserving other areas for holistic conservation or with this as the prime aim. Of course, this leaves open the question of the size of areas or the area to be reserved for holistic conservation of nature. However, it involves rejection of a completely economic approach to conservation.

At the opposite extreme to the ecocentric view is the view that ideally all wildlife conservation should be determined by economic values and that systems should be developed so that the conservers of economically valuable wildlife can be fully rewarded. Ethically, I prefer the middle path (outlined in the previous paragraph) to either of the extremes. Nevertheless, it is accepted that sometimes greater realisation of economic values can sometimes foster nature conservation and support the cause of conservationists. Nature conservationists are not necessarily inconsistent when on some occasions they support and on other occasions they oppose greater reliance on commercial or economic use as a means of supporting wildlife conservation. Conservationists need to be selective in their support of economic incentives and values for wildlife conservation if their main goal is to support biodiversity. This is the main message of this paper.

ACKNOWLEDGEMENTS

Research for this paper was partially supported by a grant of the Australian Centre for International Agricultural Research (ACIAR Project No. 40). The views expressed are not necessarily those of the Australian Centre for International Agricultural Research. I wish to thank Ms J. Wen for her research assistance.

REFERENCES

Barbier, E.B. 1991. Managing trade and environment: the demand for raw ivory in Japan and Hong Kong. *The World Economy.* 14(1): 407-430.

Bishop, R.C. 1978. Endangered species and uncertainty. The economics of a safe minimum standard. *American Journal of Agricultural Economics.* 60: 10-18.

Ciriacy-Wantrup, J.V. 1968. Resource Conservation: Economics and Policies. Division Agricultural Economics, University of California: Davis.

Demsetz, H. 1967. Towards a theory of property rights. *American Economic Review.* 57: 347-59.

de Roos, G.T. 1981. The impact of tourism upon some breeding wader species on the isle of Vlieland in The Netherlands' Wadden Sea. Med. Landbouwhogeschool, Wageningen. 81-14: 1-131.

IUCN 1980. World Conservation Strategy. IUCN: Gland, Switzerland.

IUCN-UNEP-WWF 1991. Caring for the Earth: A Strategy for Sustainable Living. IUCN: Gland, Switzerland.

Leopold, A. 1966. A Sand Country Almanac: with Other Essays on Conservation from Round River. Oxford University Press: New York.

McNeely, J.A. 1988. Economics and Biological Diversity: Developing and Using Economic Incentives to Conserve Biological Resources. International Union for the Conservation of Nature and Natural Resources: Gland, Switzerland.

North, D.C. 1981. Structure and Change in Economic History. Norton: New York.

Tietenberg, T. 1992. Environmental and Natural Resource Economics. 3rd ed. Harper Collins: New York.

Tisdell, C.A. 1972. Provision of parks and preservation of nature – some economic factors. *Australian Economic Papers.* 11: 154-62.

Tisdell, C.A. 1990. Natural Resources, Growth and Development. Praeger: New York.

Tisdell, C.A. 1991. Economics of Environmental Conservation. Elsevier Science Publishers: Amsterdam.

Tisdell, C.A. 1993. Environmental Economics. Edward Elgar: Aldershot, U.K.

Yalden, D.W. 1984. Common Sandpiper numbers and recreational pressures in the Derwent Valley. *Magpie.* 3: 38-46.

Yalden, D.W. 1992. The influence of recreational disturbance on common sandpipers Actitis hypoleucos breeding by an upland reservoir, in England. *Biological Conservation.* 61: 41-49.

Yalden, P.E. and Yalden, D.W. 1991. Recreational disturbance of breeding golden plovers Pluvialis apricarious (sic.). *Biological Conservation.* 59: 243-62.

Young, M.D. 1992. Sustainable Investment and Resource Use. UNESCO: Paris and The Parthenon Publishing Group: Carnforth.

[6]

Combining biological conservation, sustainability and economic growth: can we overcome potential conflict?[1]

Abstract

Most countries, including presumably Papua New Guinea, would like to revitalise economic growth combining it with sustainability. Is it possible? Sensible discussion of this requires us to decide what is to be sustained and in what sense. Although many different views exist, the most commonly accepted view is that sustainability involves development which ensures that the per capita incomes of future generations are no less than those of current generations. Several writers argue that in order to achieve this, special attention must be paid to the conservation of natural resources and environmental assets, including biodiversity. Both optimistic and pessimistic theories or views exist about whether economic growth and environmental sustainability are compatible and about whether the income-levels of future generations are likely to be threatened by economic growth. Changing views on this subject are discussed.

Particular attention is given to the *World Bank Report 1992* because it assembles empirical evidence to address the question of whether economic growth leads to reduced environmental quality and growing resource shortages. On the whole, it takes an optimistic view, portraying economic growth as not only compatible with sustainability but also necessary for environmental improvement. However, it is anthropocentric in outlook and the empirical evidence as far as biological resources are concerned is that their conservation has not been successfully combined with economic growth. Since 1700, human-induced species extinctions have increased at an alarming rate, as has the loss of natural wildlife habitats. Such biological losses may in the end limit sustainable economic development.

The *World Bank Report 1992* highlights a number of economic policies that may be usefully adopted to foster environmental conservation, such as policies to ensure that the private costs paid by economic agents are brought into line with the social costs of their activities. On the other hand, both the IMF and the World Bank have promoted structural adjustment policies and seem to have promoted the adoption of market-making policies beyond what is practical and rational. Therefore, Papua New Guinea may do well to improve its mixed economic systems rather than adopt a laissez-faire system or engage in a bold experiment to market all environmental goods. One thing is clear: even if economic growth and sustainability are compatible, achieving such compatibility (especially compatibility with conservation of biological resources) will not be easy for Papua New Guinea without a lot of dedication, no matter what policy-path it embarks on.

Introduction

Most countries in the world today would like to revitalise growth combining it with sustainability. Papua New Guinea is no exception. For the less developed countries, it is an attractive possibility because it would sustainably release them from their low-income status and provide welcome long-term economic and environmental hope for their people. For more developed countries suffering, as most are, from economic recession and unemployment, it might provide a sustainable way out of their economic difficulties. It is indeed comforting to believe that economic growth and sustainability can be combined. Is it realistic? Is it possible and will it happen in practice? The answers to such questions are not straightforward and different thinkers and researchers have come to different conclusions. If we are to form a considered opinion, we must at least consider the existing range of views about these matters.

A major issue at the United Nations Conference on the Environment and Development at Rio in 1992 was the desirability of sustaining biological diversity. This raises the specific question of whether biological conservation can be satisfactorily reconciled with economic growth. Furthermore, should the extent to which biodiversity is maintained be used as an indicator of sustainability? These are all difficult questions to answer.

The need to define concepts

The task of answering the above questions is often made more difficult by failure to define the concepts being considered. For example, if sustainability is a goal, then it is important to ask: sustainability in what sense? Furthermore, what is it that is to be sustained? Without deciding on such matters in advance, it is really not possible to get beyond first base. As for what should be sustained, many different views have been expressed. These include (Tisdell, 1993, Ch. 9):

- Ensuring that future generations can meet their basic needs;
- Ensuring that per capita income levels can be maintained at levels such that the per capita incomes of future generations are no less than those of present generations;
- Sustaining the maximum span of existence for the human race;
- Preserving 'community' – essential sociological bonds and interrelationships within communities, and;
- Maintaining biological diversity.

Possibly the most widely accepted concept of sustainable development amongst economists is development that ensures that the per capita income levels of future generations are no less than those of current generations. This raises the question of whether this goal is compatible with the other possible sustainability goals mentioned above, whether it can be achieved and how it might be achieved.

Some would argue that all the above possible sustainability goals are closely linked. For example, Pearce *et al.* (1989) argue that it is important to maintain the natural or environmental stock (or capital) if the income levels of future generations are not to be less than those of current generations. This involves, amongst other things, conserving biodiversity because it is a part of the environmental or natural stock. The basic philosophy underlying Pearce *et al.*'s view is that one must be wary about substituting man-made capital for natural stock. If one is careless about this, the result may be unsustainable economic growth.

Growth and sustainability – pessimists vs optimists

The debate about whether economic growth is sustainable is a very old one. For instance, in 1798, Malthus expressed the view that it may be impossible to sustain per capita incomes above subsistence level due to natural restrictions on the productivity of land and the supposed tendency of the human race to expand in proportion to the means of subsistence. This theory was refined by David Ricardo (1817) who pointed out that technological progress could be a significant factor helping to offset this tendency. Engels (1959) and Marx vigorously attacked Malthus' view, declaring that scientific and technological advance would more than compensate for any increased demand made on resources by rising populations. By the end of the 19th century it seemed that this optimistic point of view had virtually swept the field. It was to go almost unchallenged until the 1970s reaching its apogee in the 1950s and 1960s.

Models came to dominate the economic growth literature in that period in which economic growth depended upon only three main factors, namely man-made capital accumulation, technological progress and the increase in the labour force as determined by population growth. The Solow–Swan model is a good example (see Jones, 1975; Tisdell, Ch.3). In these models natural resources (let alone environmental factors) are not constraining factors on economic growth. They do not form a part of these models. These models suggest that the recipe for enhanced economic growth is a faster rate of man-made capital accumulation and a greater rate of technological progress. Environmental disaster or natural resource limitations are considered to be of no importance as barriers to sustained economic growth. Capital accumulation (with a conveniently assumed exogenous rate of technological progress) became the touchstone for economic growth and for low-income countries, a possible path for their escape from their 'low equilibrium trap'.

Furthermore, in the 20th century increasing doubts were expressed about the Malthusian theory of population increases. This further weakened the classical-economics position that population increase and natural resource limitations are key elements limiting sustainability of incomes. As income levels have risen, population levels have not continued to increase at an exponential rate. After a period of transition, rates of population increase in countries experiencing economic growth have tapered off and many developed countries are now experiencing zero or even slightly negative population growth. The empirical evidence for this is convincing and the pattern can be explained in economic terms. One should hasten to add that the transition from high to low rates of population increase is only likely to occur if economic growth occurs at a sufficient rate and for sufficient duration to raise per capita incomes substantially, and also if it is accompanied by structural changes such as greater urbanisation and industrialisation which may reduce the incentive to have a large family.

In the 1970s, however, a resurgence of Malthusian views commenced, spurred on by the first oil crisis. The Club of Rome in *The Limits to Growth* (Meadows *et al.*, 1972) argued that current rates of economic growth and population increase were unsustainable and called for urgent action to restrain both. It predicted that without such restraint, depletion of many non-renewable resources, such as fossil fuels, was imminent and that crippling pollution would become widespread resulting in economic disaster. This neo-Malthusian point of view was vigorously attacked by many mainstream economists (Tisdell, 1981). In formal terms, much of the criticism was justified. However, there were amongst the critics, many who failed to see that the economic growth solution to overcoming poverty might become a problem, that is, reduce the chances of future generations being able to achieve a reasonable standard of living.

In reality, most economists then (and probably most now, for example Tietenberg, 1992) held an optimistic point of view that economic growth is good, that it will eventually result in a stationary population and provided that the market system is allowed to operate fully, market forces will make appropriate allowances for reductions in stocks of resources. Furthermore, continuing technological progress will make for a bright future. However, it should be pointed out that the continuation of technological and scientific progress is accepted as a matter of faith. No convincing arguments are provided as to why humanity can expect continuing largesse *ad infinitum* from this cornucopia.

Beginning in 1980 with the *World Conservation Strategy* (IUCN, 1980), neo-Malthusians added a new string to their bow. Whereas the main emphasis in the 1970s had been on the depletion of non-renewable resources and pollution, the debate shifted to the disappearance of living resources, for example the extinction of species, which under normal circumstances would be renewable. Loss of living resources and loss of biodiversity became a major issue and one that was to form an important part of the Rio Conference in 1992. It was increasingly argued that such biological losses could become an impediment to sustainable economic growth.

One might say that it is all very well to talk about optimistic and pessimistic theories of the relationship between economic growth and sustainability, but what do the empirical facts indicate? Appeal to empirical observations is important even though different individuals may draw different conclusions from the same set of observations because observations are usually consistent with more than one hypothesis. The *World Bank Report 1992* assembles observations and comes to a relatively optimistic conclusion.

Does economic growth result in reduced environmental quality and resource shortages?

In order to see if economic growth, designed to achieve higher per capita incomes, is associated with a deteriorating or an improving environment and with increasing natural resources scarcity, (1) time series or (2) cross-sectional observations may be used. The *World Bank Report 1992* uses both to come to the following conclusion: Economic growth and improvement in environmental quality and increased economic availability of natural resources are not only compatible but economic growth may be necessary for such results. So in this context, economic growth in the view of the World Bank is a blessing.

The Bank provides time-series evidence to support its view that the world is not running out of marketed non-renewable energy and raw material resources. For example, it provides data showing that proven reserves of energy and mineral reserves rose in relation to annual consumption between 1970 and 1988. In addition, it has a figure (diagram) suggesting that the real long-run prices for non-ferrous metals have shown a downward trend over the period 1900 to 1990 (World Bank, 1992, p. 37). Declining real prices would indicate reduced economic scarcity. However, the data are insufficient to prove the Bank's point. In relation to non-ferrous metal prices, if the data before 1920 are ignored, there is no clear tendency for a long-run decline in such prices, and the trend could easily be a precursor to rising future prices. In any case, the question needs to be answered of why it is appropriate to project the past trend to the future.

Concerning economic growth and environmental quality, the Bank mostly relies on cross-sectional data and provides evidence that for many indicators of environmental quality; environmental quality improves with the level of income achieved by a country (see for example World Bank, 1992, pp. 11, 46, 55). This seems to be so for water quality (as measured by dissolved oxygen in rivers), and to some extent for urban air pollution levels and for access to safe water and sanitation. The main adverse environmental impacts of high-income levels are seen as rising municipal waste generation rates (per capita) and rising carbon dioxide levels (per capita). The latter adds to greenhouse gases but has a global rather than a local or national effect of perceived significance because of the major externality involved. The clear message of the World Bank is that the environmental benefits of economic growth can be expected to outweigh any disbenefits, for virtually all countries.

Encouraging evidence is also provided pointing to a slow down in rates of global population increase, suggesting that the world as a whole is completing its demographic transition and that levels of human population will stabilise in the 21st century.

A further powerful argument in favour of economic growth is the positive association between expected length of life of humans and income levels. Since mortality and morbidity appear to be significantly reduced by improved environmental quality, this suggests that from a human perspective, environmental quality has improved overall – at least in vital respects.

However, there are also some worrying environmental trends. The living natural environment is taking a 'battering'. The rate at which humans, by their activities, are extinguishing other species and reducing biodiversity is far beyond the natural rate of extinction and has increased in every century since 1700 (cf. World Bank, 1992, p. 58). Indeed, it seems that the rate of extinction of species now being brought about by humankind exceeds the rates at which mass extinction of species have occurred in the past due to unusual natural events (cf. Gould, 1990). Much of this extinction is coming about as a result of habitat destruction – the loss of natural wildlife habitats and their replacement with relatively uniform human-modified environments, modified to expand commercial and subsistence production and support a growing human population. A vast area of natural vegetation cover has been lost and in many developing countries (and in some more developed ones), the loss continues. It is estimated for example that in the Indomalayan realm from 68 per cent to 85 per cent of the land area covered by the main vegetation types has been lost. In the Afrotropical area (excluding wetland/marsh) 55 per cent to 60 per cent of the land area originally covered by the main vegetation types has been lost. The loss is continuing and, if anything, is likely to accelerate as many less developed countries in these regions embark on efforts to increase their economic growth. The outlook from a non-anthropocentric point of view is therefore gloomy. Furthermore, there is a possibility that this loss of biological resources will limit sustainable economic growth (Tisdell, 1990, 1991).

Policy matters

As pointed out by the World Bank (1992, Ch. 3), many environmental problems in less developed countries and elsewhere are made worse by inappropriate pricing and economic policies. For instance, the use of scarce natural resources such as underground water may not be priced or may be underpriced. Actual costs paid by producers (private costs) may be less than the social costs of their activities, for example where these activities have adverse environmental spillovers to others. Measures need to be taken by governments to ensure that private costs reflect full social costs. Taxes, for example, may be imposed on producers to capture the external environmental costs or damages generated by their activities. This means that their externalities are internalised and producers factor the full social cost of their activities into their decision-making thus helping to achieve a better social outcome.

In some cases, governments even actually adopt environmentally perverse industrial policies. Activities are sometimes subsidised which have an *adverse* environmental effect. Examples include subsidies for land clearing, subsidies (sometimes hidden) for logging, subsidies on pesticide use and so on. Many other actual examples could be cited.

Both market and government failures occur which adversely affect biological conservation and environmental preservation. Nevertheless, it is not apparent that the best way for countries to deal with these problems is to adopt the structural adjustment policies recommended by the International Monetary Fund and the World Bank. These call for maximum use of free markets and small government. Such a system is not necessarily better from a sustainability and an environmental point of view than current imperfect systems (Tisdell, 1992). Second, a laissez-faire policy because of market failures is unlikely to be an optimal policy for ensuring an appropriate supply of environmental goods. Policies need to be adopted by governments that are specifically targeted to nature conservation and environmental preservation. Nonetheless, this may be best done within a market framework and the policies adopted may make some use of market systems, for example involve the introduction of tradeable pollution rights. Therefore, a mixed economic system is likely to be the best available, especially if combined with freedom of information and freedom of the press. Either the adoption completely of a laissez-faire market system, or of a centrally planned economic system, is likely to lead to environmental disaster and have many other unsatisfactory consequences.

Concluding comments

The World Bank (1992), like the World Commission on Environment and Development (1987), is optimistic that economic growth and environmental improvement can be combined. Indeed, economic growth in less developed countries is seen as a prerequisite for environmental improvement, and it has been argued that the economic growth of less developed countries need complementary economic growth in developed countries (Tisdell, 1991, Ch. 12).

To support its case, the World Bank (1992) appeals to the empirical evidence relying mainly on cross-sectional data to compare environmental conditions in low income, middle-income and high-income countries. Its basic conclusion is that, except for one or two indicators (for example, emissions of greenhouse gases, such as CO_2), environmental conditions are best in high-income countries. This suggests that economic growth results in a better environment. But of course, environmental quality changes involve an index problem if the environment improves in some respects but deteriorates in others. To some extent, high-income countries depend upon resource imports from less developed ones, which enables them to export some of their environmental problems. Biodiversity loss continues and higher incomes on a global scale *may* not be sustainable under current conditions. Also, examining time series for long-run prices of non-ferrous metals and other data, the World Bank concludes that we are not running out of non-renewable energy and raw materials. Whether the Report is too optimistic, only time will tell.

Amongst other things, the Report recommends market reforms and policy changes to ensure that prices of commodities reflect environmental costs or values fully, or more fully than in the past. Efficient economic growth and environmental improvement are seen as possible and complementary. Clearly, this Report contains important lessons. For example, sometimes market systems do not perform as well as they should or government intervention has adverse environmental effects, even though many of these lessons are not new. One possible criticism of the Report is that it contains little or no discussion of values – it seems to take Western mainstream economic anthropocentric values for granted – and it could encourage complacency about economic growth by portraying mostly its beneficial effects. While there are some lessons in the Report for Papua New Guinea's formulation of national strategy, additional issues need to be canvassed.

While efforts to create a perfect market system in which environmental effects are priced laudable, such a widespread market system is unlikely to be achieved in the near future and it may prove uneconomic to market all natural or environmental resources since market-making itself also involves an economic cost. It may, therefore, be more sensible for Papua New Guinea to concentrate on ways in which it can improve its present mixed economic system rather than attempt to transform this system into a perfect market system.

Clearly there are environmental problems to be resolved in the whole of the South Pacific (see for example McKee and Tisdell, 1990, Part III). However, no matter how Papua New Guinea decides to develop its economic system, it will not be easy for it to combine biological conservation, sustainability and economic growth. While it may not be impossible, dedication, goodwill, vigilance, sensitivity and considerable effort will be needed if Papua New Guinea's natural environment is not to suffer irreparably. I wish you well with this important task, which is important not only for your country but for the whole world.

Note

1. This article originally appeared in D. Gladman, D. Mowbray and J. Duguman (eds), *From Rio to Rai: Environment and Development in Papua New Guinea*. Papers from the 20th Waigani Seminar (Vol. 6)

University of Papua New Guinea, 1996, pp. 5–16. The content of this article is the same as in the original (except for minor changes) but its presentation has been improved. Consequently, pagination is no longer the same as in the original.

References

Engels, F. (1959), 'Outline of a Critique of Political Economy', in K. Marx, *Economic and Philosophic Manuscripts of 1844*, Moscow: Foreign Languages Publishing House.
Gould, S.J. (1990), *The Individual in Darwin's World*, Edinburgh: Edinburgh University Press.
IUCN, International Union for the Conservation of Nature and Natural Resources (1980), *World Conservation Strategy*, Switzerland: IUCN, Glands.
Jones, H.G. (1975), *An Introduction to Modern Theories of Economic Growth*, London: Nelson.
Malthus, T.R. (1798), *An Essay on the Principle of Population as it Affects the Future Improvement of Mankind*, London: J. Johnston.
McKee, D. and C.A. Tisdell (1990), *Developmental Issues in Small Island Economies*, New York: Praeger.
Meadows, D.H., D.L. Meadows, J. Randers and W.W. Behrens III (1972), *The Limits to Growth: A Report for the Club of Rome's Project on the Predicament of Mankind*, London: Universe Books.
Pearce, D., A. Markandya and E.B. Barbier (1989), *Blueprint for a Green Economy*, London: Earthscan Publications.
Ricardo, D. (1817), *The Principles of Political Economy and Taxation*, London.
Tietenberg, T. (1992), *Environmental and Natural Resource Economics*, 3rd edition, New York: Harper Collins.
Tisdell, C.A. (1981), *Science and Technology Policy: Priorities of Governments*, London: Chapman and Hall.
Tisdell, C.A. (1990), *Natural Resources, Growth and Development: Economics Ecology and Resource-Scarcity*, New York: Praeger.
Tisdell, C.A. (1991), *Economics of Environmental Conservation*, Amsterdam: Elsevier Science Publishers.
Tisdell, C.A. (1992), 'Conservation, Protected Areas and the Global Economic System: How Debt, Trade, Exchange Rates, Inflation and Macroeconomic Policy Affect Biological Diversity', in *Parks for Life: Enhancing the Role of Protected Areas in Sustaining Society*, Plenary Sessions and Symposium Papers of IV World Congress of National Parks and Protected Areas, Switzerland: IUCN, Gland, pp. 35–55.
Tisdell, C.A. (1993), *Environmental Economics: Policies for Environmental Management and Sustainable Development*, Cheltenham, UK and Brookfield, US: Edward Elgar.
World Bank (1992), *World Development Report 1992: Development and the Environment*, New York: Oxford University Press.
World Commission on Environment and Development (1987), *Our Common Future*, Oxford: Oxford University Press.

[7]

Issues in Biodiversity Conservation Including the Role of Local Communities*

by

CLEMENT A. TISDELL, PhD (ANU)
Professor & Head, Department of Economics,
University of Queensland,
Brisbane 4072,
Australia.

INTRODUCTION

There is an urgent need to develop rational policies for the conservation of biological diversity. This is because: (a) the rate of reduction of biodiversity is alarmingly rapid owing to the impacts of Mankind (extensively through habitat destruction as a result of economic growth) (Wilson, 1988; Ehrlich & Ehrlich, 1992); (b) the Biodiversity Convention has come into force, thereby increasing the policy relevance of conservation strategies; and (c) there is increased availability of international aid and funding for biodiversity conservation, for example through the Global Environmental Facility. Unfortunately, however, our current knowledge about biodiversity conservation lags far behind our capacity to destroy Nature.

This paper points out some limitations of existing economic and ecological approaches to assessing conservation of biodiversity, and suggests a few possibilities for dealing with these approaches. The theoretical/structural aspects of optimal biodiversity are then briefly discussed, followed by biodiversity issues involving local communities. Illustrations are given of these issues from Xishuangbanna Prefecture in Yunnan, China.

The first issue that really needs to be settled (at least to some extent) in discussing conservation of biodiversity, is the definition or measurement of biodiversity. This matter is discussed in a useful introductory way by Pearce & Moran (1994), who distinguish between genetic diversity, species diversity, and ecosystem diversity. To measure accurately and describe such overall diversity is extremely difficult. Probably the measurement of species diversity is easiest because species tend to be discrete, but this is clearly only one dimension of a multidimensional attribute. Despite measurement problems, there is evidence that biodiversity in all its dimensions is now declining rapidly due to human impact, and that this process has been accelerating over the last few centuries and particularly decades. Amongst other things, this has led to concern that such losses could threaten the sustainability of economic development.

LIMITATIONS OF SOME ECONOMIC APPROACHES TO ASSESSING THE CONSERVATION OF BIODIVERSITY

One of the main limitations of much recent economic discussion of biodiversity is that it really does not deal with this subject, or does so only in a peripheral way. It fails to concentrate on the aspect of diversity and the value or otherwise of retaining or altering this. There has been no shortage recently of discussions and empirical work on the economic value of individual species and ecosystems, using a wide variety of approaches such as the use of CVM (contingent valuation method) as suggested by Pearce & Moran (1994).

While the use of CVM is useful for determining general and recreational values of biodiversity, it is liable to be much less useful in determining 'productivity' values. This is mainly because the general public has insufficient knowledge of the productivity influences of retention or loss of biodiversity. In many cases (some would say most) even scientists and technical experts are uncertain about the productivity relationships, but hopefully are better informed than the general public. This is an important reason for not relying entirely on CVM.

In discussing the value of retaining tropical forests for the possible future medicinal value of their plants, Pearce & Moran (1994) do not use CVM, but estimate the expected value per hectare of drugs that are likely to be derived from this retention. Their estimation is based on: (1) the market value of medicinal plants that are likely to be obtained, (2) the market value of drugs derived from these, and (3) the value of lives that should be saved by the availability of such drugs. The estimated range of values is very wide, because of both the wide range in the probability of medicinal uses and in the estimated values. At a 5% discount rate and at the upper range of the estimate, a hectare of tropical forest is estimated to be worth \$420 for this purpose, but to have a negligible value at the lower end. Note that if the principle of insufficient reason were applied to this case, the expected net present value of a tropical forest would be about \$210 per ha for medicinal purposes. According to the principle of insufficient reason, suggested originally by Laplace, events for which we have insufficient reason to suggest other probabilities should be treated as equally probable.

The model is, however, a global one and assumes that, on average, all tropical rain-forest is likely to be of equal value for medicinal purposes and that marginal and average values do not differ. Some tropical forests contain more botanic diversity than others, and therefore may have greater value for retention for medicinal purposes. In any case, the value of retaining tropical forests to maintain biodiversity for future medicinal uses, pales in comparison with their estimated value for carbon fixation. Conversion of a hectare of primary forest to agriculture is estimated to result in carbon releases causing \$4,000–4,400 in damages (Pearce & Moran, 1994 p. 42). This is a very large figure, and Pearce & Moran suggest that it would still be large after appropriate discounting.

The conservation of living resources results as a rule in a number of joint products and consequently the value of their conservation should be determined holistically, considering all foreseeable possibilities. Biodiversity is of course not only valuable for possible future medicinal applications. For example, in the case of tropical forests, retained genetic diversity may have future application to forestry tree crops and some agricultural crops. Biodiversity may also have non-use value such as existence value or as a tourist or recreational attraction. When there is a choice in conserving natural areas *ceteris paribus*, it will be an

* Based on a paper presented at a seminar held at The World Bank, Washington, DC, USA, on 18 January 1995. I wish to thank Dr M. Alauddin for his suggestions concerning this paper, and participants in The World Bank seminar for their valuable comments.

Environmental Conservation, Vol. 22, Nr 3, Autumn 1995 — © 1995 The Foundation for Environmental Conservation — Printed in Switzerland economic advantage as a rule to conserve the areas with the greatest biodiversity, which are commonly forests and their surroundings. It therefore seems quite rational to give a high priority to conserving areas with 'megadiversity', namely a high degree of biological diversity.

This raises the entire question of how we should evaluate the conservation of biodiversity as a whole. So far we do not have any satisfactory answer. Ecologists have suggested priorities based on 'degrees' of representation of living things and the rarity and imminence of their loss (*see*, for example, Tisdell, 1991 Ch. 5). Overall the preferred approach of economists has been to apply extended cost–benefit analysis to the problem. The basic proposition is that all living things and their support systems should be conserved for which the discounted total economic value is non-negative and higher than for any 'development' alternative. Thus in this indirect way, studies measuring the economic value of biological resources have implications for the conservation of biodiversity. However, some Authors have expressed considerable reservations about the cost–benefit approach (CBA) to determining the desirability of preservation of a species (Ciriacy-Wantrup, 1968; Bishop, 1978, 1979), mainly on the basis of the degree of uncertainty involved about the future value of individual species. They favour the use of a safe minimum standard (SMS).

In the absence of institutional constraints on resources available for the conservation of biodiversity, the use of the safe minimum standard criterion would result in a greater degree of biodiversity being conserved than with an expected CBA (*see* above) approach because the former will value the costs of extinction on the basis of the most unfavourable possibility whereas the latter will value it on the expected (average) possibility. Thus there is a different approach to risk-taking. On the other hand, if the resources available for conservation are institutionally constrained, the usefulness of the SMS approach becomes doubtful. Because of the constraint, SMS cannot be used as a vehicle to increase the level of conservation but can only be used to choose between the species to be conserved and other taxa etc. If this is done so as to minimize the maximum possible regret, the resulting array of species conserved is likely to have much lower expected value than would be the case if CBA was applied with a view to maximizing expected net benefits.

Uncertainty is a serious constraint to deciding rationally on the optimal conservation of biodiversity. This limits not only the application of CBA but also the application of other decision-making criteria as well. Nevertheless, we do have some pertinent knowledge and it is rational to make use of whatever knowledge we do possess. In this respect, there may be scope for applying Keynes' concept of logical probabilities (Keynes, 1921). Presumably, one of the reasons for trying to conserve the wild relatives of domesticated cultivars, such as those of Wheat (*Triticum aestivum*) and Rice (*Oryza sativa*), is that there is a high probability that their genetic material will have future economic value. Similarly, areas of great biodiversity per hectare, such as tropical rain-forest, have a high probability of future use of their genetic material due to the large amount of biodiversity present.

Observations on Some Ecological Propositions About Biodiversity

One sometimes hears the proposition that biodiversity is necessary for the sustainability of ecosystems or their stability. However, it is easy to exaggerate the fragility of ecosystems in relation to biodiversity loss. The Gaia hypothesis (implying *inter alia* that species may be so interdependent that the loss of one could eventually lead to the loss of all), may be less widely applicable than is claimed by some ecologists, even though it is possible for the loss of some species (keystone species) to threaten the functioning of a whole ecosystem. It is possible for considerable loss of biodiversity to occur, and for some ecosystems to continue to function satisfactorily in an attenuated or changed form. The Pacific islands have been used as illustrations (Ash, 1992; Thaman, 1992). However, Ehrlich & Ehrlich (1992) warn that the level of biodiversity loss which will cause an ecosystem to collapse is uncertain, and Norton (1988) also makes a similar point.

As the biological diversity of any ecosystem is decreased, the likelihood of its virtual collapse or serious attenuation increase. Having contended this, I would like to suggest that ecosystems of greater diversity are not necessarily more sustainable or more stable (Tisdell, 1994*a*). The degrees of biological tolerance of the species which belong to the ecosystem need also to be considered. Tropical ecosystems tend to be rich in biodiversity, but most of the species present in these systems show little biological tolerance and many seem to exhibit little mobility. Thus despite the higher degree of biodiversity, these systems would be at considerable risk with any environmental change. On the other hand, the ecosystems of temperate zones tend to show less biodiversity than those of the tropics, but, on the whole, the species present appear to exhibit greater biological tolerance and they may be more mobile. The species of temperate zones may therefore show greater capacity to survive than those in the tropics, should environmental conditions alter. Thus, biodiversity as such is neither necessary nor sufficient to ensure a high probability of survival of species.

The point is made by some ecologists that species diversity tends to be greater in disturbed than undisturbed environments (Smiet, 1992). Nevertheless, it would clearly be misleading to conclude that the way to increase or maintain global biodiversity is to disturb as many natural environments as possible. The maintenance of biodiversity appears to be dependent on maintaining a large variety of different environments. Uniformity of environments can be raised by increasing the area of disturbed environments and thereby reducing the relative extent of natural environments compared with those disturbed by Mankind. While some disturbance of natural environments can be expected to help maintain global biodiversity, if carried beyond a point, it will reduce such diversity. Furthermore, the impact of disturbances will depend on their nature and intensity.

Some Further Considerations in Biodiversity Conservation

The economics of biodiversity conservation depends very much on the ecological relationships involved in such conservation. For example, the scope for applying the safe minimum standard criterion to Nature conservation is reduced when it is realized that there may be no safe minimum standard ensuring the survival of a species (Hohl & Tisdell, 1993). As the population of a species increases and/or environmental factors favourable to its continued survival improves, the probability of the continued survival of the species in a fixed interval of time rises but it is unlikely to become unity, even though it might virtually do so if the time-interval is relatively short.

Fundamentally, however, the survival of species, even under relatively favourable conditions, is not certain and decision-making criteria need to take this into account. The safe minimum standard for survival of a species should relate to a minimum probability for its survival during a time-interval. Conceivably, the standard may vary with time, *e.g.* there may be a desire to raise the probability of survival of the species as time elapses.

There has been a tendency in economics, in discussing safe minimum standards and the survival of species, to concentrate on single species. This is partially explained by the degree of simplification involved. However, there is often (in fact almost always) important interdependence between populations of species and their survival, and there is increasing need to take this into account in economic modelling and decision-making. In particular, complementary relationships between species can be used to advantage in adding to biodiversity or maintaining it.

Biodiversity Issues and the Local Community

Conservation of biodiversity involves cooperation at a number of levels of government and the community. However, it is local communities which have the closest physical contact with conservation of biodiversity, and economically they are likely to be most affected by biodiversity conservation programmes. Furthermore, the co-operation of local communities is often vital for the success of biodiversity conservation programmes. If such communities only see economic losses for themselves as a result of such programmes, these can be expected to lead to political unrest, the sabotage of conservation efforts, and disregard of rules or laws adopted for conservation purposes. Even local authorities may lack the will to enforce conservation rules and laws in such circumstances.

There is often little incentive for local communities to conserve biodiversity and natural living resources because they often appropriate little, if any, of the economic benefits from such conservation. Because of externalities, many of the benefits from this conservation flow to wider communities and even to the global community, *e.g.* benefits of existence value, fixation of carbon, and so on. Even when benefits are enjoyed at the local level, these may largely be external to individuals engaging in conservation efforts.

There are at least two reasons why biodiversity may be threatened from an economic point of view: (1) those undertaking conservation efforts may appropriate an insufficient share of the total benefits of their effort to make it worth while, and (2) even if they are able to appropriate all the economic benefits from their conservation effort, these benefits may be less than the return from alternative uses of their land, resulting in lost biodiversity.

A considerable portion of the current policy discussions concentrates on methods and mechanisms to ensure that local communities and people appropriate a larger share of the total gains from their conservation of biodiversity and of living resources, whether these benefits tend to be global or more localized. Mechanisms that are being considered include:

(1) Subsidies to locals for the retention and conservation of natural areas.

(2) The payment of royalties on the use of genetic material conserved by a country or locality. This is a property rights and market approach.

(3) The utilization of the conserved living resources for non-consumptive purposes with a view to earning income. Nature-based tourism or ecotourism can in certain circumstances fulfil this role.

(4) Permitting the use of natural areas for economic activities that do not threaten biodiversity and in some circumstances may be favourable to its maintenance. These may include the gathering of non-timber products and, in certain circumstances, the limited cultivation of forested areas.

(5) Income tranfers to local people so as to reduce their need to exploit natural areas.

(6) The funding or provision of finance on concessional terms for development projects outside Nature reserves, thereby raising the incomes of locals and reducing their economic pressure to exploit Nature reserves.

A brief comment on each of these mechanisms may be in order.*

Subsidies for Retention of Natural Areas

Subsidies to conserve biodiversity, funded by the external beneficiaries of biodiversity conservation, provide a mechanism for encouraging biodiversity conservation. However, there are many complex matters to be considered in paying subsidies. These include: (a) the size of agency and transaction costs, (b) the integrity of those involved in the conservation process in ensuring that conservation is practised, (c) estimation of the size of the subsidy required, (d) delivery of the subsidy to those effective in ensuring conservation, and (e) the possible use of blackmail to extract the maximum surplus from those willing to pay the subsidy (Tisdell, 1990 Ch. 4).

Attention clearly has to be given to the size of transaction, agency costs, and effort needed to be made to minimize these. 'Integrity' also has to be considered, that is the likelihood of compliance with the terms on which a subsidy is granted. In that respect, compliance is likely to be more easily obtained if the subsidy is an annual payment (a rental payment) rather than a lump sum (discounted present value) payment. As for the required subsidy, some case-studies estimating instances have been completed. For example, Ruitenbeek (1992) has estimated this in terms of the rain-forest supply prices taking Korup National Park in Cameroon as a particular case. To do this he shows, using extended CBA, that Cameroon would make a loss on a project designed to protect the biodiversity of Korup NP and that it would need a lump-sum payment of 3,600 CFAF (US $12.71) per hectare to compensate it for this loss. Ruitenbeek suggests that this is within the range of affordability and past practice of developing countries in providing support for such conservation. A point, however, not discussed is how the subsidy delivery mechanism would operate especially at the local level, *e.g.* to compensate those with lost forest use. Ruitenbeek (1992 p. 76) makes the useful observation that the subsidy should be paid partly as a lump sum and partly on an annual basis to help cover operating expenses. He observes that 'a common problem with projects of a "social" nature in developing countries... is that local governments do not meet ongoing current budgetary needs for programs that generate few revenues'.

*Note also that there is due consideration of some of them in the preceding paper in this issue. — Ed.

Royalty Payments for Conservation

The payment of royalties for use of genetic material provides another possible incentive for biodiversity conservation. In this regard the agreement between the drug manufacturer Merck & Company and the Institute de Biodiversidad (INBio) has been hailed as an important pioneering international institutional arrangement. Merck agreed to pay INBio an upfront sum of $1 million for collection and screening of plant, insect, and soil, samples and a percentage of revenue (suggested to be 1–3%) on any of these items developed by Merck further and used commercially by Merck (Blum, 1993). A portion of the income obtained by Costa Rica will be transferred to its Ministry of Natural Resources to be used for conservation purposes. Nevertheless, as is true of most new technology, appropriation by Costa Rica is likely to be far from complete. How well rewards are linked to those actually engaging in the conservation, say at the local level, is also not clear.

Ecotourism Potentials

The charging of fees to tourists making use of biodiversity and natural resources provides another strategy for appropriating local gains from conservation and up to a point tourism development is often possible without seriously endangering conservation and biodiversity. In addition, fees or rents may be charged to tourist operators for concessions to provide tourist services. However, ecotourism projects are not always profitable. If care is not taken, they can become a financial burden on conservation authorities (Tisdell, 1994*b*). Often, conservation authorities lack business expertise in developing such projects, and they will often do well to seek the involvement of joint venturers with business skills. This is not to suggest that ecotourism cannot be profitable — Dixon & Sherman (1990) provide a number of examples of profitable Nature-based tourism — but caution is needed because financial flops can occur which burden rather than assist conservation.

Other Local Uses from Retaining Biodiversity

Local people have little incentive to support the conservation of living resources unless they can gain something from it or at least not be deprived of major benefits already enjoyed. In certain cases, it may be possible to permit limited use of natural areas by locals and still retain biodiversity. Nevertheless, Godoy & Bawa (1993) suggest that caution is needed as local people even far away from markets may reduce biodiversity by such activities. They state: 'We still do not understand the social and economic determinants of judicious uses of natural resources. Secure property rights, low population density, customary rules of use, and simple technology, seem to encourage judicious use. Extraction may be a viable activity only in areas with low population densities (Homma, 1992)' (Godoy & Bawa, 1993). The possibility of providing secure property rights to those allowed to engage in extraction in conservation areas needs further exploration.

Income Transfers and Local Development Projects

Income transfers or supplements may also provide a means to ease pressure on conservation areas, but they are probably not a socially acceptable long-term solution because they entail dependence, and their continuation requires continuing political support. Development projects which raise incomes of locals seem to be more readily accepted. These may raise the incomes of individuals in the region in which conservation is desired, or provide local people with skills which make it easier for them to migrate to higher-income areas. China's preferred strategy at the present time is to support local development projects with a view to raising local incomes and thereby hopefully reducing pressures on Nature reserves (*cf.* Wells & Brandon, 1992). Let us consider the Chinese situation, concentrating on Xishuangbanna Prefecture in southern Yunnan.

China and Strategies for Biodiversity Conservation in Xishuangbanna Dai Autonomous Prefecture

Environmental policy in China is of interest to the whole world because of China's capacity to add significantly to the global effects of environmental change (Tisdell, 1993; Hall *et al.*, 1994; Ch. 12, 1995;). It is also a country rich in biodiversity, and this biodiversity is under considerable threat (National Environmental Protection Agency *et al.*, 1994). It is, therefore, significant that the State Council adopted in 1994 *China's Agenda 21 — White Paper on China's Population, Environment and Development in the 21st Century.** This White Paper outlines policies intended to promote ecologically sustainable development for China in the next century and represents a follow-on from UNCED held in Brazil. This *White Paper* is some 244 pages in length and covers important policy questions. There is also an introduction to China's Agenda 21 (Administrative Centre for China's Agenda 21, 1994). Biodiversity conservation is stressed as one of the goals for Agenda 21, and China has devised a biodiversity conservation action plan (National Environmental Protection Agency *et al.*, 1994).

The strategy preferred at present in China for easing pressures on biodiversity conservation in Nature reserves is to try to improve economic opportunities outside of reserves and raise the income levels of people living in the neighbourhood of the reserves. China is therefore considering — and intends to test — models to promote economic development by people living in areas surrounding Nature reserves. Development and conservation in Xishuangbanna Dai Autonomous Prefecture involves such an approach. This Prefecture is located in southern Yunnan and is internationally recognized as being very rich in biodiversity.

China's approach to Nature conservation has been explained as follows: 'Most of China's nature reserves are located in poor natural areas with limited opportunities for economic development. People depend heavily on natural resources for subsistence and cash-generating activities. They continue to utilize resources from high biodiversity ecosystems set aside for protection, and increasing population and economic growth lead to overexploitation of the land and degradation of the resource-base on which the people depend. Pressures then increase to use resources in Nature reserves, and ecological damage of surrounding areas threaten the function of protected ecosystems. As a result many Nature reserves have been severely degraded since they were established and some have entirely lost the biodiversity values [which] they were intended to protect' (National Environmental Protection Agency *et al.*, 1994 p. 83).

*Cited in References as 'State Council..., 1994. — Ed.

Therefore, promotion of economic development outside of reserves is seen as important for conservation in Nature reserves. Chinese authorities believe that 'The future viability of the Nature reserve system depends on developing successful programs to address the economic needs of local people while still fulfilling the conservation goals. Instead of simply discouraging unwise development, Nature reserve managers need to cooperate with local communities to encourage the search for types of development [that will be] sustainable over the long-term and compatible with reserve management goals. The issue is whether the natural resources outside reserves can support the human population in the long-term' (*ibid.*).

While this approach seems to be promising, it is not a watertight solution to conserving biodiversity. Often measures to increase economic productivity outside Nature reserves involve intensification of land-use and a reduction of biodiversity in these areas. Such intensification, particularly in the case of agriculture, normally involves increased use of resources external to the land. This could add to pressure on the resources of a reserve, *e.g.* to use its timber for construction or the water resources in it or passing through it for irrigation and electricity generation. Higher incomes could also lead to higher effective demands for speciality items (such as special foods) which may only be available from the Nature reserve. Again the economic damage caused outside reserves by animals from reserves may rise as higher-valued and more productive agriculture is introduced. Thus social hostility to the reserve may grow. Furthermore, as economic productivity per hectare rises outside a reserve, the view may be increasingly accepted that the reserve involves an economic waste of natural resources, not because it really does but because the apparent relative disparity in productivity inside and outside the reserve increase. In any case, it would be unwise to relax measures to protect reserves as economic development in their surrounding areas proceeds. In fact, a strengthening of these measures may be needed as discussed later in this essay.

Agroforestry and Social Forestry Projects

A popular suggestion for community projects to ease pressures on Nature reserves has been to encourage local villagers to engage in agroforestry. This is one of the approaches that is being tested in Xishuangbanna, which Prefecture contains Xishuangbanna State Nature Reserve, a very important Nature Reserve consisting of five sub-reserves and with a bureau as its chief administering body. The Bureau for the Protection of this State Nature Reserve is willing to supply tree/shrub seedlings free of charge to landholders bordering the Nature Reserve if they wish to engage in agroforestry. Some financial support has been received by the Bureau from WWF for the above purposes, and trials have begun for instance in Zhong Tian Ba village bordering Mengyang Sub-reserve.

At Zhong Tian Ba, a small stand of mixed trees has been planted on a sloping site (but not a steeply sloping one). This site has been contoured and Tea (*Thea sinensis*) has been planted in the depressions of the contours with the trees being planted on the ridges. Both trees for timber and some for fruit have been planted. The trees being tested are:

Caganus cagan
Cassia siamea
Fiemngia macrophylla
Gliricidia sepium
Sesbania bispinosa
Sesbania sesban
Ligustrum lucidum.

Cassia siamea has been traditionally grown by the Dai people in their villages to provide fuel. It is a nitrogen-fixing species and enriches the soil. At Zhong Tian Ba, some *Cassia* trees have been planted at a second site on relatively flat land where there are now some mature Tea bushes and some vegetables have been planted. Agroforestry in this village is basically intended to meet subsistence needs. Whether it will be a success remains to be seen.

Inspection in October 1994 indicated that little or no attention is given to tending the young trees, most of which were being overwhelmed by weeds. It has also been suggested that, because the village does not have a serious soil erosion problem, the perceived need for agroforestry is low. However, there are no trees suitable for firewood or timber left on the land of the village, the only nearby possible source of supply being the Sub-reserve. The project appears to have been a top-down initiative and may not be fully supported by the villagers.

We should, however, note that the supply of seedlings may be one of the minor costs involved in agroforestry. Planting and tending young trees can be costly, and when once they become established they take space away from alternative possible crops, competing with them for sunlight and in many cases for nutrients. Also, a considerable initial waiting period may be required before any harvesting is possible. However, there may be symbiotic relationships with some crops, and the nitrogen-fixing properties of some tree/shrub species can be an advantage.

These relationships all need to be assessed on a holistic basis, using a farming system approach. Unfortunately, *in situ* tests involving agroforestry may require many years, and no long-term experiments have been completed in Xishuangbanna on agroforestry. Because of lack of information about the likely economic performance of agroforestry and social forestry in Xishuangbanna, some risks are involved in encouraging local villagers to engage in agroforestry or social forestry. On the other hand, social forestry has been practised for some time in parts of India, so it may be possible to draw suitable inferences from results there and elsewhere. Nevertheless, *in situ* uncertainty will remain.

The economics of agroforestry and social forestry are liable to vary with location and the economic returns from alternative forms of land-use. On degraded land, as on steeply-sloping land, productivity may be low and economic returns from annual crops may also be low. Therefore, the opportunity cost of agroforestry or social forestry on such land is low, whereas on agricultural land which continues to be very productive with current cropping systems, the opportunity cost of social forestry or agroforestry may be high. Thus, other things being equal, degraded lands and those of low productivity might justify a higher priority for social forestry or agroforestry than agriculturally more productive land. Furthermore, degraded areas may give rise to the greatest adverse external effects, *e.g.* through higher rates or soil erosion under their present use. Hence, the case for adopting social forestry or agroforestry on such land is strengthened if it reduces adverse external effects.

Some Alternative Community Development Projects and Methods to Benefit Local Communities

Agroforestry (or social forestry) is just one possible development to provide local economic opportunities and ease pressures by local people to make unsustainable use of Nature reserves. Other possibilities include:

(1) The adoption of improved agricultural techniques to increase yields or to make possible the introduction of higher-valued crops. In Xishuangbanna, many of the agricultural methods and techniques that are being used are traditional. Rice is for example harvested and thrashed by hand, while Buffalo (*Bubalus bubalis*) are used for ploughing and other draft purposes. Productivity tends to be low.

(2) Although Xishuangbanna receives a heavy annual rainfall, this is concentrated in the monsoon season. For at least six months of the year, Xishuangbanna is relatively dry. Irrigation of crops during this period would significantly increase annual agricultural production. In the longer term, however, multiple cropping can have a negative effect on yields. Furthermore, a number of the suggestions for introducing irrigation would be at the expense of conservation of Xishuangbanna State Nature Reserve. They include a proposal to dam the Lancang Jiang (Mekong River) in a manner that would submerge a portion of the Mengyang Subreserve but supply electricity and irrigation water. It has also been suggested that small dams or weirs might be constructed in the Reserve itself, to allow local irrigation on the currently farmed 'river' flats located in or near the Reserve. Conceivably this development could have an adverse impact on ecosystems in the Reserve.

(3) Opportunities for villagers to make greater multiple use of economic resources in the Reserve may be considered if these uses are compatible with conservation objectives. Currently, some multiple use by villagers is permitted in Xishuangbanna State Nature Reserve. For example, concessions have been granted for the cultivation of a local special ginger (*Zingiber* sp.) which only grows on the shaded forest floor and which is used for medicinal purposes. Its culture does not appear to compromise conservation values. However, this is not the case with all multiple uses. For example, concessions to grow Rubber Trees (*Hevea brasiliensis*) or passionfruit (*Passiflora* sp.) would compromise conservation values in the Reserve. Concessions for Rubber Tree plantations have been given in Shanyong Sub-reserve, and concessions for growing passionfruit in Menglun Sub-reserve have also been granted. Ecotourism is another possible multiple use. Ecotourism within the Nature Reserve has been used at one site to increase the economic opportunities of local villagers. A joint business venture has been started between a local farming cooperative and the management of Xishuangbanna State Nature Reserve to utilize the site at the Forest/Limestone Cliffs site near Menglun for ecotourism. The capital for developing the site, *e.g.* bridge construction and construction of walking tracks, has been provided by the local farming cooperative. This case contrasts with the forest development at San-Ca-He in Mengyang Sub-reserve, which includes no local involvement and for which the Bureau has attracted no joint venturers. There is a strong possibility that an economic loss will occur on the Bureau tourism investment there.

(4) Another possibility is to employ local people in the management of the Nature Reserve. This is in fact done now in Xishuangbanna, and village people (mainly villager leaders) are paid a retainer to act as guards of the Reserve.

(5) Still another way to increase local economic opportunities is to expand employment opportunities in urban areas and encourage migration from the countryside to urban areas. Most settlements in Xishuangbanna have economic development zones, and some are eligible for international trade concessions as a part of China's drive to increase cross-border trade with Laos, Myanmar, and Vietnam. Consequently, considerable expansions in service industries are under way. However, the capacity of Xishuangbanna to absorb a large proportion of its population in urban areas may be limited by its cost of transport of commodities to and from major markets. Such costs, combined with the small local market, may make most local manufacturing uneconomic. If, on the other hand, outward migration to larger cities such as Kunming in Yunnan becomes easier, this would ease population pressures in Xishuangbanna Prefecture.

Searching for Suitable Projects for Economic Development

Traditional cost–benefit analysis concentrates on choosing between projects the range of which is already known. However, often the more important and difficult issues are to discover and see that all promising projects are included in the set of decision possibilities. How does one go about this?

Sometimes projects are suggested or dictated by higher authorities living outside the village. This appears to have been so for agroforestry and social forestry projects in Xishuangbanna. Suggestions have also been made from above that villagers should grow Rice on hilly areas using terracing, even though opinions differ about the desirability of this. For one thing, terracing is costly. Although those villagers practising slash-and-burn agriculture are being encouraged to abandon it, few viable economic alternatives seem to have been made available to them, or discovered. It is important to find economically viable alternatives, and all alternatives should at least be subjected to preliminary economic analysis before being recommended to villagers.

An alternative to the top–down approach is to involve villagers in the search for community development projects. This may be done for example using Rapid Rural Appraisal (RRA) techniques. These involve direct interviews with villagers and on-the-spot appraisal of villages. Villagers have an opportunity to indicate the community projects or the type of projects that they most prefer. These are likely to be projects that they will be motivated to support if they are funded. Furthermore, as a result of such direct interaction, authorities may discover new and promising, potential projects which would not otherwise be considered by them. These could potentially have not only economic value in the villages where they are suggested, but in other villages as well.

It is sometimes claimed that projects suggested at the village level are likely to be more soundly based from an environmental and economic perspective than those originating from the top. However, such a generalization would appear to be misleading. In reality, the knowledge ranges of both villagers and outside 'experts' are limited, and the two factions often have very different knowledge sets. By sensibly and sensitively combining their knowledge, those two groups can usually improve their decisions relating to villages. This involves a side-by-side approach rather than either a top–down approach or a bottom–up approach. A further reason for not relying solely on the preferences of villagers for projects is that they may assess projects solely on the benefit to their own village, ignoring any adverse external effects.

Having discovered a set of development projects which have the support of the villagers and which appear to be economically viable, a government may wish to provide financial support for some or all of these. For villages in areas surrounding Xishuangbanna State Nature Reserve, it might be thought that benefits obtained by the villagers from pursuing such projects will ease their pressure to utilize the resources of the Reserve. However, there can be no guarantee that this will be so. For this reason, it may be wise to enter into a formal agreement with village leaders to the effect that, in return for governmental financial support for their community projects, they will assist in protecting the Reserve in their area. Currently, the Ministry of Forestry is exploring this strategy and is considering a revised system to encourage the reporting of poachers.

Concluding Comments

In relation to the whole procedure for conserving Xishuangbanna State Nature Reserve, the question is likely to be raised as to why conserve it at all. Possible answers include: (1) the returns from agricultural use or logging of it may be low and not very sustainable, and (2) once the Reserve has been fully utilized for commercial purposes, such as agriculture and/or logging, the problem of inadequate natural resources in the region will occur again. At best, the intensive utilization of the Reserve would be a temporary palliative or solution to natural resource shortages. Furthermore, economic benefits from its conservation would be lost. The conserved area has some economic value for tourism, maintenance of waterflows, and so on. It may have considerable existence value both for China as a whole and for individuals overseas who know about it. It is very rich in botanical specimens, some of which may have future use-values.

The benefits from using the Reserve for intensive 'development' purposes seem in all probability to be low in relation to the likely alternatives foregone. To utilize the Reserve in this way would be to pursue short-term gains at the expense of long-term benefits. Politicians are unfortunately often heavily influenced by short-term perspectives. So Nature reserves, particularly in less-developed countries, are always subject to the risk of economic incursions by special-interest groups searching for economic gains. This problem is present both in socialist and non-socialist countries.

It is apparent from the above discussion that decisions about optimizing conservation of biodiversity are both conceptually and empirically complex, and that much more economic and ecological research is needed in this area. In fact, there may be many aspects of biodiversity inter-relationships and associated evolutionary paths that are unpredictable (*cf.* Gould, 1990). It is still a major challenge, given the importance of externalities and other forms of market failure associated with biodiversity conservation, to develop effective mechanisms to provide incentives for sustaining biodiversity.

Summary

Although many publications have appeared in recent years purporting to address the economics of conservation of biodiversity, most do not address the diversity issues as such. This shortcoming appears only to have been recognized recently. Furthermore, from the literature it is clear that natural living areas — apart from conserving biodiversity — jointly give rise to other conservation benefits, and therefore, their conservation needs to be evaluated holistically.

It is suggested that when constraints are placed on available resources for biodiversity conservation, some criteria for species preservation such as those associated with SMS (safe minimum standard) may exhibit unsatisfactory features. While imperfection of knowledge is a serious limitation on rational decision-making about conservation of biodiversity, we have some knowledge and we may be able to use that to determine rational probabilities. In addition, it is important to scrutinize ecological claims about biodiversity. For example, ecosystems containing greater biodiversity may not be more sustainable than those with less diversity. It is also argued that the SMS criterion needs further development because there may be no standard which ensures the survival of any species.

Local communities are at the interface of biodiversity conservation. Because of externalities and market-failures, specific incentives are needed (and other measures may also be required) to make sure that local communities support (or at least do not sabotage) biodiversity conservation. Some possible general measures are outlined and discussed. Specific measures have been adopted in Xishuangbanna Prefecture in Yunnan to ease pressures of the local community on biodiversity conservation. These were outlined and discussed.

References

Administrative Centre for China's Agenda 21 (1994). *Introduction to China's Agenda 21*. China Environmental Press, Beijing, China: 32 pp., illustr..

Ash, J. (1992). Vegetation ecology Fiji: past, present, and future perspectives. *Pacific Science*, **46**, pp. 111–27.

Bishop, R.C. (1978). Endangered species and uncertainty: the economics of a safe minimum standard. *American Journal of Agricultural Economics*, **60**(1), pp. 10–8.

Bishop, R.C. (1979). Endangered species, irreversibility and uncertainty: a reply. *American Journal of Agricultural Economics*, **61**(2), pp. 377–9.

Blum, E. (1993). Making Biodiversity Conservation Profitable: A Case Study of the Merck/INBio Agreement. *Environment*, **36**(4), pp. 17–46.

Ciriacy-Wantrup, S.V. (1968). *Resource Conservation: Economics and Policies*, 3rd edn. Division of Agricultural Science, University of California, Berkeley, California, USA: xvi + 395 pp.

Dixon, J.A. & Sherman, P.R. (1990). *Economics of Protected Areas: A New Look at Benefit and Costs*. Island Press, Washington, DC, USA: xvii + 234, illustr., maps.

Ehrlich, P.R. & Ehrlich, A.H. (1992). The value of biodiversity. *Ambio*, **21**(3), pp. 219–26.

Godoy, R.A. & Bawa, K.S. (1993). The economic value and sustainable harvest of plants and animals from the tropical forest: assumptions, hypothesis, and methods. *Economic Botany*, **47**(3), pp. 215–9.

Gould, S.J. (1990). *The Individual in Darwin's World*. Edinburgh University Press, Edinburgh, Scotland, UK: iv + 54 pp.

Hall, J.V., Chapman, D.L., Barron, W.F. & Tisdell, C.A. (1994). Environmental problems of pacific rim development. *Contemporary Economic Policy*, **12**(4), pp. 1–22.

(Concluded on page 228)

REES, W. & BAILEY, S. (1989). *Defining Sustainable Development.* UBC Centre for Human Settlements, Vancouver, Canada: 12 pp.

REES, W. & ROSELAND, M. (1991). Sustainable communities: planning for the 21st Century. *Plan Canada*, **31**(3), pp. 15–26.

*ROSELAND, M. (1992). *Toward Sustainable Communities.* National Round Table on the Enviromnent and the Economy, Ottawa, Ontario, Canada: xii + 340 pp., illustr.

ROYAL COMMISSION ON THE FUTURE OF THE TORONTO WATERFRONT (1992). *Regeneration.* Minister of Supply and Services of Canada, Ottawa, Ontario, Canada: xxii + 530 pp., illustr.

*STREN, R., WHITE, R. & WHITNEY, J. (1992). *Sustainable Cities: Urbanization and the Environment in International Perspective.* Westview Press. Boulder, Colorado, USA: viii + 365 pp., illustr.

TOLBA, M.K. (1990). Building an environmental institutional framework for the future. *Environmental Conservation*, **17**(2), pp. 105–10.

WORLD COMMISSION ON ENVIRONMENT AND DEVELOPMENT [cited as WCED] (1987). *Our Common Future.* Oxford University Press, Oxford, England, UK: xv + 400 pp.

*Quoted by the Author in earlier drafts of his text but not cited in this final version. — Ed.

[Concluded from page 210]

WAINWRIGHT, M. (1992). *Introduction to Fungal Biotechnology.* John Wiley & Sons, Chichester, England, UK: xi + 185 pp.

WHITTEN, M.J. & OAKESHOTT, J.G. (1990). Biocontrol of insects and weeds. Pp. 123–42 in *Agricultural Biotechnology: Opportunities for International Development* (Ed. G.J. PERSLEY). CAB International, Wallingford, England, UK: xv + 495 pp.

WOODS, D. & RAWLINGS, D.E. (1989). Bacterial leaching and biomining. Pp. 82–93 in *A Revolution in Biotechnology* (Ed. J.L. MARX). Cambridge University Press, Cambridge, England, UK: 227 pp., illustr.

WORLD BANK (1994). *World Development Report 1994.* Oxford University Press, Oxford, England, UK: x + 254 pp.

WORLD COMMISSION ON ENVIRONMENT AND DEVELOPMENT (WCED) (1987). *Our Common Future.* Oxford University Press, Oxford, England, UK: xv + 400 pp., illustr.

WORLD CONSERVATION MONITORING CENTRE (cited as WCMC) (1992). *Global Biodiversity: Status of the Earth's Living Resources.* Chapman & Hall, London, England, UK: xviii + 585 pp., illustr.

[Concluded from page 222]

HOHL, A. & TISDELL, C.A. (1993). How useful are environmental safety standards in economics? — the example of safe minimum standards for protection of species. *Biodiversity and Conservation*, **2**, pp. 168–81.

HOMMA, A.K.O. (1992). The dynamics of extraction in Amazonia: a historical perspective. Pp. 23–33 in *Non-Timber Products from Forest Evaluation of a Conservation and Development Strategy* (Eds D.C. NEPSTAD & S. SCHWARTZMAN). The New York Botanical Garden, Bronx, New York, NY, USA: 176 pp..

KEYNES, J.M. (1921). *A Treatise on Probability.* Macmillan, London, England, UK: 466 pp.

NATIONAL ENVIRONMENTAL PROTECTION AGENCY *et al.* (1994). China: *Biodiversity Conservation Action Plan.* National Environmental Protection Agency, Beijing, China: v + 106 pp., illustr.

NORTON, B. (1988). Commodity, amenity, and morality: the limits of quantification in valuing biodiversity. Pp. 200–11 in *Biodiversity* (Ed. E.O. WILSON). National Academy Press, Washington, DC, USA: 521 pp., illustr.

PEARCE, D. & MORAN, D. (1994). *The Economic Value of Biodiversity.* Earthscan, London, England, UK: xiv + 172 pp., illustr.

RUITENBEEK, H.J. (1992). The rainforest supply price: a tool for evaluating rainforest conservation expenditures. *Ecological Economics*, **6**, pp. 57–78.

SMIET, A.C. (1992). Forest Ecology on Java: Human Impact and Vegetation on Mountain Forest. *Journal of Tropical Ecology*, **8**, pp. 129–52.

STATE COUNCIL OF THE PEOPLE'S REPUBLIC OF CHINA (1994). *China's Agenda 21 — White Paper on China's Population, Environment and Development in the 21st Century.* China Environmental Press, Beijing, China: ii + 244 pp.

THAMAN, R.R. (1992). Vegetation of Nauru and the Gilbert Islands: case studies of poverty, degradation, disturbance and displacement. *Pacific Science*, **46**, pp. 128–58.

TISDELL, C.A. (1990). *Natural Resources, Growth and Development: Economics Ecology and Resource Scarcity.* Praeger, New York, NY, USA: xvi + 234 pp., illustr.

TISDELL, C.A. (1991). *Economics of Environmental Conservation.* Elsevier Science Publishers, Amsterdam, The Netherlands: xxii + 234 pp., illustr.

TISDELL, C.A. (1993). *Economic Development in the Context of China.* Macmillan, London, England, UK: xiv + 218 pp., illustr.

TISDELL, C.A. (1994*a*). *Biodiversity, sustainability and Stability: an Economist's Discussion of Some Ecological Views.* Discussion Paper Nr 139, Department of Economics, The University of Queensland, Brisbane 4072, Australia: iv + 16 pp., illustr.

TISDELL, C.A. (1994*b*). *Ecotourism, Economics and the Environment Biodiversity Conservation: Studies in its Economics and Management, Mainly in Yunnan, China.* Working Paper Nr 9, Department of Economics, The University of Queensland, Brisbane 4072, Australia: vi + 21 pp., illustr.

TISDELL, C.A. (1995). Asian development and environmental dilemma. *Contemporary Economic Policy*, **13**(1), pp. 1–12.

WELLS, M. & BRANDON, K. (1992). *People and Parks: Linking Protected Area Management with Local Communities.* World Bank, World Wildlife Fund, US, and US Agency for International Development, Washington, DC, USA: xii + 99 pp., illustr., maps.

WILSON, E.O. (1988). The current state of biodiversity. Pp. 3–18 in *Biodiversity* (Ed. E.O. WILSON), National Academy Press, Washington, DC, USA: [not available for checking].

PART III

ECONOMICS OF CONSERVING WILDLIFE SPECIES

[8]

THE ECONOMIC CONSERVATION AND UTILISATION OF WILDLIFE SPECIES

CLEM TISDELL

INTEREST IN THE economic conservation and utilisation of wildlife has been heightened by the current concern of the community and economists about ecology and the environment but significant contributions to this subject were being made before the 70's. For example, H. Scott Gordon published a seminal article in the early 1950's on "The Economic Theory of a Common Property Resource: The Fishery" [5] in which he showed that when a resource is held as common property, as in the case of sea fisheries, this leads to its inefficient exploitation and may lead to the extermination of species which should be preserved on economic grounds.

Wildlife species are a replenishible (renewable) resource which become non-renewable under certain conditions, e.g., if the population of a species falls below a critical level. The chief difficulty which stands in the way of the economic conservation of many wildlife species is the impossibility of individuals holding workable property rights in them. Because of the nature of the species, it is difficult, impossible or uneconomic for individuals to identify, e.g., by branding, tagging, etc., the members of the species which they own, or to prevent others from stealing their property, or to confine the members of the species within spatial territories which are the property of the owners and subject to their surveillance. Consider for example migratory birds, fish in the ocean, and animals such as kangaroos which can only be confined at considerable cost of enclosures.

It is not always possible or economic to create effective individual property rights in wildlife species. Nevertheless, policies can be adopted to promote the economically efficient preservation and utilisation of wildlife. The purpose of this paper* is to outline the drawbacks of common-ownership and to examine some of the alternatives to it. However, it might be said at the outset that none of the alternatives are ideal although many are preferable to holding exhaustible resources as common property.

1. WILDLIFE AS COMMON PROPERTY

Where the yield of economic resources varies with their management and utilisation, their ownership as common property usually leads to economic inefficiency. As H. Scott Gordon has observed "There appears . . . to be some truth in the conservative dictum that everybody's property is nobody's property. Wealth that is free for all is valued by none because he who is foolhardy enough

* I wish to thank N. Vousden and C. Walsh of the Australian National University and my colleagues at Newcastle for discussing this topic with me.

to wait for its proper time of use will only find that it has been taken by another" [5, p. 135]. Under the rule of common property, anybody can exploit and take possession of any single member of a wildlife species. The consequences of common property have been most closely explored in the economic literature for fisheries [5, 7, 8] but clearly the principles also have application to most undomesticated animals. At least three sources of economic inefficiency arise from making wildlife common property. (i) Effort directed to current harvesting of wildlife may not be optimally allocated between sources of the harvest, (ii) too many resources may flow into harvesting as compared with requirements in other industries, and (iii) the optimal economic conservation and utilisation of a species through time is unlikely to be attained. I am assuming here that the species is harvested for its fur, meat, feathers etc., and that it must be slaughtered for this purpose. It may also be that the species has curiosity-value or some other value (e.g., via a favourable externality which stems from its existence). Elements of this type are put to one side for the moment. They are important and will be introduced towards the end of the essay. However, independently of these elements, common property creates problems for optimal conservation.

The point has been made by H. Scott Gordon [5], and by subsequent contributors such as A. Scott [7], R. Turvey [10] and Vernon Smith [8] that too many resources flow into the exploitation of resources which are held as common property. In a competitive economy, factors embark on the utilisation of common-property resources until the *average* product of each factor from this activity is equal to the value of its *marginal* product elsewhere i.e., in the competitive private-property sector of the economy. At least, this is so if resources exploiting common property tend to share equally in its bounty.

This can be illustrated from a simple case by Figure 1. Imagine that there is one variable resource, L, and that the average product (catch) from the common-property resource falls as the amount of L which is allocated to it, L^*, rises. Furthermore, suppose for simplicity that the price of the product from the common-property resource is constant. The value of the average product of the variable factor in exploiting the common-property resource might be as indicated by the curve marked *VAP* in Figure 1 and then the value of its marginal product is shown by the curve marked *VMP*. If w is the going price of the variable factor, it also indicates the value of its marginal product elsewhere. Given that the exploitative industry's demand for L is rather small in relation to the total demand for L, the industry (which involves common property) employs L_2^* of L. Owners of L find it profitable to enter the industry provided that their average income exceeds w. Hence, in equilibrium L_2^* of L is allocated to the industry. For example, owners of L find it profitable to enter the industry if L_1^* of L has entered because earnings per unit of L average out to r which is in excess of w, their earnings elsewhere. But the entry of more than L_1^* units of L into the industry is socially inefficient because the value of the marginal product of L in the industry involving common property is depressed below that elsewhere. The optimal allocation of L could, however, be

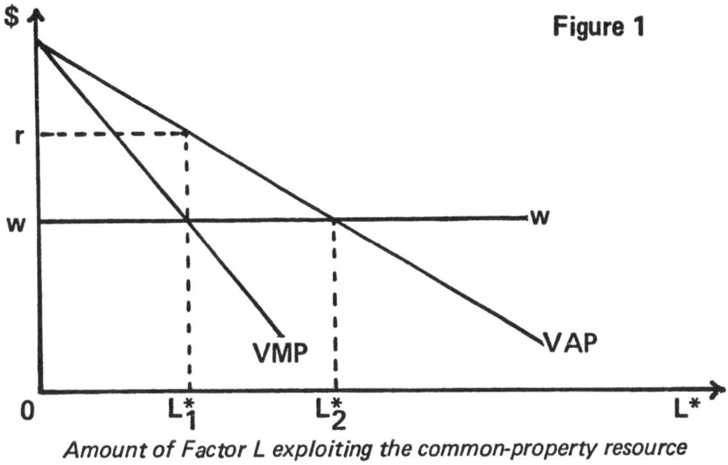

achieved by imposing a charge of $r–w$ on each unit of L which enters the common-property industry. In essence, this involves collecting a rent of $(r–w)L_1^*$, which otherwise would be dissipated by competition.

If resources are held as common-property, competition leads to economic inefficiency because rents are engulfed by the units of factors (firms) imposing external diseconomies on one another. For policy purposes, it is important to identify the sources of the diseconomies especially if several factors are involved in the exploitation of the resource.

Consider first diseconomies which arise from the level and the composition of a population of a species. The immediate impact of competitive exploitation of animals which are common property is to reduce their density and thus raise the cost of capture, e.g., because they are more costly to find and each capturing manoeuvre is likely to bag less animals. Where species are relatively sedentary, costs are raised by unco-ordinated effort since each competitor may lack knowledge of areas already worked and may waste resources searching worked areas. In cases like this, something might be said for allocating competitors to zones. H. Scott Gordon's view [5] is possibly based on the density-diseconomy factor. It also has a longer-term rationale. The population of a species may be permanently reduced and its density of coverage lowered.

Each individual finds that his own activity in slaughtering species has a negligible impact on his cost of capturing them, but the combined activity of all can considerably raise the cost of capture. Indeed, the population of a species may be so reduced that its cost of annual harvest is much higher than for the same harvest with a higher population. The annual harvest of wildlife is likely to form a backward-bending supply curve like that shown in Figure 2. The supply curve marked *SS* is a long-run one indicating both economic and bionomic equilibrium. Along this curve, rates of harvest can be maintained in perpetuity and the flow of factor services to the industry is in equilibrium for the value of their average product equals the value of their marginal product elsewhere. Note that in the illustration given in Figure 2 and with the demand for the harvest indicated by the curve marked *D*, two points of equilibrium exist. One is marked E_1 and the other E_2. Neither equilibrium is socially optimal since both involve overharvesting (the argument of H. Scott Gordon) but it is always more economical to be on the bottom branch of this supply curve than on the backward-bending branch. This is of course assuming that the species itself gives rise to no diseconomies and supposing that the backward-sloping branch of the supply curve corresponds to lower populations than the positively sloping portion. The absolute cost of harvesting is lower on the lower branch. The cost of harvesting X_1 units of the species is $B.X_1$ in equilibrium E_2 but could be reduced to $A.X_1$ if the population of the species happened to be higher.

Figure 2

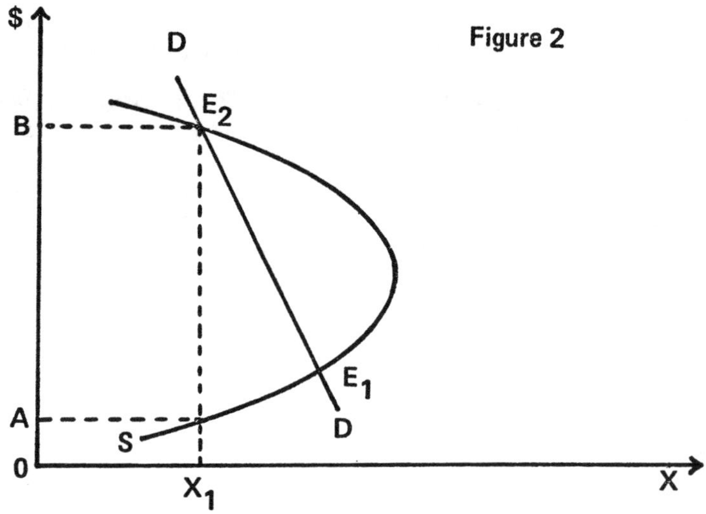

Annual Harvest of Wildlife Species

Of course, there is no guarantee that either of these equilibria will be attained. A low-population or a high-population equilibrium is possible but neither might be attained. For example, a sudden rise in demand might lead to so much entry that the species is eradicated before one of the equilibria is attained. This will be discussed below when allocation through time is considered.

Presumably diseconomies arising from the size of the aggregate population of a species can be allowed for by controlling the size of the *aggregate* annual harvest. But there may be other diseconomies which are not related so much to the size of the harvest but to crowding by the number of hunters, trappers, fishing boats, fishermen, etc. Although crowding and stock diseconomies may typically occur together, it is possible to control one without controlling the other. Crowding by hunters etc. may make it more difficult to quarry game since it is more likely to be put to flight, more care is required to avoid damage to other hunters and hunters may need to wait until others have left particular areas. To avoid economic inefficiency and a part of rent being frittered away by diseconomies of crowding, it is necessary to limit the number of hunters, fishermen, etc.

Before considering important difficulties associated with the allocation of common-property resources through time, it is worth noting that not only do too many factors flow into the exploitation of common-property resources but those factors which enter are usually misallocated. There is usually a tendency to over-work the areas in which the common-property resource is most productive, i.e., areas which under private-property would yield the greatest rent. This is illustrated by the example depicted in Figure 3.

The species is assumed to occur in two separate areas. N_1 represents the amount of factor L allocated to Area 1 and N_2 that allocated to Area 2. The average product and marginal product curves in the two areas are indicated by natural notation. Imagine that $\overline{N}_1$ of L has been allocated to the common-property industry. Given the common-property assumption, all of $\overline{N}_1$ is employed in Area 1, the area with the highest average product. But the harvest from employing $\overline{N}_1$ of the variable factor could be increased by allocating N_2^* of it to Area 2 and N_1^* to Area 1, i.e., by harvesting the species in the extra-marginal and marginal areas. However, if the common-property is competitively exploited such an allocation (which in this instance maximises output from $\overline{N}_1$ and equates the marginal product of L in both areas) cannot persist because the average product of L in Area 2, U, is less than its average product in Area 1, V. L will leave Area 2 for Area 1 until average product is T and all units of L exploiting the common-

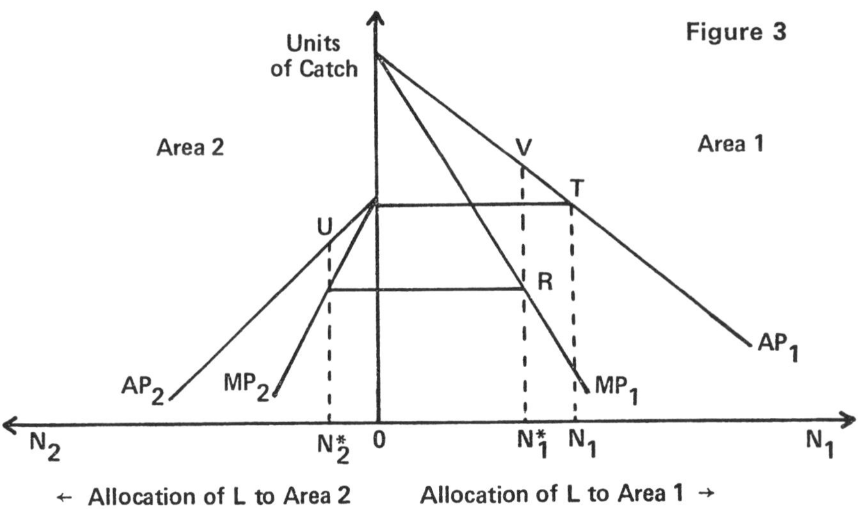

Figure 3

property resource have the same average product and the same average income. Thus resources which are employed in the common-property industry are misallocated within the industry. The allocation between areas may be made optimal in this instance by charging each unit of L which enters Area 1, V–R and not charging in Area 2. In other cases, charges for entry are required in all areas but at rates which vary from area to area depending upon the relationship between average and marginal products in the areas.

The most serious problem in the allocation of common-property resources has not yet been discussed. Where the productivity of the resource varies with the amount and nature of its stock, the stock is unlikely to be optimally allocated through time. In the case of wildlife, each hunter, fisherman etc., is merely guided in his actions by his current gains. He takes no account of their impact on the future of the species for he cannot gain appreciably by husbanding a species or sparing it now. There is no incentive for him to conserve since the fruits of his efforts will flow principally to other hunters, fishermen, etc. Because of this externality, the slaughtering of a species may increase (and a species can be exterminated) at a time when the optimal policy is to increase the population of the species.

Although this is relatively clear, it may be helpful to consider a formal example. Imagine a large but given number of hunters hunting a particular species which is common property and assume for simplicity that the demand for the produce of the species is perfectly elastic. Furthermore, assume that each hunter faces identical cost and other economic conditions and that they vary their catch identically. The current profit, π, of each hunter and the maximum present value of each hunter's future profit, K, depends on the current catch per hunter. In a particular instance, the curves for π and K might be like those shown in Figure 4. In this case, each profit-maximising hunter takes x_2 of the species in the current year. But such a large catch is at the expense of discounted future income. The optimal policy is for the hunters to maximise their present discounted income, i.e., current income plus the present value of maximum future profit, $\pi + K$. This occurs, as can be seen from Figure 5 when the current annual catch is $\bar{x}$. In that figure, the curve NV represents the marginal value of K and MT the marginal value of π and the dashed line their (vertical) sum. The socially optimal catch is between x_1 and x_2 but will not eventuate in a competitive climate.

It is possible for the marginal current profit curve, MT, to move upward at the same time as the dashed curve indicating the summed marginal curves shift downward at the x-axis, e.g., because the species becomes relatively much more valuable in the future. If this should happen, the slaughter of the species will increase at a time when efforts should be made to reduce the slaughter and increase the population of the species. A species could be eliminated at a time when the value of conserving it is increasing. A number of economic policies are available for dealing with this problem and these will be discussed below.

Other consequences also follow from the fact that no individual competitive

Figure 4

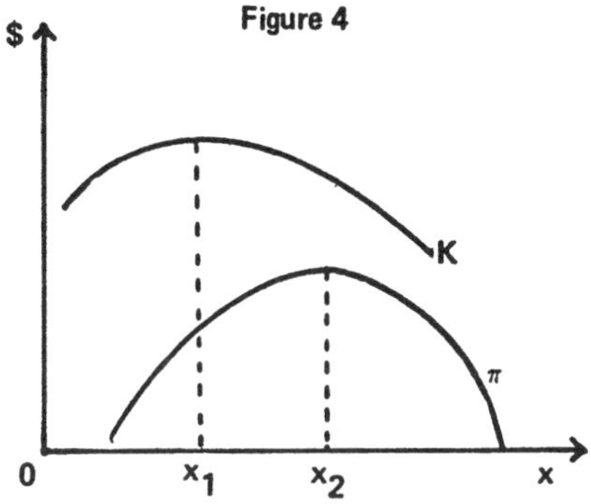

Catch per hunter in current year

Figure 5

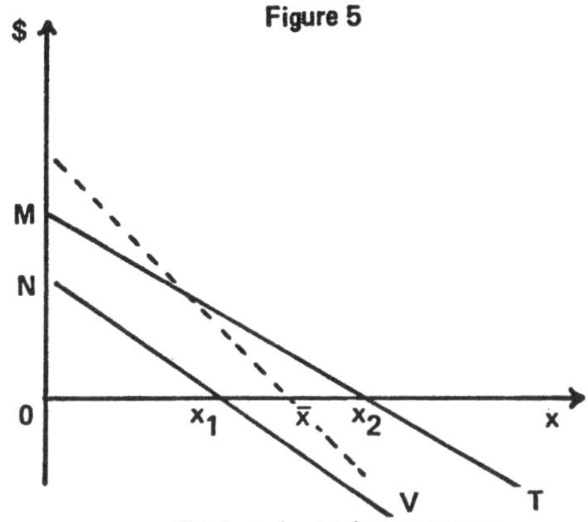

Catch per hunter in current year

exploiter of a common-property resource can gain by waiting or by deferring actions which are currently profitable to him. A hunter, for example, has no incentive to discriminate between members of a species on the basis of their future profitability. Hence, if it is currently profitable to him, he may destroy members such as younger members and females of a species although it may be collectively rational to preserve these members in view of their productivity. He may, if the animals have a breeding season, destroy them during this season even though it is collectively rational in view of future gains to refrain from destroying them during this time. Governments, in order to improve the exploitative pattern, may impose size limits on the catch (in the case of fishing minimum mesh sizes) and may declare closed seasons during the breeding periods of animals.

The external diseconomies which have been noted above influence the cost of harvesting a species. Interdependence between the levels of population and population growth of different species has been ignored. Two species can be in either competitive or complementary relationships to one another. If at least one of these species is common property such as a wildlife species, individuals have no incentive to manage it in a socially optimal fashion. If the wildlife species is either competitive with or complementary to a domesticated private-property species, there is again no assurance that the wildlife numbers will be optimally managed. Any individual gains practically nothing from husbanding wildlife which is either common-property or so mobile that others are likely to gain most from its regulation. Consequently, if a wildlife species has an adverse impact on other valuable species its numbers can remain above the socially optimal level. Conversely, it may be reduced below such a level when it has a favourable impact on other valuable species. Taking account of these externalities, it may be necessary to regulate the activity of landowners in controlling wildlife on their property, e.g., to pass laws declaring that landowners shall attempt to eradicate pests on their land, such as rabbits in Australia.

Serious economic waste can occur when economic agents obtain property rights to land or other space containing suitable habitats for wildlife species. If the land has value for domesticated species or other commercial uses which are best pursued by destroying the natural environment, it will be destroyed because the landowner can appropriate little of the value of wildlife and thus will undervalue their habitats in his private plans. Each landowner considers that his destruction of the habitat of a particular wildlife species has virtually no effect on the availability of the species to him. But all landowners by acting in this way may destroy all the habitats of the species or cause the availability of habitats to fall below a critical level so that the species becomes extinct even when its survival is in the social (economic) interest. A case can be made out for subsidising the preservation of habitats of some wildlife species of economic value. Yet in some instances a subsidy should only be paid to landowners for the preservation of possible habitat areas above a minimum size since small areas are often insufficient to ensure the survival of some species [3]. Alternatively or as well, the state might itself retain ownership of suitable habitats and attempt to preserve them. The advantages and disadvantages of alternative policies are discussed below.

2. Economic Methods for Conserving and Utilising Wildlife Species

It is often difficult to devise economic methods for the efficient conservation and utilisation of wildlife species. The circumstances of different species vary so much that variations of policy may be called for and no policy is likely to give perfect efficiency. Nevertheless, measures can be adopted which are better than the common-property alternative.

Writers such as H. Scott Gordon [5] and Vernon Smith [8] have strongly canvassed the policy of placing wildlife species (in particular areas) under the sole ownership of different exploiters. If the species occurs and remains in isolated pockets and does not come into competition with domesticated species or alternative economic activity, this policy can lead to Paretian economic optimality since all externalities are internalised by the sole-owners and they are able to appropriate marginal gains from husbanding the species and varying its rate of utilisation. The real difficulty is that these conditions are rarely met. For example, not all wildlife species can be optimally confined in independent pockets. These species cannot be put under the control of a large number of independent owners having effective individual property rights. Of course, a private monopoly for the exploitation of the whole species might be established, and this might internalise all externalities. However, this raises a number of difficulties. If the monopoly is effective, the supply of articles from the species is likely to be restricted to below the socially optimal level. Nevertheless, from a conservation angle this approach might be better than the common-property alternative.

Turvey [10] suggests that the limitations of an overall private monopoly can be overcome by setting price ceilings on the produce from the species. By this method, monopoly-profit can often be reduced and an optimal utilisation of the species can be achieved. The great difficulty of this approach is that it assumes considerable knowledge on the part of the governmental regulating authority. The ceiling price would need to be varied to allow for variations in marginal costs and in demand. However, in nearly all cases where externalities arise considerable knowledge is required by governmental regulating bodies if they are to achieve Paretian optimality.

This is certainly so if the species is common-property and is competitively exploited. The government may adopt several measures to promote the optimal utilisation and conservation of the species. These may either take the form of direct (physical) controls or of tax and similar fiscal measures. While these different methods are to some extent substitutes (this statement is defended later) Turvey [10] suggests that the tax-subsidy approach is inherently the more efficient of the two.

From the discussion of Section 1, it is apparent that a number of measures may need to be simultaneously adopted in order to promote the optimal utilisation of common-property resources which are competitively exploited. If a tax-subsidy (Pigovian) approach is taken

(i) individual exploiters ought to pay a charge[1] on the amount of their catch and this might be varied by the area of the origin of the catch if differential rents are significant, and also altered to reflect the optimal required variations in breeding stock through time.

(ii) if external diseconomies arise from the number of entrants, a tax on entry may be called for and this might need to be different in different geographical areas.

(iii) taxes on the catch of different members of a species might be varied to reflect the social marginal productivity of the various members. Taxes might for example, vary with the size, age and/or sex of the member. Or, again, taxes might be higher during the breeding season of a species to reflect the high social returns from conservation at that time.

Possible direct controls which correspond to these measures are:

(i) quotas limiting the maximum catch of individual exploiters and varied with the area of catch and by the need to alter the stock of the species,

(ii) quotas restricting the number of entrants and limitations on areas of their operation,

(iii) prohibitions on the capture of certain members of a species and/or regulations on the composition of the catch. Closed seasons or special regulations on the composition of the catch might apply during the breeding season.

Direct and indirect controls may, and indeed often are, simultaneously applied. While Turvey suggests that a tax-subsidy (Pigovian) approach is inherently superior to direct controls, this is not always the case, especially if problems of collecting the tax are taken into account. Turvey, in discussing fisheries outlines

1. A charge is required if the common-property resource has any scarcity value. In theory, it is easy to calculate the optimal charge. See, for example, references 5, 8 and 10, and the examples in Section 1.

proposals for a tax or charge on the catch of fish (a common-property resource) and then states:

> An alternative method would be to impose quantitative restriction upon the amount of fishing effort. In practice, such restriction would produce an inferior suboptimum, unless it were so all-embracing as to amount to the institution of a sole owner of the fishery. The reason is that any restriction must be framed in terms of a limit upon one or more of the resources used in the industry. But to ration the supply of any resource is to invite the substitution of other resources for it. Thus if the number of boats were limited, larger engines would be installed, bigger crews carried . . . None of this would be efficient, in terms of resource allocation; it would simply increase the total costs for all alternative levels of fishing effort. [10, p. 73]

However, it is unreasonable to condemn direct controls on the basis of this argument. The argument is specious since the corresponding direct control to Turvey's tax method is the imposition of quotas on the *catch*. If taxes are imposed on only some factors, say the entry of boats, exactly the same sort of misallocation arises as that mentioned by Turvey for direct controls. Nevertheless, it might be that in practice taxes are preferable to direct controls although I am not convinced that they always are. Tax variations generally allow more leeway than fiat for individual adjustments and might be favoured on this ground. But in some cases the cost of collecting taxes is excessive and direct controls with some policing are preferable. For example, if the catch requires little processing and does not pass through any central facility (port, factory etc.) it is almost impossible to collect taxes on the catch and vary the tax by the size of the members taken. Problems of policing can in fact sometimes tell in favour of direct controls. A rule for example, that the daily catch shall not exceed so much can be policed and occasional violations detected and punished. Recently, Baumol and Oates [1] have also argued that the Pigovian approach to regulating environmental pollution requires information which the controller rarely possesses and favour quantitative standards set by biologists, ecologists, etc., with charges to polluters being varied to meet these standards. They state that

> The basic appeal of the pricing and standards approach relative to the Pigouvian prescription lies in its workability. We simply do not, in general, have the information needed to determine the appropriate set of Pigouvian taxes and subsidies . . . [1, p. 51]

Similar problems of allowing for externalities arise in the optimal control of wildlife species. The method of approach to controlling wildlife numbers which I shall suggest below has much in common with the approach of Baumol and Oates. But it is apparent that the methods which are most efficient in any circumstances will vary with the possibility of putting them into practice.

To achieve optimality, it is normally necessary to control several variables simultaneously. For example, the total catch, the areas of catch, the distribution of members taken, the number of entrants may need to be simultaneously controlled. However, the control of some of the variables by the state may be preferable to no control. For example, the state might set bagging limits on a species and adjust these to give a desired aggregate catch. By doing so it can control stock diseconomies and improve the allocation of the stock through time. But if entry is free and bagging limits are adjusted downwards as numbers working in the industry increase, inefficiency results if the long run average costs experienced by hunters etc. are U-shaped. If the costs encountered by all hunters etc. are the same, entry will proceed until just normal profit is earned and each firm (hunter) is operating with excess capacity. In equilibrium, each firm (hunter) will be in a position like that shown in Figure 6. The cost curves there are indicated by usual notation, P is the equilibrium price of the catch given the aggregate quota and the equilibrium numbers of firms in the industry. The representative firm (hunter) bags x_1 of the species and operates below capacity. Since the costs of the total catch could be reduced if there were fewer firms in the industry the solution is inefficient. This reduction in numbers could be achieved by imposing taxes on the catch. The problem is to calculate the optimal taxes.

Figure 6

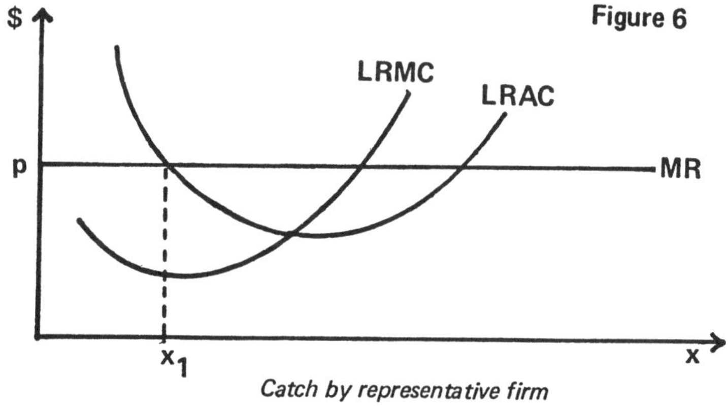

Of course, I am assuming that the species is being caught for purely commercial purposes. If the activity is for sport, the bagging limit approach might have some merit if hunters get similar satisfaction from a catch and their marginal utility from a catch diminishes with its size. However, these assumptions do not seem very realistic, e.g., satisfaction seems to differ.

There is one method which overcomes many of these difficulties and has applications to fishing, hunting etc., for commercial purposes and for pleasure. This is to issue licences for specified catches (differentiated by areas if rents differ) and make these available by competitive bids, or find by a trial-and-error process the prices which equate the supply of licences to the demand for them. Licences, for example, might be valid for one year. The total licensed catch is then varied by the controlling authority to preserve a socially optimal stock of the species, if it can. Like any sole owner, the controlling authority has to make predictions about future demand, present stock and so on. Rents accrue to the state controlling authority not a private monopolist as might be the case under alternative arrangements and rents are not frittered away by the economic wastes of competitive exploitation of common-property resources. Thus this method may be more adequate from a distributional point of view and from an allocative point of view than alternative schemes. The controlling authority might also find it socially worthwhile to husband the species, e.g., by maintaining numbers and to pay subsidies to landowners for the retention of favourable habitats for the species.

Is there a case for the state itself to provide game reserves and parks for the conservation and utilisation of wildlife species? Economists such as Dolan [4] have argued that there is no case. Tisdell [9] has put a case for the provision of natural parks by the state. The argument need not be repeated here but it recognises that parks serve multiple needs of which the preservation of wildlife is just one. Nevertheless, the economic justification for a state providing parks and reserves for the conservation and management of wildlife requires further exploration.

A strong case often exists for declaring the breeding grounds of valuable migratory animals as state sanctuaries or reserves. If these grounds happen to be privately owned, private enterprise has no incentive to utilise them in a socially optimal manner because large externalities arise. If the population of a species is increased as a result of preservation of its breeding ground or of conservation there, the owner of the ground gains little although hunters and others elsewhere may gain much. A private owner has no incentive to preserve the ecological balance of a breeding ground even if it is socially optimal to do so and he also has no incentive to refrain from taking animals at the grounds even though it might be socially more productive not to destroy them while they are breeding. State ownership of the grounds can be advantageous. However, even under state ownership there is *no guarantee* that the grounds will be utilised in a socially optimal manner. State instrumentalities are subject to political pressures and these sometimes result in solutions which are not Paretian optimal.[2]

The value of a species may depend not on the market value of the physical goods which it yields but upon the value of various intangibles which it provides. Many animals and birds have curiosity and entertainment value which is often freely available from their natural existence.[3] Passing parrots and songsters give us a delight for which there is no payment and indeed there does not seem to be any way in which their general availability can be made subject to a price payment. They, therefore, are public goods and deserve to be treated as such.

I do not think that the argument is much affected by the fact that some of the species are kept in zoos or could be kept in private aviaries. These are not perfect

2. Majority voting need not lead to Paretian optimality. See, for example, G. Tullock, "Problems of Majority Voting", *The Journal of Political Economy*, Vol. 67, 1959 and reference 9.

3. In addition, some species which have no direct economic value might be indirectly valuable because of their link with other species, e.g., they might provide food for valuable species.

substitutes for freely roaming wildlife. The alternatives involve a cost to enjoy and some individuals object to the caging of animals on principle. The birds which visit one's backyard or neighbourhood undoubtedly have additional entertainment value to those at zoos, and their upkeep, even from the social point of view, may be less.

It is clear that private enterprise will fail to preserve an optimal number of animals and species because it cannot appropriate the whole of the net value of doing so. The problem is especially acute in cases where the socially optimal policy is to permit the animals to roam at large. In some cases, species may disappear because private enterprise cannot appropriate sufficient of their value to set aside large enough reserves required for survival of the species. Again, the allowance which private enterprise makes for risk may deter it from preserving a species when its preservation is socially optimal. The risk factor may cause private enterprise to favour immediate commercial development of an area, to waiting for high returns from wildlife in the distant future. [9] In a state undertaking, a lower allowance for risk or no allowance seems appropriate because of the averaging process. [9]

Problems of co-ordination can also cause the extermination of a species under private enterprise. Cobweb-reactions can be imagined which lead to the extermination of a species. Oversupply by private enterprise might be overcompensated by undersupply. The difficulty is that should the supply of the species fall even temporarily below a critical level the species may not recover. The species may disappear because of collective error even though conservation of the species is socially optimal.

Other arguments are sometimes advanced in favour of measures to support the preservation of wildlife. Animals of various types have been incorporated in the symbols, literature and culture of all nations and many of their inhabitants are prepared to pay some premium for the conservation of such animals presumably so that their descendants will have the opportunity of coming into contact with these animals. It is not for me to question the worth of such desires. If individuals wish to keep options open for their descendants and are prepared to pay to keep these open, the problem is how are they to realise their ambitions. Collectively the individuals face a situation of the prisoners-dilemma type. Contributions by most of the group are usually required if a conservation scheme is to be effective but each individual has a selfish interest not to contribute even though he desires the collective goal. State interference and compulsion may be necessary to achieve the desired collective goal.

These arguments support (under the various circumstances stated) the provision of state parks and game reserves.[4] But not all members of a species can be brought within the ambit of a park-system and it is certainly not economic to aim for this anyway. From the previous discussion, it seems most economical to

4. Note that I do not wish to imply that culling of a species in state parks cannot be justified. Indeed, culling may be necessary to ensure the survival of a species if a park is of limited size.

have, at one and the same time, state parks, privately owned zoos, and wildlife roaming at large. Thus not only a system of state parks or reserves with an optimal management programme is required for the conservation of wildlife but also rules and economic measures to regulate their conservation and utilisation at large. While it is apparent that the "invisible hand" is defective in this area, it ought not be forgotten that there is no automatic mechanism either which makes the control of the state perfect. The control by the state is only potentially better than that of private competition. Its policies must be subjected to continual scrutiny. While the preceding analysis gives some guide to optimal policy, account may need to be taken of additional imperfections of the real world in applying it. But these imperfections do not excuse gross economic mismanagement of national and international wildlife species.

The University of Newcastle
N.S.W., Australia

REFERENCES

[1] BAUMOL, W. J. and W. OATES, "The Use of Standards and Prices for the Protection of the Environment", *Swedish Journal of Economics*, Vol. 73, 1971, pp. 42–54.

[2] BOULDING, K. J., *Economics as Science*, McGraw-Hill, New York, 1970.

[3] COSTIN, A. B., and H. J. FRITH, *Conservation*, Penguin Books Australia, Ringwood, 1971.

[4] DOLAN, B. G., *Tanstaafl: Economic Strategy for Environmental Crisis*, Holt, Rinehart and Winston, New York, 1971.

[5] GORDON, H. Scott, "The Economic Theory of a Common Property Resource: The Fishery", *Journal of Political Economy*, Vol. 62, 1954, pp. 124–142.

[6] PLOURDE, C. G., "Exploitation of Common-Property Replenishible Natural Resources", *Western Economic Journal*, Vol. 9, 1971, pp. 256–266.

[7] SCOTT, A., "The Fishery: The Objectives of Sole Ownership", *Journal of Political Economy*, Vol. 63, 1955, pp. 116–124.

[8] SMITH, VERNON L., "Economics of Production from Natural Resources", *The American Economic Review*, Vol. 58, 1968, pp. 409–431.

[9] TISDELL, C., "Provision of Parks and the Preservation of Nature—Some Economic Factors", *Australian Economic Papers* (forthcoming).

[10] TURVEY, R. "Optimization and Suboptimization in Fishery Regulation", *American Economic Review*, Vol. 54, 1964, pp. 64–76.

[9]

Kangaroos as an economic resource[1]

Abstract

Provides a broad overview of the status of kangaroo species, the Macropodidae, and public policies for their management in Australia in the 1970s. Public policies are found not to maximise the total net economic value of land use. Property-rights failures occur in relation to kangaroo species harvested for their commercial use-value, as well as for species having no such value but possessing instead mainly non-use economic value. Apart from direct use-values, this article recognises the importance of bequest values and the significance of sustaining gene pools. Implicitly, harvested species of kangaroos are conceptualised as mixed goods, that is as goods involving a mixture of excludable and non-excludable economic attributes.

Protests about the destruction and economic exploitation of kangaroos have become commonplace in Australia. For example, a petition was received on this subject at the April 1973 sittings of the House of Representatives. As a result of earlier protests, the House of Representatives Select Committee on Wildlife Conservation investigated and issued a report on the *Conservation and Commercial Exploitation of Kangaroos* and the Labor Government on attaining office announced a ban on the export of kangaroo products.

The status of kangaroos as a resource

The value of kangaroos as an economic resource can be considered from a number of points of view. From the export figures for 1970–71, I have calculated that the average price received for each undressed kangaroo and wallaby skin is $2.12 and the average price obtained per pound of meat exported is 15 cents. The average live weight for a female Red Kangaroo at 33 months is 47 lbs and 62 lbs for a male. According to the Commonwealth Scientific Industrial Research Organisation (CSIRO) the carcass weight is 77 per cent of the live weight. Hence, considering the mix of species and so on, the average carcass weight of kangaroos harvested in Australia is not likely to be less than 30 lbs: consequently, on the basis of these export prices, kangaroos used commercially are valued at $6.72 or nearly $7 on average. The harvest of kangaroos in Queensland is almost 1 million per year; in Western Australia one-quarter of a million and possibly another one-quarter of a million for the remainder of Australia. Thus, taking a conservative estimate and assuming average receipts of only $6 per kangaroo, the total value of the annual kangaroo harvest in terms of meat and unprocessed skins is of the order of $9 million per year.[2] This amounts to almost 75 cents on average for each Australian.

Comparison with other extractive industries may be interesting. The value of manganese production in 1968 was $8 million, the net value of tin mined and quarried, $12.9 million, and gold $18.3 million. Thus, merely at the extractive level, the value of the kangaroo harvest is not insignificant.

If one defines the kangaroo industry to include shooters, meat wholesalers, retailers and canners (mostly in the pet food industry), tanners, and fur processors and exporters, manufacturers, wholesalers and retailers of skin products, the industry appears more significant. In a submission to the House of Representatives Committee in September 1970, the Kangaroo Industry Association stated that the industry has a capital investment of $14 million, which includes $7 million in plant and equipment. The industry employs 5 400 people and has an annual wages bill of about $12 million.

In terms of meat and skins alone, kangaroos are a valuable resource. However, allowance should be made for their value as a tourist attraction and for their value in other respects, for example, their value in maintaining a gene pool.

Although the above overall values are of some interest, they are nevertheless of little significance from the point of view of economic analysis. To examine the economic use of resources, we need to consider the value of alternatives that are foregone. Is the present mixture of production of kangaroos and domestic livestock on the land economically optimal? Does the extra social value obtained from a greater kangaroo population exceed the value of livestock production that is foregone? Taking into account the physical possibilities for trade-off between kangaroos and domestic livestock and the relative prices of the commercial products obtained, overall it is highly probable that kangaroos are stocked in insufficient quantities to maximise the value of production and collective profit from the land. The land is relatively overstocked with domestic species. There is also a tendency to over-harvest kangaroos that have commercial value.

The explanation for these tendencies is simple. Because kangaroos are so mobile as a resource, landowners find it difficult to appropriate them and to ensure themselves of any reward for husbanding them. On all except very large properties, each landholder finds that the number of kangaroos is virtually independent of his own activity and that he can gain little by husbanding kangaroos. On the other hand, he can appropriate all gains from husbanding domestic livestock and will expand the number of these whenever this is profitable, even if the increase of his profit from the extra numbers of domestic livestock is less than the loss in collective profit from kangaroos. Furthermore, the landowner has little incentive to prevent kangaroos being taken on his property for commercial purposes. He loses nothing from this and may believe that it will lead to a marginal reduction in 'the pest'. Thus, in the absence of state interference, kangaroos do in fact become common-property resources.[3]

When a resource is common-property and has commercial value this has several undesirable economic consequences. Too many factors of production from an economic efficiency point of view are attracted to exploiting the resource and there is no mechanism to ensure its conservation for the future. Exploiters are merely guided by their short-term selfish profits and a resource, which should be conserved, may be exhausted. In contrast, when private-property rights can be effectively enforced for a resource, long-term (or discounted profit) guides business and the conservation of the resource may be ensured under the same conditions, which would lead to its disappearance when it is a common-property resource. The resource is conserved out of desire for future profits. For this reason, we do not, for example, expect cattle to become extinct in the near future, although some varieties may disappear if they become relatively unprofitable. This, of course, underlines the point that even if kangaroos can be confined and farmed that it may be relatively unprofitable to farm them and the disappearance of some species may be speeded up rather than retarded.

While kangaroos are a renewable economic resource, species become non-renewable once their population falls below a threshold level. According to Calaby[4] of the CSIRO, three of the 45 species of kangaroos present in Australia at the time of European settlement are now extinct and an additional 12 are close to extinction. The irreversibility problem alone weighs in favour of intervention by the government.

In order to determine whether kangaroos will be preserved when they can be farmed and to decide on the optimal mix of kangaroos and domestic livestock, we need to investigate the physical trade-off that is possible between kangaroos and domestic livestock. To determine this is not a simple matter because there are at least 42 species of kangaroos with marked differences in habitat requirements and inter-relationships with domestic livestock. Some of the smaller types of kangaroos have little commercial value (but not all) and are extremely vulnerable to land use by domestic stock because of habitat removal. Because cattle have eaten out long grass that provides their shelter, the populations of some kangaroo species have dwindled and others have suffered because of the clearing of rainforest and brush for the purpose of farming. The nail-tailed, hare-wallabies, some bandicoots, the Musky Rat-Kangaroo *Hypsiprymnodon moschatus* and the Parma Wallaby *Macropus parma* have suffered in this way. Because of the low commercial value of most of the species of small kangaroos and the major reduction which domestic livestock brings to their populations, mixed-land use does not appear to be profitable in their case. They are best conserved on reserves free from domestic stock.

However, there are several large kangaroos, such as the Red Kangaroo *Megaleia rufa*, Eastern Grey Kangaroo *Macropus giganteus* and Euro,[5] which tend to increase as the numbers of domestic stock increase up to a point. Domestic livestock, such as cattle, complement the numbers of these kangaroos because increased watering points are provided, sometimes the vegetation changes in favour of the kangaroos and 'marsupial lawns' are created by cattle eating the longer coarse grass. Moreover, research by the CSIRO shows that the diets of these herbivores do not overlap completely. As a consequence of this relationship, mixed land use, involving kangaroos and livestock, yields maximum biomass from the land, according to CSIRO research.

H.J. Frith, Head of the Division of Wildlife Research of the CSIRO, speaking of large kangaroos says:

> Kangaroos are animals of a particular state of botanical succession of the range. They are uncommon in country that is not grazed by stock. In much of the inland the numbers of stock and of Red Kangaroo are very definitely linked. The grazing has led to changes in the pastures that have favoured an increase in the numbers of kangaroos, and up to a point, an increase in the density of Red Kangaroos. The point does come, however, where further increase in the number of stock leads to the destruction of the range and, as a result, the destruction of both kangaroos and stock. It seems that in much of the inland we can have a relatively short-term economy, based on domestic stock alone or a long-term one based on both stock and kangaroos. (*A.C.F. Newsletter*, April 1968, p. 5)

Unfortunately, there is at the moment (early 1970s) no economic mechanism that prevents overstocking by domestic stock.[6]

Only in the case of the Eastern Grey Kangaroo is there definite evidence that it would survive if it could be farmed. Griffiths and Barker suggest that its numbers up to a point complement wool production.[7] Because the Eastern Grey eats certain plants, the growth of others is encouraged which when eaten by sheep produce better quality wool. In the case of the other large kangaroos, their preservation would depend very much on relative prices.[8]

Maximum biomass is of no economic significance and if the relative price of the mass of a kangaroo is low compared to domestic stock, mixed-land use will not occur and kangaroos may disappear. In the time available to me, I have not been able to work out the profitability of mixed-land use at current prices. The matter is complicated in that the relative growth rates of the species must be compared. The growth rate of kangaroos is slower than for sheep and this has a bearing on the proposal to farm kangaroos. Nevertheless, evidence points in favour of mixed farming in certain inland areas.

However, the possibility of farming kangaroos is still in the experimental stage. Research is continuing at the CSIRO on this. The Kangawalla Pastoral Co. near Glen Innes plans to have cattle raising and tourism co-existing with kangaroo farming. Nevertheless, the fact is that commercial farming of kangaroos is of insignificance at present and we are dependent on government policy to deal with the situation.

Policies in force and their limitations

Let us consider the public controls (existing in the early 1970s) on kangaroo harvesting in New South Wales, Western Australia and Queensland.

The National Parks and Wildlife Service in New South Wales controls the destruction of kangaroos. Any property owner wishing to destroy kangaroos must apply to the Service. An officer inspects the property and if he considers that selective culling of kangaroos would assist graziers and not endanger kangaroo species, he issues a Section 25 licence for a specific number of kangaroos to be shot. Cloth tags corresponding to this number are issued free to the landowner and must be attached to the carcasses as soon as possible.

If a farmer wishes to sell the carcasses, he must either obtain a Trapper's Licence or have a licensed trapper do the shooting for him. A licensed trapper can only operate on a property with the written permission of the owner and a Section 25 licence must be in force for that property. In order to sell his skins, a trapper must obtain 20 cent plastic royalty tags (available in unlimited number) from the Service, and ensure that both cloth tags and plastic royalty tags are attached to the skins as soon as the animals are killed. Thus, the number of cloth tags that are issued to property-holders by the Service effectively regulate the harvest.

In Western Australia, the Department of Fisheries and Fauna administers the control of kangaroos. In February 1971, controls were introduced to limit the annual commercial harvest of Red and Hill Kangaroos combined to approximately 200 000. There are 50 licensed professional shooters each authorised to take 4 000 Red and Hill Kangaroos. Royalty tags at 10 cents each are issued to these shooters. In addition, a small issue of tags is made to pastoralists.

In Queensland, the Fauna Branch of the Department of Primary Industries administers policy. Although Queensland does not operate a tagging system, it does control kangaroo harvesting. The main controls are limitations on chiller boxes and a 20 cent royalty charge for each kangaroo carcass used commercially.

In an attempt to limit the Queensland harvest, the number of chiller boxes has been reduced and controls provide for a minimum of 50 miles between boxes. In my opinion, the effect on the rate of harvesting is not great. Licences are required for operation in the industry. However, licences for shooting are apparently easy to obtain. In 1970, 2 000 licences were issued to shooters, 280 of whom described themselves as professional. In practice, kangaroos are almost open-access common-property in Queensland. [Note: This was the situation in the early 1970s.]

Rather than examine the policies of these States individually, let us concentrate on some general points. All the States impose a royalty charge varying from 10 cents to 20 cents on each kangaroo carcass used for commercial purposes. Only Queensland imposes no quantitative restriction on the take of kangaroos.

Royalty payments can be regarded as excise duties. They do not appear to be used as instruments to control the number of kangaroos harvested but seem to be designed to raise revenue for the government. Royalty payments probably have little effect upon the harvest, because they are small[9] in relation to an average value of $6 per kangaroo and the supply of kangaroos harvested might be fairly inelastic. The quantitative controls imposed in Western Australia and New South Wales and their associated tagging system give more certain control over the harvest than the mere use of royalty payments. However, these measures do not prevent the extermination of kangaroos by poisoning and loss of habitat.

The policies adopted in Queensland seem to suffer from all the shortcomings associated with open-access common-property resources. For example, too many resources from an economic efficiency point of view are devoted to the shooting of kangaroos and kangaroos are not optimally conserved through time.

I wish to stress, however, that in none of the states have measures been adopted to deal with the economic consequence of the inter-dependence between kangaroos and livestock. It is not enough to control only the harvesting of kangaroos on rangeland. To maintain an optimal mix in the use of the land, livestock numbers and habitat need to be controlled. Although there could be political objections to this on private land, there is scope for implementing policy along these lines on the considerable Crown Lands on lease.

At present it is apparent that we do not get the maximum commercial value from our land considering kangaroos as factors in the product-mix and this is in part due to the appropriability problem. However, current commercial value should not be our only consideration in conserving kangaroos. For example, it can be argued that some species should be conserved on the chance that they will be of value to later generations.

Some species of kangaroos will not survive even if appropriability by landowners is easy. Parks and managed reserves seem essential to their survival.[10] Hence, given our general aspirations, it seems likely that optimal land-use policy requires areas of commercial land use without measures to protect wildlife, commercial areas subject to controls to favour wildlife, reserves with restricted commercial access such as restricted grazing for livestock, and parks with no right of commercial utilisation of their resources (except for tourism under particular conditions). It is the balance between land uses and the methods used to control land use that are the basis of the conservation debate. While Australian policies for the control of kangaroos as a natural resource have improved, current policies (1973) are inadequate, especially in coping with the interdependence problem.

The importance of the interdependence problem can be emphasised in conclusion if we consider a point made by Senator Durack. Senator Durack stated (*Hansard*, Senate, No. 7, May 1973, p. 1222) that as a result of the export prohibition on kangaroo products,[11] widespread poisoning of kangaroos by pastoralists is planned in north-west Western Australia. However, the export ban is possibly not the major reason. Because the prices of cattle and sheep have increased greatly in the last year, graziers have an incentive to increase their stock of these animals. Up to a point, this can be achieved by reducing the kangaroo population. In this regard a co-ordinated campaign by farmers to reduce kangaroo numbers is likely to be most effective, but judging from CSIRO studies on the movements of kangaroos, (complete) poisoning on a single, large property could reduce the kangaroo population of that property by a significant percentage for a couple of years. In general, pastoralists in Western Australia have no property rights in kangaroos so the direction of their self-interest is clear, especially in the north-west of the State where properties are very large. However, from a general policy point of view the main tragedy is that current public policies concentrate merely on controlling shooting of kangaroos and fail to take account of other ways in which kangaroo populations can be reduced, for example by poisoning and competition from domestic livestock.

Notes

1. Based on an address to the Newcastle Area members of the Economic Society of Australia and New Zealand in June 1973. I wish to thank Mrs Elaine Sheehan for providing me with some useful references. This article originally appeared in *Economic Activity*, **16**(4), October 1973, pp. 32–36. The content of this article is the same as in the original (except for minor changes) but its presentation has been improved. An abstract has also been added. Consequently, pagination is no longer the same as in the original.
2. The value of kangaroo exports in 1970–71 was approximately $1.9 million which was about 20 per cent of the value of the total kangaroo harvest. Thus, allowing for rising meat prices, the export ban imposed by the Labor Government may have much less impact on kangaroo harvesting than has been commonly indicated in the press and elsewhere.
3. On small properties, a prisoner's dilemma type of problem arises.
4. J.H. Calaby, 'The Current Status of Australian Macropodidae', *Australian Zoologist*, **16**(1), 1971, pp. 5–12.
5. The Euro is also known as the Wallaroo or Hill Kangaroo.
6. There is no mechanism which prevents overstocking by domestic stock in relation to kangaroos. However, note also that an effective price mechanism, coupled with private property rights, will not prevent overstocking in comparison to the long-term carrying capacity of the land. Both uncertainties and externalities may lead to a solution which is socially sub-optimal in this regard. As a consequence, the collective environment may deteriorate, as has apparently happened in the Mediterranean Basin.
7. M. Griffiths and R. Barker, 'The Plants Eaten by Sheep and by Kangaroos Grazing Together in a Paddock in South-Western Queensland', *CSIRO Wildlife Research*, **11**, 1966, pp. 145–67.
8. Details of this and technical trade-offs between kangaroos and domestic livestock are given in C.A. Tisdell, 'Kangaroos – The Economic Management of a Common-Property Resource Involving Interdependence of Production', Section 24, ANZAAS Conference, Perth, August 1973.
9. They amount to 1.6 to 3.3 per cent of value depending upon the State involved.
10. Some economic questions are involved in deciding how large these parks should be and where they should be situated. Cost considerations cannot be ignored.
11. These were in place when this article was written but later withdrawn.

[10]

KANGAROOS: THE ECONOMIC MANAGEMENT OF A COMMON-PROPERTY RESOURCE INVOLVING INTERDEPENDENCE OF PRODUCTION

Of the 45 species of kangaroos present in Australia at the time of European settlement three are now extinct, and an additional 12 are close to extinction (5, p.17). In particular the small species such as the rat-kangaroos seemed to have been most adversely affected by farming and introduced predators whereas large kangaroos such as the red have benefited from the environmental change. However, even in their case the continuing public concern about conservation and economic utilisation seems justified. As a result of pressure from conservationist groups, the House of Representatives set up a Select Committee on Wildlife Conservation which produced, in November 1971, a short interim report (4) on kangaroos. In early 1973, the Federal Labor Government announced its intention to ban the export of kangaroo skins and products as an apparent conservation measure. This ban is now being reconsidered (*The Australian*, 10 March 1973, p.2) and a committee of the States and Commonwealth is examining the economic management of kangaroos.

Economists are naturally interested in the utilisation of resources including wildlife species. Existing economic literature (13,20,21,22,23,25) concentrates on wildlife which is common-property, in particular on fish in international waters (13,21,22,25). The literature points out that whenever a species is held as common-property (*i.e.* available for free appropriation by every individual) and has commercial value that this is liable to lead to economic inefficiencies. The species is liable to be overharvested, the allocation of harvesting activity in time and between areas is less than optimal and there is a lack of husbandry of the species even when husbandry is optimal from the collective *commercial* view. (For further details, see, for example, 23.)

Economists have suggested a number of different measures to deal with these problems. Turvey, taking a traditional Pigovian approach, argues (25) that these deficiencies can be corrected by appropriate taxes (royalty payments) on the catch and on other economic activity associated with the species. Others such as Tisdell (23) and, by inference, Baumol and Oates (3) see quotas as being more desirable in *certain* circumstances.

Again another policy measure has been canvassed by H. Scott Gordon (13) and Vernon Smith (22). They favour the replacement of the common-property form of effective ownership by private property. In their view, an individual should be granted sole ownership of a species within a region and, if necessary, a monopoly of the species. Since I have already discussed these measures elsewhere (23) I shall not do this again here.

However, each of these measures can be effective for the economic management of wildlife under particular conditions. For example, if a species occurs in isolated pockets the private ownership solution seems feasible, but does not seem to be if the species is *extremely* mobile and is in competition with domestic species. In the case of taxes and quotas, it must be physically possible to enforce these. Enforcement is likely to be easier if the catch goes through some central processing points, *e.g.*, such as a factory or a "chiller-box". In some cases, economic management of a wildlife species may call for a combination of quotas, taxes and private ownership. This could be so for kangaroos used for commercial purposes.

There are many different species of kangaroos (in fact, 42) with varying characteristics and habitat requirements so it is liable to be misleading to generalise about their economic management as a whole. Some of the smaller types are of little or no commercial value for meat and skins whereas others such as the Red and Grey Kangaroos are of considerable commercial value. In order to use our resources efficiently, a range of policies is required for controlling kangaroo populations. Some species can only survive in national parks or reserves with suitable husbandry and free of competition from domestic stock and introduced predators. Others can be successfully carried in conjunction with domestic stock, *e.g.*, the Red and Grey Kangaroos, and the efficient use of resources may require mixed land use in their case. Others such as the Euro *might* be so strongly competitive with domestic stock and of so little comparative commercial value that it would be most economic to eradicate these (except within the confines of suitable reserves). A wide range of management policies for species in parks and reserves, as well as for species roaming at large, is required (23,24). The matters involved are extremely complex and I shall concern myself in this paper principally with policy and the management of kangaroos in conjunction with domestic stock.

The economic studies of wildlife which are mentioned above do not take account of interdependence of species. While interdependence does not alter the import of their general views, it creates extra difficulties for economic management. In the case of kangaroos, their interdependence with domestic stock is important (5,7,8,9,18). Some species such as the Euro and the Red Kangaroo tend to increase with the introduction of livestock because of increased watering points and favourable changes induced in the pasture whereas other smaller species such as nail-tailed wallabies and hare-wallabies have virtually disappeared because livestock has eaten their shelter (8, p.584).

In order to devise rational policies for the economic management of kangaroos, it is important to clarify the production relationships between kangaroos and various types of livestock (and other land uses). A minor start can be made by drawing on the theory of production and the observations of zoologists and others. This is done in the next section. Existing policies for the management of kangaroos are then outlined and discussed.

II

Although the C.S.I.R.O. Division of Wildlife Research has produced much valuable knowledge about kangaroos, considerable further research is required to quantify accurately the interdependence of kangaroo numbers with domestic stock. As far as I am aware, no specific production relationships have been quantified although important qualitative results are available for some types of kangaroos. On the other hand "research into the ecology and habitat requirements of virtually all small species has barely begun." (5, p.26).

It is important to distinguish various possible "technological" relationships between kangaroos and domestic stock because the possibility of survival of kangaroos under favourable commercial conditions and even supposing a high degree of appropriability by landowners depends on these factors. Furthermore, a government concerned with the efficient use (in the sense of Pareto) of the land must take these technological (or more correctly, biological) relationships into account.

I shall concentrate on three theoretical types of transformation frontiers between species of kangaroos and domestic stock. The analysis is limited to the two-commodity case as a first step towards the study of many interdependent species. The transformation frontier indicates flows of kangaroos and livestock, i.e., the annual cull or "harvest". More specifically, the frontier indicates maximum equilibrium flows corresponding to equilibrium stocks of the species. Thus the rates of harvest on the frontier can be maintained in perpetuity given the possibilities of the land and the available techniques. The populations of the species remain steady once they reach a level corresponding to a point on the transformation frontier.

The three broad types of transformation frontiers between wildlife and domestic stock which it is profitable to distinguish are those which exhibit

(1) competitiveness throughout,
(2) one-sided complementarity, and
(3) double-sided complementarity.

Case (2) can be divided into 2(a) circumstances in which the livestock complements the wildlife species and 2(b) instances in which the wildlife species complements the production of the livestock. Of course, complementarity of production throughout the transformation frontier is possible, but this can be looked on as a special case of situation (3). Although these cases are specifically related to kangaroos and livestock they also have application to wildlife and livestock, and interdependence between species generally.

(1) *Competitiveness Throughout the Transformation Function.* The characteristic of this case is the negative slope of the product

transformation throughout i.e., the rate of product transformation is negative at all values. The transformation function itself may, for example, be strictly concave (decreasing returns), strictly convex (increasing returns), or linear (constant returns). Examples of these three regular cases are given in Figures 1 to 3 respectively.

Figure 1

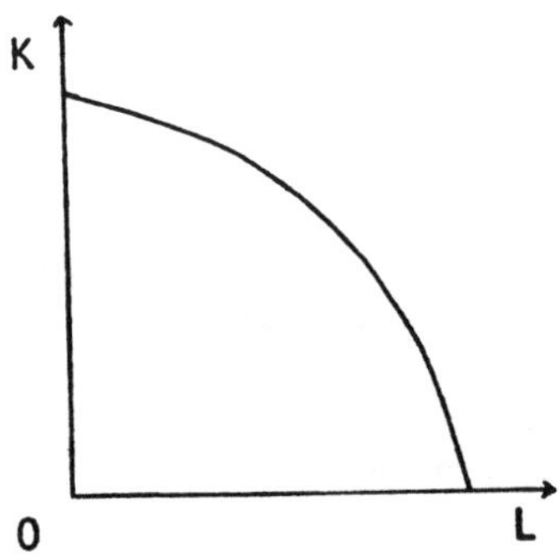

Figure 2

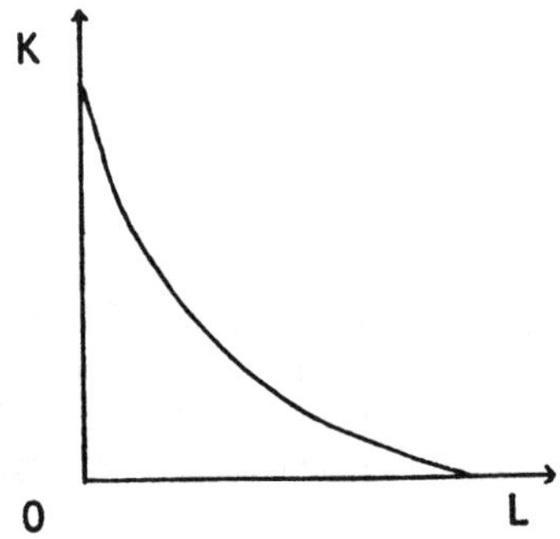

Figure 3

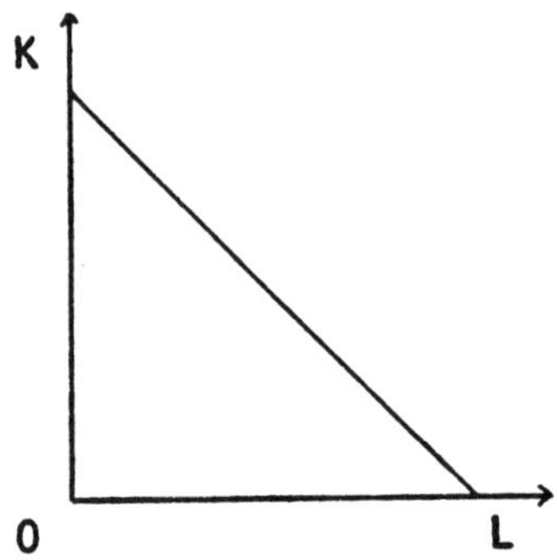

K = Quantity of Kangaroos Harvested Per Year
L = Quantity of Livestock Culled Per Year

Given the market value placed on kangaroos and livestock, mixed land use cannot maximise the value of output if increasing returns (Figure 2) occur, may (but is unlikely to do so) if constant returns is the case, and is likely (but not certain to do so) if decreasing returns occurs in joint production.[1] In other words, given constant prices for kangaroos and livestock, a corner-point solution is certain to eventuate if increasing returns occur but is least likely to come about if decreasing returns arise. In every case, if the price of livestock relative to the price of kangaroos is sufficiently high in comparison to the rate at which extra livestock can be

1. This is so since the iso-value lines are straight parallel lines.

obtained by foregoing kangaroos, kangaroos will be exterminated even if landowners can appropriate the whole of their market value.[2] But if the opposite is the case landowners will conserve and utilise kangaroos if they are able to appropriate their market value.

For the Red Kangaroo, Megaleia Rufa (Desmarest), there is some evidence that the transformation frontier *might* be like that in Figure 1. Bailey (2) found in his study the red kangaroo seemed to be in competition with other herbivores (mainly sheep and rabbits) for food. Red kangaroos did not seem to be ecologically separated in their food preferences from other herbivores either by the parts of the plant or types of plant eaten (2, p.38). However, Bailey points out that his study was conducted during a drought period when more competition might be expected. Newsome and Frith suggest (16, p.5) that while there is competition for food between domestic stock, especially sheep, at least during good years the overlap is small (17, pp.40-44). In their view, the kangaroo and sheep are largely complementary graziers (16, p.10).

Frith says in a longer statement, "Kangaroos are not in direct competition with stock at all times; to a considerable extent kangaroos and stock can run on the same land without detriment to one another and, in some cases to mutual benefit, as their grazing is to some extent complementary. Decreasing the number of Red Kangaroos will not increase the carrying capacity of the land for other stock by an equivalent amount. There will be a net decrease in the amount of protein produced by the land and there is little doubt that the maximum productivity would be achieved in the long term, by grazing some kangaroos with stock." (12, p.5).

On the basis of this information it is possible to rule out constant returns, or increasing returns in the transformation functions. Maximum biomass (productivity?) from grazing is not obtained from mixed land use in these cases.[3] A competitive relationship like that shown in Figure 1 is still possible but in view of evidence to be presented later the Red Kangaroo seems on average to exhibit one-sided complementarity with stock.

Before examining the one-sided case, consider a competitive type of production relationship which may apply to species of kangaroos which have their habitat removed either by grazing livestock or by the clearing of scrub and forest by farmers. This has happened, for example, to some species of nail-tailed wallaby, hare-wallabies and bandicoots (18, pp.584-585), and, with the clearing of rain-forest and scrub, to the musk rat-

2. The extermination is a consequence of intensive stocking of the land.

3. The equal biomass lines for kangaroos and livestock are parallel straight lines. Biomass is said to be at a maximum only for a *mixture* of kangaroos and livestock. This is inconsistent with a linear transformation frontier or a strictly convex one but is consistent with a strictly concave one.

kangaroo and parma wallaby (5, p.17, p.23). The transformation function may be discontinuous as shown by AB and CD in Figure 4. The kangaroo species disappears once livestock numbers reach some threshold and cause the habitat of the kangaroo species to fall below a level necessary to sustain a kangaroo population at all.[4] Since most of the species threatened in this way have no commercial value reserves from which livestock are excluded may be the only way to ensure their survival. It may also be desirable to subsidise the provision of suitable habitats for these kangaroos on private land.[5] Note that if these kangaroo species which have their habitat threatened have sufficient commercial value in relation to livestock and landowners can appropriate this, they would conserve the species.

Figure 4

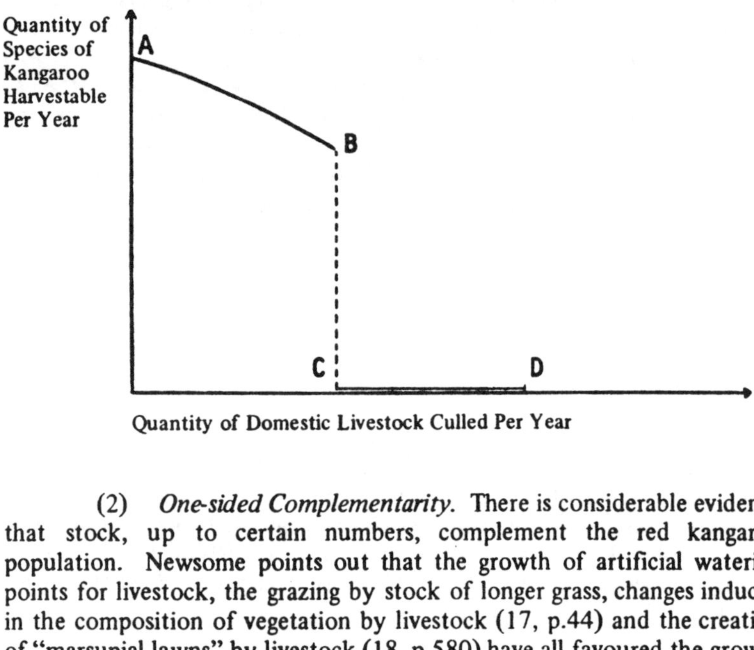

(2) *One-sided Complementarity.* There is considerable evidence that stock, up to certain numbers, complement the red kangaroo population. Newsome points out that the growth of artificial watering points for livestock, the grazing by stock of longer grass, changes induced in the composition of vegetation by livestock (17, p.44) and the creation of "marsupial lawns" by livestock (18, p.580) have all favoured the growth of red kangaroo numbers. Newsome asserts "It is a firm conclusion that the present subclimax vegetation of Australia's inland plains is supporting a higher biomass of livestock and Red Kangaroos than of either alone because of their largely different diets" (18, p.581).

The type of transformation function shown in Figure 5 is

4. The necessity of habitats to be above a threshold size if species are to survive is for example mentioned in A.D. Costin and H.J. Frith, *Conservation*, Penguin Books Australia, 1971.

5. Threshold habitat considerations would have to be taken into account in considering the subsidy. *C.f.*, C. Walsh and C. Tisdell, "Non-Marginal Externalities: As Relevant and As Not," *Economic Record*, forthcoming.

probably typical for Red Kangaroos and livestock. However, this one-sided complementarity is not sufficient to ensure the survival of Red Kangaroos given that commercial appropriation is possible. If the relative price of domestic stock becomes high enough, corner-point C maximises profit. At this point, the density of domestic stock and the associated land changes are such as to make no equilibrium harvest of Red Kangaroos possible. The population of kangaroos is extinct or on the verge of extinction.

The Euro exhibits a similar one-sided relationship to that for Red Kangaroos and livestock except that the Euro is more competitive with sheep. "... Euros have benefited in two ways from the advent of stock, through an abundance of permanent though artificial waters, and through the abundance of drought fodder." (18, p.579) Grazing by sheep has favoured the multiplication of spinifex and during drought the Euros fare much better than sheep on a diet of spinifex. The Euro has even proven itself to be very resilient in the face of large water poisoning programmes." (8, 9, 18, p.579).

Figure 5

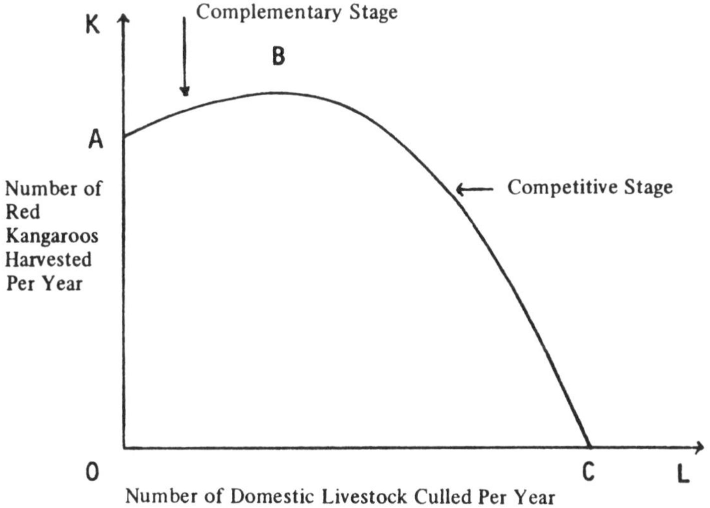

There is little evidence of one-sided complementarity from the other end, i.e. of kangaroos complementing livestock, although Griffiths and Barker (14) do not dismiss this possibility. They say "In fact in a good year, such as 1963, and given the moderate number of kangaroos which we encountered, it is not inconceivable that grey kangaroos could be beneficial to wool production by keeping in check grasses of low protein content that could otherwise get out of hand and compete heavily with nitrogen-rich dicotyledons. This is a notion that deserves investigation." (14, p.166). In the case of the Grey Kangaroo, Macropus Giganteus (Shaw), double-sided complementarity cannot be ruled out.

(3) *Double-sided Complementarity.* When kangaroos complement livestock (lower-ended complementarity) a lower-ended corner-point never maximises the value of output and the prospect for preservation of kangaroos by landowners seems favourable.[6] In the case of double-sided complementarity, such as that illustrated by Figure 6, a mixture of stock and kangaroos always maximises the value of production. It does so even if kangaroos are of no commercial value. The transformation frontier in Figure 6 exhibits complementarity in the ranges AB and DF and competitiveness in the segment BCD. The value of the land use is always maximised by a combination in the segment BCD. The biomass is also maximised in this sector but, of course, biomass itself is of little economic relevance.

Figure 6

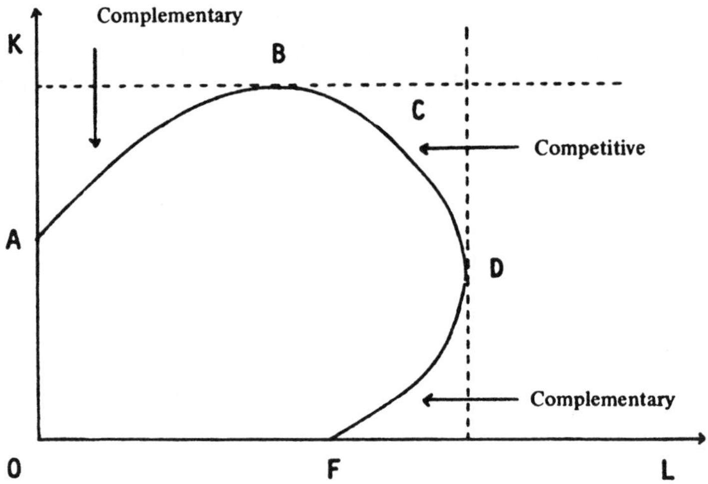

On *average* the Eastern Grey Kangaroo, Macropus Giganteus, may exhibit double-sided complementarity with stock (14). However, during drought the relationship probably becomes competitive throughout.

There is clearly a variety of transformation relationships between livestock and kangaroo harvesting which depend upon the species of kangaroos involved.

III

The above analysis has several implications and applications which it is useful to indicate before describing and analysing the policies adopted by some of the states for the management of kangaroos.

6. However, this is not certain to occur since on small properties owners find that kangaroo numbers are virtually independent of their individual action. The prospect is more likely to be realised on large properties.

First, even when kangaroos have commercial value and individual landowners can appropriate it, this does not ensure the conservation of the species unless the value of producing a positive amount of kangaroos is high enough to compensate landowners for the value of livestock forgone. If inexpensive enclosures make the commercial farming of kangaroos (6) possible, their survival is not ensured unless the "farming" of them is sufficiently profitable in comparison to livestock. Farming of the species of larger kangaroos may become profitable but some species have no value for their skins and carcasses and commercial farming of these is never likely to be profitable. Their chance of survival depends upon the provision of suitable parks and reserves which are adequately managed.

Secondly, the transformation functions indicate the extent to which conservation and utilisation of kangaroos on land can be combined with livestock on the same land. In the case of reserves, livestock numbers above a particular level endanger the wildlife species which the reserves are designed to protect.

The transformation function can be used with other information as a basis for determining "ideal" land use and devising measures to bring this about. While ideal land use may require the provision of some parks and reserves from which livestock are excluded in order to preserve species of kangaroos and wildlife, in other cases controlled grazing by livestock need not endanger species. Policies regulating the mixture of wildlife and domestic stock are also required for range or grazing land. A mixture of some species of kangaroos and domestic stock may be optimal from a social economic point of view. The problem appears to be that although Australian governments have control over the harvesting of kangaroos, they do not have (or have not exerted) much control over private land use. Since kangaroo numbers and livestock numbers (and associated investments) are interdependent, control is required over *both*.

In reserves, this dual control is no problem. Nor need it be in the long term for the considerable Crown Lands which are leased. These could be leased subject to government controls on livestock numbers and cultivation and on the preservation of habitats suitable for kangaroos (and other wildlife). It may also be that the government should institute a policy of purchasing marginal agricultural land and add this to reserves for combined use by wildlife and stock and/or subsidise the preservation of some wildlife habitats on private land.

At the moment, on range land or private land, governments control *only* the harvest of kangaroos. In these areas, they exert no control over livestock numbers and wildlife habitats. Because of difficulties by landowners in appropriating kangaroos, the commercial value of the harvest from this land is lower than is possible and long-term conservation goals (which may in part have a type of merit-good basis (23)), are not efficiently pursued. While administration costs and loss of freedom may rule out the political attainment of the otherwise economically optimal mix, no doubt existing second-best policies can be improved.

IV

Let us look at the controls on kangaroo harvesting in New South Wales, Western Australia and Queensland. Queensland has the largest annual commercial kill in Australia, about one million carcases, followed bv Western Australia with over 200,000 carcases. The New South Wales harvest is comparatively small.

In N.S.W. the National Parks and Wildlife Service controls the destruction of kangaroos. Any property owner wishing to destroy kangaroos must apply to the Service. An officer inspects the property and if he considers that selective culling of kangaroos would assist graziers and not endanger kangaroo species he issues a Section 25 licence for a *specific* number of kangaroos to be shot. *Cloth tags* corresponding to this number are issued free to the landowner and must be attached to the carcases as soon as possible.

If the farmer wishes to sell the carcases he must in addition obtain a Trapper's Licence or have a licensed trapper do the shooting for him. Any person who shoots kangaroos to sell the meat and/or skins must hold a *Trapper's Licence,* costing $5. A licensed trapper cannot operate except on a property where a Section 25 licence has already been issued and the written authority of the property owner has been obtained." (19, p.1). If a trapper wishes to sell kangaroo skins, he must obtain plastic royalty tags from the Service (available in unlimited numbers at 20c each) and must ensure that *both cloth and plastic royalty tags* are attached to the skins as soon as possible after the animals are killed.

Wholesalers and those dealing in kangaroo skins must be registered with the Service. They are not to accept kangaroos without both the cloth and plastic tags attached. When the skins are being processed the tags are to be returned to the Service. Furthermore, each licensed Kangaroo Trapper, Fauna Dealer and Skin Dealer is required to submit to the Director of National Parks and Wildlife a monthly return.

In N.S.W. significant property rights remain with landowners, even though the harvest is carefully controlled. The number of cloth tags which are issued to property-holders effectively regulate the harvest and there is nothing to prevent a landowner from selling these to a Licensed Trapper. In the case of Western Australia, the rights of landowners in kangaroos for commercial use are not so secure.

In W.A., the control of kangaroos is administered by the Department of Fisheries and Fauna. In February 1971, Western Australia introduced controls which are designed to limit the annual commercial harvest of Red and Hill Kangaroos combined to approximately 200,000. Professional licensed shooters are the mainstay of the industry. There are

50 licensed professional shooters each authorised to take 4,000 Red and Hill Kangaroos (Euros).[7] Tags at 10c each are issued to these shooters and are to be attached to the animals taken for commercial use. "In addition, small issues of tags are made to Pastoralists. These tags may be used by the Pastoralist himself or a nominated agent or a Professional Shooter."[8]

The Western Grey Kangaroo (Macropus Fuliginosus) is subject to separate control in agricultural areas.[9] Because of the rapid increase of numbers in South-West of the State, licensed part-time shooters are allowed and there could be a need for chillers in rural areas. In some shires shooting of grey kangaroos by property owners, agents or licensed shooters is possible without a damage licence but in others, if grey kangaroos are causing damage, a farmer *must* obtain a damage licence from the fauna warden before shooting can commence. In all cases, if a farmer wants to sell skins and carcases royalty tags are required in addition to the damage licence.

In the case of Red and Hill Kangaroos the rights of property-holders are minimal. They are only permitted marginally to trade in carcases and skins of these kangaroos although according to the Senate Report they are permitted to destroy any number on their property. (4, p.15, par. 76). If owners of large properties are unable to obtain any reasonable payment from professional shooters for kangaroos taken on their property, they clearly have an incentive to poison kangaroos.[10]

In Queensland, fauna policy is administered by the Fauna Branch of the Department of Primary Industries. Although Queensland does not operate a tagging system, it does control kangaroo harvesting. The main controls are limitations on chiller boxes and a 20c royalty charge for each kangaroo carcase used commercially.

In an attempt to limit the harvest, the number of chiller boxes has been reduced and controls provide for a minimum of 50 miles between chiller boxes. This indirect measure may add to the cost of harvest (although taking into account the Hotelling locational effect,[11] up to a point the opposite is possible). If the distance between boxes becomes too great many hunters may concentrate on skins, there may be a loss of

7. Information on the number of shooters and quotas supplied by letter from the Department of Fisheries and Fauna, W.A. Details on the harvesting of Red and Hill Kangaroos are given in *W.A. Government Gazette (No.39) 17 April 1970.*

8. Letter from the Department of Fisheries and Fauna.

9. These controls are set out in the W.A. *Government Gazette (No.67) 23 July 1971* and explained in a leaflet of the Department of Fisheries and Fauna, *Management Programme Grey Kangaroo*, September 1972.

10. This assumes that large landowners can obtain a reduction in kangaroo numbers by poisoning and that poisoning is relatively inexpensive.

11. H. Hotelling, "Stability in Competition," *Economic Journal*, Vol. 39, 1929, pp.41-57

carcasses and some may install refrigeration of their own. The effect on the rate or harvesting may not be great.

Licences are required for operation in the industry. However, licences for shooting are apparently not difficult to obtain for in 1970 2,000 licences were issued to shooters, 280 of whom described themselves as professional hunters. Dealers are required to record details of animals received, the shooter's licence number, and a royalty of 20c per carcass is payable by the shooter. This royalty goes into consolidated revenue.

In Queensland, property-holders have the legal right to exclude shooters from their property and seem to be in a position to appropriate kangaroos if this is technically possible.

Samples of the skulls of kangaroos are used by the Fauna Branch to determine the age structure of kangaroos in a region and the need for protective measures (such as closed seasons). A similar approach has been adopted by Western Australia for the Western Grey Kangaroo.

V

Rather than examine the policies of these States individually, let us concentrate on common and general points. All the states impose a royalty charge varying from 10c to 20c on each kangaroo carcass used for commercial purposes. Only in Queensland are there no quantitative restrictions on the take of kangaroos.

Royalty payments can be regarded as excise duties. The effectiveness of royalties in controlling the number of kangaroos shot for commercial purposes depends upon the incidence of the royalty and the size of the per-unit royalty payment. If the supply of kangaroo carcasses or the demand for them is very inelastic, the impact of royalties on the size of the harvest is minimal. It is certainly possible that the supply of carcasses if fairly inelastic considering that kangaroos may be regarded as vermin and part-time shooters get a certain amount of gratification from shooting activity. Royalty payments alone may not be very effective curbs on shooting.[12]

Quotas apply in Western Australia for the commercial take of Red and Hill kangaroos and quantitative controls are imposed in New South Wales on all shooting of kangaroos. With associated tagging systems, the quantitative method gives more certain control over the number of kangaroos used commercially, and in New South Wales over the number and distribution of kangaroos shot. However, these measures do not prevent kangaroos from being exterminated by poisoning and loss of habitat.

12. No attempt is made by the states to use royalties as a means of varying the harvest or allocating shooting activity. For example, royalty rates are not raised at times and in areas where an increase in the population of kangaroos is desired.

From an efficiency point of view, the method of allocation of quotas and limited harvest rates is interesting. For the Western Australian quota, preference is given to those engaged in the commercial shooting of kangaroos during the whole of 1968 and 1969.[13] The allocation of quotas depends upon an individual's historical involvement in the industry and may mean that new low cost shooters are excluded from the industry. An alternative system would be to auction quotas (say, in lots of 4,000 with possibly some restrictions on bidders). Any monopoly-profit then is likely to go to the State and new low cost operators are given the chance of entry.

In New South Wales, culling of particular quantities of kangaroos is allowed on properties with the permission of the Wildlife Service. The Service has adopted general guidelines on the permissible culling rate (15, p.56) and cloth tags are issued to the property-holder in corresponding numbers. Presumably, the property owner can sell these to licensed trappers if he wishes to and so appropriate some of the value of having kangaroos on his property.

As mentioned earlier, restrictions on the number of chiller boxes has been used in Queensland with a view to limiting the harvesting rate. As pointed out, this measure may not be effective in reducing the number of kangaroos destroyed and could add to the costs of the numbers used commercially.

The question of the appropriation of kangaroos by property-holders is most important. In some cases where kangaroos have *sufficient* commercial value, it can be argued that kangaroos are not optimally conserved and utilised because of the impossibility of land-holders appropriating the commercial value of kangaroos. If property-owners can only appropriate the commercial value of kangaroos (and are well informed) they would husband kangaroos like livestock. In this regard, the C.S.I.R.O. has been investigating the farming of kangaroos and means of keeping them enclosed. (6). However, as pointed out earlier using transformation functions, complete appropriability does not ensure survival of a species (in fact, it might ensure its destruction if it is regarded as a pest or is relatively unprofitable).[14] Nevertheless, the farming of *some* types of kangaroos with livestock is, in certain areas, the optimal commercial product-mix if kangaroos can be cheaply enclosed and appropriated by the property-holder.

In the absence of a cheap method of enclosure, the appropriability problem remains. The kangaroo is so mobile that on small properties the land-holder is not able to appropriate it and might truly regard the number of kangaroos present on his property to be quite

13. See W.A. *Government Gazette (No.39) 17 April 1970.*

14. The species will be regarded as a pest when it is relatively unprofitable in relation to alternatives.

independent of his policies affecting them, e.g., habitat removal, shooting. If they are profitable to harvest or fun to shoot, he will carry on these activities without thought of the future kangaroo population. If they are regarded as pests and the carcases have little or no commercial value for him, he has no incentive to adopt costly eradication measures – the neighbouring kangaroos will quickly replace those which he destroys. Thus an example of the prisoner's dilemma problem occurs.

However, on large properties of which there are several in Australia, the technical appropriability problem is not so serious. Studies which have been done by the C.S.I.R.O. indicate that some types of kangaroos used for commercial purposes have a fraction of members which are relatively sedentary. In the case of the Tero study of the movements of the red kangaroo in North-West N.S.W., in a 30-month period two-thirds of the collars attached to kangaroos for identifying movement were found within 15 miles of where the animals were released. This was so despite drought conditions (1, p.27). Other studies indicate even slighter movements of red kangaroos (7, 14).

The fraction of animals which can be technically appropriated by holders of large properties may make it worthwhile for these land-holders to husband some types of kangaroos if legal appropriation is possible. In Western Australia not even large land-holders have the right to legal appropriation of Red and Hill kangaroos for commercial purposes. In the case of a large land-holding unable to appropriate any commercial value from kangaroos, poisoning of kangaroos when these are in competition with livestock may become an attractive proposition.[15] Thus policies designed to preserve red kangaroos may have the opposite result if they deny appropriation rights to large land holdings.

Another aspect of the appropriation question should not be neglected. Appropriation by landowners enables them to earn rent from the use of their resources (or charge others rent for using these). In a competitive market economy, differential rents are necessary to the optimal allocation of resources in space. If landowners are unable to charge shooters rent or if shooting quotas are general and not optimally allocated by properties, a less than optimal spread of shooting or harvesting of kangaroos occurs. As H. Scott Gordon points out (13, see also 23) in the absence of rents or measures with equivalent effect, areas with high productivity are overharvested. This is likely to happen in Western Australia where the aggregate quota for Red and Hill kangaroos is not differentiated by area and also in Queensland where no quotas apply. This is assuming in both cases that landowners find it practically impossible to obtain payment from shooters for taking kangaroos on their properties. In Queensland it is possibly also true that since entry to kangaroo shooting seems easy, too many resources from an efficiency

15. This is because large properties can appropriate much of the value of eradicating the species on the property.

point of view are devoted to kangaroo shooting. The value of the average product of resources in the industry tends to be equated with the value of their *marginal* product elsewhere (see 13 and also 23) whereas, under certain conditions, efficiency requires equality of the value of the marginal product of resources everywhere. However, it is quite possible that marginal considerations are insignificant when compared with total considerations (Cf., 3).

In none of the states have measures been adopted to deal with possibilities arising from interdependence between kangaroos and livestock on rangeland. There seems to be no policy regulating the preservation of habitat in these areas and controlling livestock numbers. Especially for Crown Lands on lease there is scope for policies with a wider perspective.

Our knowledge about the characteristics of kangaroos, especially the smaller macropods, remains limited. Further knowledge is required and needs to be disseminated. It is to be hoped too that policies can be adopted to improve strains of species of kangaroos used commercially. The commercial possibilities and prospects of improvement of kangaroos are incompletely explored. Essentially because public goods are involved, this research needs to be done by the government.[16]

At present it is apparent that we do not get the maximum commercial value from our land considering kangaroos and wildlife as factors in the product-mix and this is in part due to the appropriability problem. But current commercial value ought not be our only consideration in conserving kangaroos (23). Some species of kangaroos will not survive even if appropriability by landowners is easy. Parks and managed reserves seem essential to their survival. Just how large these parks should be and how they ought to be managed is not a question which I have explored, although, I have looked at some of the arguments for parks and reserves elsewhere (23, 24). Nevertheless, given our general aspirations, it seems likely that optimal land-use policy requires areas of rangeland or commercial land use without measures to protect wildlife, rangeland and commercial areas subject to controls to favour wildlife, reserves with restricted commercial access, such as restricted grazing for livestock, and parks with no right of commercial utilisation of their resources (except for tourism under particular conditions). It is the balance between land uses and the methods used to control land use which are the basis of the conservation debate. While Australian policies for the control of kangaroos as a natural resource have improved, this paper points to specific inadequacies of current policies especially in coping with the interdependence problem.

University of Newcastle Clem Tisdell

16. It is, in fact, being done in Australia by the government through such organisations as the C.S.I.R.O. The only question is whether the expenditure on this research should be increased.

REFERENCES

1. P.T. Bailey, "The Red Kangaroo, Megaleia Rufa (Desmarest), in North-Western New South Wales. I Movements, "*C.S.I.R.O. Wildlife Research*, vol. 16, 1971, pp.11-28.

2. P.T. Bailey, P.M. Martensz and R. Barker, "The Red Kangaroo, Megaleia Rufa (Desmarest), in North-Western New South Wales. II Food, "*C.S.I.R.O. Wildlife Research*, vol. 16, 1971, pp29-39.

3. W.J. Baumol and W. Oates, "The Use of Standards and Prices for the Protection of the Environment," *Swedish Journal of Economics*, vol. 73, 1971, pp.42-54.

4. Commonwealth of Australia, Interim Report from the House of Representatives Select Committee on Wildlife, *Conservation and Commercial Exploitation of Kangaroos*, November, 1971.

5. J.H. Calaby, "The Current Status of Australian Macropodidae," *Australian Zoologist*, vol. 16, Pt. 1, 1971, pp.17-29.

6. J.H. Calaby and W.E. Poole, "Keeping Kangaroos in Captivity," *International Zoo Yearbook*, vol. 11, 1971, pp.5-12.

7. C.S.I.R.O., "The Red Kangaroo", *Rural Research in the C.S.I.R.O.*, No.50, March 1965, pp.11-14.

8. E.H.M. Ealey and H. Suijendorp, "Pasture Management and the Euro Problem in the North-West of Western Australia," *The Journal of Agriculture of Western Australia*, vol. 8 (Third Series) 1959, pp.273-286.

9. E.H.M. Ealey, "The Ecology of the Euro, Macropus Robustus (Gould), in North-Western Australia. I. The Environment and Changes in Euro and Sheep Populations," *C.S.I.R.O. Wildlife Research*, vol. 12, 1967, pp9-25.

10. H.J. Frith, "The Mobility of the Red Kangaroo, Megaleia Rufa," *C.S.I.R.O Wildlife Research*, vol. 9, 1964, pp.1-19.

11. H.J. Frith, "Conservation of Kangaroos," paper presented to the Symposium on Conservation held during the A.N.Z.A.A.S. Congress, Hobart, Tasmania, August 1965.

12. H.J. Frith, "Controlled Harvesting of Kangaroos," *A.C.F. Newsletter*, No. 3, April 1968.

13. H.S. Gordon, "The Economic Theory of a Common Property Resource: The Fishery," *Journal of Political Economy*, vol. 62, 1954, pp.124-142.

14. M. Griffiths and R. Barker, "The Plants Eaten by Sheep and By Kangaroos Grazing Together in a Paddock in South-Western Queensland," *C.S.I.R.O. Wildlife Research,* vol. 11, 1966, pp.145-167.

15. D.L. Lunney, "Wildlife Management – Kangaroos," *Parks and Wildlife,* vol. 1, 1972, pp.55, 56.

16. A.E. Newsome and H.J. Frith, "The Kangaroo and the Game Meat Trade," a paper of the C.S.I.R.O. Division of Wildlife Research.

17. A.E. Newsome, "The Ecology of Red Kangaroos," *Australian Zoologist,* vol. 16, Pt. 1, 1971, pp.32-50.

18. A.E. Newsome, "Competition Between Wildlife and Domestic Livestock," *The Australian Veterinary Journal,* vol. 47, 1971, pp.577-586.

19. N.S.W. National Parks and Wildlife Service, circular entitled, "Information for Persons who wish to Shoot Kangaroos, Wallaroos and Wallabies, and Those who wish to Sell the Skins and Meat of Kangaroos."

20. C.G. Olourde, "Exploitation of Common-Property Replenishible Natural Resources," *Western Economic Journal,* vol. 9, 1971, pp.256-266.

21. A. Scott, "The Fishery: The Objectives of Sole Ownership," *Journal of Political Economy,* vol. 63, 1955, pp.116-124.

22. V.L. Smith, "Economics of Production from Natural Resources," *American Economic Review,* vol. 58, 1968, pp.409-431.

23. C. Tisdell, "The Economic Conservation and Utilisation of Wildlife Species," *The South African Journal of Economics,* vol. 40, 1972, pp.235-248.

24. C. Tisdell, "The Provision of Parks and the Preservation of Nature – Some Economic Factors," *Australian Economic Papers,* vol. 11, 1972, pp.154-162.

25. R. Turvey, "Optimization and Suboptimization in Fishery Regulation," *American Economic Review,* vol. 54, 1964, pp.64-76.

[11]

ON POPULATION EFFECTS, WILDLIFE AND THE MANAGEMENT OF KANGAROOS

The purpose of this note is to comment upon some points which Waugh and Calvo raise in their stimulating article, "Kangaroos: Population Effects and Management".[1] The main thesis developed by Waugh and Calvo is that it is generally preferable to regulate the commercial exploitation of wildlife species, including kangaroos, by controlling hunting and harvesting effort rather than by placing limits (quotas) upon the maximum catch or harvest. Although quotas can have serious drawbacks, Waugh and Calvo over extoll the advantages of policies which principally attempt to control hunting or harvesting effort.

But before elaborating on this theme, let me deal with another point. In criticising the Western Australian scheme for harvesting Red and Hill kangaroos, Waugh and Calvo give the impression that the scheme involves only an annual quota. In fact the number of licensed shooters of kangaroos is limited in Western Australia so that in a broad sense the scheme places a restriction on hunting effort. In addition, each licensed shooter is allocated an annual quota. Although the Western Australian scheme has advantages over a common-property solution, it does not (as was pointed out in my earlier article in this Journal[2]) result in the optimal commercial utilisation of resources.

Calvo and Waugh favour controls on hunting effort rather than the imposition of quotas on the catch or harvest because the former policy enables the population of kangaroos to be pegged at any desired level and to be maintained at this level with stability. Corresponding to any level of population of kangaroos, there is a level of harvesting effort (a constant maximum effort in Calvo and Waugh's model) which enables this level of population to be sustained. When the maximum level of effort is constant and regulated to correspond with the desired population of kangaroos, the population always returns to the desired level if it is temporarily disturbed from this level. On the other hand, quotas upon the annual harvest do not have the property of ensuring self-regulation of the population of wildlife species to a desired level. At low levels of population, population is unstable for low levels of desired population if quotas are used. At high levels of population of a species, quotas do, however, lead to local stability of population at the desired level. Controls on effort are preferred by Waugh and Calvo because of their self-regulating effects on the population of the spec-

1. Geoff Waugh and Peter Calvo, "Kangaroos: Population Effects and Management", *Economic Analysis and Policy* (this issue)

2. Clem Tisdell, "Kangaroos: The Economic Management of a Common-Property Resource Involving Interdependence of Production", *Economic Analysis and Policy,* Vol. 4, No. 2, September 1973, pp. 59–75.

ies, especially when low levels of population of the species are aimed for.

However, controls on harvesting effort do not always ensure self-regulation or stability at low levels of population of a species. The nature of the birth rate and mortality rate curves for some species may differ from those shown by Waugh and Calvo.[3] At low levels of population of the species the birth rate may fall below the mortality rate so that in contrast to the example taken by Waugh and Calvo the two curves depicting these intersect at a low level of population as shown in figure 1 below. In figure 1, the curve marked M represents the mortality rate of the species and that marked G indicates the birth rate. G-M is the net rate of change of the population of the species. In the illustration, the equilibrium at a population of P_3, E_1, is unstable and at population P_4, E_2, the equilibrium is stable.

Figure 1

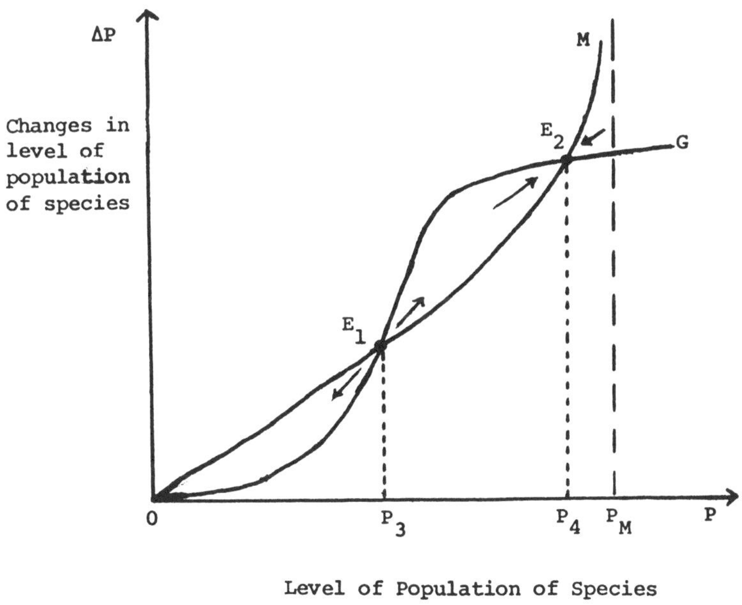

3. See their figure 1, op. cit.

If the desired level of population is above P_3 but in its neighbourhood, it is possible for random downward displacements of P (population level) to lead to an elimination of the species even if effort is controlled in the way suggested by Waugh and Calvo. Again, birth rate and mortality curves shift through time. As is well known, the birth rate of kangaroos falls during periods of drought due to their inbuilt biological mechanisms. If the birth rate falls (curve G) and harvesting effort remains at a regulated maximum figure, this may put the system into an elimination phase for the species even though it would not do this under normal conditions. In any case, a revision of optimal effort will be called for because of changed conditions. The point is that even if controls on harvesting effort are effective, the self-regulating properties may not be as ideal as suggested by Waugh and Calvo and considerable monitoring and gathering of information about the level of population and other factors would be required as with quota schemes.

However, this raises the question of whether harvesting effort can be controlled and the nature of the control mechanism. In practice, hunting effort involves the co-operation of several factors of production. Attempts to control hunting effort are usually concentrated on the regulation of one (or a few) of these factors. Thus the number of hunters may be regulated by a licensing system or the number of boats and the maximum power of equipment may be controlled, for instance in fishing. When one factor, such as the number of hunters is limited, substitution of other factors, such as capital, tends to occur and hence there may be economic inefficiency in harvesting. The actual harvest is likely to involve the use of more resources than is necessary. While the input of all factors could conceivably be limited by the controlling authority in an optimal way, the amount of information which the authority would need to achieve this would be formidable.

Again harvesting and hunting technology change with the passage of time. Technological change needs to be monitored otherwise population levels of a species could gravitate to undesired levels given the controls on harvesting effort which would otherwise exist. Moreover, hunting effort may be influenced by price changes in the co-operating factors of production and in variations in alternatives elsewhere in the economy. Such variations would also need to be monitored by the controlling authority. If undesired changes in the population of a species are to be avoided, controls on harvesting effort need to be combined with the collection of a considerable information to enable effort to be guided. The informational economy of controls on effort when compared to quotas is not as great as Waugh and Calvo suggest.

It is also difficult in some circumstances to enforce (police) controls on hunting effort and easier to enforce quotas on the harvest. For instance, licensing of shooters and limitations on their weapons requires inspectors to enforce these regulations, and it may be difficult to detect breaches. On the other hand, where the catch must pass through central processing points (chillers, factories, etc.), it may be comparatively easy to check a licensed hunter's quota.

It is clear from Waugh and Calvo's article that quota schemes do require, especially if the desired population of the species is at a low level, monitoring of the population of the species by the authority and alterations in the quota from time to time. However, it seems to me that in practice a similar need arises with controls on effort.

The Waugh and Calvo model is a selective model which illustrates a particular point. Consequently, it does not take account of the full range of problems of interdependence of species when landowners are fully able to appropriate the profit from domestic species but, at best, can only profit partially from wildlife species. In these circumstances, habitat changes occur independently of controls on harvesting effort. Resources may be in effect withdrawn from the wildlife species and schematically in figure 1, P_M may move back towards the origin and the mortality and growth rate curves alter. In other circumstances where a habitat change is favourable to a species, as seems to have been true for the Red Kangaroos, P_M could move outwards from the origin. Controls on hunting effort or quotas alone may not lead to a satisfactory solution.

While controls on harvesting effort have attractive stability features in terms of the Waugh and Calvo model, in other models the advantages are not so apparent. When other factors are taken into account, attempts to regulate the population of a wildlife species by controls on hunting or harvesting effort may require no less information than controls by quotas.

University of Newcastle Clem Tisdell

[12]

Wildlife: a national asset or pest to be managed?[1]

Summary

This paper takes account of the fact that many of the participants in the Environmental Economics Conference are non-economists. It illustrates that economics has a contribution to make in the interdisciplinary dialogue about wildlife issues.

The paper considers problems of valuing wildlife and of determining whether species of wildlife are an asset or a pest. In practice, one group of individuals may regard a species as a pest whereas another may believe it to be an asset. This conflict poses problems for managing wildlife resources and ways of dealing with the conflict are discussed. The problem is illustrated by reference to kangaroos.

The use of quotas and other means of regulating the harvest of kangaroos and other commercial species are discussed in relation to achieving a socially optimal level of harvest given that a species may be a net asset or net pest depending upon its numbers. Problems associated with the use of bounties as a means of controlling wildlife considered to be net pests, such as dingoes in some areas, are also discussed.

Whether a species is a pest or an asset

Management methods are influenced by perceptions of whether a species is an asset or a pest but, as we shall see, many species cannot be neatly categorised by these labels. For instance, there is often conflict between groups in society as to whether a species is a valuable resource to be conserved or a pest. Special attention is given to the problems of managing the resource when such conflicts arise and particularly to the use of quotas and bounties as management devices.

A species that causes some degree of commercial damage or reduces the value of something that is desired may be regarded as a pest. For instance, wild pigs are regarded as pests because, for example, they damage commercial crops. Feral cats are regarded as pests since they reduce (maybe eliminate) native species, which are desired.

Some wildlife species provide benefits (commercial or otherwise) as well as causing damages. Should we not then ask the question of whether the total benefits from a species outweigh the total costs of its damages? Should a species be regarded as a pest if its total benefits are less than the costs of its damages and as an asset if the reverse is the case? In the first case, let us call it a net pest and in the reverse case a net asset.

We cannot conclude that it is optimal from a management point of view to eliminate or reduce the numbers of a net pest, even if the cost of doing so is zero or very little. For instance, it may be possible to take suitable precautions at little cost to reduce the damages caused by what at first sight is a net pest. After such precautions, the species may become a net asset. For instance, even if eagles happened to be net pests (Fenessy, 1966), it might be possible to scare these away from lambing paddocks at little cost during lambing periods so that they then are net assets. Thus, the optimal way of dealing with a net pest may not be to reduce the population of the species.

The perception of individuals of whether and to what extent a species is a pest or an asset is important in determining whether measures are taken to destroy or conserve it. Misperception can easily exist amongst all groups interested in wildlife – landholders, nature lovers, hunters, scientists and so on. There is a lack of well-researched information about the benefits and costs of many Australian wildlife species.

Individual landowners, apart from difficulties of accurately observing the damages and benefits of species, may misperceive the value or costs of a species for a number of reasons. The spillover or externality effects of a pest may cause individual landowners to underestimate its damage, and in controlling the species they are unlikely to take into account its damage to neighbouring or other properties. Several possibilities exist:

(a) On a property the species may be below the population threshold where damage is observed (Carlson and Castle, 1972) but population on the property may roam to other properties causing commercial damage or provide a nucleus for infestation on other properties (see Figure 1).

(b) While a species may be a pest on the property, it may be relatively more damaging on other properties (for instance, because of different types of land use). Once

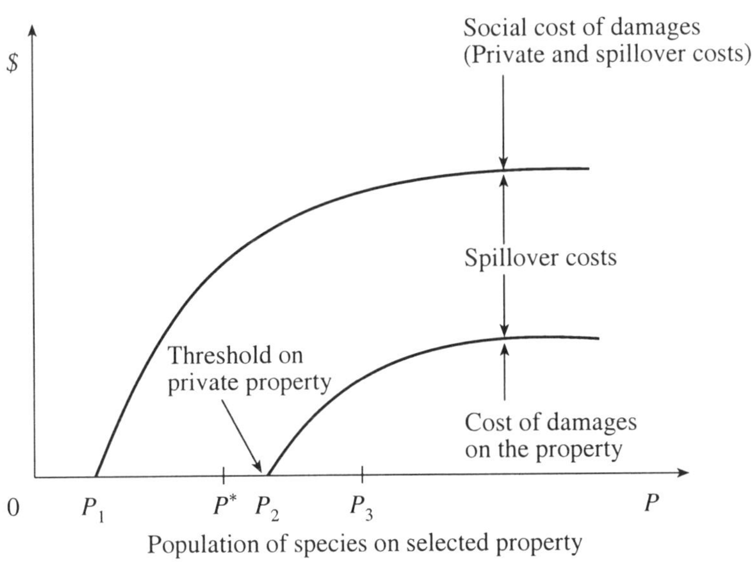

Figure 1 Misperceptions, externalities and pest control.

Note: Although the population of a species may be below the damage threshold on a property and not be regarded as a pest on the property, from a social point of view the population on the property may be a pest. This is so, for instance, for a population of P^* in the above figure.

again wrong inferences may be drawn from individual experiences and the species is unlikely to be optimally controlled.

(c) The species may be equally damaging on all properties but, because of mobility of its members, landowners may spend less on the control of the species than is socially optimal (Tisdell, 1977a). For instance, if each landholder faces a similar situation to that shown in Figure 1 and has P_3 of the species on his property, all may undertake less control than is socially optimal, since each ignores the spillover effect of the species.

As in the spatial-dimension, problems arise in the time-dimension of recognising a species as a pest and managing it optimally. The following situations are worthwhile mentioning:

(a) The species might not have been present for sufficient time for landholders to recognise it as a pest or it may have only recently migrated to an area and be below the threshold of damage. For instance, in some southern Pasture Protection Districts of New South Wales feral pigs are not considered to be a pest (Tisdell, 1978). This may be because feral pig populations have recently migrated there or have recently sprung up there. It has been suggested that landholders in southern New South Wales are not sufficiently aware of the potential pest problem that exists (Tisdell, 1978).

(b) During periods in which the population of a species is low (possibly even below the threshold point of damage) it may be easily forgotten that it is a pest and inadequate measures may be taken to keep the species under control.

The fact that different groups in society often have different views about whether a species is a pest or an asset poses problems for its management. The problem is that a species may be of different value to different individuals or to the same individual in dissimilar circumstances. Take kangaroos for example. Three basic groups would appear to have an interest in kangaroos:

(a) Landholders (agriculturalists and pastoralists).
(b) Nature lovers and tourists.
(c) Hunters, including commercial users of kangaroos.

Their interests may conflict:

(a) Tourists and nature lovers may desire the largest sustainable kangaroo population.
(b) Agriculturalists and pastoralists may wish to see numbers of kangaroos on their properties reduced to levels at which they are not a pest.
(c) Commercial users of kangaroos may wish to see the population of kangaroos managed so that their (long-term) profitability is maximised.

In many instances, the most desirable level of population of kangaroos from the commercial users' point of view is intermediate between that desired by landholders and that wanted by nature lovers. In most cases, there is no possibility of meeting the aspirations of all interested parties.

For many acceptable social welfare functions, the optimal management solution in the above circumstances of conflict involves a compromise between the interested parties. Let us consider the problem of finding a socially optimal solution.

Dealing with conflict about the value of a species

Imagine that there are two groups in society in conflict about the value of a species. For simplicity, let us assume that kangaroos are the species and that farmers and nature lovers are in conflict about the value of kangaroos. Farmers regard kangaroos as a pest and nature lovers see them as an asset.

Suppose that kangaroos are a 'shared facility' (Mishan, 1967), that is the same kangaroos as are enjoyed by nature lovers are the ones which are pests for farmers. The different values placed upon kangaroo populations by these two groups are indicated in Figure 2. The curve *EFG* represents the total increase in profit for farmers that can be obtained by reducing and holding the population of kangaroos at other than its natural sustainable level, P_N. Taking into account control costs, the most profitable population of kangaroos from the farmers' point of view is P'. The curve *KLM* represents the value that nature lovers place upon different numbers of kangaroos. The natural sustainable number, P_N, is valued most highly by nature lovers.

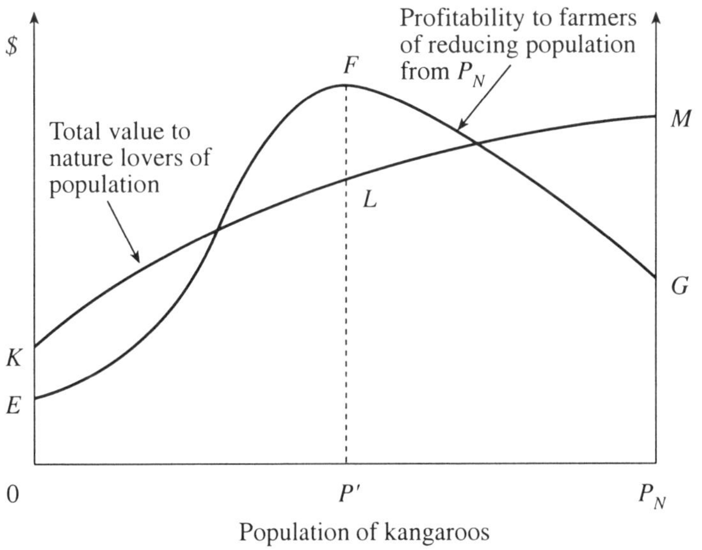

Figure 2 Total value to nature lovers and farmers of different levels of population of kangaroos.

Let us suppose that the population of kangaroos should be managed to maximise their total value. This is achieved when the marginal value of kangaroo numbers to nature lovers equals the marginal profit forgone by farmers because of an increase in kangaroo numbers. This corresponds to the point at which gainers from greater numbers (nature lovers) would be just prepared to compensate losers (farmers) for the greater numbers. In Figure 3, the optimal population is $\overline{P}$. As here, we would generally expect this population level to be intermediate between P' and P_N. It is a compromise solution.

In Figure 3, the curve *EC* represents the marginal value to nature lovers of an increased population of kangaroos and the curve *AD* represents the marginal profit forgone by farmers as a result of an increase in the population of kangaroos. These are equal for a population of $\bar{P}$. At $\bar{P}$, $BD = BC$. Alternatively, at $\bar{P}$ the marginal gain in profit to be obtained by farmers from reducing the population of kangaroos from P_N, as indicated by the curve *GC*, equals the marginal value to nature lovers of an increased population.

The shared facility solution just discussed corresponds to a situation in which all kangaroos are on rangeland. An alternative is the 'separate facilities' approach. This approach involves some land being set aside exclusively for farming and some being set aside exclusively for the conservation of kangaroos or other species. On farming land, farmers are allowed to adopt their optimal solution. In conservation areas, nature lovers are permitted their optimal solution. This corresponds to a situation where kangaroos are completely protected in national parks and other specified lands and are entirely unprotected elsewhere. If this approach is adopted, there remains the problem of how much land to set aside for each use and which land to set aside. Of course, in the case of kangaroos this approach makes no allowance for commercial users. Their presence may call for conservation measures on rangeland.

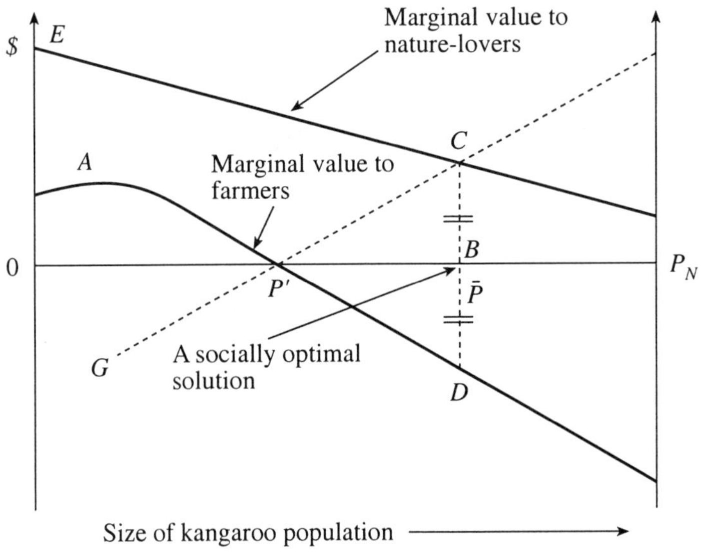

Figure 3 *Conflict is allowed for in this case by selecting a population size that maximises the value of the species. This solution is of a Kaldor–Hicks type and occurs for a population of* $\bar{P}$.

Other mixtures of land use may also be considered. For instance, some areas may be set aside:

(a) Where kangaroos (or other species) are entirely protected.
(b) Where controlled harvesting is permitted.
(c) Where no controls apply.

An 'ideal' solution is likely to be a complex one. Much more research is needed to compare the social value of the alternative solutions.

The use of quotas as a means of regulating the harvest of a species
When a wildlife species has commercial value, private hunting of it for commercial gain may occur. But the harvesting of the species is unlikely to be on a socially optimal scale. The scale may not be optimal because:

(a) The species is common-property (*de facto*).
(b) It is valued by individuals other than hunters (say, nature lovers).
(c) Is a pest for a group in society, say farmers?

The harvesting of kangaroos illustrates all of these situations.

The common-property problem and the possibility of its leading to over-harvesting has been well explored in the literature (Clark, 1976; Gordon, 1954; Tisdell, 1972). Quotas on the catch or suitable royalty payments are some of the means available to deal with that problem. I shall not deal with this problem here but concentrate on the other two considerations.

Suppose that, as shown in Figure 4, *SS* is the supply curve of harvested kangaroos and that D_1D_1 represents the demand for kangaroos for commercial use. Under these conditions, the equilibrium level of the annual harvest is E_1. However, the supply curve *SS* only indicates the marginal cost experienced by hunters. This curve needs to be adjusted to reflect the social marginal cost of harvesting. At high rates of harvesting the marginal cost to the community is likely to be in excess of that experienced by hunters because of the value placed on kangaroos by nature lovers. At low levels of harvesting, the marginal social cost to the community is likely to be less than *SS* because kangaroos are a pest to farmers and this more than balances out their value to nature lovers. Low levels of harvest imply that the population of kangaroos is allowed to reach high levels and become a serious pest. Given this relationship, the marginal social cost curve, *CC′*, crosses *SS* in the fashion indicated in Figure 4.

In these circumstances, the market equilibrium level of the annual harvest, E_1, exceeds the socially optimal level of the annual harvest, *A*, which corresponds to the point at which the marginal social cost curve intersects the demand curve for harvested kangaroos. A social optimum can be achieved by imposing a quota of *OQ* on the harvest of kangaroos or by imposing a tax or royalty charge of *AB* per kangaroo taken. Quotas are used in several Australian States to control the harvesting of kangaroos. The above circumstances (together with the interests of hunters in managing the common-property resource) provide a rationale for these quotas.

However, quotas are an ineffective management tool when either the commercial demand for harvested kangaroos falls to low levels or the marginal costs of hunting rise sufficiently. Both trends have been evident in Australia in recent years. Figure 5 illustrates the problem when commercial demand falls to low levels. Given the demand

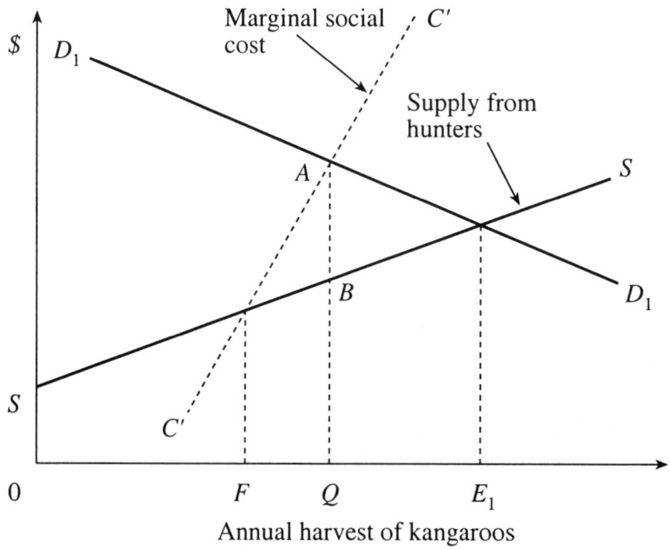

Figure 4 *Given the supply and demand conditions shown, the annual harvest exceeds the social optimum corresponding to the intersection of CC′ and D_1D_1. Optimality can be achieved by placing a quota on the harvest of OQ.*

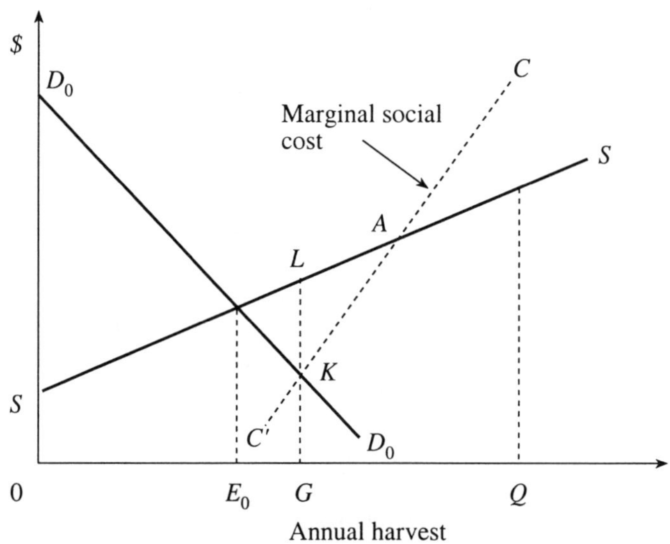

Figure 5 *When demand is low, a quota on the harvest may become ineffective. In the case shown the harvest falls below a social optimum. A bounty per kangaroo of LK would lead to a socially optimal level of harvest here.*

curve D_0D_0, the quota, OQ, is no longer filled. The equilibrium harvest OE_0 is also less than the socially optimal one since at low rates of harvest the seriousness of the species as a pest increases. This is because its population reaches high levels. The quota does nothing to ensure an optimal level of harvest. On the other hand, a bounty of *LK* on each kangaroo taken would ensure an optimal level of harvest. However, bounties raise some difficulties and I shall discuss this method of management in the next section.

A shift to the left in the supply curve of harvested kangaroos (a rise in the cost of harvesting) can also render quotas ineffectual as a management device. In the case illustrated in Figure 6, the shift of the supply curve from S_0S_0 to S_1S_1 results in the actual harvest falling below the quota of *Q*. The harvest falls to E_0. This is below the socially optimal level, *V*. Once again *V* could be reached by paying a bounty. A bounty equivalent to *AB* would achieve this result.

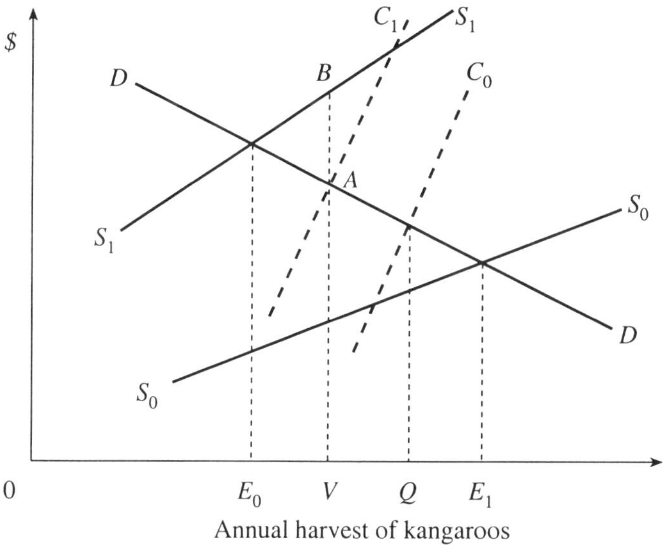

Figure 6 *Due to increases in hunting or harvesting costs, a quota may become ineffective and the rate of harvest may, as illustrated above, fall below a social optimum.*

Similarly, shifts in the external components of the marginal social cost curves (that is the value of kangaroos to nature lovers and their cost to farmers as a pest) may necessitate changes in management policies. These can also be explored in terms of simple supply and demand analysis.

It is clear that changing economic and social conditions pose difficulties for the optimal management of a wildlife species when these have commercial and other values. Wildlife authorities need to adjust their management policies to meet changing economic circumstances. To plan for the future, they also face the difficult problem of predicting economic and social conditions.

Bounties on the catch as a part of management

The above discussion indicates that bounties may have a role to play in the optimal control of wildlife species in circumstances in which their numbers are such that they are, on balance, a pest. However, bounties have received a considerable amount of criticism in the literature dealing with the control of pests (Whitehouse, 1976).

It is commonly believed that such systems tend to be too expensive in relation to the results achieved. There are undoubtedly circumstances in which control of a pest is not economic and bounties are expensive. However, in the case of species of commercial value, a bounty need not be paid on the whole catch. In the case illustrated in Figure 5, optimality would be achieved if the bounty of LK per kangaroo happened to be only paid on the marginal catch, E_0G. Administratively this might be achieved by allocating to each hunter a minimum annual target and a maximum annual target for his harvest of kangaroos. Together the minimum targets should add up to OE_0 and the maximum targets should add to OG. The bounty of LK could be paid to each hunter on the annual catch in excess of his minimum or qualifying target up to the level of the maximum catch allowed. The allocation of targets between hunters should be such as to achieve required economic efficiency conditions.

Even in the case of species of no commercial value, where bounties are being used to reduce its population it is often possible to reduce the cost of the bounty by suitably 'stepping' the payment and achieve the same result. This is illustrated in Figure 7. There the curve marked *MC* represents the marginal cost to a hunter of catching dingoes. If a bounty of $6 per dingo is paid, the hunter finds it most profitable to catch fifty dingoes per year. The cost in bounties is $300. However, suppose that the payment of bounties is stepped and $3 per scalp is paid on the first twenty-five and $6 thereafter. The most profitable catch for the hunter is still fifty per year but the cost in bounties falls 25 per cent to $225.

However, it should be observed that this stepped system would require honesty or some method of determining an individual's maximum catch. Otherwise, if animals or scalps were easy to transfer, it would pay one hunter to claim the whole catch in an area.

It is sometimes said that bounties have been shown to be ineffective since the sustained catch has risen after their introduction. This is not adequate evidence that bounties are ineffective. Higher sustainable yields may reflect a reduced population of the species. This is, for instance, implied by the Verlhust model of population growth (Christiansen and Fenchel, 1977; Clark, 1976). In many of these models, the maximum growth rate of the population is achieved at about half the carrying capacity of an area.

Difficulties arise when bounties differ by areas. This is because if transport costs are not too high, arbitrage is likely to take place. Species may be taken in areas where they are relatively easy to catch but bounties are low and transferred for collection of the bounty to areas where bounties are high. This is a problem because bounties should ideally be different between areas if dissimilar externalities exist in different areas (Tietenberg, 1974; Tisdell, 1977b) as is very likely with wildlife species.

In conclusion, let me enter a plea for more research in this area in Australia. Economic aspects of the management of wildlife species, especially Australian wildlife species, need much greater study. While some of our management problems are similar to those of other countries, we also have special problems because of the uniqueness of much of our wildlife and environment. The volume of research in

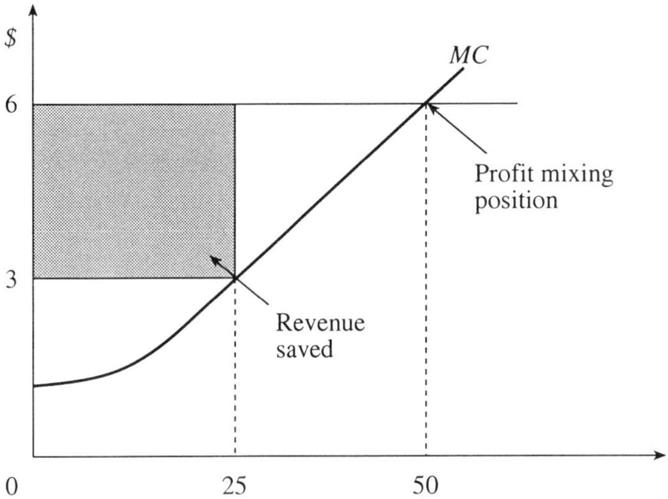

Figure 7 *A stepped bounty may be less costly than a non-stepped one and can achieve the same result.*

Australia on the economics of the management of wildlife appears to be lagging behind comparable countries such as Canada. The management of wildlife requires a consideration of economic, biological and social factors. It is perilous to ignore or play down the importance of any of these factors in decision-making about wildlife.[2]

Notes

1. This article originally appeared in Department of Science and Environment, *Environmental Economics*, AGPS, Canberra, 1979, pp. 79–87. The content is the same as in the original (except for minor changes) but its presentation has been improved. Consequently, pagination is no longer the same as in the original.
2. Postscript (added 24/08/01): Note that the supply curves in Figures 4–6 are assumed to reflect the private marginal costs of harvesting. Therefore, they assume that the government regulates kangaroo harvesting so as to appropriate rents. If, by contrast, open access is the case, the supply curves for harvesting kangaroos would be found by moving these curves towards the right. Optimal regulation should then require the open-access effect to be eliminated and after this, the externalities, as discussed, to be allowed for.

References

Carlson, G.A. and E.N. Castle (1972), 'Economics of Pest Control', in *Pest Control Strategies for the Future*, Washington, DC: National Academy of Sciences, pp. 79–99.

Christiansen, F.B. and T.M. Fenchel (1977), *Theories of Populations in Biological Communities*, Berlin: Springer-Verlag.

Clark, C.W. (1976), *Mathematical Bioeconomics: The Optimal Management of Renewable Resources*, New York: John Wiley.

Gordon, H.S. (1954), 'Economic Theory of a Common-Property Resource: The Fishery', *Journal of Political Economy*, **62**, 124–42.

Fenessy, B.V. (1966), 'The Impact of Wildlife Species on Sheep Production in Australia', *Proceedings of the Australian Society of Animal Production*, **6**, 148–56.

Mishan, E.J. (1967), *The Costs of Economic Growth*, London: Staples Press.

Tietenberg, T.H. (1974), 'On Taxation and the Control of Externalities: A Comment', *American Economic Review*, **64**, 462–6.

Tisdell, C.A. (1972), 'The Economic Conservation and Utilisation of Wildlife Species', *The South African Journal of Economics*, **40**, 245–8.

Tisdell, C.A. (1977a), 'Simple Economic Models of Pest Control – Models with Possible Application to the Control of Feral Pigs and Other Wild Animals', *Research Report or Occasional Paper* No. 33, Department of Economics, University of Newcastle, May.

Tisdell, C.A. (1977b), 'Pollution Control: A Review of the Discussion by Economists', *Proceedings Environmental Engineering Conference 1977: The Politics, Economics and Technology of Pollution Control*, Canberra, June, pp. 22–6.

Tisdell, C.A. (1978), 'Observations on the Wild Pig Problem in New South Wales – A Survey and Interpretation of Economic Aspects Based on Reports from Pasture Protection Boards', *Research Report or Occasional Paper* No. 41, Department of Economics, University of Newcastle, March.

Whitehouse, S. (1976), 'Bounty Systems in Vermin Control', *Journal of Agriculture*, Western Australia, **17**(3) (4th Series), pp. 85–9.

Conflicts about Living Marine Resources in Southeast Asian and Australian Waters: Turtles and Dugong as Cases

Clem Tisdell

University of Newcastle
Newcastle, Australia

Abstract This paper considers conflicts that arise and socio-economic problems involved in managing fugitive resources, especially transborder or transfrontier ones when economic development occurs. To do this it concentrates on the situation of turtles and of dugong in Southeast Asian and Australian waters. Particular attention is given to turtle farming and to zoning as conservation strategies and the use of marine parks for resource management. Questions are raised about the responsibilities of developed countries such as Australia for conserving species that migrate to less developed countries.

Introduction

Economic development, as in Southeast Asia, is often accompanied by intensified conflict about the use of resources, including marine resources. This is especially the case for common-access or common-property resources. "Ocean" resources are frequently held as common property, and it is therefore important to take this fact into account when discussing the utilization of marine resources (cf. Comitini 1969). Increases in population, rising per capita income with associated rising demands for goods and services, and the

Marine Resource Economics, Volume 3, Number 1
0738-1360/86/030089-00$02.00/0

introduction of new technologies are placing increasing pressures on the world's limited resources (Barney 1980). Economic growth and change in many less developed countries (LDCs) is leading to a breakdown in customary controls on the use of common property (Ciriacy-Wantrup 1963: 109; Tisdell 1983), and new social approaches to the use of these resources need to be sought. Similar problems arise for fugitive resources (Ciriacy-Wantrup 1963), which may also be transboundary (Munro 1982) or transfrontier (OECD 1974, 1976) resources—that is, moving from one jurisdiction to another. The existence of fugitive species may be endangered, and the utilization or lack of conservation of these species may be accompanied by increasing welfare or economic efficiency losses as development proceeds, as well as mounting internal and international social conflict.

Turtles and dugong are significant fugitive species in Southeast Asian and northern Australian waters and have been subjected to pressure as a result of economic development. Furthermore, turtles, and to a lesser extent dugong, are transboundary or transfrontier resources. Biologists consider the dugong to be endangered and are concerned about the prospects for survival of a number of species of turtles. Both species have functional values (e.g., they are used for food), as well as existence value for some residents of developed countries and particular groups in some LDCs; for example, the dugong has special existence value for the Kiwai people of Papua New Guinea (Hudson 1983b).

In this paper, socioeconomic problems involved in managing turtles and dugong, especially in Southeast Asia and Australia, are examined. Particular attention is given to the possible effects of turtle farming on the conservation of the green turtle. Limitations of management policies, such as those involving marine zoning, are discussed. Taking the Great Barrier Reef Marine Park as an example, marine parks involving zoning are considered as a possible management approach. Questions are also raised about the responsibility of a developed country such as Australia for conserving transboundary species, such as turtles and dugong, shared by LDCs in Southeast Asia and elsewhere. Let us first consider the situation of marine turtles and later that of the dugong.

Marine Turtles, Especially the Green Turtle, *Chelonia mydas*

There are seven recognized species of sea turtles. Of these the best known are (1) the green turtle, *Chelonia mydas*; (2) the hawksbill turtle, *Eretmochelys imbricata*; (3) the loggerhead, *Caretta caretta*; and (4) the leatherback turtle, *Dermochelys coriacea*. The normal range of these species is confined to tropical waters, and they occur widely throughout Southeast Asia and in the northern waters of Australia. All of the species are utilized in one way or another by man, and these practices have led to serious depletions of their populations.

The eggs of all these species are eaten by man and are eagerly sought after in many Southeast Asian countries. The green turtle (so-called because of the color of its fat) is especially valuable to man. Not only is it valued for its meat, oil, and shell, but also its skin is used for the leather trade and its calipee is a prized ingredient of soup (Bustard 1972; Clayton 1975; Considine and Winberry 1978). It was once numerous in tropical shallow seas but is now greatly depleted by man's predation, and it is virtually extinct in some areas of its former range. However, it is still relatively abundant in tropical Australian waters, and important rookeries occur on some northern Australian beaches. The green turtle also breeds in Southeast Asia, and three small islands off Sarawak are said to form one of the largest green turtle rookeries in the world (Bustard 1972: 26). However, there has been a significant decline in the numbers of turtles in the Sarawak area due, it appears, to egg harvesting rather than to the taking of turtles—turtle meat is not favored by Muslims in the area.

The green turtle, unlike other major sea turtles, is predominantly vegetarian except in the first year of its life. Other sea turtles are either carnivorous or omnivorous and are less edible than the green turtle, the meat of which provides a quality steak with a taste described as between that of veal and chicken. The meat is high in protein and extremely low in fat (Clayton 1975).

The loggerhead turtle is almost entirely carnivorous. Its meat, like that of all nonvegetarian sea turtles, is less edible than that of the green turtle. Nevertheless, it is sometimes eaten by people. Furthermore,

> Their eggs are relished by coastal people everywhere. As a result of the population explosion together with the general availability of power boats, this threat has increased greatly for all species of sea turtle. Uninhabited rookeries formerly never visited by people can now be visited regularly in order to collect eggs. (Bustard 1972: 29–30)

Mainland rookeries of this species and others are also being adversely affected by human encroachment and activities.

The hawksbill turtle is omnivorous. It provides tortoiseshell and has been heavily exploited for this purpose. It nests in small numbers in scattered areas, which include small islands in the South China Sea and in northern Australian waters. Unlike the green turtle, it has countless scattered nesting grounds. It is more commonly taken at sea than on land. Not only is it of value for its shell, but also its eggs are eaten, its skins are in demand, its meat is eaten by some coastal people, and a method has been found of successfully using the calipee in soup.

The leatherback turtle is the largest marine turtle and lives mostly on jellyfish. It seems to be seriously threatened by the harvesting of its eggs. The most important of its nesting grounds outside of the Americas is reported by Bustard (1972) to be in Trengganu (in eastern Malaya) where between 850 and 1,600 females are thought to nest each season. He claims that the Trengganu rookery is seriously overexploited:

> Unfortunately, the eggs are harvested as food in Trengganu and, due to very efficient marketing, virtually every nest is located and the eggs removed. To date conservation effort has not been able to secure nearly sufficient eggs for hatchery incubation to offset the tremendous drain imposed by human consumption of virtually the total egg lay. It seems certain that the Trengganu rookery is being seriously over-exploited but it has not yet proved possible to reduce the level of exploitation. (Bustard 1972: 34)

I shall concentrate on the economics of the conservation of the green turtle, the species with the widest range of uses by man.

This species is now being commercially farmed in the Cayman Islands of the West Indies and is being ranched elsewhere.

The green turtle spends most of its life at sea and lives for approximately 15–20 years, browsing in shallow waters. Mature females come ashore at night to lay their eggs in the sand at a limited number of rookeries, which can become quite crowded. Over the few weeks of the laying season in each year, mature females lay 300–500 eggs, with each nest or clutch averaging about 100 eggs. In between clutches, females return to the water near the rookeries where they are fertilized by congregating males. The turtles and their eggs are very prone to human predation in their rookeries and in the sea near them.

Young turtles hatch from the eggs approximately 60 days after the eggs have been laid and make their way to the sea on moonlit nights. They are believed to identify the sea by light refraction, and the presence of car lights or lights from human habitation can cause the young to move toward this source (and their destruction) rather than the sea. The hatching rate of eggs varies greatly but is approximately 50%. Natural predation from animals and birds takes a toll on land, and marine predators eagerly await the mass of young hatchlings reaching the sea. Of the eggs, "Perhaps 1 in 1,000 survive beach and shoreline predation and subsequent ocean life to achieve maturity" (Clayton 1975: 9).

Little is known of the movement patterns of young turtles. However, it is known that adult turtles migrate long distances. Biologists at the University of Venezuela have tracked turtle migrations of 3,219 km (2,000 miles) (Bellairs, 1969, vol. 2, p. 421), and Carr (1968) has observed movements of 2,254 km (1,400 miles) from breeding grounds in the Atlantic. In Australia, green turtles tagged on Heron Island in Queensland have been recovered in New Caledonia, more than 1,000 miles away, and north of Papua New Guinea. It seems very likely that some of the green turtles nesting in northern Australia use feeding grounds in Southeast Asia and vice versa. The extent of the intermixing of the populations is, however, uncertain. Yet there can be no doubt that this is a *fugitive species* and that it ranges beyond the territorial waters of countries in the region and into the territorial waters of other countries in the region. It is to some extent a common natural resource for the region.

The green turtle is reputed to return to the beach on which it was born on to breed (Jayewardene 1982; Clayton 1975). Indeed, some writers claim that it returns almost to the precise spot where it was born (a position analogous to that of salmon). While there is scientific evidence for return of turtles to the beaches where they were born, Bustard (1972: 133) suggests that green turtles may not return to the exact location of previous nesting but to the same general area. Carr, Main, and Smart (1973) provide strong evidence, from variations in turtle shell patterns on islands in the Torres Straits off Northern Australia, that turtles tend to return for nesting to the site of their birth or close by. The question of return is of some importance for the economics of conservation within a rookery area. If a rookery is zoned or parts of it are zoned for commercial use, to what extent would those with rights to the rookery have an incentive to conserve turtles or their eggs? To what extent can conservation at a rookery be successful? What *national* gains can be made by conserving and maintaining turtle stocks?

Stocks of the green turtle are being depleted by (1) the collection of their eggs at rookeries, (2) the capture of females while nesting at rookeries, (3) the capture of males and females in the waters adjoining rookeries—densities are high here at nesting time and mating is an important preoccupation, (4) their capture at other times, mostly in the shallow waters of their feeding grounds, and (5) the encroachment of human habitats and mining on breeding grounds, which destroy or reduce the value of these grounds. The demand for eggs, meat, shells, and other products derived from the green turtle is substantial both in local areas and in international markets. Even in the absence of any international trade, the species would be placed under pressure in Southeast Asia by local demand for eggs and other products.

Carr, while mentioning that southeastern Asia provides important nesting grounds for various species of turtles, points out the following:

> The preservation and wise exploitation of marine turtles is an international problem. All the species cross boundaries and some of them

> commute over a quarter of the world. In different parts of the world they are put to different human uses, and local conservation agencies disagree as to both the survival status of sea turtles and the steps needed to protect them. In one place only eggs are harvested; in another only the mature turtles, away from the nesting beach are hunted; in still other places, both eggs and nesting females are ruthlessly taken. (Carr 1968: 229)

Although protection measures may be taken in one area to conserve turtles, these may be thwarted by lack of controls elsewhere. For example, quotas or closed seasons on the catch of adult turtles in one area may fail to maintain a turtle population if eggs are being extensively harvested elsewhere, and vice versa.

A number of methods can be adopted to help increase the chances of survival of population of the species. Nesting grounds or rookeries (or at least some of these) can be made national parks. In the United States and Australia some such parks have been established. However, it is not so easy to establish such parks effectively in some of the LDCs. The livelihood of many coastal people can be greatly affected, and they may have few alternative employment prospects. Quotas may be placed on the egg take in particular areas, or limited seasons for collection of eggs and for the capture of turtles in particular areas may be promulgated. However, poaching is a serious problem in many LDCs. Resources for the enforcement of laws are scarce, and nonenforcement of laws sometimes indicates rational political ambivalence by governments.

Prospects for the enforcement of laws needs to be considered seriously. For example, Bustard points out,

> The hawksbill [turtle] is well known in the Fiji Islands where it has been the subject of gross over-exploitation and is greatly depleted in numbers. This has occurred despite excellent legislation on paper, which protects adult turtles of all species from November to February inclusive (the main breeding time) and the eggs of all species at all times. Poaching is rife, the adult turtles are taken for food and the eggs collected wherever possible. (Bustard 1972: 310)

Jayewardene points out that in Sri Lanka the law gives complete protection to turtles, but it is not enforced effectively:

> It is an offence for any person to possess, capture, kill, injure and take these animals or destroy eggs of turtles. The fishermen, the law enforcement agencies and the general public are well aware of these laws but the depredations continue. Soon after the law concerning turtles was promulgated, it was suspended for a period of two years on the representations made by fishermen whose livelihood was supposedly affected by the banning of their "traditional" form of employment.
>
> Now more than two years have passed but the capture of turtles and the destruction of their eggs still occurs. The penalties imposed on those who are found guilty under these laws should be harder so that they will be more of a deterrent. (Jayewardene 1982: 23, 25)

A number of writers propose heavier penalties for breaches of laws protecting turtles. Bustard (1972: 191, 192), after pointing out that ineffectively enforced protection legislation is relatively worthless (except as evidence of an enlightened government), suggests that "poachers weigh up the possibility of being caught (and convicted) against the potential gain from poaching" (p. 191). He suggests that this being the case, heavier penalties for a given probability of detection will have a deterrent effect. However, just how responsive are poachers to heavier penalties and policing? (Recent work on crime economics underlines the importance of empirically investigating such effects, see, for example, Buck et al. 1983). Is it *politically* possible to impose major penalties on turtle utilization in particular localities where this utilization is important? Is there not a low limit to the penalties that low-income earners can be *forced* to pay? (Their economic bases for paying fines are small.) Furthermore, in some countries law and order is tenuous. The fact may have to be accepted that in some developing countries and for some time yet, no effective way will be found to enforce protective legislation, except maybe in small pockets of these countries.

It might be noted that conservationist groups in Sri Lanka and Malaysia purchase turtle eggs from collectors to prevent them from being consumed, incubate them, and release the hatchlings to the sea (Jayewardene 1982; Bustard 1972). To the extent that this practice forces up the price of eggs it may lead to a rise in their collection. Only if the overall supply of eggs is perfectly inelastic does the purchase by the conservation bodies represent the total number of eggs saved from human consumption and contribute fully to conservation.

Even if one can effectively control the exploitation of sea turtles, their conservation in addition requires the protection of their rookery habitats. With the growth of coastal-based tourism and increasing human population requiring greater urban space, increasing demands are being made on rookery sites. The Mon Repos rookery near Bundaberg in Queensland provides one example where real estate developers and the local council have had a long-standing conflict with conservationists (Bustard 1972; "Housing row over turtles," *Courier Mail*, Brisbane, January 16, 1984). Archie Carr (1968: 231) points out that partly because sea turtles require peace and wild shores for breeding, large colonies have been wiped out in Florida, the Bahamas, Bermuda, and the Hawaiian Archipelago. In a situation of real estate development versus conservation of a site, it very often turns out that benefactors from conservation (e.g., nature lovers, harvesters of turtles) are scattered, and their individual gains from preventing development may be small, whereas developers have a concentrated interest in a site and stand to obtain large individual gains. The economics of politics in such cases suggests that developers are likely to succeed politically even when the net social benefit is reduced by development (Downs 1957; Olson 1965; Tisdell 1982: 530, 531). Nevertheless, developers do not always have political success.

The prospects for conservation of sea turtles in the wild are considered to be so uncertain that many look toward the farming of sea turtles as a means of conserving and utilizing turtles. Some conservationists also believe that farming of turtles will reduce incentives to harvest turtles in the wild.

A sharp distinction needs to be drawn between ranching and farming of turtles. At the present time, ranching is by far the more common activity. "Ranches" are dependent on eggs taken from the wild to produce their stock, whereas farms supply eggs from their own breeding stock and do not draw on wild populations. Conservationists, such as the International Union for Conservation of Nature and Natural Resources (IUCN), have deplored ranch-type activities except on a pilot research basis because ranches encourage an increase in the collection of eggs from the wild. On the other hand, it is claimed that higher hatching rates from eggs and survival rates can be obtained under ranching than in the wild, and if a suitable number of hatchlings are released to the wild, wild stocks of turtles will not be seriously depleted (Raj 1977: 15). Ranching is reported to be common in the Pacific—for example, in the Cook Islands. Hatchlings are reared in artificial ponds and sometimes in fenced areas of the sea. At the present time, the likely overall impact of ranching on the supply of turtle products and on the size of wild stocks is not clear but a definite risk exists of this practice leading to reduced wild stocks.

The world's first turtle farm was established on Grand Cayman Island in the West Indies by Mariculture Ltd. It began originally as a ranching venture, and year-old turtles raised at the hatchery from incubated eggs were released into an enclosed sea area to feed on sea grasses. But because of predation and other factors, this method proved to be uneconomic (Considine and Winberry 1978: 53). In 1971 operations were shifted to a new site on the island with a view to raising turtles entirely in artificial growing tanks without release of the turtles to sea areas for grazing purposes.

The original company ran into financial difficulties. The farm was taken over by a company in which the shares are owned by a West German business group, by the Commonwealth Development Finance Company of London, and in small part by the Cayman government (Fish Farming International 1979). Turtles raised at this farm are processed when they are about four years old, and 10,000 or more turtles weighing approximately 100 pounds each are supplied per year. The population of turtles on the farm fluctuates between 40,000 and 80,000 depending upon the time of the year and the emergence of hatchlings.

Although the farm originally practiced ranching, the aim of the farm was to advance to a closed-cycle operation with eggs being supplied from breeding on the farm. The farm has been successful in establishing the closed breeding cycle as a result of its husbandry experiments—the first breakthrough came in 1973 when captive wild stock mated, producing eggs and viable hatchlings. The farm has been self-sufficient in egg supplies since 1978 (Fish Farming International 1979).

The farm seems to be relatively capital intensive, it requires a high level of management, clean fresh seawater must be pumped in large volumes (using powerful diesel engines) through the holding tanks so as to replace their contents several times in one day, and the turtles are fed on imported high-protein pellets (in fact, imported from the United States) (Considine and Winberry 1978: 55). It is not a small-scale self-contained economic operation that might assist development and employment in coastal communities in LDCs and provide a viable alternative to the harvesting of wild turtles by their local communities. It would seem desirable to develop less capital-intensive farming techniques which make greater use of local materials in LDCs (cf. Weatherly and Cogger 1975; Raj 1977). More appropriate technology is required if small-scale turtle farms are to be established in coastal communities of LDCs. Nevertheless, the way is open for further development of farming techniques. The possibility exists for turtles being hatched and reared to yearlings at larger establishments and then being distributed to smaller farms for rearing to processing age.

Those conservationists who have supported turtle farming have done so for two different reasons. One group sees little chance of turtles surviving in the wild. R. E. Schroeder expresses this view as follows:

> It became clear to us that no conventional conservation methods will do much good in Central America. There is a population explosion unmatched elsewhere in the world. Grinding poverty is the rule. Law enforcement along the wild, primitive coasts is all but non-existent. The number of nesting turtles falls markedly each year. (Bustard 1972: 183)

This pattern is repeated elsewhere and has led naturalists such as Bustard to the view that the most effective method of conserving the green turtle in the long term is to farm it (Bustard 1972: 186).

Apart from farming maintaining stocks of domesticated turtles, some conservationists believe that farming will increase market supplies of turtle products, depress prices, and reduce the taking of turtles from the wild. It is theorized that successful farming operations "could so flood the market with products that pressure might be removed from wild turtles perhaps altogether" (Clayton

1975: 9). However, a consideration of simple market demand and supply analysis indicates that the impact on the level of harvesting from the wild could be small or of zero magnitude. The possibility even exists that farming might stimulate demand sufficiently for pressure on wild stocks to be raised rather than lowered. Indeed, this possibility sufficiently concerns some conservationists for them to oppose turtle farming.

If the supply curve of turtles from the wild is relatively inelastic, a variation in the market price for captured turtles makes little difference to their rate of capture in the wild. On the other hand, if the supply curve is relatively elastic, a variation in the market price of turtles has a considerable influence on the rate of capture from the wild. (In reality, many turtles are destined for purely domestic use or isolated local markets.)

If farming leads to an expansion in demand for turtle products (as it may well do), it could in fact lead to a rise in market price and place greater pressure on wild stocks. Products from the Cayman Island turtle farm are exported primarily to developed areas (Europe, the United States, and Japan), and attempts have been made to expand markets there (Fish Farming International 1979).

Some of the theoretical possibilities can be illustrated by Figure 1. There AS_W represents the supply curve of turtles from the wild and ABS_T represents the total supply of turtles inclusive of the supply from farms. Given that the market demand curve is D_1D_1 in the absence of farming, market equilibrium is established at E_1 with a supply of X_1 turtles per period. As a result of farming, however, supplies expand, and equilibrium is established at E_2. Because the market price of turtle products is now lower, supply of turtles from the wild falls from X_1 to X_0 while total supplies expand to X_3. The reduction in supply from the wild is relatively small because the supply curve AS_W is relatively steep. However, farming of turtles may bring with it an expansion in demand for turtle products. In the case illustrated, the demand curve is shown to shift up from D_1D_1 to D_2D_2, and most of the expansion of demand may be generated in more developed countries (MDCs). With an upward shift in demand, market equilibrium shifts not from E_1 to E_2 but from E_1 to E_3. The equilibrium price of turtles rises, total

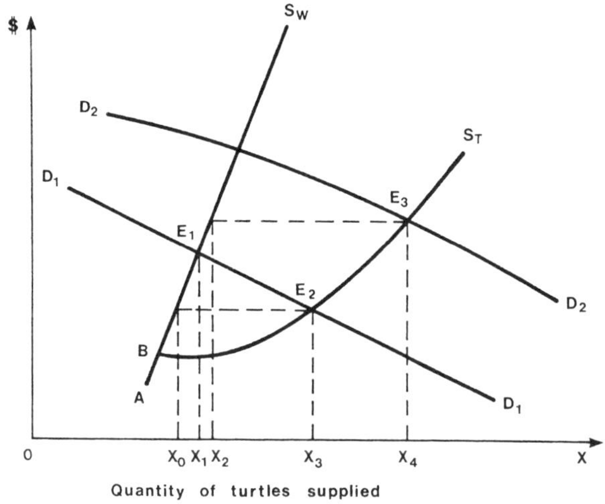

FIGURE 1. Possible influences of turtle farming on the supply and demand curves for sea turtles.

supply expands and the number of turtles taken from the wild rises from X_1 to X_2 per period.

If farming does succeed in reducing the price of turtle products, the commercial value of wild stocks of turtle will be reduced even though turtles in the wild may continue to have existence value and will be useful as a genetic reserve. However, farming by no means guarantees the continuing existence of wild stocks.

Just how valuable natural stocks of turtles are from a purely commercial point of view has not been determined. To what extent does it pay to conserve stock to obtain future yields? If the growth in the value of yield is sufficiently slow, then from a *purely* commercial viewpoint it can pay to liquidate stocks (Clark 1976: 62). From a global point of view, given the reproductivity rate of the green turtle and even allowing for high levels of natural predation, it seems likely from a purely commercial or utilitarian viewpoint that at present there is a case to maintain natural stocks of green turtles. By contrast, the slow rate of growth of populations of dugong suggests that it may not be economic to maintain their wild stocks if commercial or utilitarian considerations only are taken into account.

The Dugong, *Dugong dugon*

The Dugong (*Dugong dugon*) is the sole living species of the family Dugongidae. It inhabits shallow warm coastal waters of the Indian and western Pacific oceans. This mammal is completely herbivorous and lives on sea grasses. The major surviving population occurs in Australian coastal waters from Shark Bay in Western Australia around the north of the continent to Moreton Bay in Queensland.

The IUCN lists the dugong as an endangered species, and it is said to be "nearly everywhere declining under human hunting pressure" (Philip, Duke of Edinburgh, and Fisher 1970, p. 241). Its numbers have been seriously reduced along the east African coast. Some still occur in the Gulf of Kutch and the Andaman Islands, a relict population exists in Sri Lankan waters where overhunting has been marked, and a few are left in Burma and Malaysia. Some occur in the Palau Islands, the Carolines, the Solomon Islands, and the Marshall Islands, as well as around the coasts of New Caledonia and New Guinea, but the major remaining population is now in Australian waters, where the species is protected, except that they can be taken by aboriginal people.

The meat of the dugong is very tasty, and it is sought after by coastal people within its range. The human population explosion in the Indian Ocean and the West Pacific, the advent of outboard motors, the use of nylon nets, the desire for cash, the breakdown of traditional tabus, and the failure of customs to adjust rapidly to changing circumstances have all conspired to add greatly to hunting pressures by traditional groups on the dugong. The case of the Kiwai people, dugong hunters in the Torres Strait, Papua, as outlined elsewhere, can be used to illustrate the pattern of the rising exploitation of dugong (Hudson 1983a, 1983b; Tisdell 1983). Hudson points out the following:

> With the introduction of new technology and a greater wish to participate in the cash economy, the dugong taken by the Kiwai people of the northern Torres Strait increased by more than 100% in 20 years, the largest increase in hunting level taking place in the mid-to-late 1970s. In 1981 the dugong catch fell dramatically and analysis of the structure of the population of animals killed in the previous 3 years caused grave concern over the viability of the exploited population. (Hudson 1983a, p. 108)

Despite the fact that the dugong is a national animal of Papua New Guinea and can therefore only *legally* be hunted by traditional methods for traditional purposes, its numbers in the northern Torres Strait have continued to decline. Illegal hunting undoubtedly continues, and incidental as well as illegal capture in nets is taking its toll. The population of dugong in the northern Torres Straits is still going down (Brydget Hudson, personal communication, December 1983), despite the fact that the Kiwai people have set up the Maza Wildlife Management Area and have suggested rules to ban the hunting of dugong in this wildlife area. For one thing, dugong move between reef areas and move into and out of the management area, and are claimed by some Papuans to be taken in Australian territory by Torres Strait Islanders who are Australian citizens (Olewale and Sedu 1980). Undoubtedly the fugitive nature of the dugong reduces the effectiveness of local zones or conservation areas in protecting it, and in this case international cooperation is needed (Eaton and Sinclair 1981: 17).

Heinsohn reports that daily movements by dugong of up to 25 km are common: "Animals move in towards shore with the rising tide to feed; at low tide they rest or feed in deeper water. In calm weather they move from sheltered into exposed waters" (1983, p. 475). During the course of a year they may move their location 100 km or more. While they do not move the distance that turtles do, they are nevertheless very mobile, and a large reserve would appear to be needed to protect them effectively. The Great Barrier Reef Marine Park off the Queensland coast is possibly of sufficient size to give the species protection. In the end, it seems possible that the world's surviving stock of dugong will be confined to Australian waters.

Sadleir (1970) suggests that it might be possible to farm dugong. However, unlike the case of turtles, no progress has been made toward the farming of dugong. In fact, the dugong may be an *uneconomic* species given its slow rate of reproduction (cf. Clark 1976: 62). Reproductive maturity does not begin until 9–10 years and may be as late as 15–17 years. "Pregnancy rates are very low and the interval between the birth of calves in Queensland populations is from 3 to 6 years. Individuals may reach an age of more than 50 years" (Heinsohn 1983, p. 476). There is a gestation period of 12 months. The female gives birth to a single calf that stays with the mother for at least one year and for as long as two years. Since the net reproduction rate of the population is low, the population can only sustain very low rates of harvest.

Unfortunately, there is little ground for conserving the species if the purely economic or utilitarian argument expounded by Clark (1976: 62) is applied. It is, however, a beautiful and innocuous species, and many conservationists in MDCs value its continued existence in the wild. This observation raises issues such as the extent to which an LDC should conserve a species when it is not to its economic advantage to do so. Some of these issues are taken up later.

Aspects of Marine Parks and Zoning

The practice is growing in the Southeast Asian and Australasian region of establishing marine parks and zoning their use. The largest such marine park is the Great Barrier Reef Marine Park, of which the Capricornia section has been declared and zoned. The Cairns section (which was declared in late 1981) is now in the process of being zoned. Marine parks are unlike national parks in that they do not provide complete protection for all species—they provide for controlled use of marine resources. The Great Barrier Reef Marine Park Authority (GBRMPA) says that zones are needed "to provide suitable areas for different activities, such as fishing, diving, tourist day trips, boat anchoring, scientific research; to separate conflicting activities; and to protect areas of particular significance, such as the major breeding areas of reef animals" (GBRMPA 1982, p. 2). Actual zoning is subject to a consultative political process.

The major part of the Capricornia section is a general use zone where commercial fishing is allowed. There is very little restriction on commercial fishing in the general use *A* zone, but trawling is not allowed in the general use *B* zone, the smaller of the two, and there is some restriction on navigation by vessels of greater than 500 tons. Still smaller is the Marine National Park area for protecting natural resources. This has an *A* zone (in which recreational activities, limited recreational but not commercial fishing, and approved research are allowed) and a *B* zone that allows for public appreciation and enjoyment free from recreational activities, fishing, and collecting. There is also a single preservation zone in the Capricornia section designed "to preserve areas in their natural state, except for scientific research purposes, and to protect important turtle and bird nesting sites" (GBRMPA 1982, p. 3). In addition, certain areas are subject to periodically restricted use. These are designated as replenishment areas and seasonal closure areas. In replenishment areas, fishing and collecting may be prohibited for limited periods to enable resource stocks to regenerate. Seasonal closure areas are intended to protect some areas in which birds and turtles nest from human intrusion during the nesting season. Permits for particular activities may be required in some zones (GBRPMA 1982). Approximately 80% of the Capricornia area is without restriction except that mining and commercial spearfishing are prohibited.

The extent to which economic factors are taken into account in drawing up the zoning plan is unknown. However, GBRPMA is required to call for and take into account representations from the public on at least two occasions during the development of the zoning plan. To what extent do factors considered by some economists to be important in the economics of politics influence the final zoning adopted? To what extent can economics contribute to the planning of optimal zones? How, in fact, are conflicts between users of the reef area settled?

It might be noted that the GBRMPA has no jurisdiction above the low-water mark. The Great Barrier Marine Park is under the joint control of the Australian commonwealth government and the government of Queensland, but all territory (except for a limited number of commonwealth-owned islands) above the low-water mark is under the independent control of the Queensland government. Given the presence of ecological interdependence, some conservationists feel that it would be desirable to incorporate relevant terrestrial areas directly into the resource management area of the marine park. There is an intention to incorporate land areas in Ningaloo Marine Park in the reef region of North West Cape in Western Australia (National Parks Authority 1983). Marine and terrestrial management of resources is planned. The marine section of the park will encompass approximately 5,000 km^2. It contains important breeding grounds for turtles, and dugong are present in the area, as in the Great Barrier Reef Marine Park. It is proposed that the marine section be zoned into three general categories—general use (54%), sanctuary (9.3%), and recreation (36.7%), with recreational areas further subdivided according to type of recreation to be allowed (National Parks Authority 1983). Commercial fishing will be allowed in the general use zone but not in the recreation zone nor in the sanctuary. The sanctuary is to be left in its natural state undisturbed by man.

These two marine parks merely provide examples of the growing importance of zoning as an instrument of marine resource use in the Southeast Asia and Australia region and suggest the need for economists to consider zoning more seriously as a means of resource allocation. It might be pointed out that tourism is affected by zoning, and its environmental impact may be controlled by it. In this respect, it is worthwhile considering the Master Plan or SCETO Report for tourist development in Bali, Indonesia (Daroesman 1973; Tisdell 1984).

Concluding Observations

Conflicts over the use of marine resources within countries in the region, between countries inside the area, and with countries outside of it can be expected to intensify. For example, within countries there is conflict between commercial, subsistence, and recreational fisherman over the use of fishing resources. Furthermore, national fishermen sometimes see foreign fishing vessels, either fishing just outside the Exclusive Economic Zone (EEZ) or exploiting leases in defined areas within the EEZ in a way that threatens the available fish stocks. Conservationists, both those hoping for better management of commercial stocks and those interested in conservation for conservation's sake, come into conflict with some fishing groups, urban developers, and tourist promoters. Such conflicts cannot be expected to lessen with economic development because development raises the value of natural resources.

We need to consider the extent to which the rate of exploitation of marine resources in this region exceeds that justified by national economic self-interest and to search for practical policies to rectify the situation. Furthermore, are there fugitive resources that are not being managed to the best economic advantage of the whole region? In fact, there seem to be some such resources (turtles appear to be one) and international cooperation is needed to organize regional management policies regulating their use.

International conflict, however, may (and does) exist in the conservation of fugitive resources. Australia, for example, is in a position to conserve breeding grounds and mature stocks of some marine species that appear to migrate to Southeast Asia and parts of the Western Pacific. To what extent should Australia be expected to protect such species if it is not in its narrow economic interest to do so? Again, to what extent should LDCs be expected to protect marine species and reefs when the main beneficiaries are in MDCs? Distributional questions are involved, but these matters should not be insuperable stumbling blocks to greater conservation even though questions of foreign aid are involved—they certainly should not be a reason for failing to carry our conservation management programs that are in the narrow economic national interest (Pearson and Pryor 1978; Tisdell 1983). Marine parks and zoning are being increasingly used in the Southeast Asian and Australian region as a management technique. Economists need to investigate factors in zoning and the economic justification for zoning. In the past, this type of marine management has been left solely to biologists and ecologists (IUCN 1976).

Acknowledgments

I wish to thank Jim Marsh, Bruce Rettig, Jon Sutinen, and other participants in the workshop on marine resource economics held at the East-West Center, Honolulu, for their useful comments on the first draft of the paper. It has also benefited from comments by John Kennedy and other seminar participants at La Trobe University, Australia, and from the comments of two anonymous referees.

References

Barney, G. O. 1980. *The global 2000 report to the president of the U.S.* New York: Pergamon Press.

Bellairs, A. 1969. *The life of reptiles.* London: Weidenfeld & Nicholson.

Buck, A. J., M. Grass, S. Hakim, and J. Weinblatt. 1983. The deterrence hypothesis revisited. Regional Sci. Urban Econ. 13:471–486.

Bustard, R. 1972. *Sea turtles: Natural history and conservation.* London: Collins.

Carr, A. 1968. *The turtle: A natural history of sea turtles.* London: Cassell.

Carr, A. F., A. R. Main, and L. P. Smart. 1973. *Turtle farming project in northern Australia: Report on an enquiry into ecological considerations and report on an enquiry into organisation, management and market prospects.* Canberra: Commonwealth of Australia.

Ciriacy-Wantrup, S. V. 1963. *Resource conservation: Economics and politics,* rev. ed. Berkeley: University of California Press.

Clark, C. W. 1976. *Mathematical bioeconomics: The optimal management of renewable resources.* New York: Wiley.

Clayton, D. 1975. Farming green turtles: Keep it small and simple. *Fish Farming Int.* 2(3):9–11.

Considine, J. L., and J. J. Winberry. 1978. The green sea turtle of the Cayman Islands. *Oceanus* 21(3):50–55.

Comitini, S. 1969. The exploitation of marine resources. In *The encyclopedia of marine resources,* ed. F. E. Firth, 210–215. New York: Van Nostrand Reinhold.

Daroesman, R. 1973. An economic survey of Bali. *Bull. Indonesian Stud.* 9(3):28–61.

Downs, A. 1957. *An economic theory of democracy.* New York: Harper & Row.

Eaton, P., and P. Sinclair. 1981. *Wildlife in Papua New Guinea.* Konedobu, P.N.G.: Division of Wildlife, Department of Lands and Environment.

Fish Farming International (P. Hjul, editor). 1979. Turtle steak from Cayman Islands. *Fish Farming Int.* 6(4):44–45.

GBRMPA. 1982. *Help zone the Reef.* Townsville: Great Barrier Reef Marine Park Authority.

Heinsohn, G. E. 1983. Dugong *Dugong dugon.* In *The complete book of Australian mammals,* ed. R. Strahan, 474–476. Sydney: Angus & Robertson.

Hudson, B. E. T. 1983a. Dugongs of the Northern Torres Strait: Aerial surveys, observations during a tagging project, catch statistics, with recommendations for conservation and management. *Pacific Science Association 15th Congress Abstracts* 1:108. Dunedin, New Zealand: University of Otago.

Hudson, B. E. T. 1983b. Dugongs: Can the Kiwai survive without them? Paper presented to the 11th International Congress of Anthropological and Ethnological Sciences, Vancouver, Canada, August. 20–25.

IUCN. 1976. *Marine parks and reserves.* Morges, Switzerland: International Union for Conservation of Nature and Natural Resources.

Jayewardene, J. 1982. The conservation of marine turtles in Sri Lanka. *Tigerpaper* 9(2):21–27.

Munro, G. R. 1982. Fisheries, extended jurisdiction and the economics of common property resources. *Can. J. Econ.* 15:405–425.

National Parks Authority. 1983. *Ningaloo Marine Park: Report and recommendations by the marine park working group.* Nedlands, Western Australia: National Parks Authority.

Olewale, E., and D. Sedu. 1980. Momora (the dugong) in the Western Province. In *Traditional conservation in Papua New Guinea: Implications for today,* ed. L. Morautu, J. Pernetta, and W. Heaney, 251–255. Boroko, P.N.G.: Institute of Applied Social and Economic Research.

Olson, M. 1965. *The logic of collective action.* Cambridge, Mass.: Harvard University Press.
OECD. 1974. *Problems in transfrontier pollution.* Paris: Organization for Economic Cooperation and Development.
OECD. 1976. *Economics of transfrontier pollution.* Paris: Organization for Economic Cooperation and Development.
Pearson, C., and A. Pryor. 1978. *Environment: North and south.* New York: Wiley.
Philip, Duke of Edinburgh, and J. Fisher. 1970. *Wildlife crisis.* London: Hamish Hamilton.
Raj, U. 1977. Turtle farming in the South Pacific. *South Pacific Bulletin,* 3rd quarter, pp. 427–430.
Sadleir, R. 1970. *Animals of Australia and New Zealand.* London: Hamlyn.
Tisdell, C. A. 1982. *Microeconomics of markets.* Brisbane: John Wiley.
Tisdell, C. A. 1983. Conserving living resources in third world countries: Economic and social issues. *Int. J. Environ. Stud.* 22:11–24.
Tisdell, C. A. 1984. The environment and tourism in Southeast Asia and Australia. *Thai J. Develop. Admin.* 24:124–142.
Weatherly, A. H., and B. M. G. Cogger. 1975. Fish culture: Problems and prospects. *Science* 197:427–430.

[14]

Institutional management of an international mixed good

The IWC and socially optimal whale harvests

Yoshihiro Kuronuma and Clement A. Tisdell

This paper illustrates and discusses the applicability of the economic theory of 'common property' (*res communis*) resources to whale management. It re-examines empirical evidence about the economic irrationality of the economic management of 'common property' resources with reference to several whale stocks, and analyses the past management of whale resources by the International Whaling Commission (IWC). It shows that the collective management of whale stocks as a private good by the IWC has not resulted in collective efficiency as defined in the IWC's original convention. It also analyses the current situation, in the context of the IWC's international management of whales as a mixed good, which may be considered to be its present management objective. This discussion indicates the need for further research to determine the externality costs of harvesting (or not harvesting) each whale species, so that the IWC can achieve an optimal solution from a potential Paretian improvement perspective. At the present time a Kaldor–Hicks optimum appears not to prevail in whaling.

The authors are with the Department of Economics, The University of Queensland, Queensland 4072, Australia.

[1]According to S. Ryan, 'Scientists advising *continued on page 236*

At the 34th meeting of the International Whaling Commission (IWC) in 1982, it was decided to impose a moratorium on the harvest of all whale species. This meant a total ban on harvesting any whale species for commercial purposes, starting from the 1986 coastal whaling season and the 1985–86 pelagic whaling season, and continuing until the end of the 1990 whaling season. A decision to extend this moratorium was taken by the IWC in 1991 and 1992. In practice, this has meant that there has been no active commercial whaling, apart from aboriginal and scientific catches, since the beginning of the 1987–88 coastal whaling season and the 1986–87 pelagic whaling season. It therefore may not seem necessary at present (1993) to canvas options for the international management of whale resources from an economic perspective. However, it would be useful to analyse the past management of whale resources as a case study in the management of a 'common property' resource, not only because of the availability of data on whale management, but also because of the IWC's intention to reconsider whale management in the future.[1]

Whales involve elements of both an international private or consumptive good and a public good (ie they are mixed goods). Before the early 1970s, whale resources were not considered to be a public good, but treated rather as stocks giving rise to private goods. However, the view that whale stocks are public goods has gained in importance since the United Nations Conference on the Human Environment in Stockholm in 1972. This indicates that the partial equilibrium model discussed in neo-classical fisheries economics[2] cannot be applied directly to whales because this model does not incorporate public good values such as existence value. This suggests that this limitation to the current theory needs to be addressed.

0308-597X/93/040235-16

In the next section, the basic focus and underlying hypothesis of this paper will be discussed. A brief review of the IWC including its objectives, structure, types of regulation and enforcement policies will then be presented, followed by a discussion of empirical management procedures, some procedural issues, and the differing objectives of IWC members. The moratorium decision will be examined in order to test the hypothesis put forward in this paper and the result obtained in this section will be discussed in more detail, from the perspective of the social marginal cost of mixed-good management. Finally, the exclusion element of mixed-good management is discussed.

Basic considerations and underlying hypothesis

The formulation of appropriate management strategies for the utilization of publicly-owned natural resources has become a major problem for society. For decision makers who are concerned with maximizing society's benefits from these resources, the question of whom to assign property rights to these resources to is difficult because it involves an assessment of who can utilize the resources in the best interests of society. Such management decisions are more important for some types of resources than for others.

There are some resources for which it is uneconomic to establish private property rights, as a rule. Two such types of resources are ubiquitous and fugitive resources.[3] According to definition, ubiquitous resources such as air, wave energy, wind power and solar radiation are generally indivisible and non-excludable.[4] With such natural resources it is usually uneconomic to specify exclusive ownership or private property rights. Fugitive natural resources, such as schools of fish, are mobile and are not considered excludable until the time of capture. Property rights to such resources are normally assigned only after capture. Many of these resources are open-access resources and are available to anyone who desires them.

Because these two types of resources have different characteristics, separate approaches to their management may be required. Ubiquitous resources, while still plentiful, need no institutional regulation. They are managed as open-access (*res nullius*) resources and no private property rights are assigned to them. In fact, property rights have no meaning when there is no way of excluding anyone from using a resource. Fugitive resources are excludable at the time of capture but usually not prior to that. Definite property rights are assigned to a captured fugitive resource. For example, fishermen and hunters are owners of their prey once it has been caught. However, no property rights are assigned to the uncaptured portion of the resource. Therefore, each individual is motivated to harvest as much of the resource as possible in order to maximize his/her individual benefits from the resource. The result is that the community of users rapidly depletes the stock, because no individual is motivated to curb his/her effort in order to help perpetuate the resource. Future flows of fugitive resources are particularly susceptible to depletion as a result of overexploitation. For instance, expected high rates of return to an individual fishing firm with open access to a fish stock tend to attract investment and labour long after the rate of return from the fishery as a whole becomes negative.[5] For this reason, it is necessary to manage fugitive natural resources collectively to ensure the availability of future resource flows, and to allow society as a whole to continue to reap benefits from these resources.

continued from page 235
the IWC . . . will recommend that the population can now withstand a resumption of hunting'. Therefore, there is the potential for commercial whaling in the future (S. Ryan, 'Whale hunting may begin again', *The Sunday Times*, 5 April, No 8746, London, 1992, p 8).

[2]For example, S. Gordon, 'The economic theory of common property resources: the fishery', *Journal of Political Economy*, Vol 62, No 2, 1954, pp 124–142.

[3]S.V. Ciriacy-Wantrup and R.C. Bishop, ' "Common property" as a concept in natural resource policy', *Natural Resources Journal*, Vol 15, October 1975.

[4]*Ibid.* The article indicates that ubiquitous resources are considered non-excludable until the point is reached where their utilization becomes uneconomical. When this point of economic unviability is reached, they become excludable, and from that point on management of property rights would be necessary to ensure that the public's best interests are served. Prior to that point, however, there would be no need to establish property rights.

[5]A.R. Tussing, 'Introduction: economic policy in Alaska fisheries', in A.R. Tussing, *et al*, *Alaska Fishery Policy*, Institute of Social, Economic, and Government Research, University of Alaska, Fairbanks, USA, 1972. The so-called 'Theory of Common-Property Resources' predicts premature depletion due to dissipation of economic rent. According to Smith (V.L. Smith, 'On models of commercial fishing', *Journal of Political Economy*, Vol 77, March/April 1969, pp 181–198) it will lead to dissipation of economic rent and overinvestment and may reduce the level of the resource stock in the long run if price is always greater than the marginal cost of fishing. Many fisheries economists have also analysed not only the economic theory, but also actual case studies of the use of these types of resources. For example, as cited by J.A. Crutchfield (J.A. Crutchfield, 'Economic aspects of fishery management', in A.R. Tussing, ed, *Alaska Fishing Policy*, Institute of Social, Economic and Government Research, University of Alaska, Fairbanks, Alaska, 1972, p 19) '. . . Scott (1954), Gordon (1957 and 1962), and Gerrhardsen (1957) all stressed the fact that the absence of ownership or control by the individual units concerned would lead to serious overfishing in any fishery in which price-cost ratios are favourable at a high level of output . . .' (p 19).

Institutional management of an international mixed good

The issue is further complicated when there are international interests in open-access (*res nullius*) resources. Without international cooperative institutions, open-access resources tend to be overexploited, not only from a biological but also from an economic viewpoint, as discussed in much of the economic literature on fisheries. One possible solution to this problem is to impose a form of collective management on the resource which will change it from an open-access (*res nullius*) to a 'common-property' (*res communis*) resource. The concept of 'common-property' resources as employed here refers to a distribution of property rights in resources whereby a number of owners are co-equal in their rights to use the resource, but do not have the right to transfer it.[6] The commercial history of whale exploitation exemplifies the classic problem mentioned above. A tendency towards overexploitation can be clearly observed in the history of whaling. International cooperation was therefore required for the effective management of whale resources as private or consumptive goods, and the IWC was established for this purpose in 1946. Its creation provided an institution for the management of whale resources at an international level.

However, collective management becomes difficult when there are different international interests in a 'common-property' resource. Different values or interests may be hard to reconcile. The moratorium decision at the 34th IWC meeting illustrated a conflict between nations. Survival of the IWC as an international 'common-property' institution is apparently being threatened by international political and possibly external economic forces. Ciriacy-Wantrup and Bishop's study indirectly implies that economic history has shown that external market forces have been the main threat to 'common-property' resources.[7] Each member of the collective controlling common property may wish to see regulations relaxed believing it will gain but fail to take account of the collective effect resulting in all losing. Each may fail to appreciate the fallacy of composition. If such historical experience has predictive value, one might expect such forces to have been at work in weakening 'common-property' institutions for the private goods management of whale resources. However, it will be shown in this paper that these have not been the main forces bringing about changes in the management of whales in recent times.

The International Whaling Commission

After a series of conferences, agreement to establish the IWC was finally reached on 2 December 1946.[8] Its principles were embodied in the provisions of the International Agreement for the Regulation of Whaling (signed on 8 June 1937 in London). In 1987, its membership consisted of 41 countries,[9] seven of which were engaged in commercial whaling operations in the 1985–86 whaling season.[10] All countries engaged in commercial whaling at that time (1987), except Portugal, were members of the IWC.[11] The primary consideration in the establishment of the IWC was the necessity to manage whale resources collectively rather than allow open access to them. As stated in the preamble to the Convention in 1946, the IWC was formed 'recognising the interest of the nations of the world in safeguarding for future generations the great natural resource represented by whale stock . . .'. The preamble also states the purpose of the Convention as '. . . to provide for the proper conservation of whale stocks and thus make possible the orderly

[6]Ciriacy-Wantrup and Bishop, *op cit*, Ref 3. This concept involves institutional meaning rather than pure economic theoretical classification. This is a major reason why the author used this term. Some economists, such as J.A. Crutchfield, have pointed out that it is appropriate to use the term open access instead of making this distinction (J.A Crutchfield and G. Pontecorvo, *The Pacific Salmon Fisheries: a Study of Irrational Conservation*, Resources for the Future, The Johns Hopkins Press, Baltimore, MD, 1969, p 11). Note that the expression 'free access' can also be used; thus, there is no general agreement on this terminology yet. It should be noted, however, that Ciriacy-Wantrup and Bishop corrected the confusion about the institutional concept of 'common property'. Whereas the theory of common-property resources implied that the common-property nature of the resource led to its premature depletion, their paper argues that the common property concept was more important as a potential solution to the problem than as its cause. The concept was explained as a legal concept with an exclusion element. Moreover, Ciriacy-Wantrup and Bishop contended that the historical experience has been that uncontrolled market forces have led to deterioration of the 'commons' and that regulation was necessary for their protection.

[7]Cirarcy-Wantrup and Bishop, *op cit*, Ref 3.

[8]International Convention for the Regulation of Whaling, Washington, 2 December, 1946.

[9]Member countries in 1987 were Antigua and Barbuda, Argentina, Australia, Brazil, Belize, Chile, PR China, Costa Rica, Denmark, Egypt, Finland, France, FR Germany, Iceland, India, Ireland, Japan, Kenya, Mauritania, Mexico, Monaco, the Netherlands, New Zealand, Norway, Oman, Peru, Philippines, St Lucia, St Vincent and Grenada, Senegal, Seychelles, Solomon Islands, South Africa, South Korea, Spain, Sweden, Switzerland, UK, USSR, USA, and Uruguay.

[10]These were Iceland, Brazil, Japan, Norway, South Korea, Spain, and the USSR. In addition, two countries (Denmark, Greenland eskimos; US, Alaskan eskimos) are still engaged in whaling operations which are classified as aboriginal whaling operations. Apart from these countries, St Vincent and Grenada was engaged in small-scale whaling in the 1985–86 season.

[11]At that time, the number of whales harvested by IWC member nations was around 99% of the total world catch. Therefore, the IWC could be considered to be an international 'common-property' resource institution.

development of the whaling industry'. It is therefore evident that the IWC considered whale resources as private or consumptive goods at the time of its establishment.

Each member country appoints one commissioner as its representative on the IWC. Each commissioner has one vote. All decisions of the IWC require a three-quarters majority vote of commissioners. There are three IWC committees: a Scientific Committee, a Technical Committee, and a Financial and Administration Committee. One of the major tasks of the Scientific Committee is to provide scientific advice and recommendations to the Commission.[12] Its recommendations should take account of the state of the stocks (populations) of whale species and include recommendations about the level and method of harvesting. In the 1946 Convention (Article V, Section 1), the Commission adopted several regulations with respect to utilization of whale resources. According to Allen these regulations provide for:

(1) classification of whale stocks, and protection of certain species or stocks;
(2) catch limits by species, area and sometimes by sex for those whales which may be caught;
(3) minimum size limits and, in one case, maximum size limits;
(4) duration of whaling seasons;
(5) limitations on areas where factory ships may be used;
(6) efficient treatment of carcasses;
(7) inspection of whaling operations; and
(8) collection of data.

Decisions on these regulations are also based on a three-quarters majority vote of members. Thus, regulations governing the conservation and utilization of whale resources can be changed by a three-quarters majority vote.[13]

As far as enforcement of regulations is concerned, the Schedule to the Convention[14] provided that any whaling operations should be monitored by the government concerned, and that infractions must be reported by that government to the Commission.[15] In addition, all member countries were required to provide penalties under their own laws for infractions. This leaves countries which object to particular regulations with the responsibility of enforcing regulations that they may not believe in. This can create a loophole. In other words, the IWC has no direct international enforcement power.

Management procedures and related issues

The IWC has adopted what it calls 'new management procedures' since 1974.[16] This involves a set of rules to be applied by the Commission, on the basis of advice from the Scientific Committee, to determine which stocks should be protected and which should be exploited, and at what levels. These rules are based on a quantitative assessment of the stock of each species in different regions.[17] The rules of the IWC define the stock levels of all species based on the nature of the populations relative to maximum sustainable yield (MSY) level. The Scientific Committee prepares recommendations and/or scientific advice based on a quantitative assessment of whale stocks for catch quotas. As a result of the introduction of this procedure in 1974, a number of stocks were protected from exploitation (Figure 1) and the catch quotas for most

[12]See the rules of procedure, Appendix IV (p 26) of *International Whaling Commission Report*, 1950. For information on the roles of the other committees, see the same source.

[13]However, any country that disagrees with a regulation may file an objection with the IWC. While the objection is being considered (for at least one year, and often more), the objecting country is not considered bound by the disputed regulation. In fact, numerous objections have been filed in past years. One of the major cases was the objection by Chile, Japan, Norway, Peru, and the USSR to the 1982 decision to ban harvesting (ie zero catch) of all species of whales. By January 1987, Japan, Norway, and the USSR were still objecting to this 1982 ban. However, Japan had decided to withdraw its objection effective from the 1987–88 pelagic whaling season. This was mainly due to strong external economic pressures.

[14]*IWC Report*, 1950.

[15]According to Allen (K.R. Allen, *Conservation and Management of Whales*, University of Washington Press, Butterworths, 1980), however, one case which did not appear in national reports of infractions was when around 5 000 humpback whales disappeared from the Antarctic region in the early 1960s.

[16]*25th IWC Report*, The International Whaling Commission, Cambridge, UK, 1975, pp 40–41 and pp 49–52. Until 1973, the major method of setting quotas was based on the Blue Whale Unit (BWU). Species quotas were not introduced until 1969.

[17]According to Allen (*op cit*, Ref 15), these rules divided stocks as follows: (1) initial management stocks, which may be reduced in a controlled manner to the maximum sustainable yield (MSY) level, or some other optimum (as might be determined); (2) sustained management stocks, which are to be maintained at or near maximum sustainable yield level (or optimum, as defined); and (3) protection stocks, which are below the sustained management level, and should be fully protected. Allen also states that under the IWC: (1) initial management stocks are more than 20% above MSY level; (2) protection stocks are more than 10% below this level; (3) quotas are MSY level or above; (4) optimum level is the MSY level which gives the maximum number of animals in the sustainable catch, rather than the MSY level which gives the maximum sustainable weight.

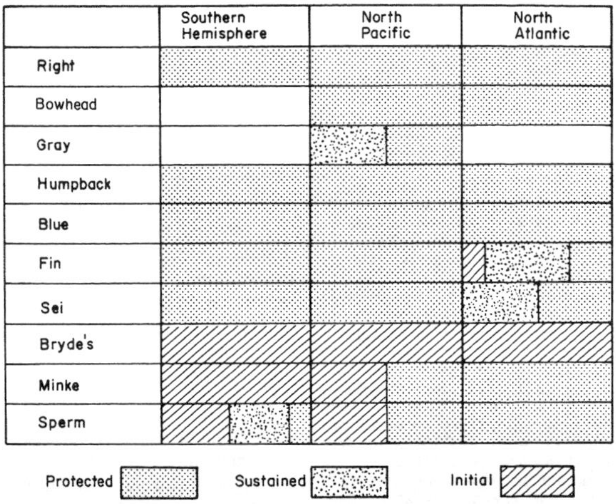

Figure 1. Classification of each species of whale in the principal ocean areas as at the 1978–79 and 1979 Seasons.[a]

[a] Although Allen has not specified, the existence of several classifications for the same species in the one area indicates sub-populations and/or sub-regions in those general areas. Empty areas indicate that a species is not found in those areas. Quotas established at the IWC annual meetings are, for example, for the Antarctic whaling season (December of the year of the meeting through April of the following year) and all coastal seasons of the year after the meeting.

Source: Allen, *op cit*, Ref 15.

species were reduced (Table 1), before the imposition of the total moratorium.

A major weakness of IWC management procedure is the IWC's scientific advisory system. Specific problems include: (1) inputs from the fields of ecology, economics and other related areas are limited, because of the emphasis on biological assessment techniques such as MSY; (2) its scope is limited to the highly consumptive objective of the IWC (ie the nature of the IWC's original objective) which operated primarily in the interests of the whaling industry; and (3) historically, scientific advice has often been neglected by the IWC.

Table 1. International whaling quotas (number of head), 1974–82.[a]

Area/species	1974–75	1975–76	1976–77	1977–78	1978–79	1979–80	1980–81	1981–82	1982–83
A. *Southern Hemisphere*									
Fin	1 000	220	0	0	0	0	0	0	0
Sei/Bryde's	4 000	2 230	1 863	771	0	264	264	244	165
Sperm	13 000	10 740	4 791	5 908	4 875	580	300	0	0
Minke	7 000	6 810	8 900	5 690	6 221	8 102	7 072	8 102	7 072
B. *North Pacific/North Atlantic*									
Fin	300	365	445	459	455	604	701	561	287
Sei/Bryde's	2 000	1 363	1 132	608	538	579	629	626	646
Sperm	10 000	8 300	7 885	7 129	4 485	1 623	1 020	450	400
Minke	–	2 550	3 024	2 955	2 952	3 904	3 915	3 915	3 795
C. *Total Commercial Quota*									
Fin	1 300	585	455	459	455	604	701	561	287
Sei/Bryde's	6 000	3 593	2 995	1 379	538	843	893	870	811
Sperm	23 000	19 040	12 676	13 037	9 360	2 203	1 320	450	400
Minke	7 000	9 360	11 924	8 645	9 173	12 006	10 987	12 017	10 867
Subtotal	37 300	32 578	28 050	23 520	19 256	15 656	13 901	13 989	12 365
D. *Aboriginal Quota*									
	–	–	–	–	–	197	206	206	206
Grand total	37 300	32 578	28 520	23 520	19 526	15 853	14 107	14 104	12 571

[a] Quotas established at the IWC annual meetings are for the Antarctic whaling season (December of the year of the meeting through April of the following year) and all coastal seasons of the year after the meeting.

Source: *The Whale Report*, Vol 5, No 3, Summer 1982, The Centre for Environmental Education, Inc (original data for IWC Annual Reports).

The first problem arises from shortcomings in the Scientific Committee's use of biological models for the estimating of the whale population. It is very important to use appropriate methods, including population models and assessment, which have been developed for individual whale species based on biological research (such as population dynamics). However, the IWC should also take into account the fact that, since its objectives are not only 'proper conservation' but also 'orderly development of the whaling industry', it is advisable, even if complicated, to at least consider socio-economic factors in conjunction with their estimate of whale populations. The Scientific Committee should consider not only biological but also socio-economic and environmental factors in its recommendations, or if the Scientific Committee's mandate is limited to estimating whale population size, the IWC should also have an advisory committee for socio-economic and environmental research.

It is also important to take ecological factors into account. For example, the krill (*Euphausia superba dana*)[18] fishery which has been developed in the Antarctic in recent years may have a significant effect on the expansion of whale populations. In addition, the methodology for determining MSY levels needs to be strictly defined,[19] as it may lead to confusion regarding recommendations for each species.

The second issue relates directly to the IWC's goal of providing for the orderly development of the whaling industry, which can be considered as a highly consumptive objective. In recent years, different objectives have gained importance and acceptance by the many members of the public. These objectives require low-consumptive usage of whales. Examples of low-consumptive usage are tourism, existence value and educational usage (museums, etc).[20] Thus, if the IWC hopes to take these objectives into account, it might need to redefine its original objectives; otherwise, it is likely to be involved in not only meaningless debate but also confusion.

IWC member countries seem to fall into three major groups. These are: (1) the whaling industry group; (2) the conservationist group; and (3) the Third World group. The major objectives of the whaling industry group are to maximize their individual socio-economic benefits from whaling. This group will take into account the level of employment, the net economic return to each country as a whole, and foreign currency earnings. But even this group needs to provide for proper conservation of whale resources to achieve its objectives. Its objectives may therefore be classified as product-oriented. However, the situation may be a little more complicated because some conservationist groups in whaling countries, for example, may object to whaling even though most individuals favour it. On the other hand, some pro-whaling groups in non-whaling countries may object to the stand of conservationists. We should take note that, empirically, this product-oriented group stresses short-term rather than long-term benefits.

The conservationist group favours low consumptive uses and the discontinuation of whale harvesting. For this group, we may identify at least three major objectives:[21] (1) ethical objectives; (2) educational, recreational, and scientific objectives; and (3) ecosystem conservation.

The first objective relates to the ethical view that marine ('advanced'?) mammals should not be killed because man is a mammal and has empathy with other mammals. The second refers to the maximization of educational and scientific benefits from the study of marine mammal populations. Note that the recreational objective here includes

[18]Krill: a small crustacean of the species *Euphasia superba dana* which is the main food of blue and minke whales (K.R. Allen, and D.G. Chapman, 'Whales', in J.A. Gulland, ed, *Fish: Population Dynamics*, John Wiley, London, 1977).

[19]At present, the IWC does not specify how this level is to be defined in a situation where a population is potentially expanding towards a new stable level. According to Allen (*op cit*, Ref 15), at least three different definitions of MSY level are possible, and each interpretation presents different problems of assessment and therefore management. These definitions are: (1) the level before expansion began; (2) the level corresponding to the potential unexploited level which would be achieved in a stable situation after all species had expanded towards their new potential.

[20]It should be noted that there are several low-consumptive values relating to whales. These include existence and bequest values. Recreational and tourism values based on whale watching may possibly be associated with existence and bequest values, but the priority seems to be to obtain maximum economic return to the industry. Therefore, it seems important to recognize these differences in values.

[21]'Conservationist' groups may not all have the same objective. The range of objectives would most likely be larger than is indicated here. The three general objectives listed are therefore only the major objectives. See Suter with regard to some basic reasons given for the conservation of whales at the time of the moratorium decision (K.D. Suter, 'Australia's new whaling policy', *Marine Policy*, Vol 6, No 4, October 1982).

Table 2. Voting record on whaling moratorium

Vote		Countries
For	25	Seychelles, Spain,[a] USA, and 22 other non-whaling nations
Against	7	Brazil,[a] Iceland,[a] Japan,[a] Norway[a], Peru,[a] South Korea,[a] USSR[a]
Abstained	5	Chile,[a], China, Philippines, South Africa, Switzerland
Absent	2	Dominica, Jamaica

[a] Commercial whaling countries in 1982.
Source: The Animal Welfare Institute, *Quarterly*, Vol 3, No 3, Summer 1982.

activities such as whale watching, but does not include any consumptive use such as sport fishing. The third objective relates to the ecological view that marine mammals should not be killed because of the effect on the ocean's food chain. A fourth reason is the high economic value given to whales for non-consumptive purposes, eg existence value, whale watching, tourism.

The primary objective of the Third World group is to obtain property rights in reserves in the global commons that are not under jurisdiction. The growing awareness of Third World countries, especially after the series of United Nations Law of the Sea Conferences on the future use of whale resources, has brought this objective to the fore. Developing countries are now more outspoken in their intention to obtain a fair share of the world's remaining resources.

The third problem, namely that scientific advice has often been neglected by the IWC, can be considered to be the result of conflicting interests among IWC member countries. This seems to be related directly to the underlying hypothesis of this paper, namely that external political and possibly external economic forces have influenced the decisions of IWC members throughout the IWC's history. This point, and the moratorium decision, will be discussed in the next section.

The moratorium

A ten-year moratorium was first proposed to the IWC in 1972 by the USA and other nations. The initiative began with the United Nations Conference on the Human Environment in Stockholm in 1972. In July 1982, the IWC decided to set zero catch limits (quotas) for commercial whaling of all whale species, effective from the 1986 coastal whaling season and the 1985–86 pelagic whaling season, and continuing until the end of the 1990 whaling season. This meant that during the period from 1986 to 1990 the IWC had to reassess the stock of each whale species (by region and by species) in order to devise proposed catch limits and MSY levels for the years from 1990 on.[22] The voting record on the whaling moratorium issue was as shown in Table 2.

Political/economic factors influenced this result. Of the commercial whaling countries, only Spain voted for the moratorium proposal. The main reason for this may have been Spain's desire to join the European Community (EC). Hence, there would have been strong economic and political pressure on Spain to vote for the moratorium proposal. China abstained because of its economic and political relations with other countries who voted on this proposal. China needed to maintain good political relations with the USA in order to strengthen its position against the USSR at that time; however, it did not want to disagree with Japan. Another interesting tendency can be seen among the relatively new IWC member countries. Belize, Senegal, and Antigua and Barbuda joined the IWC just before its 34th meeting. Many of these countries

[22] There was no drastic change after this meeting (ie at the 35th, 36th, 37th and 38th annual meetings of the IWC). However, actual commercial whaling stopped after the 1987–88 coastal whaling season. Note that Japan had stopped commercial pelagic whaling by the end of the 1986–87 whaling season.

Institutional management of an international mixed good

were represented by commissioners from the USA or the UK, who belonged to the conservationist group.[23]

There is some inconsistency between the moratorium decision and the IWC's original objective. For example, according to the Scientific Committee,[24] the gross recruitment rate for minke whales has been around 14–15%, and the natural mortality rate was only around 9.5% at the time of the moratorium decision, resulting in an increase in population. Based on these biological results, at the 34th annual meeting of the IWC, the Scientific Committee advised that the minke whale quota should be between 2 467 and 9 867 head for the 1982–83 pelagic whaling season in the southern hemisphere. The Technical Committee voted for a 2 467 minke whale quota, which was proposed by St Lucia. The final decision, made by an IWC vote, was for a 7 072 minke whale quota for 1982–83. This seemed to be consistent with the IWC's objectives. In 1993, the moratorium covers all whale stocks. However, this seems to ignore the fact that some stocks, such as Antarctic minke whales, were considered by the Scientific Committee at the 34th annual IWC meeting to be able to sustain commercial whaling. Reconsideration of stocks by species and by region may be required. Otherwise, the IWC will lose its role as an international 'common-property' resource institution which manages whaling in the interests of the whaling industry.[25]

The case of the 1981–82 sperm whale quota is another example. According to the 32nd IWC Annual Report, the Scientific Committee used two methods to estimate sperm whale stocks in the Northwest Pacific. These were the length-specific Cooke and Beddington (CB)[26] technique and the age-specific Shirakibara and Tanaka (ST)[27] technique. Since the two estimations of stocks were different but 'reasonable', the Scientific Committee could not make a recommendation to the Commission. As a result, the IWC was unable to reach a decision at the 33rd meeting in 1981 and at a special meeting held in March 1982 on the harvesting quota.[28] Such problems will not arise if the moratorium continues.[29] However, the question remains as to how we can investigate and/or develop 'reasonable' techniques for the reassessment of stocks without actual catch data.[30]

It seems that some external (international) market economic threats had an impact on the introduction of the moratorium. Examples include the measures taken by the USA (1) the Pacwood-Magnuson Amendment to the Fishery Conservation and Management Act;[31] and (2) the Pelly Amendment to the Fisherman's Protective Act.[32] The first law provides for an automatic 50% reduction in fishing allocations within the USA's 200-nautical-mile (nm) Fishing Zones (FZs) for those countries which are certified by the Secretary of Commerce as acting in violation of whale conservation programmes. The second law provides that the US President may prohibit import into the USA fish products from a country which acts in such a way as to diminish the effectiveness of any international fishery conservation programme. If these measures had been actively enforced at that time, they would have had a great effect on certain whaling countries, such as Japan and Iceland.[33] These laws provided economic penalties which reinforced the moratorium. Other international problems, such as trade and political problems, could follow for a country such as Japan if it ignored the moratorium.

It seems clear that political factors had more influence in the weakening of IWC than narrow economic considerations such as those

[23] *Asahi Newspaper* (Tokyo), 28 July 1982. At the time of the 36th (1984) IWC annual meeting the Seychelles' commissioner was British, and three commissioners from the USA represented Antigua and Barbuda, St Lucia, and St Vincent and Grenada. K. Arai, 'Kokusai hogei jouyaku to wagakuni no hogeigyo (No 2) (International whaling treaty and Japanese whaling industry)', *Gyosen (Journal of Fishing Boats)*, No 258, 1986, pp 25–35.

[24] *29th IWC Report*, The International Whaling Commission, Cambridge, UK, 1975. Report on the special meeting on Southern hemisphere minke whales, pp 349–358.

[25] In reality, however, it seems that community attitudes have changed since the IWC introduced the moratorium; thus, its original objective seems no longer to be appropriate. Moreover, it seems that the character of the IWC has already changed, although it has not yet changed its original objective.

[26] Cooke and Beddington, 'Development of an assessment technique for male sperm whales based on the use of length data from the catches, with special reference to the Northwest Pacific stock', *31st IWC Report*, International Whaling Commission, Cambridge, UK, 1981, pp 747–760. See also *32nd IWC Report*, International Whaling Commission, Cambridge, UK, 1982, pp 239–245.

[27] Shirakibara and Tanaka, 'Population Estimation of the Northwest Pacific Stock of Sperm Whales', *32nd IWC Report*, International Whaling Commission, Cambridge, UK, 1982, pp 249–50, and also *31st IWC Report*, International Whaling Commission, Cambridge, UK, 1981, SC/33/S, p 5.

[28] As a result, however, Japan was given a 1983 whaling season quota of 450 sperm whales in the North-west Pacific.

[29] There has been no actual recommendation by the Scientific Committee since the 37th IWC annual meeting in 1985.

[30] Although several different methods for the estimation of whale populations and for obtaining other scientific information without catching whales, such as blood sampling and sighting, have been proposed and implemented none of these methods seem to provide accurate scientific information yet. It also seems that the most appropriate method may differ for different species and regions.

[31] Public Law 94–265, Fishery Conservation and Management Act of 1976 and its Amendment of 1979.

[32] Public Law 94–265, Fishery Conservation and Management Act of 1976 and its Amendment of 1979, section 205.

[33] In 1981, the economic return to the Japanese fishing industry from fishing inside the US FZs was more than ten times the revenue of the Japanese whaling industry.

suggested by Ciriacy-Wantrup and Bishop.[34] The potential US measures were considered to be very powerful external economic enforcement and/or penalty mechanisms at that time. It is therefore possible to conclude that political factors in association with external economic pressures had a role in influencing the IWC member countries to vote for the moratorium. The decision was not in accordance with the industry private good or consumptive objective of IWC. It should be noted, however, that the reason that the IWC departed from its earlier private good objective does not seem to be the same as that suggested as a possible reason for the failure of such an organization by Ciriacy-Wantrup and Bishop. This is because Ciriacy-Wantrup and Bishop seem to assume a situation in which commercial producers want to have larger quotas or do not abide by quotas; hence, the common-property management solution fails as in the cartel case. Moreover, it should be stressed that the political factors represent changing values.[35] These changing values presumably resulted in the IWC's departure from its original objectives.

Mixed good management by the IWC

As discussed in the preceding section, the broader implications of Ciriacy-Wantrup and Bishop's work, that political factors associated with external market forces have been the main threat to 'common-property' resources and their institutional management, still require further research. It may be possible to elaborate on this point from the perspective of mixed good management by an international institution (eg the IWC). Whale resources are a mixed good (ie both a private or consumptive good and a public good). From the point of view of the whaling industry, the resource has been utilized as a private good. This indicates that whales were harvested and marketed under conditions of exclusion and competition. However, the world community has increasingly viewed whale resources as a public good, or at least as having some of the characteristics of public goods, since the early 1970s. According to Brown and Jackson,[36] the characteristics of a pure public good are: it can be consumed or enjoyed without the available supply being reduced, and once it has been supplied, it is impossible to exclude individuals from consuming it. This implies that whale resources *cannot* be utilized and marketed under conditions of exclusion and competition from the public good perspective. As mentioned above, the characteristics of whale resources as a public good include existence and bequest values.[37] Other non-consumptive uses include whale watching and tourism.

The above development implies that even if economic efficiency is achieved by the whaling industry in exploiting the whale resource as a private good,[38] market failure would result due to the public goods characteristics of the resource. Tisdell[39] examines the management of wildlife as a mixed good using the following figure (Figure 2). In Figure 2, the D curve represents the value per unit of harvested whales. The S curve shows the private marginal costs of whaling. The intersection of these two curves (a in Figure 2) indicates the optimal consumptive exploitation of whales from an economic viewpoint when only consumptive goals prevail. This occurs when the quantity X_s of whales is harvested annually and sold at a price of P_{Xs} each. As discussed in Tisdell, if this supply curve (S) represents optimally regulated whale

[34]Ciriacy-Wantrup and Bishop, *op cit*, Ref 3.

[35]Note that this does not indicate that economic logic is absent. The new values can, up to a point, be assigned a monetary value. In addition, the *economic cost* to a large number of IWC nations of supporting a moratorium on whaling is low or zero, because they have no whaling industry and consume little or no material parts of whales, but the non-consumptive value they place on whales is relatively high. Therefore, it seems important to be able to compare non-consumptive and product-oriented economic values, by whale species and their areas of abode (note that the following are excluded from this discussion in order to avoid further complications: economic costs of some of those nations may be relatively large for conservation activities, and also some nations may by supporting a moratorium obtain some direct benefits from leading conservation countries).

[36]C.V. Brown, and P.M. Jackson, *Public Sector Economics*, 3 ed, Basil Blackwell, Oxford, 1986.

[37]See more detailed discussion of these values, see D.W. Pearce, *Cost-Benefit Analysis*, 2 ed, St Martin's Press, New York, 1983; D.W. Pearce, and C.A. Nash, *The Social Appraisal of Projects. A Text on Cost-Benefit Analysis*, Macmillan, London, 1981; J.V. Krutilla, 'Conservation reconsidered', *American Economic Review*, Vol 57, 1967, pp 777–786; B. Weisbrod, 'Collective-consumption services of individual-consumption goods', *Quarterly Journal of Economics*, Vol 78, 1964, pp 471–477; and C.A. Tisdell, *Economics of Environmental Conservation: Economics for Environmental and Ecological Management, Developments in Environmental Economics*, Vol 1, Elsevier, Amsterdam, 1991.

[38]This is discussed further in Kuronuma (Y. Kuronuma, 'International economic management of highly migratory marine living resources: the cases of Southern bluefin tuna and Antarctic minke whales', PhD thesis, Department of Economics, The University of Queensland, Australia, 1992, chapter 11) in relation to Antarctic minke whale resource management from the private good perspective.

[39]Tisdell, *op cit*, Ref 37.

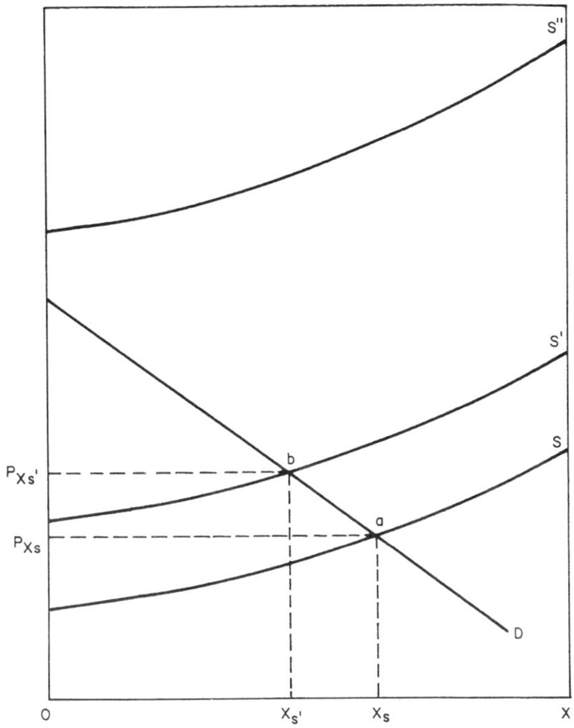

Figure 2. Mixed good management and whales.
Source: Tisdell, *op cit*, Ref 37.

resources in relation to its contribution of private goods, the quantity X_s of whales indicates an efficient harvest level from the perspective of private goods management. However, if the social marginal cost of whaling (S′) is higher than S, the private goods market equilibrium would be obtained at b, where the quantity $X_{s'}$ of whales is harvested at $P_{Xs'}$ price per unit of whales. The difference between $P_{Xs'}$ and P_{Xs} reflects the externality costs of whaling per unit of whales to be harvested,[40] eg the marginal valuation put on whales for existence purposes and other non-consumptive uses.

Tisdell also discusses the case of the S″ curve, where the social marginal cost curve for whaling is so high that no commercial whaling is optimal. The moratorium decision by the IWC in 1982 and again in 1991 *may* represent this situation. If this is the case, it indicates that because the externality costs of whaling (the difference between the S″ and S curves) are so high that it is impossible for commercial whalers to operate and obtain a social optimum. However, as discussed in Tisdell, it may be possible that the management policy for the harvest of whales by the IWC is not optimal in the potential Paretian improvement (Kaldor–Hicks) context because of political factors. It is possible to view

[40] *Ibid*.

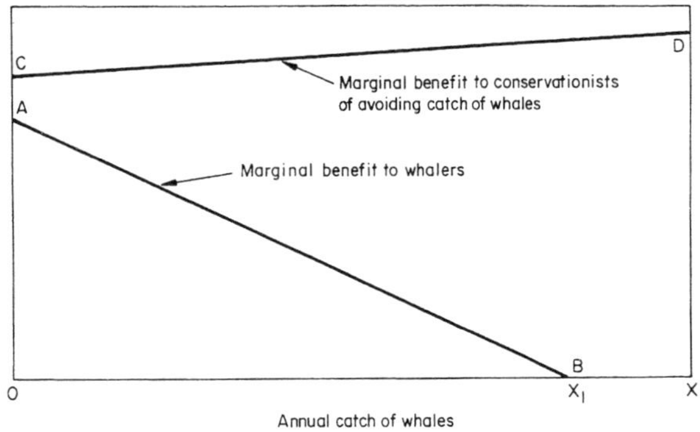

Figure 3. In this case a ban or moratorium on whaling is Kaldor–Hicks optimal.

this as the non-optimality of a voting system based on a three-quarters majority from a Kaldor–Hicks (a potential Paretian improvement) perspective. Commercial whaling nations who voted against the moratorium in 1982 were certainly worse off because no compensation was obtained from those nations who voted for the moratorium. Only those nations who voted for the moratorium were better off, hence a Paretian improvement did not occur. In relation to some whale species it seems possible that a Kaldor–Hicks deterioration occured.

It has been observed by Tullock[41] that straight majority voting usually does not result in a Kaldor–Hicks optimum. As a rule (*but with the exception to be specified*) scope exists for a potential Paretian improvement when majority rule is the sole *desideratum* of social choice, and side-deals cannot be struck between parties. In the case of the IWC if (non-consumptive) conservationist nations are in the majority (three-quarters majority in this case) a moratorium will prevail. If whaling nations have a three-quarters majority, whaling will occur in accordance with their wishes – ideally, from their viewpoint, one that maximizes discounted net value to them of consumptive exploitation of whales. But from a Kaldor–Hicks point of view, the first situation will only be ideal if the marginal evaluation curve of conservationists for avoiding all levels of whale harvesting exceeds the marginal evaluation of whales for harvesting whales. This case is illustrated in Figure 3. Curve CD indicates the marginal benefits to conservationists of preventing different levels of whale harvesting, and curve AB represents the marginal benefit to whalers of harvesting whales.

In the case shown, if conservationists have a three-quarters majority, no harvesting will prevail and this will be socially ideal from a Kaldor–Hicks viewpoint. On the other hand, if whalers have a three-quarters majority, the level of harvest of whales will be X_1 annually and a Kaldor–Hicks optimum will not prevail.

However, empirically, we cannot be sure that the situation shown in Figure 3 prevails. It is feasible, at least for some species of whales, that the marginal benefit curves intersect. This may be so for minke whales but not so say for very large whales such as sperm whales or southern right whales. In the former case, some harvesting of whales will be optimal for a Kaldor–Hicks viewpoint as illustrated in Figure 4. In the

[41] G. Tullock, 'Problems of majority voting', *Journal of Political Economy*, Vol 67, 1950, pp 571–579.

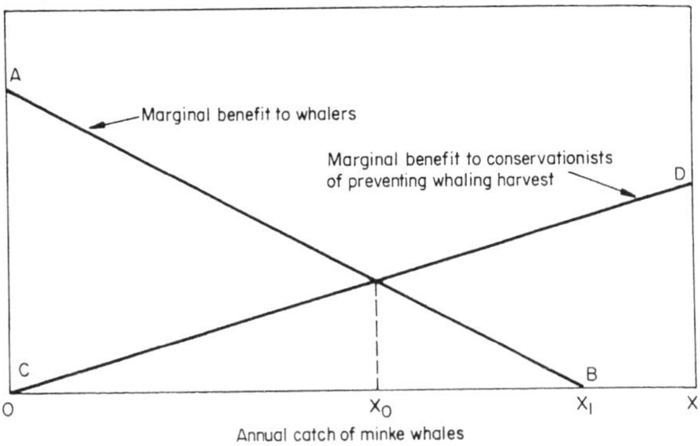

Figure 4. In this case a ban or moratorium on the harvest of minke whales is not Kaldor–Hicks optimal, but a smaller harvest than whalers desire is needed for Kaldor–Hicks optimality.

case shown, an annual harvest of X_0 minke whales is optimal from a Kaldor–Hicks point of view. This is lower than the harvest collectively desired by the whaling industry, namely X_1, but is still a positive level of harvest.

Given the characteristics of minke whales (and possibly some other species of small whales), there seems to be empirically a high probability that a situation similar to that in Figure 4 prevails. The IWC ban on the harvesting of such species is not Kaldor–Hicks optimal.

For completeness, a third case can be added, as illustrated by Figure 5. The marginal benefit to conservationists of preventing whale harvesting is indicated by OCD, and AB represents the net benefits to whalers of harvesting. In this case, harvesting is Kaldor–Hicks optimal. No restriction needs to be placed upon the collective harvest of whales for consumptive purposes. It would be optimal for a body such as the IWC to manage this species of whales, say minke whales, purely as consumptive or private goods.

The question of who should compensate whom or who should have the property rights in whales has not been specifically discussed above.

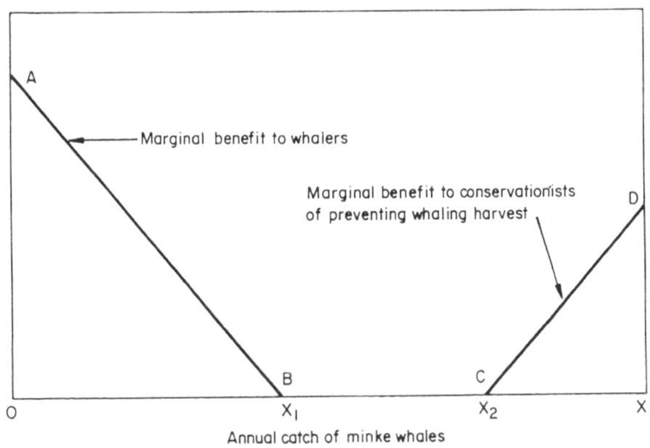

Figure 5. A case in which harvesting of a species of whales purely for consumptive purposes or as a private good is optimal. This however, still requires the collective management of these whales as common property.

If whalers have a fundamental right to hunt whales, then in principle conservationists would need to be able potentially to compensate them for reducing their harvest. If conservationists have the rights to the whales, then whalers would need to compensate conservationists for allowing any harvest of whales or an increase in the harvest of whales. If on the other hand, it was decided that whales should belong to Third World countries, then whalers would need to make a payment to these countries and/or conservationists may also need to make such a payment. It is not, however, possible to canvas this option fully here.

It should be noted that some differences in the Kaldor–Hicks optimum are likely to arise depending upon whether rules are based on willingness to pay or to accept compensation for changes in levels of whale harvesting. This complication, however, does not change the fundamental point of view presented here.

Different degrees of existence value, or more generally non-consumptive value may occur for diferent species of whales. For example, in terms of Figure 2, the marginal social cost of harvesting humpback whales might be represented by the S″ curve, while that of harvesting minke whales might be represented by the S′ curve. The impact of the humpbacked whales in its natural habitat on human beings may be greater than that of minke whales;[42] therefore, the humpback whale may have greater non-consumptive value to human beings. Further consideration of this point, such as differences in value according to whale species, size of whales, living area of whales, etc would be required for the IWC to achieve optimal global management of whale resources as a mixed good.

Exclusion element of mixed good management

A private good is generally characterized by both competition in consumption and exclusion in a market system.[43] The optimal condition for maximizing the sum of producer surplus and consumer surplus for a private good would be satisfied at the market equilibrium where the supply and demand curves for this good intersect. The supply curve represents the marginal cost of production of the private good, and the demand curve depicts the marginal utility of consumers; thus, the optimum will be obtained where the value of marginal utility and marginal cost curves intersect. In order to obtain this optimal solution both of the characteristics of a private good (ie competition in consumption and exclusion under the market system) must exist.

As noted in the preceding section, by contrast, the characteristics of a pure public good (or a collective good) are that it can be consumed or enjoyed without the available supply being reduced, and that once it has been supplied, it is impossible to exclude individuals from consuming it.[44] Optimal production conditions for public goods are found where the sum of all individuals' marginal benefits equals the marginal cost to society.[45] In the case of private goods, however, the marginal benefit to each individual would be equal to their marginal cost. The difference occurs because pure public goods cannot be utilized and marketed under conditions of exclusion and competition. This concept of exclusion is depicted in Figure 6. The horizontal and vertical axes show the consumption of goods by individuals A and B respectively. It is assumed that each individual consumes only one good. In the case of pure public goods, the consumption of individuals A and B would not affect each

[40] *Ibid.*
[41] G. Tullock, 'Problems of majority voting', *Journal of Political Economy*, Vol 67, 1950, pp 571–579.
[42] For example, much whale-watching focuses on humpback whales because of their nature; therefore this species has more opportunity to increase its existence value or non-consumptive value to human beings.
[43] Tisdell, *op cit*, Ref 37.
[44] Brown and Jackson, *op cit*, Ref 36. For further discussion of the concept of public or collective goods, see Mishan (E.J. Mishan, *Introduction to Normative Economics*, Oxford University Press, Oxford, UK, 1981, chapter 56). It should also be noted that some economists such as Layard and Walters (P.R.G. Layard and A.A. Walters, *Microeconomic Theory*, McGraw-Hill, New York, 1978) distinguish between different types of pure public goods.
[45] See Bowen for an account (H.R. Bowen, *Toward Social Economy*, Rinehart, New York, 1948).

Institutional management of an international mixed good

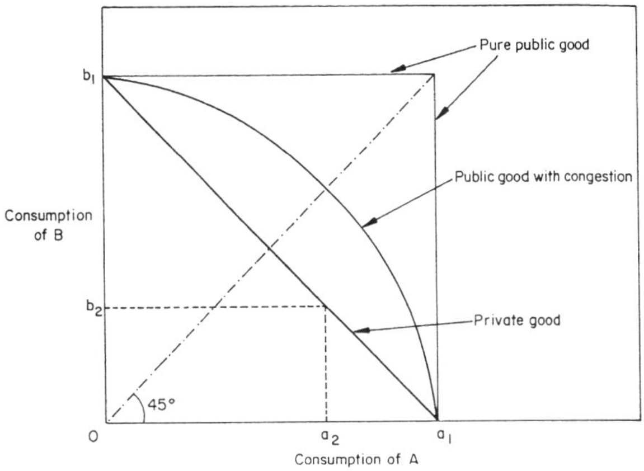

Figure 6. Exclusion and non-exclusion in the consumption of private and public goods.

Source: Adapted from A.B. Atkinson and J.E. Stiglitz, *Lectures on Public Economics*, McGraw-Hill, New York, 1980.

other. That is, A's consumption would always be $0a_1$, and B's would always be $0b_1$ in Figure 6. This indicates that each individual's consumption would always be equal to that of the other, and equal to the supply of public goods.[46] However, in the case of a private good, if B consumed $0b_1$, A's consumption would be zero, and vice-versa, because of the exclusion element of such goods. This suggests that the sum of each individual's consumption of the private good would equal the supply of that private good.

The above discussion of both types of good provides some basis for the analysis of the case of mixed goods. As noted above, mixed goods have some of the characteristics of both private and public goods. The main characteristic of such goods is that the consumption of a mixed good as a private good is not affected by the consumption of the same good as a public good, whereas the consumption of a mixed good as a public good is affected by the consumption of the same mixed good as a private good. This can also be observed in Figure 6. Let us assume that consumer A only consumes a particular mixed good as a public good, and consumer B only consumes the same mixed good as a private good. If consumer B consumes $0b_2$ of this good, then consumer A can only consume $0a_2$, and not $0a_1$, of this good. This indicates that if A wanted to consume for example $0a_2$ of this mixed good, A would try to *eliminate* $0b_1 - 0b_2$ worth of B's consumption. Thus, the concept of mixed goods does involve an exclusion element from the perspective of both private and public goods. Consumers A and B could also be considered to be particular groups, such as consumers who only take into account non-consumptive values (eg existence value) and consumers who only take into account consumptive values (eg neo-classical economic efficiency) respectively. The moratorium decision made by the IWC in 1982 indicates $0a_1$ consumption of whale resources as a mixed good with the characteristics of public goods. In this case, all of B's consumption was eliminated. As noted above, it may be possible to view this situation as the non-optimality of a three-quarters majority vote from a Kaldor–Hicks perspective. This is because those countries in whaling at the time of the decision were not compensated, and some former whaling nations

[46]For further discussion of public goods from a general equilibrium perspective, see Samuelson (P.A. Samuelson, 'The pure theory of public expenditure', *Review of Economic and Statistics*, Vol 36, 1954, pp 387–389; P.A. Samuelson, 'Diagrammatic exposition of a theory of public expenditure', *Review of Economics and Statistics*, Vol 37, 1955, pp 350–356).

still want to harvest whales as private goods. As already stressed, for example, the impact of the humpback whale in its natural habitat on human beings may be greater than that of minke whales; thus, it could be suggested that $0a_1$ consumption of humpback whales and $0a_2$ consumption of minke whales, both as public goods, would be optimal for this group of consumers. This is why it was emphasized that further research on the differences in value between whale species is necessary in order to determine an effective means of international management of these species.

Concluding remarks

Whale resources have been managed as an international common property resource by a global management body, the IWC, with the aim of achieving conservation and economic efficiency. Management by the IWC was required at first to control the total number of whales harvested as a private good (consumptive good), in order to control whale stock size from a biological perspective. However, the IWC policy was unsuccessful because of problems, which included the use of Blue Whale Units for allocation of quotas and because the IWC often ignored the scientific advice of its own Scientific Committee.

Because of political factors and the need to consider values other than private-good economic efficiency, the IWC decided to implement a total moratorium in 1982 as a form of mixed-good management policy for whale resources. Although the moratorium is still in force, discussions in this paper indicate the need for further research to determine the externality costs of harvesting each whale species, so that the IWC can achieve an optimal solution from a potential Paretian improvement perspective.

Whale management requires the continuation of the IWC (or the establishment of another institution) as an international mixed good management body. This is because the global public-goods nature of whale species seems to indicate that some supply of the resource for public-goods consumers is required. At the same time, this supply is influenced by the utilization of whale resources as private goods (consumptive goods). From this perspective, whale resource management seems to require a global common property institution. Moreover, a major problem for most existing international institutions, particularly conservation bodies, seems to be finding a sustainable way of meeting their administration costs. Because whale resources are considered to be an international mixed good, contributions to administration costs may be collected from both groups of consumers. As noted above, the extent of the public goods character (or non-consumptive value in this case) of whales may vary according to species. If this is true, then, for example, group A in Figure 6 may be willing to sacrifice $0a_1 - 0a_2$ worth of the resource as a public good so that group B can consume $0b_2$ of the resource as a private good. An international management body could then collect a fee and/or tax from whalers to cover all or part of its administration costs. At the same time, each member country in group A might also pay an annual membership fee for this purpose. This payment would vary because it would depend on how much each country was willing to pay towards management costs. There could also be a free-rider problem. One way of stabilizing such payments would be the collection of a tax from each individual public-goods consumer in group A or contributions from their governments. This would be possible if non-consumptive utilization such as whale watching, museums, existence value and educational use could be evaluated in dollar terms. However, it may be that many conservationists will reject the Kaldor–Hicks criterion as a social rule. The question would then become the ethical one of whether they ought to accept this criterion. More probably, however, they may claim that they have a right to whales, and that whalers should pay. The group to which property rights should be assigned is basically an ethical question not an economic one. However, since both parties, whalers and conservationists, benefit by whale management, there could be a case for both to contribute to the expenses of managing whale resources.

Marine Resource Economics, Volume 9, pp. 141–158
0738-1360/94 $3.00 + .00

Economics of Antarctic Minke Whale Catches: Sustainability and Welfare Considerations

YOSHIHIRO KURONUMA

National Research Institute of Fisheries Science
Ministry of Agriculture, Forestry and Fisheries
Yokohama
Japan

CLEMENT A. TISDELL

Department of Economics
The University of Queensland
Brisbane
Australia

Abstract *Clark's bioeconomic model is applied to Antarctic minke whales (AMW), the backbone of the commercial whaling in 1982 when the International Whaling Commission (IWC) opted for a ban on whaling commencing 1985/86. The moratorium appears not to be justified from the point of view of saving AMW from extinction or for maximising the net present value of returns to whalers. Catch quotas before the moratorium are found to be lower than needed for survival of the species and for sustainability of the harvests and returns. It seems that the IWC catch quotas and the moratorium were determined not by conventional bioeconomics, but by other factors such as political pressure from conservationists who suffered adverse externalities from whaling. Nevertheless, even taking such externalities into account, the present moratorium seems not to be Kaldor-Hicks optimal.*

Keywords Antarctica, bioeconomic modelling, common property, conservation, externalities, minke whales, welfare and conservation, welfare and whaling, whale management, wildlife management.

Introduction

The main objective of this paper is to apply the economic theory of common-property resources to international whale management, and in particular, to consider the management of Antarctic minke whales (AMW) as an international private good from a bioeconomic perspective. Another objective of this paper is to analyse conservation issues in relation to international whale management in the context of resource economics, not only from the viewpoint of Pareto efficient

We wish to thank two anonymous referees and the editor of *Marine Resource Economics* for their useful comments on an earlier draft of this paper. This draft was mainly completed while Dr. Kuronuma was a research scholar at the University of Queensland.

resource allocation but also from the perspective of international mixed good management.

Kuronuma and Tisdell (1993) discussed the influence of non-market forces on the International Whaling Commission (IWC). However, they did not consider the question of whether or not commercial whaling was economically sustainable under the existing constraints (*e.g.* resource quotas, whaling costs and revenues, and the size of the resource stock) before the imposition of the moratorium. In other words, Kuronuma and Tisdell (1993) did not examine the issue of whether or not the Antarctic minke whale was really facing the prospect of extinction at that time as a result of harvesting of it as a private (consumptive) good. In order to consider this, a conventional dynamic bioeconomic model (the Clark model) will be utilised in this paper. The Clark dynamic model seems to be appropriate for analysing species such as whales which have a low growth rate, and this model has previously been applied to baleen whale harvesting. Although there are many factors which should be taken into account in the model, such as both biological and economic uncertainties, the main purpose of this application is to consider the possibility of bioeconomic management of an international private good, within the context of Clark's assumptions, at the time before the imposition of the moratorium. The focus of this paper is on the AMW not only because of the availability of data on AMW resources, and the possibility that this species might again be commercially exploited in the future, but also as a comparative case study in mixed good management.[1]

In the Clark model (1976-a), the objective of whaling is assumed to be to maximise the present value of discounted net economic revenue from the targeted whale resources. This model has theoretical and quantitative links with both economics and biology. However, conservationists might consider that the above objective gives rise to negative externalities. The decision to impose a moratorium on whale harvesting can be considered to be an extreme means of eliminating a negative externality. But this extreme solution may not be optimal. In other words, the majority decision of the IWC to impose a moratorium on AMW whaling may not be optimal from a socio-economic perspective. From a neo-classical economic perspective, a compromise solution is usually the optimal means of correcting negative externalities, if a Kaldor-Hicks (or potential Paretian improvement) approach is adopted (Tisdell, 1987). A Kaldor-Hicks or potential Paretian improvement occurs when the gainers from a change *could* compensate the losers from it and be better off than prior to the change. The Kaldor-Hicks criterion supposes that changes of this nature increase economic welfare and are desirable even if actual compensation is not paid to the losers. When no further changes of this nature are possible a Kaldor-Hicks optimum exists. The Paretian criterion however, requires compensation to be paid because it supposes that an increase in economic welfare occurs provided at least one person is made better off by a change and none are made worse off. A Paretian optimum occurs when it is impossible to make any one better off without making someone else worse off.

Furthermore, although whale species have been excluded from management by coastal water nations, it seems that the IWC has failed to achieve a Paretian optimum, and has not exhausted all possibilities for a potential Pareto improve-

[1] Note that the public goods aspect of whales, including the AMW case study, were discussed to some extent in Kuronuma and Tisdell (1993).

ment. This assumes the adoption of the Kaldor-Hicks criterion.[2] It is essential to analyse the issue theoretically, because not only does scientific and aboriginal whale harvesting still occur, but there is also the possibility that commercial whaling may take place again in the future. Low consumptive uses of whale resources,[3] such as tourism and museum-related uses, and other types of values[4] also influence the optimal rate of whale harvest.

In the next section, a Clark-type bioeconomic model will be applied to the Antarctic minke whale in order to test the hypothesis of Kuronuma and Tisdell (1993). Their hypothesis is that harvesting of some species of whale is sustainable and that it may be compatible with a Kaldor-Hicks optimum. Furthermore, the decision to impose a moratorium on harvesting of whales was not dictated by bioeconomic factors. Aspects of AMW management will be discussed in the third section, based on the results of the second section, and the fourth section will discuss the conservation aspect of whale management within the context of correcting negative externalities. This section will also consider the aspect of mixed good management.

A Bioeconomic Model and Its Application

The economic model of fishery resources, which combines economic components (Gordon, 1954) with a biological model (Schaefer, 1954, 1957), may also be applied to whale resource management. Using this model, Clark (1976-a, 1981, 1985) derived the following set of equations:

$$dx/dt = rx\,(1 - x/K) - qEx \tag{1}$$

$$P(x,E) = TR - TC = qpEx - cE \tag{2}$$

where

x = number of whales in population at year t
r = intrinsic growth rate
K = carrying capacity
E = effort (catcher-boat days per annum)
q = catchability coefficient
$P(x,E)$ = net economic revenue (per unit of time)
p = price of one unit of output (one Antarctic minke whale)
c = cost of one unit of effort

[2] Theoretically, a corner-point solution is possible even from a Kaldor-Hicks perspective. This would imply no whaling.
[3] See Copes (1981) for more discussion of low consumptive uses, including measurement of the value of whale resource use.
[4] These include existence, option, and bequest values. For more detail see Pearce (1983), Pearce and Nash (1981), Krutilla and Fisher (1975), and Fisher (1981). Although such values have been the subject of much discussion in recent years, the *main* focus of this article is on the correction of negative externalities in relation to an international common-property resource.

As predicted by this static model, fishing effort expands until open-access equilibrium is reached where economic rent equals zero. This condition occurs when equations 1 and 2 equal zero.

Under conditions of sole ownership, the maximisation of the present value of discounted net economic revenue can be considered to be the first priority objective of whale management. If $\delta > 0$ is a constant which denotes the discount rate, the objective of the dynamic model can be expressed in the following equation (Clark, 1976-a):

$$PV = \int_0^{\infty} e^{-\delta t} P(x,E)\, dt$$

$$= \int_0^{\infty} e^{-\delta t} \{p - c\, [x(t)]\} h(t)\, dt$$

where:

PV = present value
δ = continuous discount rate (per annum)
h(t) = harvest rate

This management goal, rather than an objective like MSY, incorporates a trade-off between short-term and long-term benefits. Several important parameters for analysing the economic aspects of whaling are discussed in Clark (1976-a, 1981, 1985: see Appendix A-1 for these parameters and equations).

After determining the basic parameters (see Appendix A-1), Clark (1976-a, 1977, 1981, 1985) applied the above model to Antarctic fin and blue whales. In this study, we will focus only on the Antarctic minke whale, which was one of the more important commercial species in the recent history of the whaling industry, particularly for Japan and the USSR, until the total moratorium was imposed.

Table 1 was derived from equations 1 and 2, assuming the following values for the parameters:

r = 0.06
K = 700,000
q = 1.0 (a normalisation condition for units of E)
p = ¥ 2×10^6
C = ¥ 10^{10} (operating cost)

Although it is possible to imagine a range of different values for these parameters, these particular values were chosen for the following reasons. The biological figures are based on recent (30th–39th) IWC annual reports. The IWC estimated that the possible growth rate of the AMW population was between 0.06 and 0.14, and the population (x_0) of AMW in the 1984/85 season was estimated at between 450,000 and 1,000,000 whales. Because of the uncertainty of the scientific estimation, the lowest values of these parameters are used in this study. Price and cost figures are based on data from a Japanese company for the 1984/85 season, although there were three countries (Japan, the USSR and Brazil) involved in AMW operations at that time. This is because the operating costs of the Japanese company (including labour costs), and the Japanese market price for AMW, were higher than those of the other countries. It should be noted that the cost figure does not include capital costs, particularly the cost of factory ships themselves.

Table 1
Costs, Revenues and Present Values Corresponding to the Clark Model: Antarctic Minke Whales

(1000 head)	(unit: billion Japanese yen))						PV(P_s)		TPV	
x_1	R_1	C_1	P_1	R_s	C_s	P_s	= 5%	= 10%	= 5%	= 10%
450	0	0.0	0	19.30	0.21	19.10	381	191	381	191
350	200	2.51	197	21.00	0.30	20.70	414	207	611	404
250	400	5.88	394	19.30	0.39	18.90	378	189	772	583
150	600	11.00	589	14.10	0.47	13.70	273	137	862	726
80	740	17.30	723	8.50	0.53	7.97	159	79.7	882	802
50	800	22.00	778	5.57	0.56	5.01	100	50.1	878	828
10	880	38.10	842	1.18	0.59	0.59	11.8	5.91	854	848
5	890	45.00	845	0.60	0.60	0.0	0	0	845	845

Adapted from Clark's methodology (1981).

This is because Japanese factory ships were over 35 years old in 1984. However, if Japan decided to build a new factory ship, the effect of this extra cost may be closer to the case where C = ¥ 10^{11} in Appendix A-2. The choice of these parameters therefore seems reasonable at this stage given the best available information. However, the results of sensitivity analysis are recorded in Appendix A-2, in order to examine some different values of the parameters and see how these would affect the model.

Table 1 sets out the relevant characteristics of Clark's model when it is applied to AMW resources. The population x_0 of Antarctic minke whales in the 1984/85 whaling season is assumed here to have been 450,000,[5] and this is assumed to decline to the level x_1 under a hypothetical management system. Based on equations A1 and A2 (see Appendix A-1), the costs (C_1) and the revenues (R_1) corresponding to various levels of x_1 can be obtained (Table 1). Then the net depletion revenue (P_1) can be obtained as $P_1 = R_1 - C_1$ (see equation A3 in Appendix A-1). The net depletion revenue is the net discounted revenue earned by depleting an initial population of AMW to a desired or actual steady level of net economic yield. It is important to notice that the net depletion revenue achieves its maximum value at $x_1 = 5{,}000$ whales, where the unit harvest cost C/x_1 equals the unit price p. This is the so-called open-access equilibrium and/or break-even population level for Antarctic minke whales in this particular case.

Because the Schaefer (1957) model underlies the bioeconomic model used here, the open-access equilibrium population would be sustainable. However, for low levels of population no net recruitment may occur for biological reasons. This may be in excess of 5,000 for AMW so open-access harvesting could bring AMW to extinction.

The IWC appears to have set a protected stock level for AMW of 225,000. This in its view may represent a safe minimum population for survival of AMW—any smaller population would involve a positive risk of extinction of AMW. Whether this is in fact the rationale used by IWC is unclear. Furthermore, the concept of

[5] These estimates are thought to be reasonable approximations to AMW stock sizes because the best scientific estimate showed the stock to be between 450,000 and 600,000 whales in the 1989 IWC report (39th Annual Report).

Table 2
Antarctic Minke Whales: Optimal Population Level and Optimal Annual Sustainable Yields

Annual Discount Rate (%)	Optimal Population Level (x_1*)	Optimal Sustainable Yield (Y*)
0	352,000	10,500
1	295,200	10,200
2	238,300	9,400
3	182,300	8,100
4	128,300	6,300
5	79,200	4,200
10	12,000	700
$+\infty$	5,000	290

Adapted from Clark's methodology (1976-a, 1981).

a safe minimum population level may be flawed (Hohl and Tisdell, 1993a). However, for the purposes of this paper 225,000 AMW will be regarded as the safe minimum population level for the species.

The gross sustainable revenue (R_s) and sustained harvest cost (C_s) can be obtained from equations A6 and A7 (see Appendix A-1). R_s is maximised when x_1 = 350,000 whales, and this is the MSY point for Antarctic minke whales. Net sustainable revenue (P_s) is maximised at a population of x_1 = 352,500. This indicates that net economic yield or economic rent is maximised at a higher population level than the biological optimum (MSY).[6] The results of equations A6 and A7 (see Appendix A-1), *i.e.* the present value of net sustainable economic yield [PV(P_s)] and the total present value (TPV), can be observed from the last two columns of Table 1, at hypothetical annual discount rates of 5% and 10%. The population level which maximises total present value at a discount rate of 5% is x_1 = 79,238 (Table 2). This population level is far below the MSY level of 350,000 Antarctic minke whales. The behaviour of the model can also be observed in Figure 1. It clearly shows that there is an economic incentive to over-exploit this resource in order to obtain a higher TPV. The optimum population levels at other discount rates can be derived from equation A8 (see Appendix A-1) and are given in Table 2. According to Clark (1977, 1981), the benefits from sustainable yield (P/δ) dominate the total present value if the discount rate is small. On the other hand, if the discount rate is large, the net depletion benefits (P_1) dominate the TPV. Because the growth rate of AMW is relatively low, the initial population of AMW may exhibit a high level of optimal depletion.

From the empirical model, it can be shown that the IWC protected level of population of AMW of 225,000 would maximise the net present value (NPV) obtained by whalers if the interest rate is 2.354%. For a higher interest rate, a lower population of AMW would maximise NPV, *e.g.*, at a 5% rate of interest, 79,2000 (see Table 2). In the period concerned the real interest rate exceeded 2.2% so the IWC's protected stock level was above what whalers would have jointly

[6] It should be noted that this applies only to the sustainable yield phase, not the initial depletion phase (Clark, 1981).

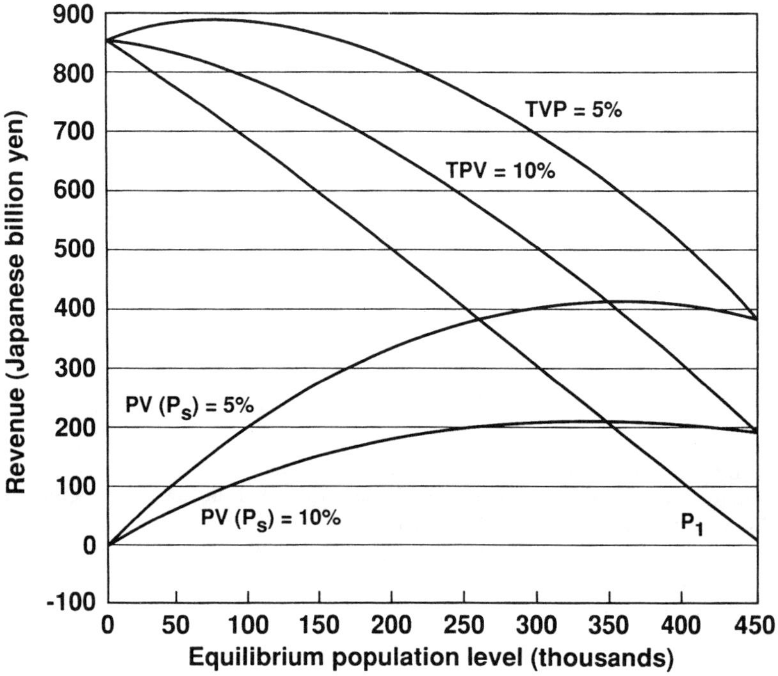

Figure 1. Net Depletion Revenue (P_1), Present Value of Sustainable Yield (PVP_s), and Total Present Value (TPV).

desired to maximise their NPV, if survival of AMW was assured for population levels below 225,000. At an interest rate of 2.2% or less whalers would maximise their joint NPV for a AMW population of 225,000 or more and the IWC's criterion for continuous commercial whaling would be satisfied. Historically 2.2% is a low discount rate especially in a resource industry as uncertain as pelagic whaling (Clark, 1976-b). However, the IWC could factor interest rates into its estimates of the optimal population level and the optimal sustainable yield (harvest level) in the future.

The Management of Whale Resources

In the previous section, the bioeconomic aspects of Antarctic minke whales were discussed. It was shown that at a discount rate of zero, static MEY would occur at a population of around 352,500 AMW, MSY could be obtained at 350,000 AMW, and open-access equilibrium would occur for a population of around 5,000 AMW. Under dynamic (MEY) analysis, optimal harvest (satisfying the IWC constraint of AMW stock being sustained of at least 225,000)[7] would be possible at a

[7] See Japan Whaling Association (1980) for the classification of stock levels of the IWC.

Table 3

Antartic Minke Whales: IWC Yearly Quotas and Actural Annual Catches (unit: head) (Quota Year: December–April)

	Allocated National Quota					Actual Catch			
Year	Japan	USSR	Brazil	South Africa	Total	Japan	USSR	South Africa	Total Catch
1975/76	3,017	3,017	642	134	6,810	3,017	3,017	776[a]	6,810
1976/77	3,950	3,950	1,000		8,900	3,950	3,950	1,000	8,900
1977/78	2,400	2,600	690		5,690	2,400	2,600	690	5,690
1978/79	2,733	2,733	755		6,221	2,733	2,733	739	6,205
1979/80	3,279	3,879	944		8,102	3,279	3,879	902	8,060
1980/81	3,120	3,120	832		7,072	3,120	3,120	749	6,989
1981/82	3,577	3,577	948		8,102	3,577	3,577	854	8,008
1982/83	3,224	3,223	625		7,072	3,224	3,223	625	7,072
1983/84	3,027	3,028	600		6,655	3,027	3,028	N.A.	6,055
1984/85[b]	1,941	3,027	342		5,310	1,941	3,027	N.A.	4,968
1985/86[c]	1,941	3,028	—		4,969	1,941	3,028	—	4,969
1986/87[d]	1,941	3,028	—		4,969	1,941	3,028	—	4,969
1987/88[e]	273	—	—		273	273	—	—	273

Notes:

a 75/76 South Africa quota was transferred to Brazil because S.A. had stopped whaling operation.

[b] 84/85 Scientific Committee's Recommendation 4,224
- Brazil (Area II) 342
- Japan (within IWCs quota) 1,941
- USSR (USSR's own decision) 3,027
- Total Quota 5,310

[c] 85/86 IWC Moratorium
- Japan (USA—Japan Agreegment) 1,941
- USSR (USSR's own decision) 3,028
- Total 4,969

[d] exactly same as c

[e] One factory ship with a special permit (scientific research permit)

Source: 23rd–29th Annual Reports of IWC, 1972–1989 and personal communication with Japan Whaling Association.

discount rate of between 0–2.2%,[8] with a sustainable yield of around 10,000 AMW per year.

These results indicate that continued harvesting of AMW is sustainable at low (shadow) discount rates if our assumptions hold and whalers act as a cartel maximising NPV. On the other hand, if higher discount rates are adopted continued harvesting will lead to a significant reduction of the AMW stock. This section will compare actual data on AMW management with the findings of the previous section.

Table 3 shows the yearly quotas and actual catches of Antarctic minke whales, by country, for the years 1975/76–1984/85. The actual AMW catch varied from 5,000 to 9,000 whales, depending upon the IWC's yearly quotas, over the decade before the implementation of the moratorium. The figures for the 1984/85 whaling season show that 4,968 AMW were caught during this season. An effective discount rate in the 0–2.2% range indicates a sustainable yield of around 10,000 AMW (Table 2). This implies that the objective or effect of IWC management in the 1984/85 whaling season was to increase the population level by allocating

[8] Historically real rates of interest have normally exceeded 2.2% in most countries.

limited quotas.[9] Because total catch figures were equal to and/less than the total quotas allocated by the IWC, the IWC's management of AMW resources seems to have been effective if we assume that its objective was to increase the population size. Therefore, we may conclude that the moratorium decision was influenced by other than bioeconomic factors. This is because, if the IWC's objective for management of AMW has been concerned only with 'the proper conservation of the AMW stock and the orderly development of the whaling industry', the IWC could have allowed whaling to continue under a quota system, at quota levels similar to those in 1984/85.

In fact since the estimated population of AMW in 1984/85 was at least 450,000 and therefore well above its protected level of 225,000, much higher catches could have been allowed by IWC and stocks maintained above their protected level. Furthermore, at this level, the AMW population would be capable of sustaining an annual catch of around 9,000 head annually. This level is well in excess of the quota/catch for 1984/85 and exceeds annual quotas and catches in all of the years from 1975/76 onwards (see Table 3). Therefore, clearly IWC seems to have been motivated in its decisions on the catch (and the moratorium on whaling) by factors other than those designed to maximise the net present value to whalers of AMW and/or the survival of AMW populations for the purposes of whaling. In the next section it is argued that its management decisions also do not seem Kaldor-Hicks optimal when the welfare of 'conservationists' are taken into account.

From the above, it seems the actual rate of harvesting AMW was considerably less than that which would have maximised the NPV of the whalers. This actual rate of harvesting was equivalent to the rate that would prevail at a very low rate of interest, that is, an interest rate lower than that which occurred historically. There are several possible reasons why the NPV of the whaling industry might not have been maximised: 1) the mixed good nature of whale resources, particularly public good considerations, may have already influenced quota allocations before the moratorium decision; 2) the whaling effort for the AMW catch may not yet have reached an equilibrium (*i.e.* this could have taken some time because of the transfer of capital [Bjorndal and Conrad, 1987]); 3) the Japanese objective might not have been to maximise NPV, but to 'maximise' NPV under existing socio-economic constraints including maintenance of employment in whaling; 4) for strategic reasons, the Japanese whaling operators may not have wanted to reveal their desire for a higher catch to obtain greater economic gain in the longer term. In relation to the last matter, conservation lobbyists might have sought an even greater reduction in the whaling quota, or even a moratorium, if whalers had pursued unconstrained NPV maximisation. There is of course also the possibility that the parameters estimated for the above model are not accurate but we do not believe that the errors are so substantial as to make this the main reason for NPV not being maximised. Possibly further refinement of the model along the lines in Clark (1985) would also not alter this conclusion.

A good deal of attention has been paid in the economic literature to the safe minimum level of population of a species (*i.e.* the minimum level of the standing stock to prevent species being driven to extinction). In reality, the minimum

[9] This is because the IWC had been allocating total quotas of less than 10,000 AMW since harvesting started in the 1971/72 season.

viable population of a species level will vary with environmental fluctuations and can be difficult to determine (Hohl and Tisdell, 1993a). This indicates that to a certain extent the minimum sustainable population is uncertain. However, management decisions regarding AMW must be made despite this uncertainty. This raises the question of how to make optimal decisions under uncertain conditions. From the whalers' viewpoint, however, it might be much simpler if they considered the 'protected stock' level, which is one of the three IWC stock classifications to be the 'extinction' level of certain stock, because no commercial whaling would be allowed if stock falls below this level. The minimum viable population for the survival of the Antarctic minke whaling industry would thus be 225,000 AMW given this approach.

Correction of Negative Externalities

The bioeconomic management of AMW as an international private good was discussed in the preceding sections. Bioeconomic analysis links biology and economics through the maximisation of the present value of the discounted net economic revenue; however, this objective ignores any spillover or external benefits from saving the species (Tisdell, 1990). The correction of negative externalities in the context of neo-classical resource management can be applied to the conservation issue in relation to the international management of whales if there is a possibility of compromise between whalers and conservationists. It is obvious that unless negative externalities are somehow corrected, the result will be a Pareto or Kaldor-Hicks inefficient resource allocation.

Corrective action will be needed to achieve the optimum whale catch which will involve a compromise between whalers and conservationists. In economic theory, there are several types of public policy prescription for the correction of negative externalities.[10] Some of the basic corrective measures are: 1) a Coasian private contracting solution (a market-oriented prescription); 2) a Pigouvian solution (a taxation/subsidy oriented solution); 3) a Lindahl equilibrium with competitive markets for correction of the negative externality; and 4) other forms of institutional regulations and direct controls.

The first two measures (Coasian and Pigouvian) are similar in the sense that both aim to achieve Pareto efficient resource allocation by obtaining the optimal equilibrium level of the externality, where marginal damage cost equals the marginal net social benefit. In other words, the Pareto optimum level of pollution is where the marginal net benefit of additional pollution is equal to the marginal cost of providing it. In its strong version, the Coasian theorem argues that a Pareto-relevant negative externality will be eliminated through voluntary exchange between the parties involved (*e.g.* between whalers and conservationists) as long as property rights are well specified,[11] costless transactions are possible, and the income effect is zero so that marginal values are not affected by changes in property rights (Coase, 1960). In this situation, a unique equilibrium is determined irrespective of the initial assignment of property rights or legal liability according to Coase. But in practice initial assignment of property rights does affect the equilibrium substantially (Kuronuma and Tisdell, 1993; Hohl and Tisdell, 1993b)

[10] See Tisdell (1982) chapter 13 for more detail.
[11] Property rights in whales are not well defined in practice.

and depending upon this assignment quite a different economic welfare solution can result.

The strength of the Coasian solution as a policy tool for dealing with negative externalities lies in its powerful conclusion that as long as there are benefits to be gained from trade, bargains will be struck in the market to eliminate these potential gains from trade, thereby arriving at an optimal equilibrium level of the externality, without government interference. This result, however, can only be achieved if there are no impediments to trade in the form of prohibitive transaction costs, and if institutions conducive to trade are maintained in the economy (Randall, 1983).

The question arises, then, as to whether or not it is possible to apply this prescription to the issue of international whale management. Theoretically speaking, it would be possible; however, as Fisher (1981) noted, non-fulfilment of Coase's underlying assumptions would limit its 'practical applicability'. First of all, the assumption of no transaction costs (or barriers to trade) may only be applicable to a two-party setting where each party is either an individual or a firm. In many externality situations (including whaling), many parties and individuals are involved, and transaction costs are therefore prohibitive. There are varying objectives, even amongst conservationists, in relation to whale management.[12] Even granting that only two groups exist, and that transaction costs are very low between, let us say, a group of conservation-minded nations and a group of whaling nations, there is still no assurance that an optimal equilibrium level of the externality will be attained. This is because some members of the IWC may have an incentive to hide their true preferences and thus understate their willingness to contribute to the collective effort to compensate whaling nations in the case of whaling rights (or overstate their demands for compensation in the case of victims' rights). Even in a two-party setting, there would be the possibility of strategic behaviour on the part of the whaling nations, such as deliberately increasing the level of the whale catch in order to extract a higher payment from the other party, providing that no legal liability is imposed on the whaling nations for inhibiting the reduction of the whale catch. When the reduction of rights affects marginal values, the equilibrium solution becomes dependent on the original assignment of property rights. An increase in the rights of whaling nations may

[12] There are many international conservation groups, such as Friends of the Earth, Project Jonah and Greenpeace. According to Shuter (1982), their basic reasons for promoting the conservation of whales at the time before the moratorium decision were as follows:

- Whales are highly evolved social mammals with brains that rival the human brain in complexity of development. The structure of the whale's brain is such that there is the potential for high intelligence. Studies of the small whales in captivity support this view.
- The method of killing whales with explosive harpoons, often after an extensive chase, is an example of cruelty that would require extreme need to justify, particularly as there is evidence to support the idea of strong social ties between members of the group.
- There are substitutes for products derived from whales. Many users have already changed to substitute products.
- The history of whaling is tragic, with right, bowhead, humpback, and blue whales suffering a drastic decline in numbers, and the numbers of fin and sei whales also being heavily reduced. Today whalers hunt sperm and minke whales, which represent the last sizeable stocks of great whales.
- The harvesting theory on the basis of which whales are killed has been rejected by many scientists because of the difficulty in estimating population sizes and the risk involved in using such a simplistic, ecologically unsound theory.

result in less abatement (a higher catch) at the optimum, while a shift in favour of the conservation group would have the opposite effect.

Given the inapplicability of the Coasian solution in cases where the necessary assumptions are violated, there is often resort to government and/or institutional intervention through taxation or regulation. The imposition of a Pigouvian tax on whalers for example which is equivalent to the marginal damage at optimal avoidance or Pareto-optimal level, and the distribution of this tax revenue in a lump sum to the conservationists, will achieve the same result as the contracting (Coasian) market solution.[13] One strength of this solution is that the tax provides a continuing incentive to whalers to cut back on whale harvests by imposing direct controls (Fisher, 1981).

The Pigouvian tax oriented solution to the problem of negative externalities, while theoretically appealing for achieving the optimum, may not be a practical policy tool. There are administrative and transaction costs involved in any activity by an authorised institution (or government). Thus, it becomes necessary for that institution to ascertain whether the action can be taken at a cost which is less than the gains from achieving an optimum resource allocation. In order for the authorised institution to determine the optimum equilibrium and thus the optimum tax to be imposed, it must be able to estimate the marginal damage cost and marginal net social benefit curves (*e.g.* marginal cost as seen by whaling nations, and marginal value to conservationists, respectively).[14]

Determination of the lump sum subsidy to whalers, for example, involves knowledge of a benchmark level of whale catches; which is very difficult to determine without whalers misrepresenting their true marginal benefit curve. Moreover, the level of the lump sum subsidy could influence whalers' decisions in the long run (whether to go out of business or indulge in more whaling activities). The next stage would be to determine how to achieve the optimum, which could become complicated depending upon the nature and scale of activity of the whaling party or parties. Even if the two curves could be clearly determined, in the case of whale management, there is no international organisation which could correct negative externalities by collecting a tax and thereby achieving an optimum equilibrium.[15] Thus, as concluded by Turvey (1963), the imposition of a tax upon the party creating the diseconomy is very complicated and *a priori* prescription of such a tax is not wise.

The third policy prescription, the Lindahl equilibrium solution, involves a competitive equilibrium which would result if a market for resource use was created, for example, through a market for 'whale harvest rights'. This would mean allocating catch rights to conservationists (and/or non-whaling nations), setting a market price for these rights which was equal to the marginal damage of

[13] Again, this assumes that marginal values are not affected by redistribution; hence, the optimal solution is independent of the initial assignment of property rights. Note that while a Pigouvian subsidy is theoretically equivalent to a tax in situations where the income effect is zero, in practice, the two have different allocative effects.

[14] According to Turvey (1963), this involves an evaluation of all the alternatives open to society and examination of their effects on polluters and the adjustments polluters could make to reduce the loss.

[15] This might be one major reason why Clark (1981) recommended the establishment of a 'Marine Mammal Authority'. See also Gulland (1988).

the whale catch (or marginal cost as seen by the whalers) and allowing whalers to purchase the number of rights that would maximise their profits.[16] Roumasset (1979) indicated that this solution would be equivalent to imposing a Pigouvian tax on polluters (*e.g.* whaling nations) and giving the proceeds in a lump sum to the recipients of pollution (*e.g.* conservationists). Fisher (1981) also compared the 'auction' of pollution rights and taxation. Although, in principle, both should have the same result, the 'auction' of whaling rights has the advantage of automatically adjusting to changing standards of environmental quality and inflation. As discussed previously, the limitations of the taxation solution may also apply to the 'pollution rights' approach, because of the types of information and administrative costs involved. It should be noted that several problems may occur if this solution is adopted. Tisdell (1982) states that these problems include "the possibility that competition for pollution rights may not be perfect, equilibrium in the auction market may not be readily achieved, or the pollutants emitted may not form a common pool but may have different externalities and concentrations in particular areas" (Tisdell, 1982, p. 404).

Other forms of government intervention could involve direct control or regulation of whaling catches. To accomplish this, the government (or authorised institution) would need to determine the individual cost functions of each whaler and on this basis impose whatever type of regulation was necessary. In this respect, a tax would be less costly to implement because it would be the same for all whalers once the amount had been determined. In cases where the desired whale catch level was zero (*i.e.* a moratorium), for example, and where rapid reduction in catch levels was desired (possibly due to environmental conditions), direct controls would be desirable (Fisher, 1981). It seems that the IWC's system of control is a variation on this policy prescription (*e.g.* a quota system). The moratorium decision can be viewed as an extreme form of quota system.

In most of the above-mentioned government (or authorised institutional) intervention options for correcting negative externalities, a crucial aspect is the availability of knowledge about the damage function involved. This knowledge is needed in order to design an institutional intervention scheme which can achieve Pareto optimality within the context of neo-classical economics. As stated above, such information is difficult to obtain, and the cost involved may well outweigh the benefits to be gained from correcting the situation. Moreover, some conservationists will reject the Kaldor-Hicks criterion as a basis for making social decisions. In that case, one is driven back to trying to obtain agreement on ethics.

Conclusion

This paper indicates that, from the perspective of conventional bioeconomic analysis, commercial harvest of Antarctic minke whales could have continued at the catch levels of the 1984/85 whaling season on a sustainable basis. This result indicates that factors other than biological and economic concerns influenced the

[16] There are similarities between this and the individual transferable catch quota system. Moreover, the question arises of whether all quotas should be given to conservationists, or to the whalers, or whether some should be allocated to each group. The answer to this may depend upon the choice of decision-makers and/or the community.

decision to impose a moratorium[17]. As discussed in Kuronuma and Tisdell (1993), the decision was strongly influenced by political and non-market forces.

Clark's simple model suggests that owners of the natural stock of a renewable resource which has a low growth rate might have a strong economic incentive to deplete that stock. This suggestion is borne out by the analysis of AMW in this paper, particularly when higher discount rates apply. Whale resources are an international common-property resource with the characteristics of a mixed good. It is appropriate to consider such resources as being owned by the international community (*e.g.* the IWC[18] which includes many nations and is not involved in any whaling activities[19]). In the real world, considerations other than economic ones exist. It seems that the 1982 moratorium decision may have involved non-economic considerations or a failure to balance the purely economic interests of whalers and conservationists.

At present, it seems that there is no scope for compromise between the objectives of conservationists and whalers, because they involve different value judgments. From a neo-classical economic perspective, however, it may be possible to reach a compromise if this issue can be considered as one of correcting negative externalities. Although this view assumes economic efficiency as its first priority, it is one way of approaching the issue. However, it may be that many conservationists will reject the Kaldor-Hicks criterion as a social rule. The question then would be an ethical one rather than an economic one. In practice, it is important to have accurate information on both whale resources and economic factors. In addition, it is necessary to establish an international organisation (or to give authority to the IWC) to correct for negative externalities if it is decided to implement a neoclassical economics approach. One solution might be to establish a Marine Mammal Authority along the lines suggested by Clark (1981, pp. 18–19). It would operate subject to some species preservation constraints. Since "to a large extent the economic future of Mankind appears to be intertwined with the conservation of other species and the preservation of their life support systems . . ." (Tisdell, 1990, p. 21), there are many factors which need to be taken into account in economic research on the management of such resources in the future.

References

Annual Report of International Whaling Commission. 1950, 1972–89 (1st, 23rd–39th Annual Report). The International Whaling Commission. Cambridge, Britain.

Bjorndal, T. and Conrad, J. M. 1987. Capital dynamics in the North Sea herring fishery. *Marine Resource Economics*. 4(1):63–74.

[17] This statement can be supported only if our assumptions, including biological and economic parameters, hold.

[18] The IWC can be considered to be a central body of international common property in relation to whale resources, although in its early years it was the representative of whaling nations. There is no doubt, however, that nations other than IWC members would consider whale resources to be open-access resources. In this context, this argument would only apply to IWC members.

[19] Legally speaking, since the imposition of the moratorium, none of the IWC member countries are commercial whaling nations. It should be noted that almost no member countries of the IWC are involved in any whale resource-oriented activities (e.g., economic and educational use).

Clark, C. W. 1976-a. *Mathematical Bioeconomics: The Optimal Management of Renewable Resources*. John Wiley & Sons. New York, London, Sydney, Toronto.

____. 1976-b. A delayed recruitment model of population dynamics, with an application to baleen whale populations. *J. Math. Biol.* 3:381–391.

____. 1977. The economics of whaling: two species model, in G. S. Innes (ed.) *New Direction in the Analysis of Ecological Systems*. Part I. Simul. Counc. Proc. Ser. 5(1): 111–119.

____. 1981. Economic aspects of renewable resource exploitation as applied to marine mammals, in *Mammals in the Seas*. Vol. III. Food and Agriculture Organisation of the United Nations. Rome.

____. 1985. *Bioeconomic Modelling and Fisheries Management*. John Wiley & Sons. New York, Chichester, Brisbane, Toronto, Singapore.

Coase, R. H. 1960. The problem of social cost. *Journal of Law & Economics*. 3:1–44.

Copes, P. 1981. Some aspects of evaluating low-consumptive uses of marine mammal stocks, in *Mammals in the Seas*. Vol. III. Food and Agriculture Organisation of the United Nations. Rome.

Fisher, A. C. 1981. *Resource and Environmental Economics*. Cambridge University Press. Cambridge, UK.

Gordon, S. 1954. The economic theory of common property resources: the fishery. *Journal of Political Economy*. 62(2):124–142.

Gulland, J. 1988. The end of whaling? *New Scientist*. No. 1636: 42–47 (29 October).

Hohl, A. and Tisdell, C. 1993a. How useful are environmental safety standards in economics?—The example of safe minimum standards for species. *Biodiversity and Conservation*. 2:168–181.

____. 1993b. Resource-use conflicts related to environmental and ethical stances in contemporary economic thought. *Discussion Paper* No. 116. Department of Economics, University of Queensland, Brisbane, 4072, Australia.

Japan Whaling Association. 1980. *Whale Stock: Research and Management*. Japan Whaling Association. Tokyo.

Krutilla, J. V. and A. C. Fisher. 1975. *The Economics of Natural Environments*. The Johns Hopkins University Press. Baltimore, Maryland, USA.

Kuronuma, Y. and C. A. Tisdell. 1993. Institutional management of an international mixed good: The IWC and socially optimal whale harvests. *Marine Policy*. 17(4):235–250.

Pearce, D. W. 1983. *Cost-Benefit Analysis*. 2nd edn. St. Martin's Press. New York.

Pearce, D. W. and C. A. Nash. 1981. *The Social Appraisal of Projects. A Text on Cost-Benefit Analysis*. Macmillian. London.

Randall, A. 1983. The problem of market failure. *Natural Resources Journal*. 23:131–148.

Roumasset, J. A. 1979. Sharecropping, production externalities, and the theory of contracts. *American Journal of Agricultural Economics*. 61(4):640–647.

Schaefer, M. B. 1954. Some aspects of the dynamics of populations important to the management of the commercial marine fisheries. *Inter-American Tropical Tuna Commission Bulletin*. 1:27–56.

____. 1957. Some consideration of population dynamics and economics in relation to the management of the commercial marine fisheries. *J. Fish. Res. Bd. Canada*. 14(5):669–681.

Shuter, K. D. 1982. Australia's new whaling policy. *Marine Policy*. October.

Tisdell, C. A. 1982. *Microeconomics of Markets*. John Wiley & Sons. Brisbane, New York, Chichester, Toronto, Singapore.

____. 1987. Tourism, the environment and profit. *Economic Analysis and Policy*. 17(1): 13–30.

____. 1990. Ecological economics and the environmental future. *Discussion Paper in Economics*. No. 28. Department of Economics, The University of Queensland, Australia.

Turvey, R. 1963. On divergences between social cost and private cost. *Economica*. 30(August):309–313.

Appendix

A-1 The Clark Model (1976-a, 1981)

The initial 'depletion' stage produces a gross revenue of R_1 and a cost of C_1 given by:

$$R_1 = p\,(x_0 - x_1) \tag{A1}$$

$$C_1 = c \int_{x_1}^{x_0} dx/x \tag{A2}$$

where x_0 is the existing population level, and x_1 is the equilibrium population level; therefore, the net depletion revenue is:

$$P_1 = R_1 - C_1 \tag{A3}$$

The gross sustainable revenue and the corresponding sustained harvest cost are:

$$R_s = prx_1 * (1 - x_1/K) \tag{A4}$$

$$C_s = cE_s = cr * (1 - x_1/K) \tag{A5}$$

and the present value of the sustained future net economic yield is:

$$PV(P_s) = \int_0^{\infty} e^{-\delta t}P\,dt = P_s/\delta \tag{A6}$$

The total present value is the sum of A6 and the net depletion revenue A3:

$$TPV = PV(P_s) + P_1 \tag{A7}$$

The optimal equilibrium population level x_1^* is given by:

$$x_1^* = K/4 * (\lambda + \sqrt{\lambda^2 + \mu}) \tag{A8}$$

$$\textit{where} \quad \lambda = c/pqK + 1 - \delta/r$$

$$\textit{and} \quad \mu = 8c\delta/pqKr$$

The optimal equilibrium population level x_1^* does not depend upon the initial level

x_0, but upon the ratio, δ/r, between the economic discount rate and the biological growth rate. Clark (1981) stressed that in the case of a population which is initially in a depleted state relative to its optimum, (i.e. $x_0 < x_1^*$), the optimal policy requires a moratorium until the population recovers to the optimal level x_1^*.

A-2 AMW Sensitivity Analysis

The following values for the different parameters are assumed in this paper, section 2 as the original set of values:

$$r = 0.06$$
$$p = ¥\ 2 \times 10^6 \text{ (Japanese yen)}$$
$$C = ¥\ 10^{10} \text{ (Japanese yen)}$$
$$X_0 = 450{,}000 \text{ AMW}$$
$$K = 700{,}000 \text{ AMW}$$

Although the choice of these values for the different parameters uses the best estimates based upon the information available, the following sensitivity analysis has been conducted (A–Table 1) in order to examine the possible effects on the model of using different values for some of these parameters. Details of the full analysis are available from the authors upon request.

The first column of the table shows a range of different values for some of the original parameters. The first row shows the original results of the bioeconomic application described in the text (section 2). The next four rows provide the results of four different values for the biological parameters (r and K). As can be clearly observed from the last two columns (δ and Y*) of these four rows, different values of the biological parameters strongly affect both the discount rate and the possible optimal sustainable yield. This can be clearly seen in the cases where r = 0.02 and r = 0.14. In the case where K = 1,000,000 AMW, a moratorium is required. This is because this population is initially in a depleted state relative to

A—Table 1
Results of AMW Sensitivity Analysis

Case	MSY	MEY	Open-access Equilibrium	δ Possible discount rate[a] (%)	Y* Possible optimal sustainable yield (AMW head)
r = 0.06	350,000	352,500	5000	0–2	10,500–10,200
r = 0.02	350,000	352,500	5000	0–0.3	3,500–3,400
r = 0.14	350,000	352,500	684	0–3	24,500–23,500
K = 500,000	250,000	252,500	5000	0–1	7,500–7325
K = 1,000,000	500,000	502,500	4995	—	—
p : × 2 (p = ¥4 × 10⁶)	350,000	351,250	2507	0–1	10,500–10,225
p : × 1/10 (p = ¥2 × 10⁵)	350,000	375,000	50,012	0–2	10,446–10,070
C: × 10 (C = ¥10¹¹)	350,000	375,000	50,012	0–2	10,446–10,070
C: × 1/10 (C = ¥10⁹)	350,000	350,250	513	0–1	10,500–10,200

[a] Discount rates in this range would satisfy the IWC's criteria for both 'sustained' and 'initial' management stocks.

the optimum (i.e., $X_1^* = 502{,}500 > X_0 = 450{,}000$). These results indicate that it is very important to have accurate biological data on AMW in order to determine management options. The values of the economic parameters (the last four rows) show the results of four different values of price and costs. These changes do not greatly affect the discount rate (δ) or the optimal sustainable yield (Y^*) (i.e. the range of δ is between 0 to 2%, and the range of Y^* is between 10,500 and 10,070 AMW). As predicted by the model, however, both an increase in price and a reduction in cost would result in a lower open-access equilibrium level (i.e., 2,507 AMW), and a lower MEY level (i.e. case $2 \times p$: 351,250 AMW, case c/10: 350,250). This behaviour indicates the classical depletion process in an open-access fishery (eventually leading to extinction in this particular case). An increase in cost ($10 \times c$) and a reduction in price (p/10) have exactly the same effect. (MEY increases to 375,000 AMW and OA equilibrium also increases, to 50,012 AMW.) Note that these particular cases produced exactly the same results, due to proportional changes in price and cost.

Economic Analysis & Policy Vol.29 No.1, March 1999 **59**

OPTIMAL AUSTRALIAN DUGONG POPULATIONS AND CONSERVATION PLANS: AN ECONOMIC PERSPECTIVE

Clem Tisdell
Department of Economics
The University of Queensland
Qld 4072

Australia provides one of the last refuges globally for the sea mammal *Dugong dugon*, an inhabitant of the Queensland coast and other northern Australian waters. In response to declining dugong numbers, some ecologists have strongly advocated extensions of dugong protected areas in Queensland. In these areas, gill net fishing is banned. This raises the question of what is the optimal population of dugong (and similar species) and whether economic factors should play a role in its determination. Ecologists recommending extended dugong protected areas pay no attention to economic factors so their analysis is far from holistic. As discussed, economics is relevant to assessing the cost-effectiveness of alternative conservation strategies and social cost-benefit analysis can throw further light on the social dimensions of the problem, even though A.C. Pigou's view that welfare economics only yields partial answers should be heeded. Furthermore, even application of precautionary principles and safe minimum standards requires account to be taken of economic considerations, as recognised by amendments to the Endangered Species Act of the US. The ecologists in this dugong protection case ignore all such considerations.

1. INTRODUCTION

Two important ecological reports, *The Dugong (Dugong dugon): An Action Plan for its Conservation* (Marsh *et al., n.d.*) and *A System of Dugong Sanctuaries for the Recovery and Conservation of Dugong Populations in the Great Barrier Reef World Heritage Area* (Preen and Morissette, 1997) have been prepared in recent times on the status of the dugong in Australia. Each is accompanied by proposals to foster conservation of populations of dugong. The latter report proposes ten dugong sanctuaries for the southern Great Barrier Reef and Hervey Bay (see Figure 1). Banning of gill nets is recommended in these sanctuaries.

Of the two reports, that by Marsh *et al. (n.d.)* is the least categorical. It points out that while dugong numbers have declined in The Great Barrier Reef (GBR) region south of Cooktown, 'the causes of the decline are unknown, but could include habitat loss, incidental drowning in commercial gill nets and indigenous hunting', (p.2). It states that 'apart from dugongs drowned in shark nets in Queensland, there are *no* quantitative data on anthropogenic impacts' (pp.1-2).

FIGURE 1

LOCATION OF THE TEN DUGONG SANCTUARIES PROPOSED FOR THE SOUTHERN GREAT BARRIER REEF AND HERVEY BAY (SHOWN IN BLACK)
(Preen and Morissette, 1997)

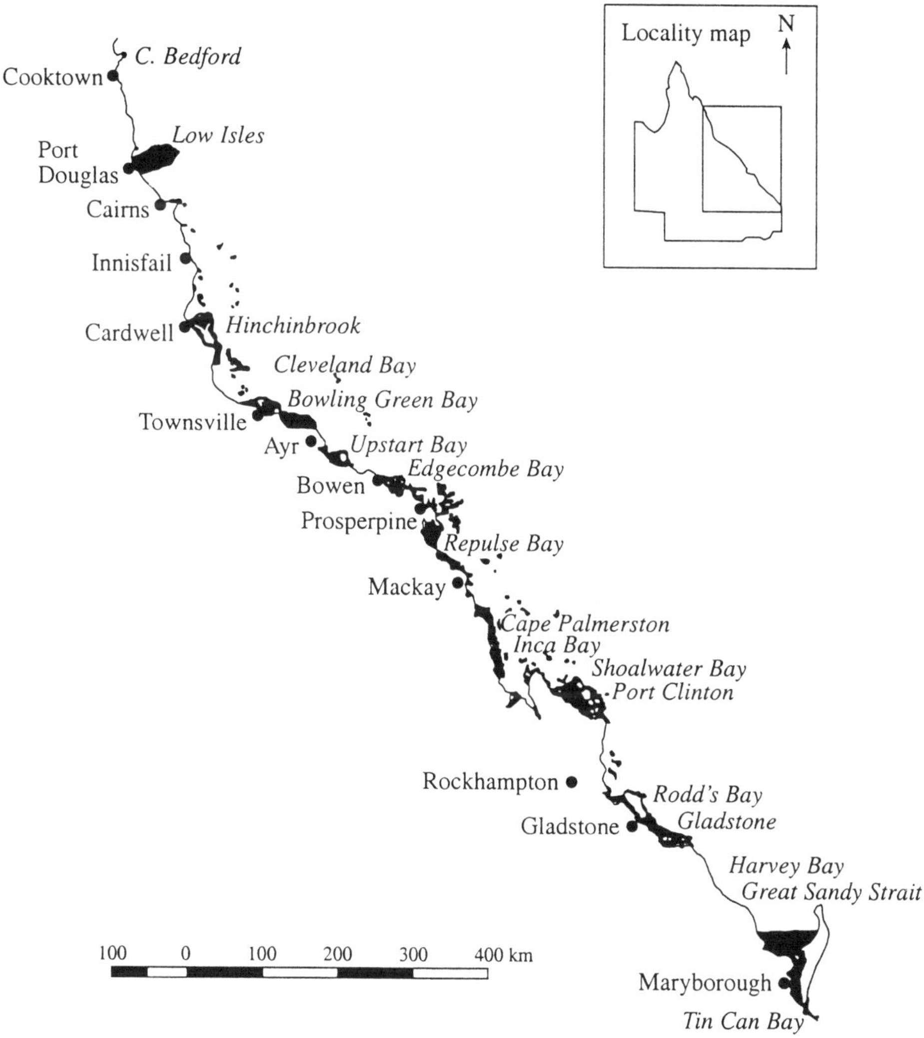

A well thought out list of research priorities essential for informed management of dugong populations are set out (Marsh *et al., n.d.,* pp.5-6).

Despite the fact that this research has not been completed Preen and Morissette (1997) make major policy recommendations for a system of dugong sanctuaries which are expected to impact adversely on the livelihood of a large number of fishermen in Queensland, as well as resulting in displacement of fishermen and possible crowding of fishermen in areas not set aside as dugong sanctuaries. Flow-on adverse economic consequences for local communities in regional coastal Queensland are anticipated. They make these recommendations with a view to achieving an optimal population of dugongs. For them this seems to imply the requirement that dugongs be not critically endangered locally anywhere within their current population range in Australia. This however, begs the question of how the 'optimal' population of dugongs is to be determined.

2. THE OPTIMAL POPULATION OF DUGONGS

Figures given by Marsh *et al.,* indicate that Australia's total dugong population is of the order of 83,000 head. Most of this population is located in the 'top' of Australia from the north of Cape Bedford in Queensland around to Shark Bay in Western Australia. The population in the southern Great Barrier Reef region is estimated to be relatively low at about 1,600 head and in *this region* dugong is listed by Marsh *et al. (n.d)* as a critically endangered species. However, this is unlikely to be the classification of the World Conservation Union (IUCN). The IUCN Red Book describes a critically endangered species as a one 'facing extremely high risk of extinction in the wild in the immediate future'. Because dugongs in the southern GBR probably do not form an isolated distinct population, they are unlikely to achieve separate classification as critically endangered under IUCN criteria. In any case, the dugong is not endangered throughout the whole of its population range in Australia according to Marsh *et al. (n.d.)* (see Figure 2) even though it may be endangered in some localities. The exact contributors to low numbers of dugong in the southern GBR region are not clear as yet, although a cyclone in the Hervey Bay area in 1992 significantly lowered dugong numbers there by reducing the extent of seagrass meadows (Zann, 1995, p.24). Periodic destruction of seagrass meadows by cyclones and then their subsequent recovery along with that of the size of local dugong populations appears to be normal.

Preen and Morissette (1997, p.8) state 'To allow dugong populations to recover to their optimum sustainable level all significant dugong habitat, both past and present, should be protected in sanctuaries. Protection of only a subset of dugong habitats, like those that contain substantial dugong numbers may prevent dugong extinction in the southern GBR, but will not allow for recovery'. Elsewhere they also speak of the optimal sustainable population of dugong, but nowhere does their concept of the optimal population appear to be defined.

From their text, it is clear that Preen and Morissette want not just to maintain the minimum population of dugong required to ensure the reasonable probability of survival of dugong in Australian waters as a whole, but want to conserve at least the minimum populations of dugong throughout their whole range in Australia considered necessary for their survival in every region where they now occur. Their aim is to try to *prevent any local* extinctions of dugong populations. Whether or not their proposals are sufficient or more than sufficient to prevent local extinctions is a matter for ecologists. What is the probability that local extinctions will occur without the DPAs proposed and where would these extinctions occur? What difference do the restrictions make to these probabilities? Could similar reductions in probabilities be obtained by alternative means and at lower cost? No specific information seems to be available in relation to these questions.

FIGURE 2

MAP SHOWING THE STATUS OF THE DUGONG IN VARIOUS PARTS OF AUSTRALIA ACCORDING TO THE IUCN (1995) CRITERIA AS INTERPRETED BY MARSH *ET AL.* (N.D.)

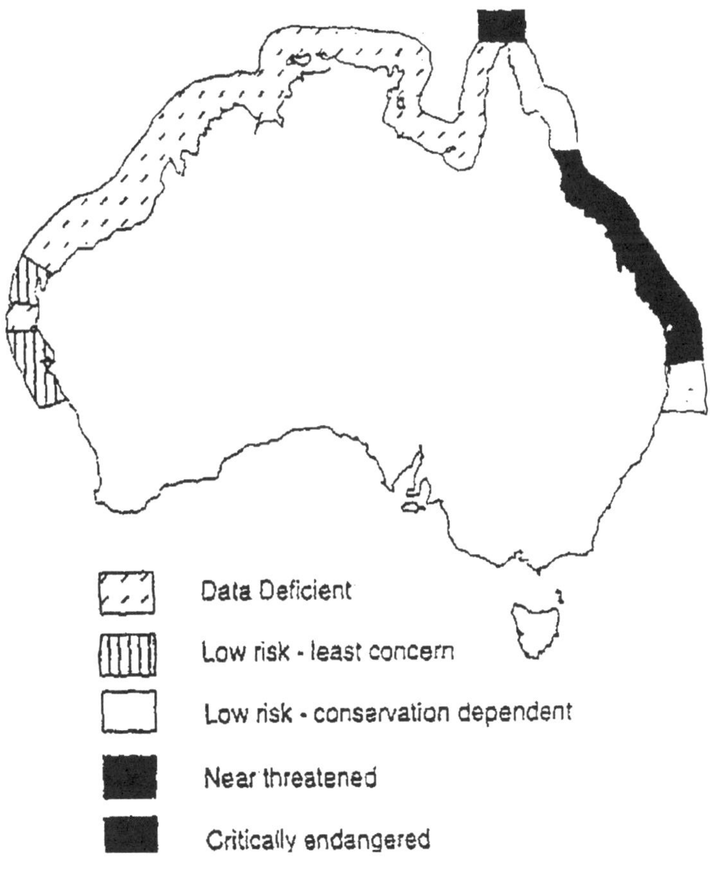

Preen and Morissette (1997) *seem to* waiver between several ideas about optimal populations of dugong in the southern GBR region, which is the main focus of their attention and policy recommendations. These are:

(1) The minimum populations of dugong required to ensure the survival of dugong throughout their range in the southern GBR region, taking into account the mobility of these animals.

(2) The (maximum sustainable) population which would emerge in the absence of anthropogenic disturbance.

(3) A dugong population somewhere in between these limits.

What we are not told is what criterion is used to decide that these populations are optimal. From what point of view or points of view are they optimal? From the point of view of dugongs? How is the human interest factored in? Are humans to be considered as part of the ecological system or not? What human values should be factored into the optimisation problem and how? Without account being taken of these factors, proposals for optimisation of dugong populations are narrowly based and unclear. Economic and social evaluation is not included in the problem by Preen and Morissette unless they assume that saving of dugongs is of infinite value.

Although Preen and Morissette mention Australia's obligations under international conventions as providing support for their proposal, there is no discussion of how legally binding these conventions are and how Australia's obligations are to be interpreted. In any case, it is doubtful if the international Convention on Biodiversity Conservation obligates nations to 'save' species *throughout their entire range*.

In addition, note that there is usually no minimum population of a species that guarantees its future existence (Hohl and Tisdell, 1993). All that one can conclude is that the probability of survival of a species can be expected to rise as its habitats and its population are more fully protected. So we have to ask what probability of survival of a species, in this case dugong, are we aiming for and why? The above theory implies that application of the *precautionary principle* and requires an assessment of the risks and uncertainties associated with the alternative management options. No attempt to do this has been made in the policy recommendation of Preen and Morissette.

However, it should be pointed out that Wills (1997, p.313), regards the precautionary principle as a strong form of the safe minimum standard. He points to the 1973 Endangered Species Act (ESA) in the USA (as an example of its application) in relation to which the US Supreme Court ruled that 'Congress intended the ESA to protect listed species regardless of cost. This led to ESA being amended to grant exemptions where 'overriding economic or national-interest concerns were deemed to outweigh species preservation' (Wills, 1997, p.314). Wills goes on (p.314) to summarise his point of view as follows:

> 'The apparent wastefulness of ESA is not conclusive evidence against a precautionary approach, but rather against precautionary policies that take no account of the value of alternatives sacrificed. Remember that humanity has gained in the past and will continue to gain from ecosystem conservation'.

Natural scientists considering optimal dugong populations have failed to consider financial and social costs and benefits of their policies. It seems that even the safe minimum standard rule as now sometimes interpreted requires that consideration be taken of the social and economic costs of species preservation (cf. Randall, 1993). Preen and Morissette do not, however, consider any of this literature and seem quite unaware of even the seminal work of Ciriacy-Wantrup (1968).

3. ECONOMICS AND THE OPTIMAL POPULATION OF SPECIES, IN THIS CASE, DUGONG

Economics, not considered in the reports mentioned above, can be factored into decisions about optimal population or conservation of species in two ways. These are:

(1) *cost minimisation* in relation to some standard or target for the population of a species and,

(2) *economic optimisation* of the population of the species.

Neither of these approaches have been applied in determining the optimal population of dugong in Australia or in the GBR region.

Cost minimisation or cost effectiveness involves searching for strategies which will minimise the cost of achieving the population of dugong aspired to. This for example, would involve search for conservation strategies which would minimise costs imposed on fishermen. Has for example, the best configuration of DPAs been proposed to achieve protection of dugong populations and minimise the cost imposed on fishermen? Should research be undertaken to search for effective methods to deter dugong from entering the area of gill netting? Are there techniques available or which could be developed to reduce unwanted incidental catch? Why is such research not being funded and why is there not a programme for such research? The incidental catch problem is a widespread problem and more attention needs to be given to it from a scientific research point of view.

The second approach to this type of problem adopted by some economists is to treat it as an economic optimisation problem using social cost-benefit analysis (Cf. Campbell *et al.*, 1997). For this method to be applied, it is ideal if all social costs and benefits can be expressed in monetary units. If this is not possible, then one goes as far as is practical in quantifying social costs and benefits in monetary terms and makes a list of the 'intangibles' that cannot be quantified so these can be taken into account in the final judgement.

This approach is illustrated by diagrams which look at *possible* costs and benefits of reducing the incidental catch of dugong by fishermen. There are several possibilities to consider. Firstly, it is possible that the economic costs imposed on fishermen in terms of reduced profit, income foregone, and so on exceeds the willingness of conservationists to pay for any reduction in the incidental catch of dugong in an area. This would imply that on purely economic grounds no reduction in the incidental catch of dugong would be justified. This case is illustrated in Figure 3. Line DEF represents the additional costs imposed on fishermen of having to reduce their incidental catch of dugong and line ABC represents the additional benefits to conservationists (e.g., their marginal willingness to pay) for a reduction

Economic Analysis & Policy Vol.29 No.1, March 1999 **65**

FIGURE 3

NO REDUCTION IN THE INCIDENTAL CATCH OF DUGONG IS OPTIMAL (ECOMONIC) IN THIS CASE

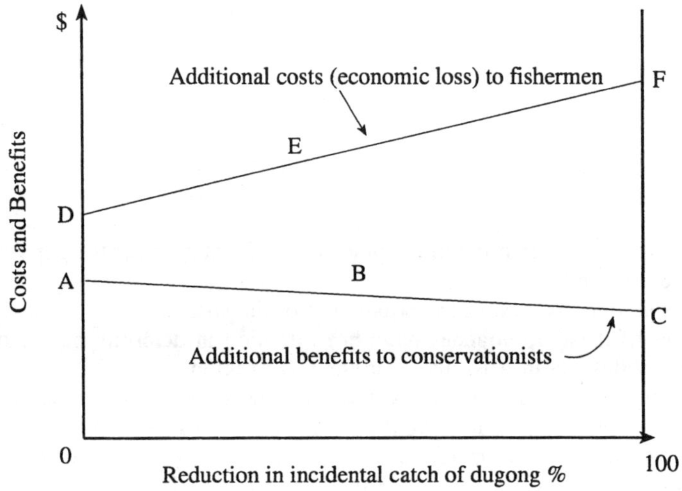

FIGURE 4

IN THIS CASE, SOME REDUCTION IN THE INCIDENTAL CATCH OF DUGONG IS ECONOMIC SOCIALLY BUT ANY GREATER REDUCTION RESULTS IN A SOCIAL DEADWEIGHT LOSS.

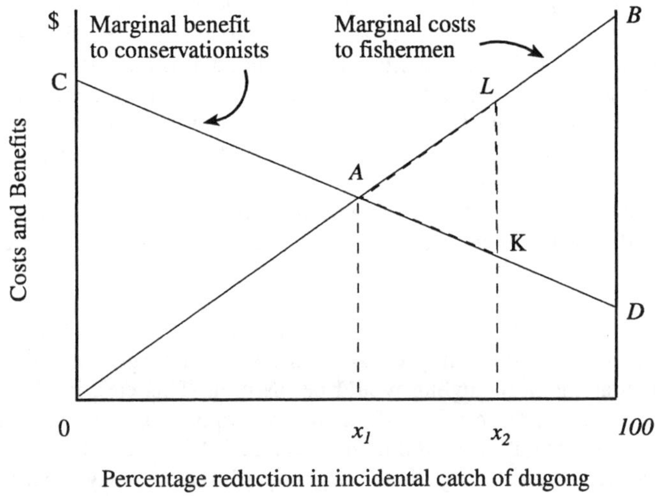

in the incidental catch of dugong. In this case, it is not economic to reduce incidental catch of dugong. This is because the cost imposed to fishermen always exceeds the *economic* benefit to conservationists.

Although in the case illustrated in Figure 3 no reduction in the incidental take of dugong is economic, if a new method of reducing the incidental take of dugong happened to be developed, this could reduce the cost to fishermen of reducing the incidental catch of dugong. Consequently, it may become economic to reduce the incidental catch of dugong. Such a new method would move the line DF downward possibly sufficiently far to intersect line AC, other things constant. This intersection point would correspond to the optimal economic reduction in the incidental catch of dugong after the introduction of the technique. A reduction in the incidental catch of dugong would then be economic. New techniques of this kind result in a 'win-win' situation, that is, benefit both conservationists and fishermen. However, little or no sustained research appears to have been undertaken to find such methods.

Figure 4 illustrates a case in which it is economic from a social point of view to reduce the incidental catch of dugong. Line OAB represents the additional costs to fishermen of reducing their incidental catch of dugong and line CAD represents the additional benefit to conservationists of doing this. In this case, a reduction in the incidental catch of dugong by x_1 per cent maximises social net economic benefit; for this reduction the marginal benefit to conservationists equals the marginal cost imposed on fishermen[1]. If the incidental catch of dugong is reduced

---

1 The optimality condition can easily be outlined in mathematical terms. If $h(x)$ represents the costs imposed on fishermen of reducing the incidental catch of dugong and if $g(x)$ represents the benefit to conservationists, then the net social benefit (NSB) of reducing the incidental catch of dugong is NSB = $g(x) - h(x) = f(x)$. The necessary condition for maximisation of this (given an interior solution) is $\frac{df}{dx} = \frac{dg}{dx} - \frac{dh}{dx} = 0$. This implies that the rate of change of benefits to conservationists should be equal to the rate of increase in costs imposed on fishermen.

The second order condition for the maximum is that $f'' < 0$. Since $g'(x)$ is downward sloping and $h'(x)$ has a positive slope, this condition will be automatically satisfied if the first order condition is met.

Mathematically the optimisation problem is straightforward. In practice, the main problem is to estimate the functions accurately from an empirical point of view. Furthermore, there is scope for philosophical argument about how best to specify benefits to conservationists. Should for example willingness to pay form the basis of such estimates or should willingness to accept compensation be used for specification (Tisdell, 1991)? Observe that deadweight social loss (DSL) represented by the hatched area in Figure 4 would mathematically be obtained as follows:

$$DSL = \int_0^{x2} h'(x)dx - \int_0^{x2} g'(x)dx.$$

Economic Analysis & Policy Vol.29 No.1, March 1999 **67**

further, a social deadweight economic loss occurs. If, for example, authorities require and achieve a reduction in the incidental catch of x_2 per cent, the social deadweight loss is equal to the equivalent of area of triangle AKL, the hatched area in Figure 4. It is clear from the above discussion that without proper attention to the costs and benefits of reducing the incidental catch of dugongs, a social economic loss can occur. It is even possible for regulation to be socially less favourable than no regulation from an economic standpoint.

In addition, if the measures, means and techniques for reducing the incidental catch are *prescribed,* they may not be the most efficient or cost-effective , from an economic point of view. For example, the prescribed methods may, in relation to the case illustrated in Figure 4, result in higher extra costs being imposed on fishermen so that their marginal cost curve is higher than shown by line OAB. For ease of illustration, a similar diagram to Figure 4 is provided as Figure 5. The prescribed methods may result in extra costs being imposed on fishermen, and when these are accounted for, their marginal costs might be as shown by line OEF.

If this is so and authorities reduce the incidental catch by x_2 per cent, the deadweight economic loss from regulation is equal to the equivalent of the shaded area, the area of triangle OLM, plus the equivalent of the area of the hatched triangle

FIGURE 5

PUBLIC REGULATION FO INCIDENTAL CATCH CAN BE EXCESSIVE FROM AN ECONOMICS POINT OF VIEW AND ADD UNNECESSARILY TO THE COST IMPOSED ON FISHERMAN

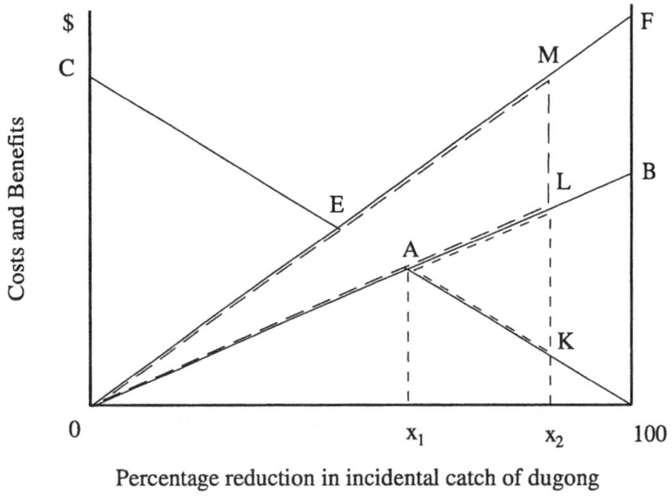

AKL[2]. Consequently, 'social loss' is raised by even more than the area of triangle AKL due to cost-effective methods not being prescribed. There is a high risk of this occurring as far as the policy recommendations of Preen and Morissette for attaining 'optimal' population of dugongs are concerned.

Observe that the steeper is the additional cost imposed on fishermen of having to reduce the incidental catch of dugong (that is the steeper is the marginal cost curve, OF, in Figure 5), the smaller is the optimal reduction in the by-catch of dugong.

If an economic approach to optimality is adopted, it is important to evaluate the social economic costs and benefits of reducing the incidental catch of dugongs. Policy measures must be formulated by weighing up these two components; (costs and benefits). Clearly, from a social economic standpoint, too much reduction in the by-catch can be forced on fishermen, and excessive costs can be imposed upon them if strategies or policies are proposed without economic assessment. These types of assessments are missing in the reports prepared by Marsh, *et al.,* and Preen and Morissette.

4. CONCLUDING COMMENTS

From the above, it seems that *not* even the *precautionary principle* requires hasty emergency action to be taken to save dugongs from imminent extinction in Australian waters. Even the likelihood of local extinctions could be a subject for serious debate. Note also that proper attention to the precautionary principle requires an assessment of the risks and uncertainties associated with alternative management options, something which has not been done by policy-makers in this case.

A decision to create or extend dugong protected areas and tighten controls on fishing effort is bound to have major economic repercussions regionally. Therefore, there is a need to assess economic factors, take these into account and gather further ecological evidence before coming to policy conclusions. This has not been done in most cases by those making recommendations for management of dugong.

While economics cannot be the sole arbiter on social decisions, it is nevertheless unreasonable to ignore economics, especially given that many of the impacts of regulations are likely to have irreversible economic consequences. The economic issues should be explored further, more ecological research is needed and in particular research is needed to find cost-effective methods of maintaining populations of dugong. Hasty decision-making in this area seems both unwise and unnecessary.

---

2 Let $r(x)$ represent the extra cost imposed on fishermen by regulation, that is costs in excess of the efficient ones. Then the total economic loss from regulation equals

$$\int_0^{x_2} r(x)dx$$

plus DSL as specified in note 1.

REFERENCES

Campbell, H.F., McIlgorm, A. and Tsmenyi, B.M. (1997) 'Fishing Management, Environmental Protection and Trade Liberalization', *International Journal of Social Economics*, Vol. 24, pp.128-138.

Ciriacy-Wantrup, S.V. (1968) *Resource Conservation: Economics and Policies*, 3rd edn., University of California, Division of Agricultural Science, Berkeley, CA.

Hohl, A. and Tisdell, C.A. (1993) 'How Useful are Environmental Safety Standards in Economics? The Example of Safe Minimum Standards for Protection of Species', *Biodiversity and Conservation*, Vol. 2, pp.168-181.

Marsh, H., Corkeron, P., Breen, B. and Morissette, N. (*n.d.*) *The Dugong (Dugong dugon): An Action Plan for its Conservation in Australia* (Draft Report), Department of Tropical Environment Studies and Geography, James Cook University, Townsville, Australia.

Preen T. and Morissette, N. (1997) *A System of Dugong Sanctuaries for the Recovery and Conservation of Dugong Populations in the Great Barrier Reef World Heritage Area and adjacent Southern Waters*, Department of Tropical Environment Studies and Geography, James Cook University, Townsville.

Randall, A. (1993) 'Thinking about the Value of Biodiversity' in K.C. Kim and R.D. Weaver, *Biodiversity and Landscape*, Cambridge University Press, Cambridge.

Tisdell, C.A. (1991) *Economics of Environmental Conservation*, Elsevier, Amsterdam.

Wills, I. (1997) *Economics and the Environment: A Signalling and Incentives Approach*, Allen and Unwin, St. Leonards, NSW.

Zann, L.P. (1995) *Our Sea, Our Future: Major Findings of the State of the Marine Environment Report for Australia*, Department of Environment, Sport and Territories, Canberra.

[17]

Conserving Asian elephants: economic issues illustrated by Sri Lankan concerns

Ranjith Bandara and Clem Tisdell[1]

Abstract

Provides background on the nature and status of the Asian elephant *Elephas maximus* and compares it with the African elephant *Loxodonta africana*. An overview is also given of the literature examining economic issues involved in the conservation of elephants. It is found that much more attention is concentrated on the African elephant than the Asian one, even though populations of Asian elephants may be in greater danger. The analysis then focuses on Sri Lanka, as a case study, and outlines the decline in wild elephant populations in this country, and considers reasons for it. Elephants are viewed as a mixed economic good, and the total economic value of Asian elephants is discussed. Pitfalls of total economic valuation analysis are noted. These are pertinent to the conservation of elephants because elephants have both positive and negative attributes and human management of their population involves cost. The question is taken up of whether Sri Lanka's present protected areas have the capacity to ensure the survival of its population of wild elephants. It is found that they do not have this capacity, and that the long-term survival of its wild elephant populations depends on their being able to use private land as well as protected areas. So the long-term conservation of wild elephants calls for integrated policies involving both public and private landholders. This is true for many mobile wild species.

Introduction and background

Economists have mostly concentrated on economic issues involved in the conservation of the African elephant *Loxodonta africana* rather than the Asian elephant *Elephas maximus*. However, in many respects, the survival of the Asian elephant is more precarious than that of the African elephant. Throughout its range, the populations of Asian elephants have declined in recent decades. As a result, IUCN (1996) declared this species of wildlife as one of the most seriously endangered species of large mammals. The geographical distribution of the Asian elephant in earlier times was a wide one, stretching from the Tigris and Euphrates valleys of present day Syria and Iraq to China (from southern China up to the Yellow River) in the east, and to Sumatra in Indonesia in the south (Daniel, 1996). At present, its distribution is highly fragmented and occurs only in thirteen countries in Asia such as India, Sri Lanka, Nepal, Bhutan, Bangladesh, Myanmar, China, Thailand, Laos, Cambodia, Vietnam, Malaysia and Indonesia. The entire Asian elephant population in these countries is estimated to be between 34 000 and 54 000 (De Silva, 1998). In comparison, the population size of the African elephant is about 600 000, and African elephants range across 33 countries in Africa. Nevertheless, this is only about 60 per cent of the elephant population of Africa of about 20 years ago (Hoare, 2000). However, the population decline of the Asian elephant has not been as sudden as that of the African elephant, rather gradual erosion over the centuries has occurred, which accelerated in the second half of the 20th century.

Although the population size of the Asian elephant is considerably less than that of the African elephant, Asian elephants have experienced a greater degree of habitat loss and fragmentation than their African counterparts. This is largely due to human impacts: (a) the increased utilization of the natural habitats of elephants for agricultural development schemes; and (b) the expansion of human settlements into elephant habitat. Continuing loss of habitat is quite difficult to control because of increasing human populations in Asia and demands for higher per capita income (Daniel, 1996). A likely corollary to a decrease in the range available to a species is a decrease in its resource-base, and for such a wide-ranging species as the elephant, this means that the animal has reduced flexibility to buffer the effects of local depletion of its resources by moving to other areas (Corze et al., 1998). The example of Sri Lanka is illustrative. The human population of Sri Lanka increased from about 2.5 million at the beginning of the 20th century to over 18 million at its end. Moreover, at present Sri Lanka's population growth is about 1.2 per cent per annum, and the size of its population is expected to exceed 25 million by the year 2025 and to reach 35 million by the year 2050 (Marshall, 1996). On the other hand, since 1900 the forest cover of the country has declined from 70 per cent to about 24 per cent (Legg and Jewell, 1995). This situation has confined the majority of Sri Lanka's elephant population to protected areas in the Dry Zone. If the present trend in deforestation and human population growth continues unchecked, the elephant in Sri Lanka will soon be confined to these protected areas. Whether they will be able to survive in such restricted areas in the long term is uncertain. This situation, as pointed out by Laws (1981) in the case of the African elephant, has developed in Sri Lanka from one where 'human islands existed in a sea of elephants, to a sea of people with elephant islands'.

As in many other Asian countries, the elephant population in Sri Lanka underwent a marked reduction starting from the mid-nineteenth century. About 12 000 elephants are thought to have inhabited the island in the mid-nineteenth century. Although the exact size of the present day elephant population is unknown, most estimates place it between 3 000 and 5 000 elephants (De Silva and Attapattu, 1997; De Silva, 1998; Weerakoon, 1999). About 90 per cent of this population is located in the protected area network of the country and altogether this area amounts to 8 220 km^2. This is equal to about 12 per cent of the total land area of Sri Lanka. However, most of the protected areas involved are small in size and they have been established on an *ad hoc* basis. As a result, they are not large enough to support a viable population of elephants on their own (Desai, 1998). A recently conducted survey confirmed that although some elephants range completely within some parks, a portion of the herd ranges outside the boundary of parks (Weerakoon, 1999). Habitat fragmentation and the subsequent loss of feeding grounds has been recognised as one of the major reasons for this latter phenomenon (Santiapillai and Jackson, 1990; De Silva, 1998; Weerakoon, 1999).

Habitat fragmentation generally leads to smaller and more isolated animal populations. Smaller populations are then more vulnerable to local extinction, due to stochastic events, and they are more susceptible to the negative effects from inbreeding depression (Shaffer, 1981). On the other hand, such isolated elephant populations more frequently confront humans in the vicinity of natural habitats of elephants such as national parks or protected areas (Sukumar, 1989). Desai (1998) emphasises this point further by arguing that the level of conflict and the extent of crop and property damage increases with the extent of habitat loss of the individual elephant ranges. However, taking into account the small size of Sri Lanka, its already large commitment to conservation, the economic aspirations of its growing human population, and its socio-economic conditions, it may be impossible in the future to increase the size of its protected areas to any substantial degree.

The home ranges of the Asian elephant vary between 47.5 km^2 and 183.6 km^2 (Fernando, 1997). Weerakoon (1999) has reconfirmed these figures, and he distinguishes the difference between the home ranges of male and female elephants. According to his estimates, the home ranges of male elephants range between 47.5 km^2 and 157.9 km^2 while the home ranges of female elephants range between 53.6 km^2 and 183.6 km^2. These estimates demonstrate that the land area required to support a minimum viable population of Asian elephants is large, larger than any single protected area currently existing in Sri Lanka or likely to exist in the future. Therefore, the crux of Sri Lanka's problem in conserving elephants is that confinement of elephants to Sri Lanka's protected areas is incompatible with the long-term survival of its wild elephant population. Furthermore, such confinement may be an uneconomic strategy or an unworkable one. Thus, it seems that the survival of Sri Lanka's elephants depends on their being able to utilise private lands as well as protected areas. This inevitably results in conflicts with farmers because elephants can be quite destructive of crops and farm property.

The survival of wild elephants in Sri Lanka, and in Asia generally, depends to a large extent on successful public policies for managing such conflict. This article briefly outlines the nature of the current and changing status of the Asian elephant, makes some comparisons with the African elephant and provides some details on the status of *Elephas maxima* in Sri Lanka. In this analysis, the Asian elephant is considered as a mixed economic good possessing use and non-use values. Moreover, this article examines the sufficiency or otherwise of Sri Lanka's protected areas for the survival of its wild elephant population as well as the mobility of such animals. This provides the necessary background for assessing Sri Lanka's policies for conserving wild elephants. The issues raised are pertinent to other Asian countries, as well as to situations of other species of roaming wildlife which cannot be, or are not, confined to protected areas, and to those species which need to use extra land in addition to protected areas in order to survive.

An overview of the main economic issues involving the conservation of elephants

Economic issues involving elephant conservation attracted considerable attention in the economic literature after the implementation of the decision made under the Convention on International Trade in Endangered Species (CITES) in 1989 to restrict international trade in elephant products (Simmons and Kreuter, 1995; Tisdell and Zhu, 1996; Mendelssohn, 1999). Most of this literature has focused on three important economic aspects of elephant conservation. One has been the likely impact of the ban in trade in ivory and elephant derived products on the conservation of elephants (Dublin and Jachmann, 1992; Bulte and Kooten 1999a, b; Khanna and Harford, 1996; Barbier et al., 1990; Barnes, 1996; Bulte and Kooten, 1996). Dublin and Jachmann (1992) examine the impact of the ivory ban on illegal hunting in six elephant ranges in Africa. Sugg and Kreuter (1994) outline the effects of the ivory ban on the elephant population in Africa. Khanna and Harford (1996) and Bulte and Kooten (1996) provide a detailed account of the economic efficiency of the ivory trade ban in preventing illegal trade. Simmons and Kreuter (1995) use a political economy framework to examine economic issues involved in the ivory trade ban. In this analysis, they try to analyse who owns the elephants in Africa under the CITES recommendations. The work of Bulte and Kooten (1999a) examines the opposing and supporting arguments for the trade ban using empirical results from Kenya.

The second economic issue considered in the elephant-conservation literature is the extent to which provisions of some communal property rights to elephants can support their conservation and reduce poaching (Balakrishnan and Ndhlovu, 1992; Kiss, 1990; Simmons and Kreuter, 1995; Treves and Sanderson, 1995; Skonhoft, 1998; Dickson, 1999; McPherson and Nieswiadomy, 2000). The works of Kiss (1990), and Simmons and Kreuter (1995), provide detailed accounts of the economic viability of community-based conservation programs in Africa. Skonhoft (1998) examines the conflict between wildlife conservation and the cost and benefit obtained from it in east Africa assuming that local communities share in the profits from utilisation of elephants in protected areas. He finds that such sharing arrangements do not necessarily result in a net economic benefit for the local people. Dickson (1999) analysed the argument favoring the assignment of property rights in wildlife to local communities in the context of Communal Areas Management Program for Indigenous Resources (CAMFIRE) in Zimbabwe. In this analysis, in order to examine the success of the integrated conservation and development program, he used two related assumptions based on a participatory approach to wildlife. McPherson and Nieswiadomy (2000) outlined the merits and demerits of the community-based wildlife conservation program using a political economy framework.

The third issue canvassed in the economic literature on elephant conservation is the assessment of the total economic value (TEV) of elephants. The works of Brown and Henry (1989), Geist (1994), Barnes (1996) and Gowdy (1997) provide a detailed analytical framework that can be used for the estimation of the economic value of elephants. Barnes (1998) investigated the direct economic use value of the elephant population in Botswana, in terms of the present value of 15 years of gross output and national income discounted at 6 per cent. Elephants used for viewing were the *status quo*. Uses examined included elephant-viewing, possible introduction of safari hunting tourism, licensed hunting by Botswana citizens, elephant cropping (culling) for ivory, hides and meat, and combinations of these. Mendelssohn (1999) assesses whether the rigorous application of economic valuation techniques to land-use decisions and to policy and project analysis could result in an increased and more targeted level of investment in elephant conservation in Africa. In his analysis, he also highlights the practical problems associated with the application of cost–benefit analysis and market analysis.

The nature and status of the Asian and African elephants: a comparison

The elephant is the largest living land animal. There are two broad species of elephants: the Asian elephant *Elephas maximus* and the African elephant *Loxodonta africana*. A summary of the physiological differences between Asian and African elephants is presented in Table 1. The Asian elephant is divided into three sub-species. The Sri Lankan sub-species *maximus* has the darkest skin, the Asian mainland sub-species *indicus* has medium darkness of skin, and the Sumatran sub-species *sumatranus* has the lightest skin colour and least depigmentation (patches on the skin). The Asian elephant inhabits a variety of habitats, mainly forest, but also grasslands, marshes, lake shores and transitional zones between forest and open habitats. They prefer grasses. However they also consume bark, roots, leaves, and stems of trees, vines, and shrubs. Most of an adult's activities involve searching for and eating food. They eat in the morning, evening and at night, but rest during the hottest part of the day. On average, this species of wildlife consumes about 150 kg of vegetation and drinks about 140 litres of water a day but only about 44 per cent of what is consumed is actually digested. Moreover, they rarely forage in one area for more than a few days in a row.

Table 1 The physiological differences between Asian and African elephants

Attribute	Asian Elephant	African Elephant
Weight	3 000–5 000 kg	4 000–7 000 kg
Height at shoulder	2–3.5 metres	3–4 metres
Skin	Smooth	More wrinkled
Highest Point	Top of head	Top of shoulder
Size of ears	Smaller	Larger
Number of ribs	Up to 20	Up to 21
Shape of back	Convex	Concave
Shape of head	Dorsal bulges	No bulges and dish
Tusks	Males only	Both sexes have tusks
Trunk	Fewer rings and more rigid	More rings and less rigid
Tip of trunk	One finger	Two fingers
Hair	More hair	Less body hair
Heaviest recorded tusk	39.0 kg	102.7 kg

The Asian elephant is slightly smaller in size than the African elephant. It can grow to be 2–3.5 metres in height and 4–6 metres in length. It is tallest at the arch of the back. It weighs between 3 000 and 5 000 kg. Only the males have tusks and these are smaller than those of the African elephant, and are not present in all males. The ears are small and do not cover the shoulders. The forehead has two humps and the trunk has a single lobe at its tip. The front feet have five toes while the back feet have four. Asian elephants can reach speeds of 40 km/h while running and 6.4 km/h while walking. They are an oddity among mammals because they grow until they die, which is usually around the age of sixty.

Asian elephants have a long history of association with humans. This species of wildlife still has a particular place in human society, and its history, culture, folklore and mythology in most Asian countries. Especially in the past, thousands of elephants were domesticated for use in transportation and logging in most areas of India, Burma, Thailand and Sri Lanka. At present, about 10 000 or fewer elephants are used as working animals in these countries.

During the last half of the 20th century, the wild Asian elephant population declined to an estimated 34 000–54 000 individuals (Santiapillai and Jackson, 1990). As a result, since 1976 this species of wildlife has been listed as endangered in Appendix I of CITES. The main reason for this reduction in numbers is the increase in human population and human demands on natural resources that destroy the habitat of the elephants (Daniel, 1996). Competition with humans for basic resources has had a dramatic effect on the distribution and migration habits of Asian elephants, which are prepared to travel great distances in search of water and adequate vegetation.

There are two sub-species of the African elephant: the Forest elephant *Loxodonta africana cyclotis* and the Savannah elephant *Loxodonta africana africana*. The African Forest elephant is smaller than the Savannah elephant, and lives in the equatorial forests of central and western Africa. The Savannah elephant is found throughout the grassy plains and bush lands of the continent. The African elephant is the world's largest living terrestrial mammal (shoulder height to 3–4 metres; weight to 4 000–7 000 kg) and it has a social structure organised around females and calves. In the Savannah sub-species, each family unit usually contains about ten individuals, although several family units may join together to form a 'clan' consisting of six to seventy members led by a large female. Forest elephants live in much smaller family units. Small, temporary associations of males also exist; the members of such groups join and leave at will. Adult bulls are often seen with cow-calf groups. Sexual maturity is reached at about 10 years in males and females, although males become sexually active much later. Usually, a single calf is born after a gestation period of 22 months. Females can remain fertile until 55–60 years old. Both the male and female African elephant can live up to an age of 60 to 70 years and have the lowest metabolic rate of any placental mammal. Home ranges vary in size between 14 and 3 120 km^2, depending on the availability of food and water resources. A fully-grown African elephant eats up to 200 kg of grass, leaves, roots, fruits and bark daily. Unlike the Asian elephant, both sexes carry tusks. The ivory tusks and prehensile trunk are distinguishing features of the African elephant. The longest recorded tusk of an African elephant was 3.8 metres long and 94.5 kilograms in weight. The large, columnar feet of the African elephant allow it to move surprisingly quickly over rough ground, reaching speeds of 25 mph in short bursts.

Although it is difficult to assess population numbers accurately, it is believed that a population of 3–5 million African elephants may have existed between 1930 and 1940. During the 1970s and 1980s, their population is estimated to have declined significantly. Probably fewer than 600 000 animals remain today. Most of this decline is believed to be the direct result of unsustainable off-take by the illegal ivory trade, coupled with habitat loss due to human population pressure. Historically, the illegal ivory trader was possibly the greatest threat to African elephant populations and still remains a potential threat today. Most elephant ranges in Africa extend outside protected areas, and human–elephant conflicts occur when farming activities take place within the elephant range. Often elephants raid fields and destroy crops. It is predicted, that as human populations continue to grow, habitat loss and degradation through activities such as logging and agriculture will become the major threats to the survival of the African elephant. WWF (1997) has identified five issues that need to be addressed in order to conserve African elephants. They are: (1) slowing the loss of natural habitat; (2) strengthening activities against poachers and the illegal ivory trade; (3) reducing conflict between human and elephant populations; (4) determining the status of elephant populations through improved surveys; and (5) enhancing the capacity of local wildlife authorities to conserve and manage elephants.

The present status and historical overview of the decrease in elephant population in Sri Lanka

Although recent estimates indicate that the size of the current elephant population in Sri Lanka is between 3 000 and 5 000 elephants, scientific evidence to ascertain the exact number is inadequate (De Silva, 1998). Despite some conflicting earlier evidence (Norris, 1959; McKay, 1973; Schultz, 1984), Desai (1998) argues that the size of Sri Lanka's population of elephants has been decreasing since the early 1800s. Moreover, in his analysis he also argues that this decreasing size of the elephant population has had a significant impact on the current distribution of the elephant population in the country. This distribution is shown in Figure 1.

Desai (1998) establishes three phases of the decrease in the elephant population of Sri Lanka by reviewing the literature on the economic history of Sri Lanka under the British. The first phase was the domestication of the elephant as an export commodity in the early to third quarter of the 1800s. During this period, elephants were regarded as a harvestable resource to be exploited and thousands of wild elephants were captured and exported (Marshall, 1996). This export trade flourished until the third quarter of the 1800s. According to Deraniyagala (1955), between 1853 and 1872, approximately 2 500 elephants were exported. However, the actual number of elephants removed from the wild for domestication during this period would be much higher if elephant mortality during the process of capture, training and transport is taken into account.

The second phase of the decrease in Sri Lanka's elephant population occurred with the expansion of the plantation industry in Sri Lanka between the 1870s and 1940s. During this period, elephants were still regarded as resources and exports continued. However, with the expansion of the plantation industry, elephants were considered to be a pest and a bounty was paid for their destruction with a large number of elephants being shot throughout their range, especially in the Central Province. Both sport and bounty hunting accounted for the removal of thousands of elephants during this period. For instance, in the Northern Province bounties were paid for the killing of 3 500 elephants in mid-1887 and in Hambanthota, bounties were paid for the killing of 2 000 elephants between 1878 and 1882 (Olivier, 1978). This trend continued until Sri Lanka's political independence in 1948.

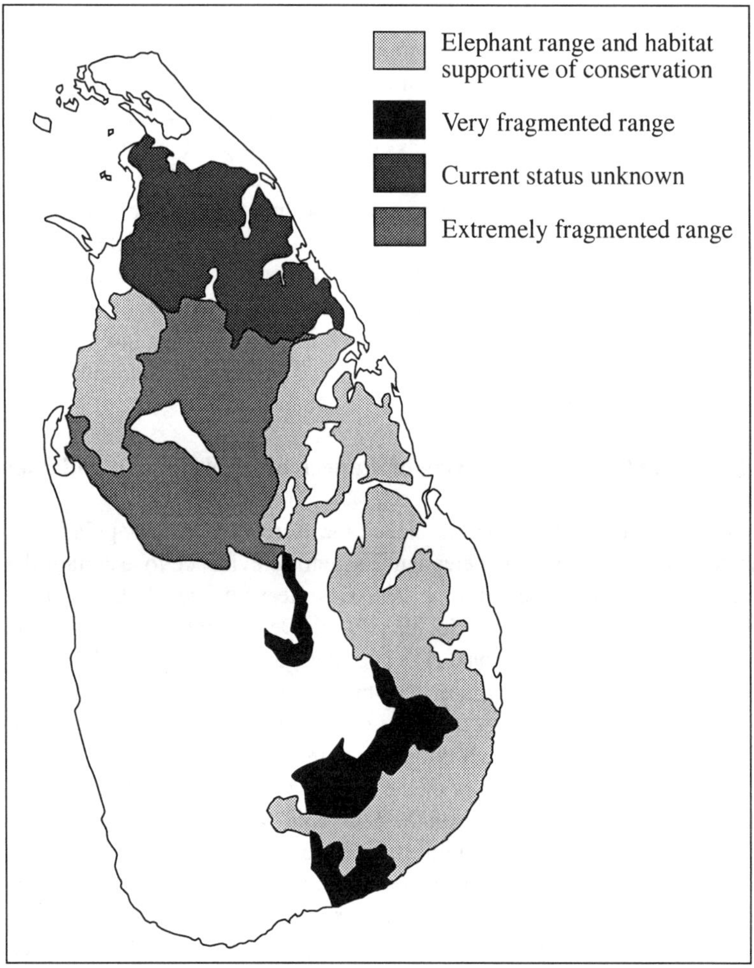

Figure 1 Generalised elephant distribution in Sri Lanka in 2000, as estimated in the GEF Project, Department of Wildlife Conservation, Sri Lanka

The third phase covers the current post-independence period. During this period, the largely undeveloped Dry Zone area in the east of Sri Lanka was targeted for development. The Dry Zone contained the last large tract of elephant habitat in Sri Lanka containing a major elephant population (De Silva, 1998). The main development scheme in this zone was the accelerated Mahaweli Development Program, the objective of which was to develop 260 000 ha of new land for agriculture using irrigation facilities. Land-use changes on this scale resulted in tremendous fragmentation of the habitat of elephants in this area and enhanced the conflict between humans and elephants. The present human–elephant conflict in the Mahaweli and North West region is a direct consequence of such drastic and large-scale land-use change over a very short period of time. As the elephant was a protected species during this period, elephants in areas designated for development were simply driven off agricultural land into adjacent patches of habitat. Jayewardene (1994) has given a concise and clear picture of the development of the Mahaweli river basin (including the North West region), its impact on elephants and the actions adopted for controlling elephants. Santiapillai (1994) estimates elephant mortality in Sri Lanka for the period between 1951 and 1970. According to his estimates, during this period a total of 1 163 elephants perished in the wild, of which 639 (or 55 per cent) were killed by farmers in defence of their crops. More recently, De Silva (1998) updated the estimate of elephant mortality in Sri Lanka and revealed that on average about sixty elephants perished annually in the period between 1970 and 1998. Primarily elephants were killed during this period because of their interference with agriculture and with other human activities. Ivory poaching was simply a by-product.

While elephant habitat was reduced and fragmented to a fraction of its original size, what remained of the elephant population was left largely intact. Displacement, shrinking habitats, lack of adequate natural resources and increased overlap in land-use between man and elephants, all contributed to the increasingly severe conflict between humans and elephants. This conflict is a symptom of a deeper problem, namely that of habitat loss and the resulting displacement of elephants. This problem was further compounded by habitat fragmentation, which created a mosaic of elephant habitats and agricultural areas where patches of environments were widely interspersed within agricultural areas. This is typical of many elephant ranges in the region. It indicates that legislation to protect a species, though well intended, does not achieve much in the absence of effective habitat protection. Effective habitat protection in turn depends upon far-sighted land-use plans prepared and implemented well ahead of large-scale development interventions. This has hardly happened anywhere and often even 'committed' (promised) safeguards have been overlooked. It is the ecosystem, the species and its habitat that need to be protected if conservation is to succeed. As elephants have neither the space nor the resources they require, they resort to crop raiding and often involuntarily kill humans and destroy property.

The Asian elephant as a mixed good with positive and negative attributes

Compared to African elephants, little attention has been given to estimating the economic value of Asian elephants (Barnes, 1998). However, the range of economic values of the Asian elephant appears to be wider than those of the African elephant. A close association between Asians and elephants dates back for more than 2 000 years (Jayewardene, 1994) and there are strong traditional cultural ties between Asians and the elephant. The elephant enjoys a quasi-religious status in the long-established Buddhist and Hindu traditions of these societies (Rudran et al., 1995). The widespread emotional attachment of Asians to the elephant (and its plight) is indicated by its press coverage. Because of the deep and widespread cultural and emotional attachment of the people to the elephants, it is regarded as a 'flagship species' for conservation in most countries in Asia (De Silva, 1998). De Silva (1998) and others believe that the elephant can be used as a 'flagship species', to pave the way for not just elephant conservation but also to support biodiversity conservation in general in this region.

The Asian elephant is a mixed economic good because some attributes are marketable whereas others are not. Furthermore, it has both positive and negative (pest) attributes.

Changes in the relative values of these components have a considerable impact on social decision-making about the conservation of elephants.

The concept of total economic value (*TEV*) provides a framework to capture the positive aspects of the economic value of elephants (Barnes, 1996). In the *TEV* framework, economic value of any given environmental amenity is categorised into two major components, namely, use value (*UV*) and non-use value (*NUV*). The *UV* may be broken into two major sub-groups such as direct use value (*DUV*) and indirect use value (*IUV*). In addition, *NUV* may be divided into two components: option value (*OV*) and existence value (*EV*). Therefore, a basis for the estimation of the *TEV* of elephants is:

$$TEV = UV + NUV, \text{ or}$$
$$TEV = DUV + IUV + OV + EV$$

However, it is evident that these values are not easily aggregated in a straightforward fashion. For example, conservation of elephants in their natural state involves direct costs of providing a protected area, and this may include paying guards and rangers to protect and maintain the area and may perhaps involve the cost of establishing a 'buffer zone' for surrounding local communities. In this process, the direct use options of elephants and some land are sacrificed, if non-use value options are chosen. Therefore the opportunity cost of non-use value options are the benefit that would have been obtained if use value options were chosen. Such costs are easily identified as they often comprise marketable outputs and income sacrificed. It is not surprising therefore, that governments and donors usually concentrate on these costs – the direct costs plus the foregone benefits of conservation when choosing to retain the elephant in its natural or a managed state. However, many of the values of natural or managed environmental resources are not bought and sold on markets, and thus are generally ignored in private and public development decisions. For example, the market value of environmental resources converted to some commercial use usually does not reflect the lost environmental benefits. Likewise, conservation decisions of any wildlife are therefore often biased in favour of those uses that do have market outputs. Thus, the failure to account fully for the economic costs of conversion or degradation of environmental resources is sometimes a major factor resulting in inappropriate conservation policies.

The total economic valuation framework, as applied to the positive attributes of Asian elephants, is summarised in Table 2. Positive use values of elephants are classified according to whether they are direct or indirect. The former includes the productive or consumptive values of elephants as resources for such commodities as ivory, hide, other elephant products, recreation and tourism. These are all private goods because they can be marketed. However, they may not all be marketed fully, for example, viewing of elephants. Marketable uses may be important in both domestic and international markets. In general, the value of marketable goods and services is easier to measure than the value of non-marketable direct uses. Often policy-makers only take account of marketable uses of species such as elephants. Indirect use values of elephants are usually not marketed. Indirect use values are difficult to quantify and are often ignored in elephant conservation and management decisions. For instance, conservation of elephants in their natural state helps the conservation of several other species that are directly or indirectly benefited by habitat association with elephants.

Table 2 List of positive use and non-use economic values for Asian elephants

Use Values		***Non-use Values***	
Direct Use Values	Indirect Use Values	Option and Quasi-Option Values	Existence Values
Ivory and ivory carving Elephant safaris and tourism Hides and hire Sale of elephant calves	Markets generated for local agricultural products and other services by tourism Ecological role as a flagship species (?) Habitat impacts favourable to conservation of other wildlife	Future possible demands for an elephant product and services such as educational and scientific Expected value of the information derived from delaying exploitation of the elephant	Intrinsic or pure existence value Biological diversity Social, historical, cultural and religious value Bequest value

The non-use value of elephants (these are non-marketable goods) can be categorised into two broader categories: option and existence values, including bequest value. Option value arises because individuals may be uncertain about their future demands for elephant products and services or their availability in the future. In most cases, the preferred approach for incorporating option values into the analysis is through determining the difference between ex-ante and ex-post valuation. This can be done by developing well-specified models of individual choice, through reasoning about how marginal utility of income differs in the various contingency states. If an individual is uncertain about the future value of the elephant product and services, but believes it may be high or that current exploitation and conversion may be irreversible, then there may be quasi-option value derived from delaying the development activities. Quasi-option value is simply the expected value (if the situation is not so uncertain as to prevent the assignment of probabilities to future outcomes, as it may well be) of the information derived from delaying exploitation and conversion of the elephant today. Some economists believe that quasi-option value is not a separate component of benefit but involves the analyst in properly accounting for the implications of gaining additional information. Quasi-option value can be estimated by taking into account the conditional value of information. In contrast, however, there are individuals who do not currently make use of any values of elephant but nevertheless wish to see them preserved ‘in their own right’. Such an 'intrinsic' value is often referred to as existence value. It is a form of non-use value that is extremely difficult to measure, as existence values involve subjective valuations by individuals unrelated to either their own or (arguably) others' use, whether current or future. It may reflect the view that humankind has a stewardship role in relation to nature or involve 'deep ecology' concerns. An important subset of existence values is bequest value, which results from individuals placing a high value on the conservation of elephants for future generations of humans.

However, Table 2 does not contain all the characteristics of elephants that influence their total economic value, and it might also be noted that some deep ecologists would object to attempts to value elephants in monetary terms. Table 2 does not allow for negative economic attributes of elephants. These include the economic costs of damage to agricultural crops, to fences, and sometimes farm buildings as well as, occasionally, human injury or death. These negative economic values must be offset against the positive economic values of elephants to obtain Net Total Economic Value (*NTEV*), as previously pointed out by Tisdell and Zhu (1998), see also Tisdell (1979).

Suppose that the *NTEV* of elephants is solely a function of the size of their total population, X, even though this is unlikely to be solely so in practice. It is assumed for the purpose of showing the maximum of *NTEV* is not likely to correspond to the social economic optimum, using the Kaldor–Hicks criterion. This is because the economic cost of varying the elephant population must be taken into account in determining the social economic optimum.

Let

$$NTEV = f(X) \tag{1}$$

and imagine that in the absence of control $X = X_0$. The total cost of varying the population of elephants, X, may depend on whether the size of the population is to be increased or decreased. Represent it by

$$C = C(X) \text{ for } X \geq X_0 \tag{2}$$

for an increase, and by

$$R = R(X_0 - X) \text{ for } X \leq X_0 \tag{3}$$

for a decrease.

Consider the case when *NTEV* reaches a maximum for $X \geq X_0$, say at X_2. Then social economic welfare derived from the elephant population *might* be raised by outlays to increase the population of elephants. An increase is desirable in the case illustrated in Figure 2. In Figure 2, the net social economic welfare, W, from the population of elephants,

$$W = NTEV - C(X) \tag{4}$$
$$= f(X) - C(X) \tag{5}$$

reaches a maximum for $X = X_1$. This occurs when the marginal *NTEV* from increasing the population of elephants equals the marginal cost of doing so. In the case shown in Figure 2, this is so for $X = X_1$. X_1 involves a smaller population of elephants than that which maximises *NTEV*, X_2 in this case which in turn could be expected to be lower than the population of elephants that maximises *TEV*.

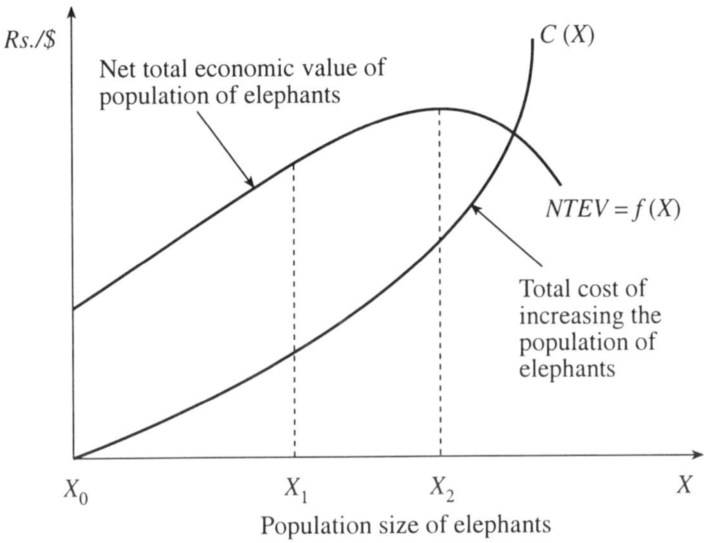

Figure 2 *A situation in which Kaldor–Hicks optimum is achieved by increasing the number of wild elephants in a country*

Note that in some cases where the maximum of *NTEV* occurs for an increase in the population of wild elephants, a Kaldor–Hicks social welfare optimum may be achieved by non-intervention to alter the current level of population of elephants because the extra cost of increasing the population exceeds the extra benefits. In this case, the optimum remains at X_0, and a corner-type solution exists.

Observe also that if the maximum of *NTEV* occurs for $X \leq X_0$, it is possible that reducing the population of elephants could increase *W*. Once again, this will depend on the costs involved. This case can be illustrated using a similar figure to Figure 2. However, in this case the reduction in the level of the elephant population is treated as the independent or controlled variable and is the variable on the abscissa.

This analysis can be adapted to consider other types of wildlife that have positive as well as negative (pest) economic values. Clearly unbalanced economic analysis results if only the positive attributes of a species (that also has some negative consequences) are considered, and if the costs of managing a species are ignored. In such cases, one cannot rely for policy advice on *TEV* narrowly conceived. Nevertheless, at the same time, it has to be recognised that the extended analysis itself is an abstraction both from the viewpoint of its welfare or value assumptions and its portrayal of ecological relationships.

Given that one wants to maintain or increase the population of elephants in a country, it is necessary to consider how this can be achieved. Is it possible for example to maintain the current population of elephants in Sri Lanka by confining them to the existing protected areas in Sri Lanka? If the 'answer' is 'yes' then that would raise the further issue (not discussed here) of how can it be done, and would the cost exceed the benefit? If protected areas are insufficient on their own from an ecological point of view to ensure the survival of wild elephants, their enclosure in protected areas is not an option for conserving elephants in the wild. Consider this matter for Sri Lanka.

Limited capacity of Sri Lanka's protected areas to ensure the survival of elephants and issues raised by mobility of elephants

The protected area network in Sri Lanka, as in most countries, has been established on an *ad hoc* basis. Many protected areas were previously hunting reserves. The ecological requirements of elephants were often not met when defining the boundaries of these reserves. As a result, its protected areas (PAs) have insufficient carrying capacity to support sustainably their current elephant populations. At present about 12 per cent of land area in Sri Lanka is designated as PAs for the conservation of elephants and this is a little over 8 000 km^2. However, there are only three PAs larger than 500 km^2 and about 49 per cent of the PAs are less than 100 km^2. Adding to the small size of the PAs is the fact that they need to support elephant populations whose ecological requirements are relatively large. Even though the PAs were small in the past, there was extensive forest cover outside the PAs. Moreover, this forest cover provided corridors between the PAs for elephants. This in turn ensured that elephants had suitable habitat and were therefore not in serious conflict with the human population (Fernando, 1993). At present, most of the forested areas outside the PAs have already been lost or are being lost rapidly and what remains is fragmented and degraded (Jayewardene, 1996). Therefore, the connectivity between the PAs has been lost to a large extent. As a result, the elephant population in Sri Lanka is scattered and isolated in disjointed ranges. Possibly all PAs in Sri Lanka have insufficient carrying capacity to support and maintain a viable long-term population of elephants merely on their own and the survival of elephants depends on their being able to use land areas outside PAs as well as in PAs. Furthermore, considering the large land area already committed for conservation in Sri Lanka, it may not be possible to create larger and new PAs in the future.

Nevertheless, many believe that even under such limited circumstances, it is possible to implement successful elephant conservation programs. It has been suggested that any such endeavour requires maintaining a minimum genetically viable population and providing for individual home ranges in terms of the size of the habitat (Sukumar, 1989). An effective breeding population (N_e) of 50 animals is required for short-term conservation of elephants. Based on age and sex ratios in the population this would translate into a total population of 200 elephants. A recent radio telemetry study of elephant ranging behaviour in Sri Lanka has shown that in order to achieve this target, an individual home range as large as 160 km^2 is required (Weerakoon, 1999). Assuming that at least ten non-overlapping home ranges are included in the conservation effort, one would have to allow at least another 25 per cent more area as the home ranges cannot be squeezed in, and a larger area would be required depending on the shape of the home ranges. This implies an area of 2 000 km^2 and would certainly support a viable population in the short term. However, the largest national park in Sri Lanka is Wilpattu which is 1 316 km^2 in size, followed by Ruhuna (978 km^2), Madura Oya (558 km^2), Victoria – Randenigala (420 km^2) and Somawathiya (377 km^2). These are all less than 2 000 km^2. Thus, even the largest national park in Sri Lanka is of insufficient size to ensure a viable population of elephants on its own in the biological short-term. For this purpose, it is essential that elephants in Sri Lanka be able to use areas outside of PAs as well as within them if elephant populations are to remain naturally viable. This is even more imperative if effective long-term conservation of wild populations of elephants in Sri Lanka are to survive.

For long-term conservation without management intervention, an effective breeding population (N_e) of 500 is suggested (Sukumar, 1989). This in turn would translate into a population of 2 000 elephants. There is only one such population known in Asia and that is in the Nilgiri Biosphere Reserve in south India (Desai, 1998). The reserve covers an area of 5 520 km^2 (total contiguous forest is over 10 000 km^2) and supports a population of over 3 000 elephants. Given the size of the PAs and the elephant population, a conservation program of this scale is unlikely to be possible for a country like Sri Lanka. It may be more practical in Sri Lanka to target conserving several smaller populations and manage these as a single meta-population. In order to achieve such an objective, integrated policies for the management of elephant populations are needed. It is clear that the continued survival of Sri Lanka's wild elephant populations depends upon them being able to use land other than protected areas, including private agricultural land for their survival. Effective elephant conservation must be based upon this reality, and this situation is likely to require the payment of adequate compensation to farmers to tolerate damage from elephants.

Towards integrated economic policies for the conservation of Asian elephants

Most policy actions adopted in Sri Lanka to conserve elephants and alleviate human–elephant conflict are transient measures and have been taken largely to tie over a particularly critical time on an *ad hoc* basis. De Silva (1998) summarised the important actions that have been taken by the Sri Lankan Department of Wildlife Conservation and other government and non-government organisations during this period. However, overall management strategies for elephant conservation in Sri Lanka are inadequate, as has been highlighted by several researchers (Thouless, 1994; Fauna International, 1995; Desai, 1998). Therefore, it is necessary to develop a specific overall policy for elephant conservation. There is no doubt that such a policy must ensure the survival of elephants as well as allow for the welfare of the people in the vicinity of elephant ranges. In achieving these objectives, it is necessary to take into account ecological consequences of agricultural development decisions as well as a number of environmental consequences previously ignored by policy-makers. On the other hand, it is also important to consider adequate incentive programs such as farmer insurance schemes and subsidies to farmers to tolerate the presence of elephants in non-protected areas such as agricultural fields in the vicinity of protected areas.

In the past, most elephant conservation programs and attempts to mitigate human–elephant conflict in Sri Lanka have failed to accomplish the combined objectives of ensuring elephant survival as well as maintaining human welfare simultaneously. For instance, the policy of protection has favoured the establishment of national parks and nature reserves, supported by legislation that prohibits or restricts the local communities from their usual access into these areas (Shan, 1995; Tacconi and Bennett, 1997). Access has traditionally belonged to these local communities. In addition to their not obtaining any significant part of the revenue from the commercial park activities, the acquisition of land for establishing these parks in many countries has often directly displaced many rural communities (Barbier, 1992; Skonhoft and Solstad, 1996). Villagers are often prevented from eliminating 'problem' animals in order to protect their crops and livestock by the existing anti-poaching laws and other enforcement (Barbier et al., 1990). As a consequence, local communities have been alienated to a large extent from the wildlife. Furthermore, since they bear the real cost of conservation without obtaining any significant benefit from it, it is easy to understand why a rather negative attitude to wildlife preservation has emerged among the rural communities. Combined with a dense and rapidly growing population and scarcity of arable land, this frequently translates into direct involvement in illegal encroachment of local communities into the national parks and other restricted areas (Skonhoft and Solstad, 1998).

Economic benefits from wildlife conservation rarely trickle down to farmers and landowners in the vicinity of protected areas. Rural people believe that the authorities ignore their elephant-related losses while denying them the right to kill raiding elephants and gain some compensation by utilising elephants to supplement farm incomes. They view the apparent lapse in control of problem animals by authorities as avoidance and as part of official wildlife-protection policy, rather than as a genuine operational gap traceable to lack of resources. Moreover, their chronic frustration encountered as a result of cumbersome and ineffectual government procedures when claiming compensation for economic damage caused by elephants in Sri Lanka and elsewhere (Tisdell and Zhu, 1998) compounds this conflict. In addition, villagers perceive the government's failure to pay adequate compensation on grounds of management problems as a denial of rights. These perceptions suggest that if the law remains overprotective of wildlife, and if those who benefit from wildlife are unwilling to share losses and costs, wildlife may not be sustained on private land in the long run. Misconceptions about factual matters also contribute to the intensity of the conflict. Therefore, an effective outcome in elephant conservation requires policies that integrate economics and conservation, and private and public land uses, rather than just pursuance of narrowly defined conservation strategies.

Conclusions

Available protected areas are insufficient in size to ensure the survival of many species of large, mobile terrestrial animals requiring extensive territories for their continued survival. Given the extent of human demands to use land for purposes other than nature conservation, these areas are unlikely to be extended in the foreseeable future to sufficient size to ensure a high chance of survival of such species. This seems to be to the survival of the Asian elephant. Protected areas in Sri Lanka are fragmented and none are of sufficient size to provide a reasonable chance of long-term survival of the Asian elephant in a natural state. Thus survival of this species in Sri Lanka requires its use of protected and non-protected areas, and this is true almost without exception throughout Asia. Therefore, public policies for the survival of Asian elephants must provide appropriate economic incentives for the holders of unprotected lands to tolerate the presence of elephants, if the Asian elephant is to have a reasonable chance of long-term survival. Thus, an integrated approach (taking account of elephants on private as well as public land) to public conservation policy is needed. This is so whether one adopts the goal of maximising the net total economic value of this species after allowing for management costs, or modifies this goal so as to take account of nature as a merit good. Otherwise there may be only one place in Asia where the Asian elephant could survive in the long-term, namely in the Nilgiri Biosphere Reserve in India.

Note

1. School of Economics, The University of Queensland, Brisbane 4072 Australia. The first draft of the material in this chapter appeared in the series, *Economics, Ecology and the Environment*, Working Paper No. 59, June 2001, The University of Queensland, Brisbane.

References

Abel, N. and P. Blaikie (1986), 'Elephants, People, Park and Development: The Case of Luangwa Valley, Zambia', *Environmental Management*, **10**, 735–51.

Balakrishnan, M. and D. Ndhlovu (1992), 'Wildlife Utilisation and Local People: A Case Study in Upper Lupande Game Management Area, Zambia', *Environmental Conservation*, **2**, 135–44.

Bandon, K.E. and M. Well (1992), 'Planning for People and Park: Design Dilemmas', *World Development*, **20**, 557–70.

Barbier, E. (1992), 'Community-based Development in Africa', in T. Swanson and B. Barbier (eds), *Economics for the Wilds*, Washington, DC: Island Press.

Barbier, E., J.C. Burgess, T. Swanson and D.W. Pearce (1990), *Elephants, Economics and Ivory*, London: Earthscan Publications Ltd.

Barnes, J.I. (1996), 'Changes in the Economic Use Value of Elephants in Botswana: The Effect of International Trade Prohibition', *Ecological Economics*, **18**, 215–30.

Barnes, J.I. (1998), 'Economic Influences on Elephant Management in Southern Africa', Paper presented at the Workshop on Cooperative Regional Wildlife Management in Southern Africa, University of California, Davis, 13–14 August.

Bateman, I.J. and I.H. Langford (1997), 'Non-users Willingness to Pay for National Parks: An Application and Critique of the Contingent Valuation Method', *Regional Studies*, **20**, 571–82.

Bell, R.H.V. (1987), 'Conservation with a Human Face: Conflict Reconciliation in African Land Use Planning', in D. Anderson and R. Grove (eds), *Conservation in Africa: People, Politics, and Practice*, Cambridge: Cambridge University Press, 79–101.

Brown, G.M. and W. Henry (1989), *The Economic Value of Elephants*, LEEC Paper, 89–12, IIED/London Environmental Economics Centre, London.

Bulte, E. and G.C. Kooten (1996), 'A Note on Ivory Trade and Elephant Conservation', *Environmental and Development Economics*, **1**, 433–43.

Bulte, E. and G.C. Kooten (1999a), 'Economic Efficiency, Resource Conservation and the Ivory Trade Ban', *Ecological Economics*, **28**, 171–81.

Bulte, E. and G.C. Kooten (1999b), 'Economics of Antipoaching Enforcement and the Ivory Trade Ban', *American Journal of Agricultural Economics*, **81**, 453–66.

Burton, M. (1994), 'Alternative Projection of Decline of the African Elephant', *Biological Conservation*, **70**, 183–8.

Burton, M. (1999), 'An Assessment of Alternative Methods of Estimating the Effect of the Ivory Trade Ban on Poaching Effort', *Ecological Economics*, **30**, 93–106.

Chain, H.C., P.K.S. Kumara, W. Piyadasa, G.A.P. Ganagoda and V.H. Perera (1998), 'Domesticated Working Elephants in Sri Lanka', in *Proceedings of the National Symposium on Elephant Management and Conservation*, Sri Lanka: Colombo.

Corze, H., A.K.K. Hillman and E.M. Lang (1998), 'Elephants and their Habitats: How do they Tolerate Each Other?', in C.W. Fowler and T.D. Smith (eds), *Dynamics of Large Mammal Populations*, New York: John Wiley and Sons, pp. 227–37.

Curtis, B. (1989), 'How to Save Elephants', *Washington Post*, 14 October, A22.

Daniel, J.C. (1996), 'Conservation of Asian Elephants', *Gajah*, **16**, 9–16.

Deraniyagala, P.E.P. (1955), *Some Extinct Elephants and their Relatives, and the Two Living Species*, National Museum of Ceylon, Sri Lanka: Colombo.
De Silva, M. (1997), Report: *National Consultancy on Elephant Management*, GEF Project UNO/SRL/001/SRL, Department of Wildlife Conservation, Sri Lanka: Colombo.
De Silva, M. (1998), 'Status and Conservation of the Elephant and the Alleviation of Man–Elephant Conflict in Sri Lanka', *Gajah*, **19**, 1–24.
De Silva, M. and N. Attapattu (1997), 'Alleviation of Wild Elephant–Human Conflict and Conservation of Elephants in the North-western Region of Sri Lanka', (Mimeo), Department of Wildlife Conservation, Sri Lanka: Colombo.
Desai, A.A. (1991), 'The Home Range of Elephants and its Implication for their Management', *Journal of Natural History*, **88**(20), 145–56.
Desai, A.A. (1998), *Conservation of Elephants and Human–Elephant Conflict*, Technical Report, Department of Wildlife Conservation, Sri Lanka: Colombo.
Desai, A.A. and N. Baskaran (1996), 'Impact of Human Activities on the Ranging Behaviour of Elephants in South India', *Journal of Natural History Society*, **93**(3), 145–56.
Dickson, B. (1999), 'The Precautionary Principle in CITES: A Critical Assessment', *Natural Resource Journal*, **39**, 211–28.
Dixon, J.A. and P.B. Sherman (1990), *Economics of Protected Areas*, Washington, DC: Island Press.
Doughley, G. and H.P. Parker (1990), 'Projected Decline of the African Elephant', *Biological Conservation*, **54**, 183–8.
Dublin, H.T. and H. Jachmann (1992), *The Impact of the Ivory Ban on Illegal Hunting of Elephants in Six Range States in Africa*, Switzerland: WWF, Gland.
Fauna International (1995), *Elephant Management Plan 1995*, Colombo: Fauna International.
Fernando, A.B. (1993), 'Recent Elephant Conservation Efforts in Sri Lanka: A Tragic Story', *Gajah*, **10**, 19–25.
Fernando, J.M.P. (1997), *Genetics, Ecology and Conservation of the Asian Elephant*, Unpublished MSc Thesis, Oregon: University of Oregon.
Geist, V. (1994), 'Wildlife Conservation as Wealth', *Nature*, **386**, 491–2.
Gibson, C.C. and S.A. Marks (1995), 'Transforming Rural Hunters into Conservationists: An Assessment of Community-Based Wildlife Management Programs in Africa', *World Development*, **23**, 941–57.
Gowdy, J. (1997), 'The Value of Biodiversity: Market, Society and Ecosystems', *Land Economics*, **73**, 25–41.
Hoare, R. (2000), 'African Elephants and Humans in Conflict: the Outlook for Co-existence', *Oryx*, **34**(1), 34–8.
Hoffmann, T.W. (1975), 'Distribution of Elephants in Sri Lanka', *Loris*, **13**(5), 278–80.
Hoffmann, T.W. (1978), 'Distribution of Elephants in Sri Lanka', *Loris*, **14**(6), 366–7.
IUCN (1996), *Red List of Threatened Animals*, Switzerland: IUCN, Gland.
Jackson, P. (1997), *Conservation of Asian Elephants*, Switzerland: IUCN, Gland.
Jayewardene, J. (1990), 'Elephant Conservation in Sri Lanka', Part IV, *Tigerpaper*, (FAO), **17**(2), 16–21.
Jayewardene, J. (1994), *Elephants in Sri Lanka*, Colombo: The Wildlife Heritage Trust of Sri Lanka.
Jayewardene, J. (1996), 'Elephant Management and Conservation in Mahaweli Project Area in Sri Lanka', *Gajah*, **21**(2), 303–13.
Khanna, J. and J. Harford (1996), 'The Ivory Trade Ban: Is it Effective?', *Ecological Economics*, **19**, 147–55.
Kiss, A. (1990), 'Living with Wildlife: Wildlife Resource Management with Local Participation in Africa', *World Bank Technical Paper No. 130*, African Technical Department Series, Washington, DC: The World Bank.
Laws, R.M. (1981), 'Elephants as Agents of Habitat and Landscape Change in East Africa', *Oikos*, **21**, 1–15.
Leader, W.N. (1993), 'The Cost of Conserving Elephants', *Pachyderm*, **17**, 30–34.
Legg, C. and N. Jewell (1995), 'A 1:50,000-scale Forest Map of Sri Lanka: The Basis for a National Forest Geographic Information System', *Sri Lanka Forester*, (Special Issue), 3–24.
Marshall, A. (1996), *The State of World Population*, Washington, DC: United Nations Population Fund.
McKay, G.M. (1973), *Behavior and Ecology of the Asiatic Elephant in Southern Ceylon,* Sri Lanka: Department of Wildlife Conservation.
McNeely, J.A. and K.R. Miller (eds) (1994), *National Parks, Conservation and Development: The Role of Protected Areas in Sustaining Society*, Washington, DC: Smithsonian Institution Press.
McPherson, A.M. and M.L. Nieswiadomy (2000), 'African Elephants: The Effects of Property Rights and Political Stability', *Contemporary Economic Policy*, **18**, 14–26.
Mendelssohn, G. (1999), 'The Relevance of Economic Valuation for Species Conservation Policy: The Case of the African Elephant', in M. O'Connor and C. Spash (eds), *Valuation and Environmental Theory, Method and Practice*, Cheltenham, UK and Northampton, US: Edward Elgar, pp. 123–42.

Norris, C.E. (1959), *Preliminary Report on Ceylon Elephant Field Survey*, Part II, Times of Ceylon, Sri Lanka: Colombo.
Olivier, R.C.D. (1978), *On the Ecology of the Elephant*, Unpublished PhD Thesis, University of Cambridge, UK.
Rudran, R., J. Jayewardene and W.A. Jayasinghe (1995), 'A Need for an Integrated Approach to Elephant Conservation', *Proceedings of the Seminar on Asian Elephants*, Bombay: Oxford University Press.
Santiapillai, C. (1994), 'Elephant Mortality in Sri Lanka', *Gajah*, **12**, 48–54.
Santiapillai, C. and M. De Silva (1997), 'An Action Plan for the Conservation and Management of Elephants in Sri Lanka', *Gajah*, **18**, 1–24.
Santiapillai, C. and P. Jackson (1990), 'The Asian Elephant: An Action Plan for its Conservation', *Gajah*, **12**, 58–84.
Schultz, D. (1984), 'Another River Dammed', Department of Wildlife, Sri Lanka: Colombo.
Shaffer, M.L. (1981), 'Minimum Population Size for Species Conservation', *BioScience*, **31**, 131–4.
Shan, A. (1995), *The Economics of Third World National Parks: Issues of Tourism and Environmental Management*, Cheltenham, UK and Brookfield, US: Edward Elgar.
Shoshani, J. and M.P. Kahl (1998), 'A Recap of African Elephant Research and Conservation in Historical Perspective', National Symposium on Elephant Management and Conservation, Department of Wildlife and Conservation, Colombo, Sri Lanka.
Simmons, T.R. and U.P. Kreuter (1995), 'Who Owns the Elephant? The Political Economy of Saving the African Elephant', in T.L. Anderson and P.J. Hill (eds), *Wildlife in the Marketplace: the Political Economy Forum*, Lanham, MD: Rowman and Littlefield Publishers, pp. 148–62.
Skonhoft, A. (1998), 'Resource Utilization, Property Rights and Welfare: Wildlife and Local People', *Ecological Economics*, **26**, 67–80.
Skonhoft, A. and J.T. Solstad (1996), 'Wildlife Management, Illegal Hunting and Conflicts: A Bioeconomic Analysis', *Environment and Development Economics*, **1**, 165–81.
Skonhoft, A. and J.T. Solstad (1998), 'The Political Economy of Wildlife Exploitation', *Land Economics*, **74**(1), 16–31.
Sugg, I.C. and U.P. Kreuter (1994), *Elephant and Ivory: Lessons from the Trade Ban*, Institute of Economics Affairs, IEA Studies on the Environment No. 2, London.
Sukumar, R. (1989), *The Asian Elephant: Ecology and Management*, Cambridge: Cambridge University Press.
Sukumar, R. (1991), 'Minimum Viable Population for Elephant Conservation', *Gajah*, **11**, 48–52.
Tacconi, L. and J. Bennett (1997), *Protected Area Assessment and Establishment in Vanuatu: a Socioeconomic Approach*, Australian Centre for International Agricultural Research, Australia, Canberra.
Thouless, C.R. (1994), *Accelerated 'Mahaweli' Development Program*, Vol. IV, USAID, Colombo, Sri Lanka.
Tisdell, C.A. (1979), 'Wildlife: A National Asset or a Pest to be Managed?', in Department of Science and the Environment, *Environmental Economics*, 79–87, Canberra: A.G.P.S.
Tisdell, C.A. and X. Zhu (1996), 'Protected Areas, Agricultural Pests and Economic Damage: Conflicts with Elephants and Pests in Yunnan', *Biodiversity Conservation: Studies in Economics and Management Mainly in Yunnan, China*, No. 26, Department of Economics, Brisbane: University of Queensland.
Tisdell, C.A. and X. Zhu (1998), 'Protected Areas, Agricultural Pests and Economic Damage: Conflicts with Elephants and Pests in Yunnan, China', *The Environmentalist*, **18**, 109–18.
Treves, L.N. and S. Sanderson (1995), 'Property, Politics and Wildlife Conservation', *World Development*, **23**, 1265–75.
Waithaka, J. (1998), 'Human–Wildlife Interaction in Kenya', *Pachyderm*, **25**, 30–42.
Weerakoon, D.K. (1999), *Ecology and Ranging Behaviour of Wild Elephants and Human–Elephant Conflict in Sri Lanka*, Unpublished Report, Department of Zoology, Sri Lanka: University of Colombo.
Whyte, I.J. (1996), 'Studying Elephant Movements', in K. Kangwana (ed.), *Studying Elephants*, AWF Technical Handbook.
WWF (1997), *Conserving Africa's Elephant: Current Issues and Priorities for Action*, World Wide Fund for Nature, Switzerland: Gland.

PART IV

CONSERVATION AND USE OF NATURAL AREAS

[18]

PROVISION OF PARKS AND THE PRESERVATION OF NATURE—SOME ECONOMIC FACTORS*

CLEM TISDELL

University of Newcastle

I. Introduction

Public concern about the preservation of parks, natural areas and wildlife species seems to have increased in recent years. In Australia, for example, there has been vocal opposition to oil exploration on the Great Barrier Reef, to the mining of some beaches for rutile and other minerals, to the development of coal mines in the Blue Mountains and on the South Coast of New South Wales and so on. Conservationists have also pressed their case for more and larger parks to help with the preservation of native animals [5] such as kangaroos and wombats and there have been a number of governmental enquiries into environmental problems. Similar evidence of this concern can be quoted for most economically advanced countries.

Interest in economic factors and the environment has been given a new fillip, and indeed a separate field of economic study, ecological economics, is now emerging. This field owes much to the writings of Kenneth Boulding [1]. Recently, E. Dolan in a small book, *TANSTAAFL: The Economic Strategy for Environmental Crisis* [6], brought together several ideas in ecological economics and presented some challenging views of his own about conservation and the public interest. For example, he claims that the supply of parks and wilderness areas is more likely to be in the vicinity of a social optimum if their provision is in private rather than public hands. In his view, policy should be directed towards "getting the government out of the business of *protecting* the wilderness." [6, p. 97]

Within Australasia, governments have assumed the main responsibility for supplying parks and natural recreation areas and this is so in many other regions of the world. In view of the points raised by Dolan and others ought this policy be altered, *e.g.*, so that beaches become private property? Is private enterprise likely to provide a socially better quantity and quality mix of recreational areas and parks than the government?

This question is difficult to answer on an *a priori* basis but it is worthwhile considering factors which have a bearing on the answer. The discussion indicates serious obstacles to preserving a satisfactory environment in advanced economies.

A number of reasons are first given for suspecting that private enterprise will fail to supply an optimal quantity and spectrum of parks. The factors which are discussed include monopoly, externalities and neighbourhood effects, and irreversibility and uncertainty. My suggestion is that when all of these elements are considered markets or private enterprise will undersupply natural parks. But this raises the question of whether the government will supply an optimal quantity if

* I wish to thank E. Sieper for pointing out a problem in an earlier formulation of this paper.

it accepts the responsibility of providing natural parks. My argument suggests that this is unlikely, and it is a moot point whether the approach of government is likely to be socially preferable to that of private enterprise. But in order to deal with this matter, one needs adequate theories of the political process. While the contributions of Buchanan and Tullock [9] are encouraging in this respect, the traditional view of economists that the State is a monolith willing and able to carry out the plans or prescriptions of economic idealists is unsound. Government must be considered in its complexity with its multiple bodies and interests, conflicts and shortcomings.

II. Monopoly Elements and the Private Provision of Parks

Dolan [6] is, on the whole, correct in claiming that parks are not pure public or collective goods.[1] Exclusion is possible and they might be profitably operated by private enterprise. While exclusion possibilities provide a conceivable basis for the profitable provision of parks by private enterprise, it does not ensure that parks will be optimally provided by private enterprise.

The first possibility is that although exclusion is possible it may be relatively unprofitable to collect admission fees. Taking into account the cost of collection, private enterprise may find that development of its land is more profitable even though the net social advantage lies with free access to the land in its natural state. Or again consider the case of a landowner who wishes to retain a wilderness area or has no development possibility for it. Suppose that he does not find it profitable to collect fees from visitors to the area. He might make its use free. On the other hand, complete exclusion might involve little cost or use might be reduced at little cost *e.g.* by signs indicating that trespassers are prosecuted. This will appeal to the landowner if there is likelihood of any unfavourable externality to his adjoining property. Exclusion is liable to occur though it is unwarranted from the social point of view in the sense that potential users could compensate the landowner for his potential loss. State operation of the park with free access to potential users may be called for. However, let us now consider the performance of private enterprise if the cost of collecting fees is a minor one.

The performance depends upon the number of individuals supplying park facilities and the state of competition. In view of the heterogeneous nature of the commodity some degree of individual monopoly is likely to be common. Take the case of an individual who owns a natural feature and has no competitors in the immediate neighbourhood. He has a monopoly which may arise from the differentiation of his product as well as from spatial factors.

If a landowner has a monopoly in the provision of natural parkland in an area, how much of his land will be set aside as natural parkland and how does this quantity compare with the socially optimal quantity? Let us deal with this in a simplified manner. For a park of any given size, it is supposed that the marginal cost of an extra entry to the park is zero. Thus the socially optimal number of entries is the number for which the extra value of entry is zero *i.e.*, the number

[1] Natural parkland or other parkland can give rise to a pure public commodity. For example, parkland which is overlooked by residences and so affords their occupants excellent views might be in this category. There is likely to be no economic way of making the view subject to a payment.

for which the demand curve is zero. However, assuming a downward-sloping demand curve for entry and that the monopolist is unable to discriminate between entries, he finds it most profitable to restrict entry to the level at which his marginal revenue is zero. He is unable to appropriate the whole value of the park to consumers.

As the size of the park varies, it is reasonable to suppose that the demand curve for using it will alter and almost certainly increase. Consequently, the monopolist's maximum revenue (equals profit from parkland) changes with the size of the park as does the maximum amount which consumers are willing to pay for the optimal social use of the park. It seems likely that both of these curves as functions of the size of the park increase at first at an increasing rate but eventually exhibit diminishing marginal values. Examples of their corresponding marginal curves as a function of park size are shown in Figure 1 by the curves *PMR* and *ABD* respectively. Since the monopolist is unable to appropriate the whole of the extra (potential) value of the extra parkland to consumers, *PMR*

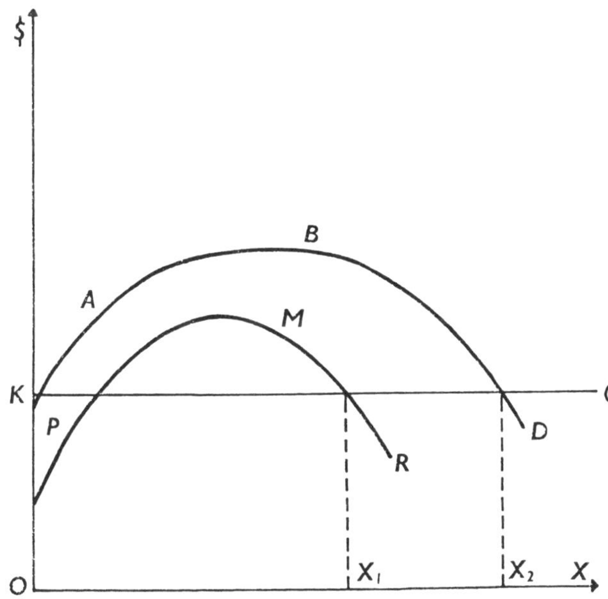

ACRES OF NATURAL PARKLAND

FIGURE 1

is below *ABD*. Consequently, the monopolist provides less than an optimal quantity of parkland. For example, let *KC* represent the marginal opportunity cost of natural parkland. It might be the return from using the land for meat production. The monopolist maximises his profit by supplying only X_1 acres for parkland although X_2 acres are socially optimal. Any land which the landowner has in excess of X_1 is used for the next best alternative, e.g. meat production.

A landowner's monopoly may vary greatly and Dolan suggests measures to strengthen it. In order to get the government out of the business of preserving nature, Dolan describes "excess-taking"[2] as a useful mechanism [6, p. 98]. By this system, a developer is not only sold the immediate tourist attraction but also an adjoining area. On developing the tourist attraction, *e.g.*, a ski run, the developer is able to utilize the adjoining land in any way that he wishes *e.g.*, he might dispose of it for ski lodges. But this method may also enable the entrepreneur to eliminate competition and undersupply the recreational facility in his area.

Owners who obtain monopolies in addition to underproviding parks and recreational facilities may underutilize such facilities as are provided. In the absence of price discrimination, this social underutilization is liable to occur since the monopolist, in order to maximise his profit, fixes a fee which is in excess of marginal cost.

III. Externalities, Neighbourhood Effects and Spillovers

Natural parks are not pure public goods but do give rise to externalities of various kinds. While some of these externalities are favourable, others may be unfavourable. Wind, water erosion and flooding may be less if natural land cover remains than if agricultural development takes place [8]. Also the cost of purifying water for any nearby population is liable to be lower and the supply of water less variable if natural cover is left in a catchment area. On the other hand, the risk of serious fire damage to nearby properties may be increased and marauding animals from the reserves may damage nearby crops and fences.[3]

The above spillovers are fairly obvious. However, there are others which although less direct are of considerable importance. Research by psychologists and sociologists indicate that crowding of human populations into cities tends to breed aggressiveness and violence and that the influence is more marked if individuals are unable to retreat to comparatively open spaces. If this is so, it provides a sound basis for subsidising the use of beaches, natural parks and so on. By increasing the use of these facilities, one reduces crime and the general viciousness of society. In my opinion, this is a favourable externality of considerable importance.

Again, other problems of appropriation occur. Owners may have no incentive to preserve animals and species of little commercial value and may not build reserves of sufficient size to ensure their survival in a natural state. For example, nocturnal animals may fail to be tourist attractions. Nevertheless, the preservation of such species may be of interest to scientists. Dolan suggests that scientists be given grants to pay for the preservation of these species.

[2] Excess-taking arises, for example, if a developer is assigned the obligation to provide a particular facility in a park and in consideration is granted the exclusive right to develop an area in the vicinity of the facility in whatever (commercial) manner he wishes. The developer is thereby enabled to appropriate the whole or part of the quasi-rents from the provision of the main facility. I understand that Thredbo Village in The Kosciusko State Park has been developed on a similar principle.

[3] Kangaroos in Australia sometimes break fences and foul drinking water for stock. They also compete to some extent with domestic stock for food, but the extent of the competition is debatable. See *Conservation and Commercial Exploitation of Kangaroos, Parliamentary Paper No. 219,* An Interim Report from the House of Representatives Select Committee on Wildlife Conservation, Commonwealth Government Printing Office, Canberra, 1971, p. 35.

In the absence of state interference, the externalities mentioned above are liable to lead to the underprovision of natural parks if their supply is left to private enterprise. While it might be possible to subsidise private suppliers of parks, the determination of the appropriate subsidy is likely to be difficult.

IV. Irreversibility and Uncertainty

It is frequently argued that, once natural areas are destroyed, it is almost impossible to restore them at a later time. Given this irreversibility, there ought to be some weighting against commercial development of natural areas. But, as Dolan contends, this irreversibility is likely to be taken into account by private owners [6, p. 91]. He then goes on the claim that "the irreversibility argument turns out to work not in favour of extending our national park system as it now exists but of turning it into a system of private parks to provide surer protection for the future" [6, p. 92]. While agreeing that private enterprise does take account of irreversibility, I believe that, given irreversibility and allowing for uncertainty, the likelihood of private enterprise preserving less than a socially optimal quantity of natural land is high.

This conclusion follows if firms on the whole are risk averters, if the variance (or risk element) of returns increases with time, and if the expected return from natural land tends to rise above "cultivated" or developed land with the passage of time. For simplicity, two alternative paths are indicated in Figure 2. Path 1 is the expected return from natural land and path 2 that from the same land if developed.[4] The irreversibility argument implies that the choice of path 2 excludes

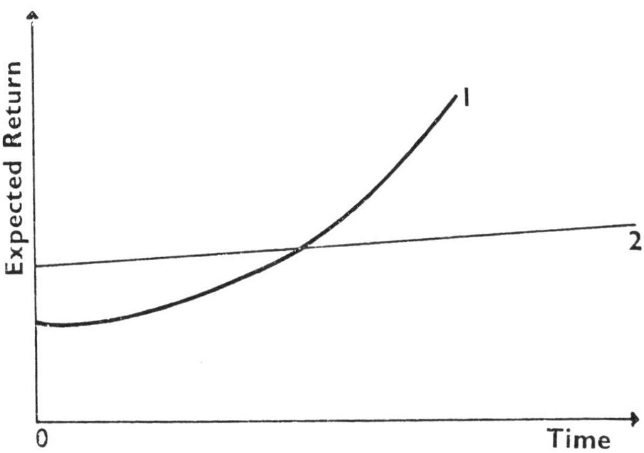

FIGURE 2

[4] The expected return from parkland is assumed to increase at a faster rate than for developed land because (a) technological progress in the supply of parkland is absent or slow whereas that for the products of development are greater and (b) the demand for parkland may be more responsive to income and population increases than for alternative products from the land. Ranken and Sinden have recently reported their empirical results on the demand for outdoor recreation but these do not permit us to draw a comparison like that made in (b). See R. L. Ranken and J. A. Sinden, "Causal Factors in the Demand for Outdoor Recreation", *Economic Record*, vol. 47, 1971.

the possibility of returning to path 1. If uncertainty (risk) is a regular compounding function of time then it might be allowed for by adding a premium to the interest rate. Assume that the appropriate premium for risk is the same for each project. The addition of the premium increases the probability that the present discounted value of the plan for path 2 exceeds that for path 1, *i.e.*, that development gives a higher adjusted present value than leaving the land in its natural state. Furthermore the greater is uncertainty about the future returns and the greater is the premium, the more likely is it that the entrepreneur will choose commercial development since the addition relatively favours the *adjusted* present value of development. The choice in favour of development is likely to be made even if the *expected* present value of virgin land is higher than developed land.

If the returns from the various projects of society are not perfectly correlated, then risk in aggregate is less than the riskiness of individual projects. By pooling arrangements, it might be possible to reduce individual risks to the aggregate level. State ownership makes pooling and sharing possible even when private ownership is unable, as Arrow shows [1, 2], to take full advantage of pooling and sharing possibilities. If pooling is fully effective, a social optimum requires that *expected* returns from projects be maximised and this is unlikely to happen under private enterprise.[5]

In belittling the irreversibility argument, Dolan also suggests that irreversibility is rare. For example, he claims that land can be reafforested after a fairly short interval of time. However, there are causes where reversibility is impossible, *e.g.*, where species have disappeared. Furthermore, the above argument still has some force if processes cannot easily be reversed.

The so-called options argument [10] is sometimes urged as a basis for interference. It is claimed that consumers wish to have an option (for themselves and their descendants) of being able to use natural parks in the future but that they are unable to give economic force to their wish. While entrepreneurs will take account of the probable demand for natural parkland, individual owners are faced by risks and if they are risk-avoiders this will lead to the undersupply of natural parkland. Prospective consumers would be willing to pay a sum for an extra supply if only this could be organized.

V. The Government and the Provision of Parks

The above discussion indicates that private enterprise cannot be relied upon to provide an optimal quantity of parks and that it is, indeed, liable to provide an insufficient quantity. If private enterprise cannot be relied upon to provide an optimal quantity of parks, is the government likely to do better?

[5] The appropriate rule for the socially optimal allocation of resources under conditions of risk and uncertainty is far from clear, especially since second best problems arise. Hirschleifer has maintained [2] that the overall expected (net) returns from resources should be maximised. With certainty-equivalent returns in the private sector tending to be below the expected value of returns, it can be shown that this rule may require the public sector to add a premium to the riskless interest rate in evaluating its investments On the other hand, Arrow and Lind [2] contend that a social optimum requires a Paretian optimum with respect to expected utilities whatever are the constraints in the system. Under this assumption, it may be optimal for the public sector to equate marginal expected returns from its projects with the riskless rate of interest despite the presence of risk aversion in the private sector.

Assuming that social decisions are reached by majority voting, Dolan claims that the government will oversupply natural parks. If general tax revenue is used to finance projects which offer a special benefit to a fraction of the population, "except in the limiting case where all political decisions are made under the rule of unanimity, each such project will be funded beyond the point where the marginal cost of the project equals its marginal benefit" [6, p. 85]. Dolan then suggests that since there is not unanimous support for the provision of natural parks, natural parks will be overprovided. However, one can reasonably doubt Dolan's proposition and more possibilities exist than Dolan recognizes. Consider majority voting.

If the marginal net evaluation curve of each developer is the opposite of the marginal net evaluation curve of each conservationist then natural parks will be overprovided if conservationists are in the majority, but underprovided if developers are in the majority. In the former case, conservationists will press conservation until their (summed) marginal net evaluation is zero and in the latter case developers will secure development of land until their (summed) marginal evaluation is zero. Note, however, in neither case does majority voting lead to a Paretian optimum. All parties could reach an improved situation by a reorganization. This can be seen with the aid of Figure 3.

In Figure 3, *OAU* is the marginal evaluation of a developer and *DCT* that of a conservationist. On the above assumptions, and given *OD* acres of land, *OC* acres of land are conserved if conservationists are in the majority but only *OA* acres if developers are in the majority. In the first case, the sum of the marginal evaluation curve of conservationists is zero whereas the sum for developers is

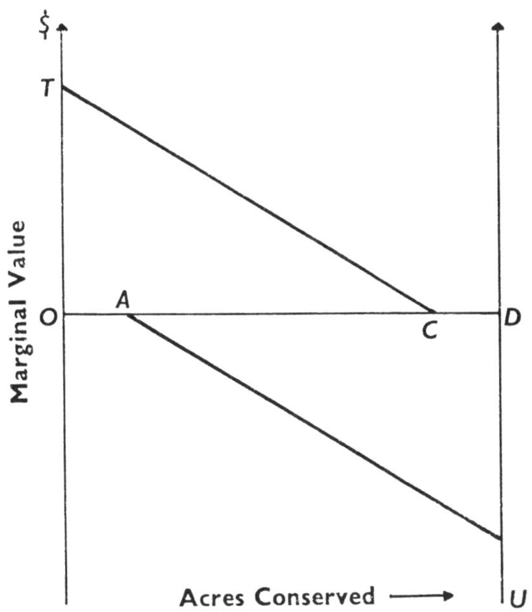

FIGURE 3

negative. Developers could bribe conservationists to reduce the quantity of natural parkland and still gain. The opposite situation exists if developers are in the majority. Majority rule results in a sub-Paretian optimal outcome. (This also occurs under less restrictive conditions.) As Tullock points out [10], logrolling[6] can lead to a Paretian improvement in these cases. Certainly majority rule does not necessarily result in a social optimum.

However, there is at least one special circumstance in which majority rule always leads to a Paretian optimum. It is the unlikely case in which the quantity of land is sufficient to satisfy the demands of both conservationists and developers so that no conflict arises. It occurs in the above example if $OC \leqslant OA$.

If majority rule prevails, natural parks are liable to be overprovided if conservationists are in the majority and to be undersupplied if developers are in the majority. The balance of numbers can only be decided by empirical observation.

Yet one might be deservedly sceptical about the relevance of the assumption of majority rule. Social decision-making is mostly delegated and voters rarely vote on particular issues but more often for a general policy. Each aspect of the general policy rarely has the support of the voter. Under this system conservationists can have varying degrees of influence, *e.g.*, if in the minority and a swinging vote they might obtain oversupply of natural parkland, or again if in the majority but not swinging the opposite might occur. Political decision-making is complex.

Again, many decisions of government are made by administrators who are often remote from the representative process. The types of decisions which they make also affect conservation and need study. Do administrators take a narrow departmental view? If so, how can a government organize effective countervailing forces in its administration? How can a ministry for conservation be an effective countervailing force?

The study of government is just as necessary to the study of economics as the study of markets even though the former may be the more difficult subject. As we have just seen, both the market and governments are liable not to provide an optimal quantity of natural parks. The above argument suggests that private enterprise will undersupply and that government will not necessarily oversupply natural parks. Both market failure and failure of the state seem possible but a firm conclusion cannot be drawn in the absence of adequate theories of government.

REFERENCES

1. K. J. Arrow, "Insurance, Risk and Resource Allocation", in *Aspects of the Theory of Risk-Bearing* (Helsinki: The Academic Bookstore, 1965).
2. K. J. Arrow and R. C. Lind, "Uncertainty and the Evaluation of Public Investments", *American Economic Review*, vol. 60, 1970.
3. K. J. Boulding, *Economics as Science* (New York: McGraw-Hill, 1970).
4. A. B. Costin and H. J. Firth, *Conservation* (Ringwood: Penguin Books Australia, 1971).
5. M. F. Day, "The Role of National Parks and Reserves in Conservation", in Costin and Frith, *op cit.*
6. B. G. Dolan, *TANSTAAFL: Economic Strategy for Environmental Crisis* (New York: Holt, Rinehart and Winston, 1971).

[6] Logrolling arises if there is trading of favours (political exchanges) among politicians.

7. W. Schwartz, ed., *Voices from the Wilderness* (New York: Ballentine Books, 1971).
8. J. A. Sinden, "An Economic Case for Conservation", in Costin and Frith *op cit.*
9. G. Tullock, "Problems of Majority Voting", *Journal of Political Economy*, vol. 67, 1959.
10. R. Zeckhauser, "Resource Allocation with Probabilistic Individual Preferences", *American Economic Review*, vol. 59, 1969.

[19]

Economics of wilderness[1]

Intangibles

The economics of wilderness is a complex subject. To deal with some of the issues raised by the supply of, demand for, and allocation of wilderness, economists have had to develop new analysis and additional theories.

One difficult issue is to decide what is wilderness and what are the desired attributes of wilderness areas; for discussion of the problem of defining wilderness areas, see Robertson (1972). The *Concise Oxford Dictionary* describes wilderness as a desert, or an uncultivated and uninhabited tract or part of garden left wild. We may ignore the last mentioned meaning in this context. To what extent must an area be uncultivated and uninhabited to be considered a wilderness area? While some needs or desires may only be met by absolute wilderness (leaving a tract to nature) other desires may be satisfied by allowing some economic development (building of roads, forestry, some housing and even some farming) while at the same time preserving some of the natural features of the land. In the case of absolute wilderness areas, the question of whether man should intervene is an open one. Should exotic and invasive species in these areas such as lantana be destroyed, should wild pigs be eradicated, should a wildlife species be managed so as to increase the species' chances of survival in the wilderness area? This depends upon the attributes desired from the tract of land.

Different individuals and the same individual at different times desire dissimilar characteristics from wilderness areas. Some of the intangibles obtained from wilderness and preserving wilderness are:

1. The possibility of obtaining solitude.
2. Of escaping from man-made or man-dominant environments and of obtaining renewal or regeneration from contact with Nature.
3. Of deriving challenge and adventure from meeting Nature on more equal terms than usual.
4. Of gaining knowledge or satisfying curiosity by studying Nature.
5. Of obtaining the idealistic satisfaction of acting in the role of man-the-preserver.
6. Of enjoying visual and related benefits.

The possibility of keeping various options open (options for oneself, for others now, or for others in the future), such as arise from the preservation of species or conservation of unique features, must also be considered amongst the intangible benefits of preserving wilderness.

Market prices do not register the total value of these intangibles. Market mechanisms are likely to underprice the worth of wilderness and result in the conservation of an inadequate amount of wilderness when this is entrusted to private supply.

Private ownership of property and its allocation to wilderness[2]

When property is privately owned and owners seek their own profit, less than a socially optimal amount of land is likely to be devoted to wilderness. In deciding on the use of their land, landowners are guided by the gains that they are able to appropriate from using their land. In the case of the use of the land for agricultural or pastoral purposes, for example for cattle production, landowners are able to appropriate all or virtually all of the social value of production of these goods at the margin. The prices of these goods closely reflect their social value.

A landowner can only appropriate a part of social value of providing wilderness. He can impose a charge upon those who use his wilderness area. However, their demand to use the area can be expected to be less than the total demand for or value placed on the area. For instance, non-visitors to the wilderness area may have an option demand for the area. They may be prepared to pay a sum to keep the option open for their visiting or benefiting from the wilderness area or to keep the option open for others, including future generations, visiting or benefiting from the wilderness area. Nevertheless, they may not be prepared to donate sums of money to a *private owner* for this purpose because there is always a chance that he will not continue to preserve the wilderness. Any legal action against the owner is likely to be hampered by the realisation that the gains of any plaintiff are likely to be small (though the gains of all injured parties combined may be great) and much in excess of his possible costs of action.

The existence of risk and uncertainty and their attitudes to these may also lead private owners of wilderness areas to prefer the development of these areas to their conservation, even though the latter is the better social policy. Short-term higher and more certain gains to be obtained from development may be preferred to greater long-term but more uncertain gains from leaving the land area as wilderness. In a social context and taking account of the law of large numbers, it may be appropriate to ignore uncertainty or place less emphasis on it in decision-making than is done by a private individual. Thus, private ownership leads to the development of more land than is socially optimal.

Wilderness: private or public good?

Economic theorists have distinguished between private goods and pure public goods and have suggested that markets are likely to supply private goods efficiently, but not public goods. A private good has the characteristic that the more one individual consumes of it, the less there is for any other individual. Radio is a good example of a public good – in the case of a pure public good, its consumption by any additional individual does not reduce the possibility of its consumption by others. Thus, any number of individuals with separate radios can tune into the same radio station without reducing its availability to others. In the case of a pure public good any number of people can jointly enjoy it. This is reviewed by Herfindahl and Kneese (1974).

However, wilderness is neither a private good nor a pure public good. It can be enjoyed *jointly* up to some level of carrying-capacity. Once the number of visitors to the area exceeds some level, the utility of existing visitors is likely to be reduced by additional visitors and the wilderness area damaged. In this respect it has the characteristic of a club-type good (see Buchanan, 1965). It might, however, be argued that some of the characteristics of wilderness are of the pure public good variety. The option of being able to visit the area may be shared by many and not be diminished in value by being shared by greater numbers.

For many individuals the preservation or provision of wilderness is a *merit* type *good* (see Head and Shoup, 1969, 1973). These individuals desire to increase others consumption of this good by interference with the allocation mechanism. Three types of situations may be distinguished:

1. The case in which a group of individuals wish to subsidise from their income the consumption or enjoyment of others of wilderness experiences. This group obtains utility from the consumption of others. They are prepared to subsidise the provision of wilderness from their own pockets. This approach is not restrictive of the freedom of others.
2. This case is similar to the previous one except that the approach is less philanthropic. All may be compulsorily levied to subsidise the provision of wilderness. The non-demanders of wilderness are made worse-off by the intervention while those who regard it as a merit good are made better off.
3. This case is an altruistic one, but involves minding the business of others. Compulsory contributions to the provision of wilderness or the subsidisation of wilderness experiences are considered to be justified because a fraction of the population underestimates the value to them of wilderness and of wilderness experiences.

A liberal approach or philosophy is inconsistent with cases (2) and (3). In case (2), State intervention serves special interests and in case (3), State intervention is the handmaiden of a group that believes that it knows the interest of others better than they themselves.

Property rights

Wilderness areas may be held in a number of alternative ways. They may be held:

1. As private property;
2. As common property;
3. As State property; and
4. As club property.

Each form of ownership has its limitations.

As pointed out earlier, private owners are not able to appropriate all relevant gains from the provision of wilderness. Apart from those limitations already mentioned, they are unlikely to obtain a payment for environmental services such as reducing the turbidity and maintaining the purity of water, lowering erosion rates and helping maintain the gene pool by preserving species. Private owners of wilderness could be subsidised by the State so as these externalities are taken into account by them, but this may be difficult to arrange politically. Alternatively, the State could impose conditions upon the owners of the property disallowing development or only allowing restricted development of the land. Some may, however, oppose this on the basis that it involves an undue interference with the rights and liberties of landowners.

From a conservation point of view, the approach of holding wilderness areas as common property is one of the least attractive. In this case, there are no regulations on the common use of property. Individuals may over-harvest natural species such as wildlife and excessively exploit resources in the area.[3] Uncoordinated and unzoned use of the area (by trail bikes, motor vehicles, nature-lovers, walkers) may needlessly reduce the satisfaction obtained by all users of the area.

When wilderness areas are state property, these may be supplied and managed in a socially optimal way. A benevolent state would appear to be in the best position to put into effect the idealistic or utopian allocations suggested by economists. In such an allocation, not only the benefits that can be appropriated from wilderness areas should be taken into account, but also other benefits which cannot be appropriated. Charging for the use of wilderness areas (if it is worthwhile to charge at all when the costs of collecting fees are taken into account) should be such as to promote efficient use of the area rather than maximise profit. When a private owner has a partial monopoly from ownership of a wilderness area, he may unduly restrict access to it to maximise his profit. The state need not do this. The state can protect wilderness areas against destructive individuals. By contrast, wilderness is unprotected when it is common property. The state can take account of the social relevance of externalities, option factors, uncertainty and merit considerations in supplying wilderness.

It would be folly to believe that the state is perfect. Public servants may be biased and ill-informed and political pressures are likely to stand in the way of ideal solutions. A study of political factors would appear to be an essential pre-requisite for assessing the likely performance of the state in providing wilderness areas (see Mosley, 1973).

Some writers are enthusiastic about the possibility that wilderness can be optimally preserved by individuals voluntarily clubbing together for this purpose (see Dolan, 1971: Ch. 7). Individuals form and subscribe to clubs to purchase wilderness areas and preserve these and then members can jointly use the facility.

There are, however, a number of reasons why club ownership of wilderness is not likely to result in an ideal solution. There are costs involved in forming clubs (of contacting potential members and so on), which can be high when potential members are scattered and often fall unevenly on sponsors. A club may fail to form when it is optimal for it to do so, and even if a club is formed, its members are unlikely to appropriate all relevant gains from its provision. Externalities, some merit good and option characteristics are unlikely to be taken into account.

One of the least satisfactory features of clubs is that they are likely to restrict their membership and use of facilities to levels below a social optimum. Clubs tend to be too exclusive from the point of view of using resources efficiently.

This can be illustrated by Figure 1. Assume that a club is in existence and has a *unique* wilderness area.[4] For simplicity, suppose that all club members obtain the same utility from the facility and let their total utility be a function of club membership, n. Utility per head (net of costs) as a function of club membership can be expressed as U/n. In Figure 1, this reaches a maximum for a club membership of n_1 and supposing that a club aims to maximise the utility *per member*, n_1 is the optimal club size. However, the membership or participation that maximises the total utility to be obtained from the wilderness is greater. The marginal utility, rate of change of utility, $\frac{dU}{dn}$ as a function of club membership is indicated in the example shown in Figure 1. In this case, n_2 is the socially optimal number of members or participants for sharing the wilderness area if total utility from the facility is to be maximised. The loss in total utility from the club solution is indicated by the shaded area in Figure 1.

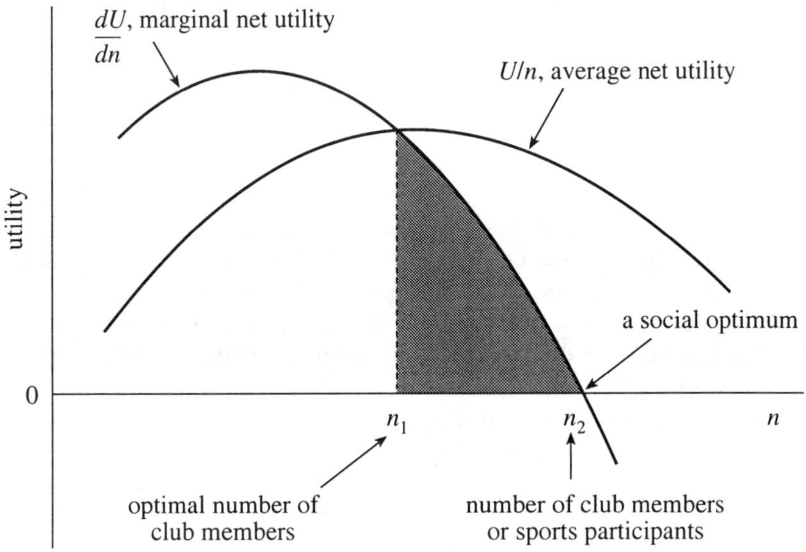

Figure 1 A club can result in overly restrictive access to a facility from a social point of view

Incidentally, it might be noted that n_2 is not the common-property solution. Common-property ownership could result in more than n_2 individuals using the area. In the case shown in Figure 2 the common property solution could result in up to n_4 individuals using the facility, thus rendering it valueless. However, the numbers available to use it may be less than n_4. It is then possible (if the only variable of significance is the number of participants) that total utility is greater for the common property solution than the club one. Any common-property use for a number of users between n_1 and n_3 in Figure 2 gives greater total utility than the club approach. The position of n_3 is determined by making the area with light shading equal to that with dark shading.

One may of course argue about whether total utility should be maximised, even granting that utility can be measured and that comparisons of interpersonal utility are possible for the purposes of meaningful discourse. Despite such qualms, it seems clear that a club can maximise its gains at the expense of a wider group. However, this does not mean that it is better for wilderness not to be provided than for it to be supplied by clubs.

Estimating the demand for wilderness – travel cost and other methods

The Clawson method (Clawson, 1959) has been widely used to estimate the recreational demand for wilderness areas, and demand estimated by this method has in turn been

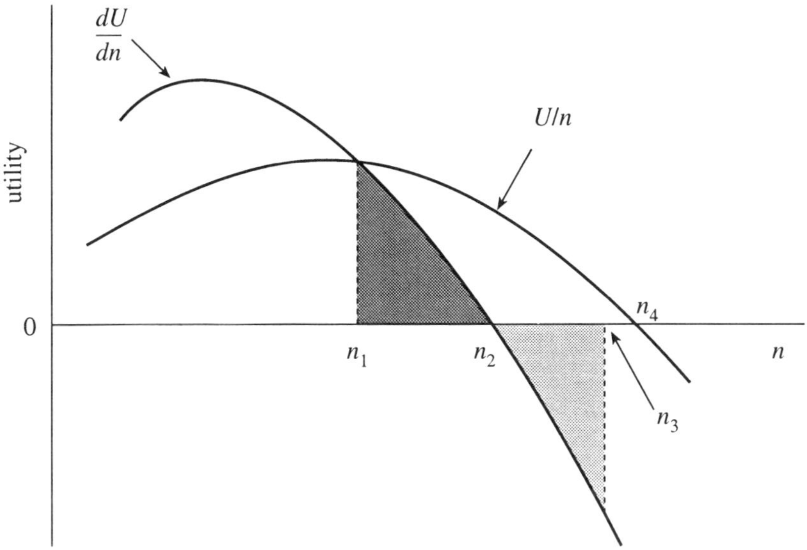

Figure 2 *Open access to a wilderness area can be socially preferable to access through membership of a club*

used to measure benefits from wilderness areas.[5] The Clawson method involves a cross sectional method of estimation. The analysis treats the cost of gaining access to an area (travel costs plus entry fees) as the price variable influencing the demand for visits to the area. Visitors over a period of time to the wilderness area are interviewed and data obtained upon the place from where their journey commenced and the cost of their travel. The frequency of visits from residential zones at different distances from the park is then calculated and related to access costs (in the case where fees are not charged, travel costs). Assuming that on average the demand of individuals in each zone for visits to the park or wilderness area is the same in relation to the cost of access, the demand curve for visits to the wilderness area can be constructed.

There have been a number of criticisms of the Clawson method, not all of which can be repeated here. For instance, the method may overestimate the value of the park because the whole travel experience may generate the observed visits to the park. The cross sectional sample may exhibit systematic bias. For example, those with higher education and more income may be located more distant from the park and since visits may also be positively related to these variables, the estimated demand curves may not accurately reflect demand. Again, the demand for visits to a wilderness area may vary with the degree of crowding in the area. Estimates of the demand curve for visits obtained when the degree of crowding is low are likely to give inflated predictions of demand as use rises. This in turn can easily result in the value of improvements, such as road improvements that lower transport costs, being exaggerated. There is also the difficulty that it is not only current demand that needs to be taken into account in evaluating the demand for a wilderness area. Future demand enters most evaluations and this is not always easy to predict. Demand may shift because of population variations, changes in income and alterations in preferences, for example, and these changes may be imperfectly predictable.

On the other hand, it needs to be stressed that the demand for visits to a wilderness area, no matter how accurately measured, only measures a part of the value of a wilderness area. Externalities, the keeping open of options, see Fisher et al. (1972) and Tisdell (1972), merit good considerations and the value of maintaining a gene pool are not taken into account.

Apart from the Clawson method, indifference curve and utility analysis has been used, for example, by Sinden (1974, 1976) to derive the demand for wilderness-type areas. These approaches, as a rule, involve interviewing or experimenting with individuals to determine their preferences. They are usually costly, and individuals may fail to reveal their true preferences. Demand curves for wilderness obtained by these methods are also subject to most of the limitations that apply to those obtained by the Clawson method.

Cost–benefit analysis and wilderness provision

Cost–benefit or C–B analysis is the term applied to methods that systematically weigh up the costs and benefits of economic alternatives. An overview of C–B analysis is given by Mishan (1971) and by Herfindal and Kneese (1974). As a rule an attempt is made to express all relevant costs and benefits in money terms or equivalents. C–B analysis does not provide one with a ready-made technique of assessing the comparative value of different alternative uses of resources.

It can only be an adequate guide to the choice of the best policy if all relevant costs and benefits are taken into account and correctly or appropriately assessed. The 'rubbish-in rubbish-out' relationship clearly applies to this analysis. Furthermore, there can be genuine disagreement about how to express benefits and costs in money terms. For instance, how satisfactory is it to use consumers' surplus as an indication of benefits to consumers? How does one measure the benefits of a policy when some individuals are made worse off as a result of a change and others better off? In the end, C–B analysis raises all the awkward questions raised in welfare economics.

Nevertheless, C–B analysis is a rational approach to considering the alternative uses of resources and the cost of foregoing alternatives. An alternative to it is not to consider systematically the cost and benefits of the alternative use of resources, an approach that is unsatisfactory. However, C–B analysis is not the only rational method for considering the optimal allocation of resources. Multivariate analysis involving a lexicographic or hierarchical ordering may, for instance, be used for rational choice. Multivariate analysis assumes that all valued things cannot be reduced to a common measuring rod such as money.

In most C–B analysis, there is a need to take account of time and uncertainty. The stream of benefits and costs involved in maintaining a wilderness area and of the alternatives to this will vary through time. How does one take account of the fact that benefits more distant in time are likely to be of less value than more immediate benefits? Normally this has been done by discounting future benefits and costs by a discount factor varying with the rate of interest and the extent to which the gains and benefits occur in the future. However, problems have arisen in deciding on the appropriate rate of interest to apply. In practice, there is a range of interest rates and the rate on long-term government bonds (which is often used) varies with the passage of time and may itself be subject to manipulation by the government. The view has also been expressed that individuals discount the future too heavily and that the appropriate rate of social discount should be lower than that observed in practice. The need for discounting is not disputed by most economists, but some admit that they do not like social discounting in certain cases. One such case occurs when the application of a discount rate indicates that it is optimal to eradicate a species.

There is also some controversy about how best to allow for uncertainty about future costs and benefits. One approach is to adjust the interest rate in the discounting factor upwards to allow for greater degrees of uncertainty. This method is not always defensible. The procedure is *ad hoc*. Another approach is to attempt to find the certainty equivalents to the uncertain situations, that is the assured gain considered to be just as good as the set of uncertain gains. Whose preferences should count in this regard? Should the government make as much allowance for uncertainty as private individuals? Arrow and Lind (1970) have persuasively argued that the government should make less allowance for uncertainty. For one thing, the government has the benefit of the law of large numbers on its side. The issues are, however, not completely resolved. The type of allowance made for uncertainty of benefits from wilderness and for the gains from alternative uses of the land can sway choice between the alternatives.

Controlling and rationing the use of wilderness areas

The charging of fees or prices provides one means of rationing the use of wilderness areas. Where fees are effective in restricting entry to a wilderness area, they ensure that those individuals, who place greatest store on visiting the wilderness area in relation to their income or means, gain access. Allocation of access is on the basis of private demand. While it is true that willingness to pay determines entry, ability to pay is also a determinant.

If a fee is charged for entry to a wilderness area, it is necessary to determine its appropriate level. Should it be determined so as to maximise receipts or profit? Should it be determined so as to encourage a socially optimal amount of utilisation of the wilderness area? In the latter case, if crowding is not a problem, the fee should be sufficiently low to ensure that no individual, for whom the value of visiting the wilderness area is in excess of extra cost generated, is dissuaded from visiting it. Where crowding is a problem, higher fees may be charged to take this into account. In some circumstances, multi-part pricing (discounts for an increased number of visits such as season tickets) is a useful method of maintaining economic efficiency in the use of an area and increasing the amount of finance received from visitors.

Alternatives to using pricing for rationing include:

1. Regulation of entry by administrative rules. For example, entry permits may only be given to a restricted category of persons, for instance scientists from a particular field, members of approved clubs, etc.
2. Means of access, such as roads to the area, may be deliberately left in poor condition to deter visitors.

Within a wilderness area, there is also the problem of dealing with the conflicting interests of users. There are several ways in which conflict between users of a wilderness area can be reduced. These include:

1. Zoning of uses.
2. Limitations on use for particular purposes.
3. Rules limiting the acceptable behaviour of users.

Sometimes zoning (separation) of activities is better than allowing these to be jointly carried on in restricted ways. In some circumstances all parties prefer zoning (separation) to a mixed approach entailing restrictions on their activities. However, there has been little economic analysis of this problem, although Mishan (1967a, b) raised it.

Some wider issues

There is always the danger that an economist may take too partial a view of the conservation of wilderness. An economist *qua* economist in the tradition of Robbins (1952; and Tisdell, 1977b) is expected to take values as given and not to influence these. In dealing with the preservation of wilderness areas, he may, for instance, take society's values about population growth and the growth of production as given even though he may realise from a wider stance that such values pose a great threat to wilderness.

There is, however, a growing group of economists who advocate a more general (less partial) stance by economists, for example Doeleman (1976). They are not arguing about whether the discount rate should be adjusted downward as Pigou does, or not used at all as suggested by Frank Ramsey, but are firmly advocating a conservationist ethic and are drawing implications from it. These approaches are discussed, for instance, by Scott (1973), and Page (1977) has recently given one of the clearest expositions of the high conservationist approach.

The values of the high conservationists and the difficulties, which they see in the traditional economic approach to decisions about wilderness, are well expressed in a part of J. Doeleman's comments on the draft of this paper. He says:

> A general and fundamental objection exists in my mind. Taking a wide view, I think it is fair to say that we live in an age – taking the last one or two centuries – in which wilderness by whichever definition has been so greatly reduced that only some petty remnants remain of the variety and complexity evolved in nature over millions of years. Much has already been lost irreversibly as a result of the substitution for simple man-made environments. What remains is under serious threat, including the ocean environment, the Amazon wilderness in South America, the Great Barrier Reef in Australia and so on. It is noteworthy that what remains almost invariably remained because of negative reasons such as inaccessibility or inhospitality of the environment. Positive decision to reserve wilderness is to date almost exclusively linked to grounds of low opportunity costs. With modern communication, transportation and production technology, opportunity costs are rising. They are further rising as a result of demographics and economic growth. The point I am driving at is that we might wish the discussion in the paper not merely to be directed at questions of *supply and demand* for wilderness and the shortcomings of its equating mechanisms, but also to the *salvation* of wilderness. The presented analysis, therefore, is not invalid or less than useful. On the contrary. However, I do claim it is incomplete. The salvation of wilderness requires

> *absolute* standards (absolute at least in the context of centuries rather than millions of years). Such standards, based on our roots in nature and our ethical responsibilities to future generations, should not be compromised under the pressures of demographic, technological and economic growth as they will without doubt if the proposed philosophy in the paper is adopted. Even allowing for 'optional demand', internalisation of externalities, adequate resolution of public good allocation, full knowledge and so on, the optimal supply of wilderness will depend on the number of people competing for it, the technology at their disposal and the purchasing power and preferences of these people. All these factors appear to lead inevitably, I think, to the further annihilation of wilderness and the facts to date are indisputably supporting this unpalatable view. If then the standard of wilderness supply cannot be compromised, it follows that demographic technological and/or economic dynamics need to be compromised instead. (Doeleman, pers. comm.)

Economists do need to take a wider perspective, especially when they act as social philosophers rather than technocrats. Technocrats are needed, but it would be a sad day for mankind if economists were all reduced to the status of technocrats unable to support any particular values. (The opposite situation could well also be disastrous.)

The values of society can be influenced and do alter, at least in the long term (Passmore, 1974). As Downs (1973) points out, the costs and benefits of organising politically in a democracy and the myopic view of the elected (because of the relatively short periods of office of the government and the myopia of the electorate) result in distorted conservationist decisions (Scott, 1976 and Tisdell, 1972). Furthermore, conservationist values in society may be distorted by the economic process and the nature of economic organisation (Tisdell, 1977a). All conservationists' questions cannot be answered by the traditional economic approach and by appeal to predominate values in society. For instance, as asked in a recent paper (Tisdell, 1979), are we justified in eliminating a species if on balance the species is shown to be a nuisance?

The economics of wilderness is a wide subject and this paper has only been able to touch upon the fringes of it. It raises questions at the frontier of economic thought and many of these questions are as yet unresolved. Economists have gone a considerable way in systematising the issues involved in the decision to allocate areas to wilderness-type use and in determining the use of these areas.

Notes

1. The content of this article is the same as in the original (except for minor changes) but its presentation has been improved. Consequently, pagination is no longer the same as in the original.
2. For a discussion of the issues raised in this section, see Tisdell (1972) and Sinden (1977).
3. The occurrence of over harvesting of wildlife when it is common property is well recognised. See Gordon (1954), and more recently Scott (1973) and Clark (1976).
4. For a theoretical discussion of some further cases of the resource use by clubs, see Tisdell (1977).
5. For a general discussion of this method see Whitby et al. (1974) and Tisdell (1976). For an Australian application of the method, see Greig (1976).

References

Arrow, K.J. and R.C. Lind (1970), 'Uncertainty and the evaluation of public investment decisions', *American Economic Review*, **60**, 364–78.

Buchanan, J.M. (1965), 'An economic theory of clubs', *Economica*, **35**, 1–14.

Clark, C.W. (1976), *Mathematical Bioeconomics*, New York: Wiley.

Clawson, M. (1959), 'Methods of measuring the demand for and value of outdoor recreation', *Resources for the Future*, Reprint No.10, Washington, DC.

Doeleman, J.A. (1976), 'Notes on the art, science and relevance of cost–benefit analysis', *Board of Environmental Studies Research Paper No. 5.*

Dolan, E.G. (1971), *TANSTAAFL: An Economic Strategy for Environmental Crisis*, New York: Holt, Rinehart and Winston, Ch. 7.

Downs, A. (1973), 'The political economy of improving our environment', in J. Bain (ed.), *Environmental Decay*, Boston: Little Brown.

Fisher, A.C., J.V. Krutilla and C.J. Cichetti (1972), 'Alternative uses of natural environments: the economics of environmental modification', in J.V. Krutilla (ed.), *Natural Environments*, Baltimore: Johns Hopkins Press, 18–53.

Gordon, H.S. (1954), 'Economic theory of a common property resource: the fishery', *Journal of Political Economy*, **62**, 124–42.

Greig, P. (1976), 'Cost–benefit analysis in recreation planning and policy making', in D. Mercer (ed.), *Leisure and Recreation in Australia*, Melbourne: Sorrett.

Head, J.G. and C.S. Shoup (1969), 'Public goods, private goods and ambiguous goods', *Economic Journal*, **79**.

Head, J.G. and C.S. Shoup (1973), 'Public goods, private goods and ambiguous goods reconsidered', *Public Finance*, **28**, 384–92.

Herfindahl, O.C. and A.V. Kneese (1974), *Economic Theory of Natural Resources*, Ohio: Merrill, Columbus, 48–50.

Mishan, E.J. (1971), *Cost–Benefit Analysis*, London: Allen and Unwin.

Mishan, E.J. (1967a), *The Costs of Economic Growth*, London: Staples Press.

Mishan, E.J. (1967b), 'Pareto Optimality and the Law', *Oxford Economic Papers*, November, 255–87.

Mosley, J.G. (1973), *Changing Government Policy on Resolution of Land-use Conflict*, Melbourne: Australian Conservation Foundation.

Page, T. (1977), *Conservation and Economic Efficiency – An Approach to Materials Policy*, Baltimore: Resources for the Future.

Passmore, J. (1974), *Man's Responsibility for Nature: Ecological Problems and Western Tradition*, London: Duckworth.

Robbins, L. (1952), *An Essay on the Nature and Significance of Economic Science*, 2nd edn, London: Macmillan.

Robertson, L.F. (1972), 'Wilderness and tourism', in A. Rapaport (ed.), *Australia as Human Setting*, Sydney: Angus and Robertson, 213–36.

Scott, A.D. (1973), *Natural Resources: The Economics of Conservation*, 2nd edn, Toronto: McClelland and Stewart.

Scott, A.D. (1976), 'Is the government the guardian of future generations?', A paper presented to *Environmental Economics Conference*, organised by Department of Environment, Housing and Community Development and Centre for Resource and Development Studies, Australian National University, Canberra, 29–30 May, 1976.

Sinden, J.A. (1974), 'A utility approach to the valuation of recreational and aesthetic experiences', *American Journal of Agricultural Economics*, **56**, 61–72.

Sinden, J.A. (1976), 'Utility analysis in recreational research', in D. Mercer (ed.), *Leisure and Recreation in Australia*, Melbourne: Sorrett.

Sinden, J.A. (1977), 'Provision and use of national parks in Victoria: empirical tests of the Tisdell propositions', *Australian Economic Papers*, **16**, 175–93.

Tisdell, C. (1972), 'Provision of parks and the preservation of nature: some economic factors', *Australian Economic Papers*, **11**, 154–62.

Tisdell, C. (1976), 'National Parks: economic issues', in D. Mercer (ed.), *Leisure and Recreation in Australia*, Melbourne: Sorrett.

Tisdell, C. (1977a), 'Coalitions and clubs – aspects of their formation and economic efficiency', in R. Henn and O. Moeschlin (eds), *Mathematical Economics and Game Theory: Essays in honour of Oskar Morgenstern*, Berlin: Springer-Verlag, 446–56.

Tisdell, C. (1977b), 'Dissent from value, preference and choice theory in economics', *Research Report or Occasional Paper No. 35*, Department of Economics, University of Newcastle.

Tisdell, C. (1979), 'On the economics of saving wildlife from extinction', *ANZAAS Conference*, Section 24, University of Auckland, New Zealand.

Whitby, M.C., D.L.J. Robins, A.W. Tansey and K.G. Willis (1974), *Rural Resource Development*, London: Methuen.

[20]

THE PROVISION OF WILDERNESS BY CLUBS

by
CLEM TISDELL (*)

Abstract

It has been argued that wilderness can be optimally preserved by clubs. Apart from the more obvious difficulties involved in forming clubs and their failure to take account of externalities, clubs are likely to be too exclusive to maximise social welfare. Because of their exclusiveness, clubs are likely to result in a less than socially optimal use of wilderness from a Kaldor-Hicks point of view. Indeed, the common-property solution may result in greater social welfare than the club approach. The argument can be generalized to the provision of other facilities (apart from wilderness) in limited supply.

Some writers are enthusiastic about the possibility that wilderness can be optimally preserved by individuals voluntarily clubbing together for this purpose [1]. Individuals form and subscribe to clubs to purchase wilderness areas and preserve these. Club members can then jointly use the facility.

There are however a number of reasons why club ownership of wilderness or similar resources is not likely to result in an ideal solution. There are costs involved in forming clubs (of contacting potential members and so on). These costs can be high when potential members are scattered and often fall unevenly on sponsors. A club may fail to form when it is

---

(*) University of Newcastle, Dept. of Economics, Newcastle, N.S.W. 2308, Australia.

(1) See E. G. DOLAN, *TANSTAAFL: An Economic Strategy for Environmental Crisis*, Holt, Rinehart and Winston, New York, 1971, Ch. 7.

optimal for it to do so. However, even if a club is formed its members are unlikely to appropriate all relevant gains from its provision. Externalities, some merit good and option characteristics are unlikely to be taken into account.

But one of the least satisfactory features of clubs is that they are likely to restrict their membership and use of facilities to levels below a social optimum. Clubs tend to be too exclusive from the point of view of using resources efficiently.

This can be illustrated by Figure 1. Assume that a club is in existence and has a *unique* wilderness area. For simplicity suppose that all club members obtain the same utility from the facility and let their total utility be a function of club membership, *n*. Utility per head (net of costs) as a function of membership can be expressed as U/n. In Figure 1, this reaches

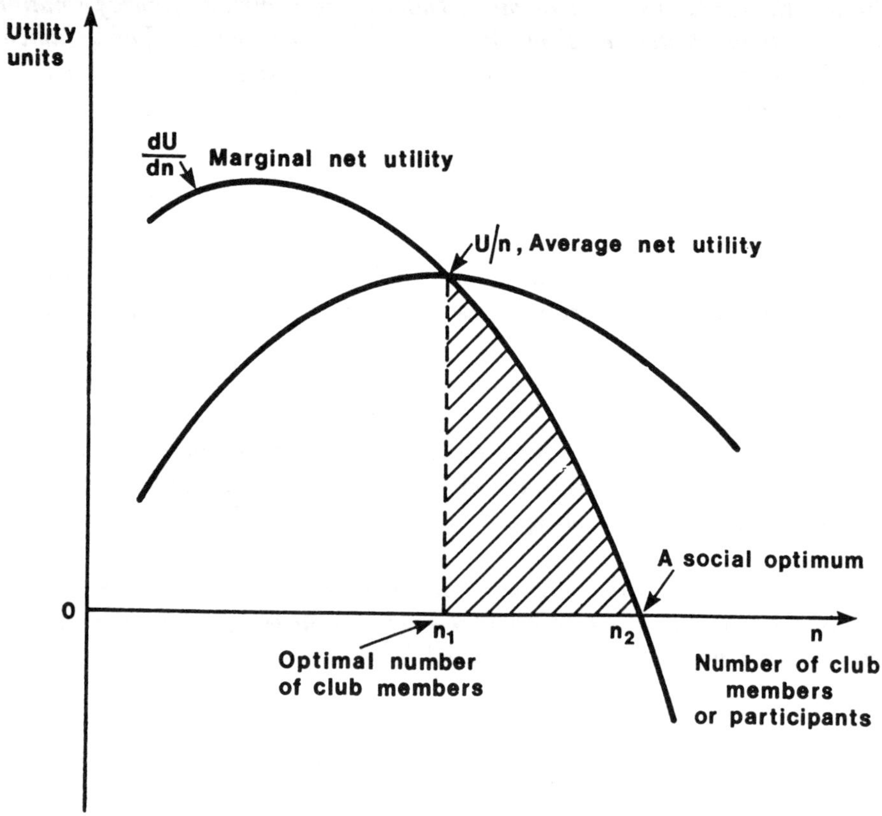

FIGURE 1. - A club can result in overly restrictive access to a facility from a social point of view.

a maximum for a club membership of n_1 and supposing that a club aims at maximising the utility per member, n_1 is the optimal club size. However, the membership or participation which maximizes the *total* utility to be obtained from the wilderness is greater. The marginal utility, rate of change of utility, $\frac{dU}{dn}$ as a function of club membership is indicated in the example shown in Figure 1. In this case, n_2 is the socially optimal number of members or participants for sharing the wilderness area if total utility from the facility is to be maximised. The loss in total utility from the club solution is indicated by the hatched area in Figure 1.

Incidentally, it might be noted that n_2 is not the common-property solution. Common-property ownership could result in more than n_2 individuals using the area. In the case shown in Figure 2 the common property solution could result in up to n_4 individuals using the facility, thus rendering it valueless. However, the numbers available to use it may be less than n_4. It is then possible (if the only variable of significance is the number of

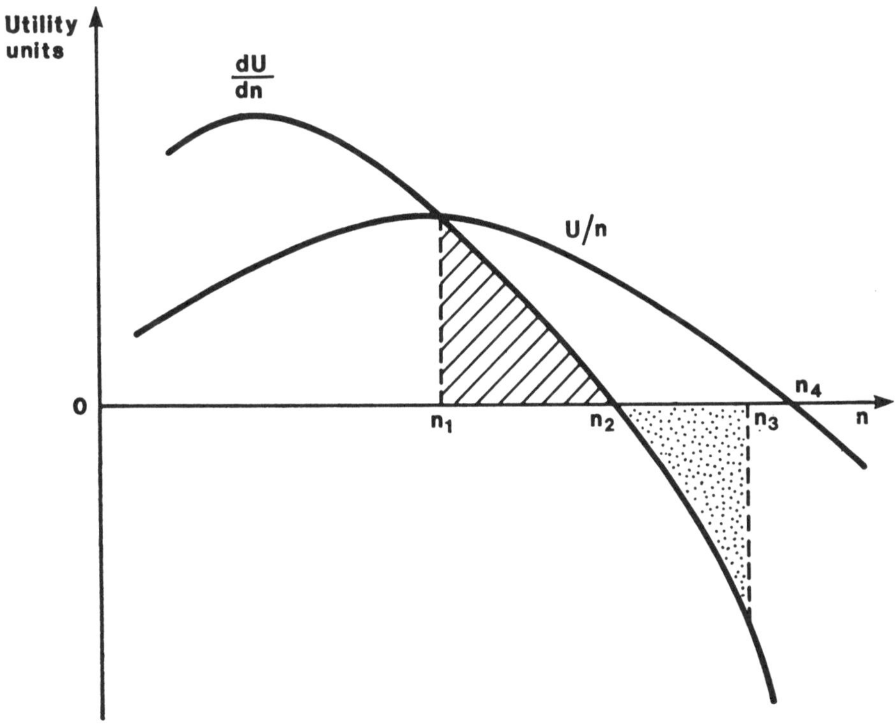

FIGURE 2.

participants) that total utility is greater for the common-property solution than the club one. Any common-property use for a number of users between n_1 and n_3 in Figure 2 gives greater total utility than the club approach. The position of n_3 is determined by making the area of the dotted area equal to the hatched area.

One may of course argue about whether total utility should be maximised, even granting that utility can be measured and that comparisons of interpersonal utility are possible for the purposes of meaningful discourse. Despite such qualms, it seems clear that a club can maximise its gains at the expense of a wide group (2). However, this does not mean that it is better for wilderness not to be provided than for it to be supplied by clubs.

LA PROTEZIONE DELLA NATURA PER MEZZO DEI CLUB

E' stato asserito che la natura incontaminata può essere protetta dai club in modo ottimale. A parte le piú ovvie difficoltà connesse alla creazione dei club e il fatto che essi non tengono conto delle esternalità, i club sono probabilmente troppo esclusivi per massimizzare il benessere sociale. Per la loro esclusività è probabile che i club determinino un uso della natura non ottimale socialmente dal punto di vista di Kaldor-Hicks. In verità, la soluzione della proprietà comune può dare un maggiore benessere sociale di quella dei club. Il problema può essere esteso alla protezione di altre risorse di cui v'è scarsità (oltre la natura incontaminata).

(2) For a theoretical discussion of some further cases of the resource use by clubs see C. Tisdell, « Coalitions and Clubs - Aspects of Their Formation and Economic Efficiency » in R. Henn and O. Moeschlin (eds.), *Mathematical Economics and Game Theory: Essays in Honour of Oskar Morgenstern,* Springer Verlag, Berlin, 1977, pp. 446-456. The possibility of a club resulting in a Pareto sub-optimal solution has been pointed out by Y-K. Ng, « The Economic Theory of Clubs: Pareto Optimal Conditions », *Economica*, Vol. 40, 1973, pp. 291-298 in his critique of J. Buchanan, « An Economic Theory of Clubs », *Economica,* Vol. 32, 1965, pp. 1-14. Given the assumption in my paper that the supply of the good is not perfectly elastic, my view is close to Ng's as expounded in E. Helpman and A. Hillman, « Two Remarks on Optimal Club Size », *Economica,* Vol. 44, 1977, pp. 293-296.

Coastal Management, Volume 17, pp. 37–53
Printed in the U.K.

0892-0753/89 $3.00 + .00

Policy Issues Related to the Establishment and Management of Marine Reserves

CLEM TISDELL

University of Newcastle
N.S.W., 2308, Australia

JAMES M. BROADUS

Marine Policy and Ocean Management Center
Woods Hole Oceanographic Institution
Woods Hole, Massachusetts 02543

Abstract *Several hundred marine reserves now exist and their number is growing. The demand for additional marine reserves can also be expected to grow, especially since they seem to be relatively undersupplied compared to terrestrial biosphere reserves. Basic socioeconomic reasons are given as to why governments should establish marine reserves. Management problems are illustrated by reference to the Great Barrier Reef Marine Park and to the National Oceanic and Atmospheric Administration's (NOAA) governing of Title III of the Marine Protection, Research and Sanctuaries Act. The nature, clarity, and precision of objectives as set out in legislation are discussed, and the importance for management of public and political support is considered. Using economic analysis, an approach different to that used by some ecologists for determining the optimal size of reserves is outlined and the view of Soulé and Wilcox favoring many large reserves is modified. The natural difficulties involved in managing marine reserves are highlighted by comparison with land-based parks. Zoning and multiple-use are common features of marine reserves and require important management and policy decisions to be made about optimal (or at least satisfactory) zoning and multiple-use arrangements. Issues that ought to be taken into account and techniques for making such decisions are discussed, and it is suggested that there should be greater input from the social sciences in the management of marine reserves.*

Keywords Australia, marine parks/reserves, economics

Introduction

A large number of marine protected areas are scattered about the globe, and the list is growing. Silva *et al.* (1986), updating an earlier list prepared by Bjorklund (1974), note more than 500 such areas. However, to put that figure in perspective, over 3,500 major protected areas existed in 1985 (World Resources Institute and International Institute for Environment and Development, 1986). Hence, the number of marine reserves is less than a seventh of the total number of protected areas, a very low fraction when one considers that the major part of the earth's surface is covered by ocean. Furthermore, the definition by Silva *et al.* (1986) of a marine protected area is very broad; they "include as marine protected areas those terrestrial areas containing or bordering shorelines, estuaries or wetlands. Thus, a land-based national park, whose boundaries encompass an oceanic shoreline, thereby affording coastal protection, will appear in the listing as will the more obvious examples of a protected coral reef" (Silva *et al.*, 1986).

Given the growing number of marine reserves, the rising demand for marine nature preservation and the need to protect more marine areas, it is important to identify and discuss relevant policy issues in the establishment and management of marine reserves. In this paper marine reserves are regarded as marine protected areas containing mainly a marine component, rather than a terrestrial one. Of particular interest are those marine protected areas that are completely marine based, such as the Great Barrier Reef Marine Park (GBRMP).

Policy decisions about marine reserves can be separated for discussion purposes into two broad sets: (1) decisions about whether or not to establish a marine reserve (the establishment decision), and (2) decisions about how to manage it once it is established. However, these decisions are interdependent because the intended nature and objectives of management of a reserve can affect its prospect of being established. For example, in some instances there may be more political support for establishment of a marine reserve if it is to be managed for multiple-use rather than for a single purpose. In this paper, establishment decisions are considered first; then management decisions are discussed in the context of objectives or aims that may be set out in relevant legislation, the physical difficulties of managing marine reserves compared to land-based ones, problems posed by multiple-use, and the potential input of social science.

Reasons for Establishing Marine Reserves and Objectives of Their Management

Welfare economics and market-failure arguments support government establishment of marine reserves to protect nature. Private enterprise cannot be expected to establish such reserves because it is unable to extract a substantial fraction of the social gains from them, as is the case for land-based national parks (Tisdell, 1972). There are two essential points to consider in relation to government provision of marine parks. First, some, but not all, aspects of a marine reserve are *nonrival* in consumption, i.e., the marginal opportunity cost of providing the reserve to an additional person is zero. Hence, the appropriate charge for these nonrival aspects is zero. Only when there is congestion is it appropriate to charge at the margin. Second, account must be taken of excludability. It may be difficult to exclude some people from enjoying the benefits of marine reserves, particularly intrinsic values. Even if access to the reserve can be controlled and enforced, the size or mix of activities in the reserve under private enterprise will tend to focus on the provision of those resources that can most easily be appropriated. This is not necessarily the socially optimal mix.

Welfare economic arguments in favor of public provision of marine reserves include: (1) the public good characteristics of marine reserves in protecting nature possessing existence value (Krutilla and Fisher, 1975; McConnell, 1983), (2) the desire of individuals to keep their individual options open (option value) (Weisbrod, 1964; Bishop, 1982), (3) the value of retaining a larger gene pool to take advantage of new discoveries, and more generally the value of retaining resource flexibility for future generations (Arrow and Fisher, 1974), (4) avoidance of large losses that may occur when common access is the only practical alternative to complete protection of a marine area, (5) the external benefits that may come from conserving species in an area, e.g., they may provide a replenishment source for species caught commercially elsewhere, and (6) discounting and risk arguments favoring conservation. It might also be noted that an additional compelling reason for the establishment of marine reserves is that they provide an alternative and, in some cases, a more efficient approach to extractive activities.

It might well be thought that legislation enabling the establishment of marine reserves or sanctuaries would provide adequate guidelines for their selection. However, this has not proven to be the case. In Australia there is no umbrella legislation for the creation of marine parks because states have jurisdiction over coastal waters. In the United States, although Title III of the Marine Protection and Sanctuaries Act enables the federal government to establish marine sanctuaries, it provides no definitive guidelines or criteria for their establishment, but merely indicates that they can be designated "for the purpose of preserving or restoring such areas for conservation, recreational, ecological or aesthetic values." This has meant that the NOAA, the body administering the legislation has, as outlined by Harvey (1983), had to develop its own guidelines, which has proven to be difficult. As a result of experience the criteria have been modified over the years to reduce the influence of vested interests and increase operational predictability (Harvey, 1983, p. 187).

From American experience as outlined by Harvey (1983), it is clear that political strategies are important in the designation of sanctuaries and the timing of designation. It may be more important to consider an area early for a sanctuary where development incompatible with conservation is imminent, rather than to spend time assessing an area that is potentially more important for conservation but under no imminent threat from development. Politics and dynamics have to be taken into account in practical strategies for the creation of marine reserves and sanctuaries. Thus there are further complications to be allowed for in the analysis. The task of developing a comprehensive analysis applicable to establishment of marine reserves is a daunting one.

Rational management should reflect the aims or objectives for these reserves. But as set out in relevant legislation, the aims or objectives are usually somewhat vague so considerable scope is permitted to administering authorities to make them more precise. Opinions differ about the desirability of such imprecision. On the one hand, it can be argued that legislatures do not have the resources or expertise to fully grasp the issues that the resource manager may encounter, nor can legislation anticipate changes in demand, tastes, and preferences. If precise aims are set by legislation, agencies may be compelled to manage resources or enforce regulations in a socially nonoptimal way. On the other hand, imprecision may lead to uncertainty and lack of direction for an agency, higher bargaining and transaction costs, and greater scope for political pressure on the agency by particular self-interest groups.

NOAA has faced uncertainty about legislatively determined objectives in its administration of Title III of the Marine Protection, Research and Sanctuaries Act, especially in relation to the management of marine reserves for multiple-use. In that respect Harvey (1983, p. 170) points out that "The notion of 'multiple-use', expressed by Congress as the basis for the management of marine sanctuaries, differs both in concept and application from the conservationist profile of the national park system. Leading issues have included the absence of definitive guidelines for the selection of sanctuary sites, the definition and application of a 'multiple use' management philosophy, and a determination of the appropriate relationship of Title III to other environmental statutes."

The Great Barrier Reef Marine Park Act 1975 is also imprecise about objectives. It has been suggested (by a referee) that if more precise objectives had been spelled out in the Great Barrier Reef Marine Park (GBRMP) Act that with changing use patterns and information they may have become so dated and inflexible as to be useless now. The object of the GBRMP Act is "to make provisions for and in relation to the establishment, control, care and development of a marine park in the Great Barrier Reef Region." Later sections relating to zoning plans make its intent clearer, but there is still considerable room for interpretation. It requires GBRMP Authority to prepare zoning plans having regard to the following objects as set out in section 31(7):

(1) The conservation of the Great Barrier Reef.
(2) The regulation of the use of the Marine Park so as to protect the Great Barrier Reef while allowing the reasonable use of the Great Barrier Reef Region.
(3) The regulation of activities that exploit the resources of the Great Barrier Reef Region so as to minimize the effect of those activities on the Great Barrier Reef.
(4) The reservation of some areas of the Great Barrier Reef for its appreciation and enjoyment by the public.
(5) The preservation of some areas of the Great Barrier Reef in its natural state undisturbed by man except for the purpose of scientific research.

Given the scope for interpreting the intent of the act, the Great Barrier Reef Marine Park Authority (GBRMPA) has formulated the following as its main goal: "To provide for the protection, wise use, appreciation, and enjoyment of the Great Barrier Reef in perpetuity through the development and care of the Great Barrier Reef Marine Park" (Kelleher, 1986, p.16). As stated, this is a very broad aim providing little guidance for actual management. For example, it does not indicate in the case of conflicts between the objectives the extent to which one objective is to prevail over the other. However, as one referee suggested, it may be unrealistic, given current and unforseen uses and the vast areas involved, to be more prescriptive. Graeme Kelleher, chairman of GBRMPA, in elaborating on this goal places great emphasis on managing the reef for ecological sustainability. He claims that the authority has come to the view that "activities depending on the reef's renewable resources should generally be held at or below maximum sustainable intensities indefinitely" (Kelleher, 1986, p. 16).

Although it is difficult, given the interdependence of ecological processes, to determine maximum sustainable levels of activity and although economists suggest that *maximum* sustainable use is not usually socially optimal (Tietenberg, 1988, p. 262; Tisdell, 1988a), actual physical and ecological considerations are only part of the problem. Bodies managing marine reserves must be able to sustain themselves within a political context. They need continuing government support and funding. This in turn depends on the attitude of the general public to policies pursued by such authorities, and the support or opposition of pressure groups representing vested interests. This is especially the case for a large reserve such as GBRMP, which is subject to multiple-use, including commercial use for fishing and tourism.

The importance of political support for the future of GBRMPA has been stressed by Kelleher (1986, p. 16). He says,

> If the reef is to be protected, more than physical aspects of the reef need to be considered. Administrative arrangements also must be durable. In Australia, the major determinant of administrative survivability of organizations like the Authority is public support. In the long run government support flows from it. Recognizing that the Authority and the Marine Park concept already have a degree of public support, the Authority must act in ways that sustain or increase that support.

Public education and information programs are believed to be important in this respect, but consideration and allowance must be made for interest groups such as commercial interests. In the latter respect Kelleher notes:

> The Authority does not make decisions lightly that adversely affect existing commercial or amateur activities. If those activities are already consistent with conservation of the reef, then the Authority is likely to take decisions that support them and which prevent them from becoming destructive. (Kelleher, 1986, p. 18)

In order to maintain public support for the GBRMP, GBRMPA promotes public appreciation of the existence value of the Great Barrier Reef and nationalistic pride in the GBRMP and close involvement in zoning plan development. The chairman of the GBRMPA has pointed out that many Australians treasure the Great Barrier Reef for "its uniqueness, biological diversity, beauty and grandeur. The successful management of the reef depends primarily on maintaining and encouraging these values in the hearts and minds of these Australians" (Kelleher, 1986, p. 13).

Of course, additional elements such as equity and existing rights in marine areas need to be considered when establishing and managing marine reserves (Salm and Clark, 1984, see Ch. 2). Furthermore, as emphasized by Lien and Graham (1986, p. 5), marine reserves may be set aside for a variety of *immediate* ends: (1) conserve habitat, (2) protect species habitat, (3) conserve important breeding areas, (4) conserve aesthetic values, (5) protect cultural and archaeological areas, (6) provide sites for interpretation, education, tourism, and recreation, (7) provide areas for research, (8) provide areas for monitoring the impact of human activities, and (9) serve as areas to train personnel for the management of protected areas. As discussed earlier, these ends require governments to take action to establish and manage marine reserves.

Size and Interrelationship of Marine Reserves

It is one thing to specify grounds for governments providing such reserves in principle, and another to determine the ideal extent, size, and nature of such reserves. Conservationists have given consideration to this issue and it is useful to note the views of Soulé and Wilcox (1980). They suggest (p. 4) that the value of a system of nature reserves in protecting a particular biota depends on the number of reserves, size of reserves, and density (or proximity) of reserves. They claim that everyone is agreed that many large reserves are ideal from the biogeographical standpoint. They argue that "all viewpoints (factors) converge on the same conclusion—reserves should be manifold, large and (for most purposes) dispersed" (Soulé and Wilcox, 1980, p. 4). But this conclusion ignores the choice or trade-off problem. If the overall area that can be reserved for nature conservation is limited, it may be necessary to choose between a few large reserves and many small ones, or combinations in between. In other words, the total area that the community may be prepared to set aside for protection would be inadequate to provide simultaneously for many reserves of large size. Land available for reserves may be only sufficient to provide for a few large reserves, or a combination of very few large reserves and several small ones, or many small reserves, or other patterns of a similar nature. Consequently, the preferred option may not be attainable and so the problem of choice needs to be addressed.

Implications of economic factors for the size of reserves in different locations can be considered by using a theoretical example. The example highlights valuation factors that do not appear to have been considered by conservation biologists in the past, but their importance is being increasingly recognized (Laist *et al.*, 1986, p. 226). Suppose (for simplicity) there are two locations at which nature reserves can be established and the size at each location can be varied. If there is no restriction on the combined area of two reserves, then taking account of the opportunity cost of resources tied up in nature (or marine) reserves, each reserve should be expanded in size until its marginal value for conservation equals the marginal opportunity cost of reserving the area for conservation. Note, however, that in reality benefits and costs are influenced not only by the size of the reserve but by the uses allowed in it.

Mathematically, letting Y_i represent the net benefit from setting aside an area at site i for a reserve, and letting B_i represent the gross benefits or value and letting C_i indicate the cost of doing so, the problem is to select a size, x_i, for the i-th reserve (that is, for each reserve) that maximizes

$$Y_i = B_i(x_i) - C_i(x_i)$$

Note that this formulation assumes that within each potential reserve, each hectare is homogeneous in its characteristics. This is very often not so in practice and complicates the analysis (cf. Tisdell, 1988b). However, let us suppose for simplicity that the homogeneity assumption holds. The necessary condition (but not sufficient) for Y_i to be at a maximum is then

$$dY_i/dx_i = dB_i/dx_i - dC_i/dx_i = 0$$

This is satisfied when the reserve at site i is of a size such that

$$dB_i/dx_i = dC_i/dx_i$$

For a maximum to occur, it is necessary in addition for the second derivative of the net benefit derived by expanding the size of the reserved site i to be negative.

The optimal size of a reserve can be illustrated in Figure 1 for location one. The curve ABC represents the marginal valuation of an area reserved at location one, and DBF represents the marginal value of opportunities foregone by such reservation, that is, the marginal cost of reserving the area. It is ideal from an economic viewpoint to reserve an area of size x_1' at location one.

An arithmetic case can be used to illustrate the optimal size in the static case further. Suppose that in an area being considered for a reserve, the gross value of the first hectare reserved is \$10,000 and that each subsequent hectare added to the reserve adds \$5 less in value than the preceding hectare. Assume that the opportunity cost of each hectare added to the reserve is \$5,000. This might consist of \$1,000 per hectare for management expenses plus \$4,000 in profit foregone from fishing assuming that fishermen are excluded from the reserve and lose this much in profit. Under these conditions, a marine reserve of 1,000 hectares maximizes net benefits. This is so because the marginal benefit of increasing the size of the reserve can be expressed as $10{,}000 - 5x$ where x represents the size of the reserve in hectares and the marginal cost is 5,000. Solving the equation $10{,}000 - 5x = 5{,}000$ yields the solution of 1,000 hectares.

Although determining these actual curves can be complex (and in practice there may be a case for determining them on different defensible bases so as to obtain rationally a minimum and maximum size for a reserve), there appears to be no superior way to approach the problem. Nevertheless, this method emphasizes that there are two sides—the value of an area from a conservation point of view and the benefits foregone by

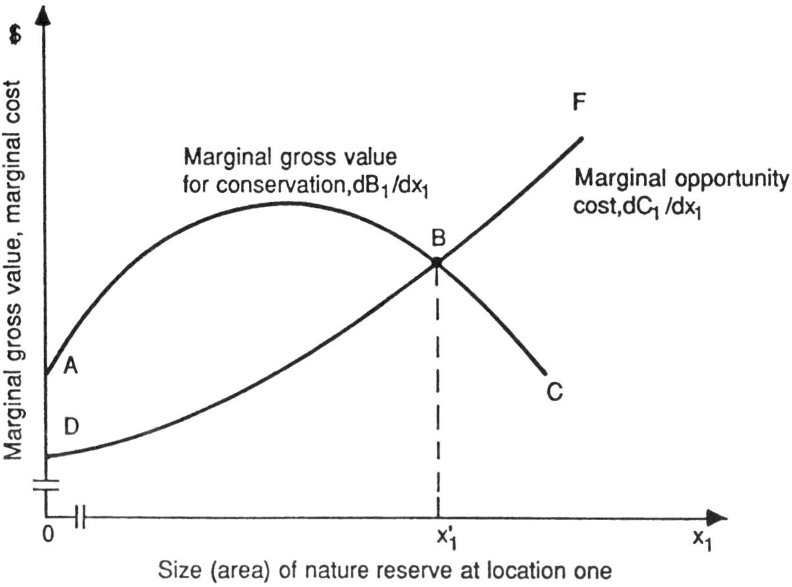

Figure 1. Determination of the optimal size of a marine reserve (when there is no area constraint on reserves) using marginal opportunity costs and the marginal value of an area for conservation.

reserving an area. This is not always clearly recognized by ecologists. For instance, the World Conservation Strategy indicates that areas that are very productive in supplying food for human consumption should be reserved for this purpose, rather than used for nature conservation (cf. Tisdell, 1983). However, this only looks at the opportunity cost side of the equation. If such areas are also very valuable in conserving species, this may mean that whereas curve DBF in Figure 1 is high, so is curve ABC. In that case, reserving all the area for food production may be short-sighted. It is likely to be rational to do this only if curve ABC is low in relation to DBF (indeed, if it falls below it). It also seems irrational in considering the size of nature reserves (including marine reserves) to consider their value only from a conservation point of view, that is, curve ABC in Figure 1 neglecting curve DBF. Furthermore, when considered in a cost-benefit setting, a small reserve can sometimes be optimal.

One can also see limitations to the Soulé and Wilcox (1980) recommendation that reserves all be large if we consider a slightly different choice problem. For example, cost-benefit optimization of the size of individual reserves might be subject to the condition that the combined area of reserves is not to exceed a particular figure, e.g., number of km^2. Such a constraint might be imposed by the government. On the assumption that it is optimal to set aside for reserves the maximum combined area allowed for them, optimization requires that the available combined area be allocated between locations so that the marginal net value (value for conservation less opportunity costs) of an extra area or section of reserve at any location is equal to that at all other locations. Use of this rule indicates that there is no a priori way of deciding the optimal relative size of reserves in advance, and so throws further doubt on the value of the recommendation by Soulé and Wilcox (1980). For example, consider the case in which two locations are available and the combined area available is $X^* = \hat{x}_1 + \hat{x}_2$. If the *net* marginal benefit function HIJ shown in panel (a) of Figure 2 applies at location one and KLM shown in panel (b) applies at location two, the economically optimal size of the reserves is x_1 at location one and x_2 at location two, that is, one large reserve and one small reserve is optimal. Even if the curves shown in Figure 2 were just marginal value of conservation curves, a similar size distribution applies because of the combined area constraint. Whereas from a conservation angle it would be better to have both reserves much bigger, this is not a realistic possibility because of the combined area constraint. Note also that in the absence of a combined size constraint, the optimal size of the reserves would be x_1' and x_2', the sizes at which the marginal net benefit from expansion of each reserve is zero. These sizes are larger than in the constrained situation.

The above models are extremely simplified conceptions of a complex problem. They are intended to highlight the limitations of generalizations in the literature about the optimal size of reserves. In order to develop operational models along these lines, attention has to be given to the specification of costs and benefits and to the complexity of possible biogeographical patterns for reserves.

In practice, it is difficult to calculate cost and benefits because of uncertainty about the natural world, e.g., the population of species in a particular area and economic uncertainty, such as about prices. Again, some benefits and costs are more tangible than others (Hufschmidt *et al.*, 1983). NOAA found it virtually impossible to calculate net benefits of a reserve in the northern Channel Islands off the coast of Southern California (Hoagland, 1983, p. 3). In establishing the Channel Islands National Marine Sanctuary and prohibiting oil and gas exploration and development there, NOAA was unable to obtain reliable estimates of opportunity costs (Harvey, 1983). As Harvey (1983, p. 188) points out, several ranges of associated costs and benefits may need to be calculated and this hinders the task of making a concise determination.

In estimating costs and benefits, one may try to determine directly the costs and benefits experienced by individuals or groups, e.g., contribution to commercial value of living marine resources, recreational value, and so on. This is the approach favored by

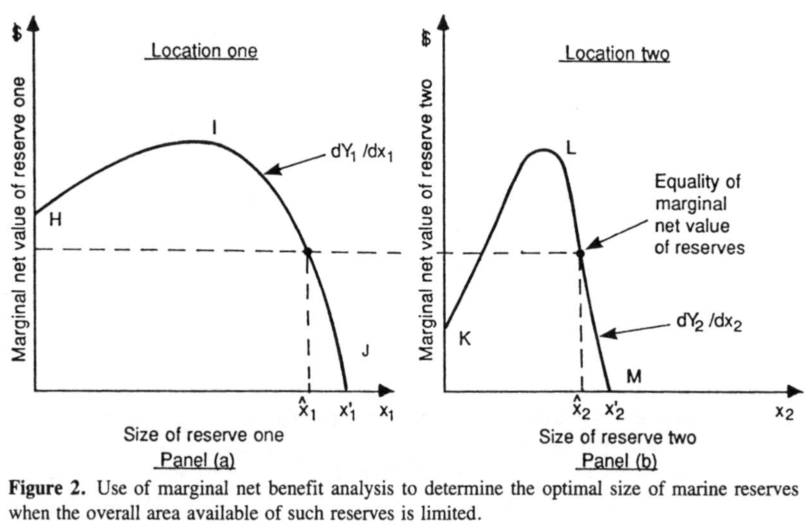

Figure 2. Use of marginal net benefit analysis to determine the optimal size of marine reserves when the overall area available of such reserves is limited.

some economists. Or, especially if funds for obtaining such information are limited, one may appeal to ''guesstimates'' of costs and benefits by a group of experts, that is, adopt an indirect approach. It seems that valuation of zones in the Great Barrier Reef Marine Park (GBRMP) has been done largely by the latter approach (cf. Cocks, 1984), but uncertainty remains a problem for rational zoning in this case (Cocks, 1984, p. 377).

The difficulties of using cost-benefit analysis for marine-use planning are well set out by Laist *et al.* (1986). Information about many aspects is usually sparse, e.g., species composition, abundance pollution effects, and so on, and it can be difficult to identify economic values and resource characteristics needing consideration. Nevertheless they conclude, considering the case of corals, that ''without a close accounting of the value of coral resources and the benefits of management actions, it is difficult to determine the appropriate level of public expenditure to dedicate to coral conservation effort'' (Laist *et al.*, 1986, p. 226).

Again, many biogeographical aspects (not taken into account in the above models) need to be considered, such as proximity of reserves to one another and the provision of corridors between reserves through which animals can pass with relative protection. Furthermore, it might be noted that there is little point in having a large marine reserve if resources for, say, enforcement of rules are thereby spread too thinly. In some cases it is better to have a smaller reserve that can be managed effectively (cf. Laist *et al.*, 1986, p. 225).

Natural Constraints on Managing the Resources of Marine Reserves Compared to Land-Based Parks

For several reasons, marine reserves are more difficult to manage than terrestrial ones. First, the environmental nature of marine over terrestrial reserves makes it more difficult to manage marine reserves. It has been claimed that marine ''ecosystems are the largest functional units of the natural world characterized by recycling of materials and properties of homeostasis'' (Ray, 1976, p. 27). Such characteristics complicate management. Consider two aspects: (1) fewer difficulties are likely to be encountered in controlling access to and human use of resources in land-based national parks than in marine reserves, and (2) it may be easier to manage animals in a terrestrial park than in a marine reserve.

In a marine reserve, boundaries are unlikely to be clearly marked or as discernible as in a terrestrial park. Hence, individuals are more likely to engage in forbidden activities in a marine zone out of ignorance, e.g., fishermen may not be aware that they have entered a zone where fishing is forbidden.

Compared to most terrestrial parks, particularly in developed countries, marine parks have a very large number of possible entry points. Consequently collection of fees for access to marine reserves is more difficult. Also, checking on what is being brought into and what is being taken out of a marine reserve is more difficult. This makes it harder to control illegal activities. On the other hand, air surveillance is easier in marine reserves compared to tree-covered terrestrial parks.

The management of animals within a marine environment appears to be harder than on land. This is especially true in relation to migratory species or those that range over considerable distances. First, humans, being terrestrial animals, are not well adapted for observing marine animals under water so they may have less information about the state of marine animal populations than on land-based ones. Second, if the size of a marine reserve is small in comparison to the range of animal movement to be protected, populations of the animals concerned may be put at risk by their capture outside the reserve. Nevertheless, particularly if the marine reserve is a breeding ground where congregating animals would be at great risk of capture and if the chances of capture are much lower outside the reserve, the reserve may play a positive role in preserving the population of species. The migratory stock of marine reserve, however, cannot be fully protected. Whereas many land-based animals are migratory and many have movements that range over long distances, it has proven to be easier technically to deal with this problem than in the sea. Fencing of land-based national parks, such as Kruger National Park in South Africa, to restrict migration and movement of animals has proven to be feasible. However, the policy of containment of populations has also required culling of animal populations, e.g., of elephant and Cape buffalo, so as to maintain balance with other resources. Fencing of or containment of migratory or mobile species within the boundaries of marine reserves appears on the whole to be impractical at present. However, it is reported that the crown-of-thorns starfish can be excluded from small areas by fencing. Furthermore, the Fish and Wildlife Service is said to be planning to contain sea otters in California in specified zones. In every case, one would have to consider the consequences of confining a species. For example, if its food source is moving and migration is in response to this, confining the dependent species could seal its doom.

To deal with the problem just noted, it has been suggested that marine reserves might be moved with the migrating animals (A. Gaines, pers. comm., August 1986), and in fact existing U.S. laws allow for this, e.g., the Endangered Species Act and the Marine Mammal Protection Act. Whereas this is theoretically possible, there are practical difficulties such as making the changes in boundaries known. One may also wonder what benefit this method of protecting a species would have over that of either prohibiting the capture of a species or restricting the quantity of the catch of it. Furthermore, a more realistic approach might be to establish strategically located reserves in different parts of the species migratory range (as is done for manatees in northwest Florida) to protect habitats essential only on a seasonal basis.

The movement or migration problem has proven to be a thorny issue when protected species move from a reserve in one country to nearby countries and are captured. For example, there were complaints of dugong moving from the Maza Wildlife Management Area in Papua New Guinea to nearby Australian Territory to be taken by Torres Strait Islanders (Olewale and Sedu, 1980; Tisdell, 1986). Hopefully, problems similar to this will become less with the Torres Strait Agreement, which was ratified between Australia and Papua New Guinea in 1985 (Anon., 1985).

It is clear that the mobility of marine systems over large distances is one of the main aspects to consider compared to terrestrial reserves. Ray (1976) makes the position clear: "The scale of marine systems confounds thinking based on terrestrial models. The largest ecosystems by far are marine and we cannot aspire to include them, *in toto,* in parks and reserves. Certain exceptions to this statement exist, of course but this is a general pattern with which we must cope. Whereas large-scale mobility or migration of major ecosystem biomass is more the exception terrestrially, it is the rule at sea. Whole fractions of ecosystems move great distances limited only by behavioural and physiological tolerances, or by the sessile or sedentary habit of some species" (Ray, 1976, p. 27).

It can also be argued that terrestrial ecosystems are to a greater extent involved in the third dimension than terrestrial ones and that aquatic animals are more closely connected to their environment than land animals (Ray, 1976, p. 27). "Most aquatic animals are not 'sealed off' by virtue of a relatively impervious skin as land animals are. Most aquatic animals are in physiologic continuity with water and are generally very susceptible to foreign substances, pollutants or nutrients which enter their bodies with facility, then quickly are incorporated into the trophic structure'' (Ray, 1976, pp. 27–28). There are also other natural properties of marine ecosystems compared to terrestrial ones as set out by Ray (1976) that complicate their management.

There is another factor in practice that can complicate the rational management of marine reserves. Under international convention, it may be impossible to exclude foreign shipping from using the reserve or areas adjacent to it. In the case of zoning of GBRMP, it was accepted that existing shipping lanes could not, for political reasons and under international shipping conventions, be relocated in the zoning plan (Cooks, 1984, p. 373). Such constraints subject reserves to the risk of oil spills, for instance. By contrast in a land-based area, the country concerned has complete sovereignty and can prevent passage of vehicles.

International law may affect the optimal location of marine reserves. In 1982 the United Nations opened for signature the Law of the Sea Convention, which in articles 55–75 establishes a 200-mile jurisdictional zone called the Exclusive Economic Zone (EEZ). Within this zone the coastal state not only is given the sovereign rights to explore, exploit, conserve, and manage all the living resources therein, but also is assigned similar rights respective to nonliving resources of the seabed, its subsoil, and the superjacent waters there. Important, too, in article 56 the coastal state is given limited rights of jurisdiction pertaining to the establishment of and use of artificial islands, installations and structures, marine scientific research, and the protection and preservation of the marine environment. All these considerations will be directly relevant to the creation, protection, and management of marine reserves should they be situated beyond the 12-mile territorial waters of the coastal states, in declared national EEZs. Complications in protecting EEZ-sited marine reserves may arise, however, in that article 58 preserves within the EEZs the high seas freedoms of navigation and overflight, and guarantees the right to all states to engage in other internationally lawful uses of the sea, including the operation of the ships and aircraft within the breadth of the EEZ. These high seas freedoms as applied to the EEZ clearly constrict the ability of the coastal state to legislate jurisdictional zones for marine preserves characterized by limited access or nonentry qualifications. Obviously, the problem there is that of a maritime ''Catch-22'' situation. That is, freedom of navigation allows for all vessels to have the legal right to sail unimpeded through EEZ areas; however, this unrestricted shipping traffic at the same time also invites the enhanced possibility of serious accidents occuring in EEZs that involve ships, e.g., oil spills.

Significantly article 58 also provides that all states must give appropriate regard to the rights and duties of the coastal state and shall comply with its lawful rules and regulations as well. If restrictions were to be applied to international shipping in EEZs for purposes of preserving and protecting the marine environment via the creation of reserves, it might well be this latter authority that gives due legal right for coastal states to do so.

Multiple-Use and Zoning of Marine Reserves

As a rule marine reserves are subject to multiple-use, and one of the uses may be shipping. In the case where a marine reserve has only a single purpose, such as complete protection of biota within it, there are no complicated decisions to be made about zoning.

However, in the single-purpose case consideration might be given about whether to surround the marine reserve proper or completely protected area by a buffer zone, that is, a zone in which activities are restricted such as mining for oil or the passage of certain ships. So, as in the case of biosphere reserves (UNESCO, 1985), zoning problems are soon encountered.

Some marine reserves—the Great Barrier Reef Marine Park is a good example—are subject to zoning of use in order to cater more effectively for multiple-use. Multiple-use can be a source of conflict, which can be reduced (1) by limitations or restrictions on activities carried out in the same area, or (2) by spatial or temporal separation of activities, or (3) by a combination of these approaches. For example, in some areas only one activity may be allowed, but in other areas multiple activities may be permitted, subject to limitations on one or more of these activities.

Whereas multiple-use may represent the best way to use resources in a marine reserve (and there is likely to be considerable pressure for use as opposed to complete protection if the reserve is large or if it contains valuable commercial resources such as oil and gas), multiple-use also creates problems for management. Relevant groups denied access or substantial access to commercially valuable resources by zoning or exclusion generally are likely to engage in political campaigns and advocacy to change the situation. This has happened in the United States. Congress indicated that multiple-use should be allowed within marine sanctuaries. Oil and gas interests ran substantial campaigns against their exclusion from such sanctuaries. Susan Harvey (1983, p. 189) comments that the multiple-use goal in the absence of a definitive programmatic division contributed to attempts by external groups to use the statutes regulatory authority to serve vested interests. If legislation governing marine reserves was more specific about aims, there would be less scope for pressure on administering authorities by vested interests, even though there may be more pressure on the legislature.

Under the Great Barrier Reef Marine Park Act 1975, GBRMPA is specifically *required* to prepare zoning plans, to call for public representations on draft plans, to submit a finalized plan to the minister (who *may amend* it) who in turn must submit the plan to Parliament for consideration. There is, therefore, considerable scope for public influence. The act is, however, clear in several respects about its intent. It prohibits drilling or mining in the GBRMP except for approved scientific purpose. This is not surprising since the main impetus to the establishment of GBRMP came from conservation groups wishing to avert the imminent threat of mining for oil on the reef (Wright, 1977). Section 37(2) of the act, quoted earlier, gives some guidance to the type of zones required. For instance, among other things it requires "the preservation of some areas of the Great Barrier Reef in its natural state undisturbed by man except for the purposes of scientific research." The relevant legislation constrains the decisions of park managers without providing them with a complete guide to policy formulation.

Rational methods of determining most suitable areas or zones for particular uses are subject to important limitations (Hopkins, 1977) and their use might not give results compatible with the intent of legislation governing GBRMP. Whereas the chairman of GBRMP claims that as far as the Barrier Reef is concerned,

> Experience has shown that in many cases it is not difficult to decide on the most appropriate zoning for individual reef and inter-reef areas. The combination of their natural qualities, location, and present and predicted usage patterns often makes the choice obvious. (Kelleher, 1986, p. 17)

It is clear from Cocks (1984) that present zoning patterns are not perfectly determined. Let us consider zoning broadly in GBRMP and then some details as raised by Cocks (1984).

Zoning on the Great Barrier Reef involves public consultation on zoning as a first step and (1) an analysis of available resources and (2) an outline of the usage or demand on resources. These are used to produce overlay maps. Before final zoning is determined, the draft zoning plan is released to the public. In the final plan, account is taken of the reactions of the public as well as that of government departments and agencies.

Broadly, there are three major categories of zones in the GBRMP, subject to subdivisions into types A and B. These are: (1) preservation and scientific research zones (only human activity for *controlled* scientific research is permitted); (2) national park zones (scientific, educational, and recreational use permitted); and (3) general use zones (commercial and recreational fishing allowed subject to some limitations). In addition, there are a number of areas such as species replenishment regions that are effectively short-term zones. Many of these broad zones (such as general-use zones) cover large areas and encompass no other types of zones.

Because a complicated and fine patchwork of zones allocations has been avoided in the GBRMP, this makes it easier for the public to conform with zoning regulations. In drawing up the zoning plan, GBRMPA took the view that it is "normally impractical to zone parts individual reefs in different ways" (Cocks, 1984, p. 373).

There is a need in drawing up realistic zoning patterns to take account of the limited abilities of individuals for dealing with complex regulations and, in the case of GBRMP, leave room for effective input by pressure groups or vested interests. Zoning of GBRMP is required by legislation to involve an interactive process with the public and government departments. The problem of zoning the GBRMP cannot be solved by backroom optimization procedures even though such procedures could conceivably be used to draw up draft plans. For the GBRMP "zoning plans are largely based on how well they satisfy expressed and inferred demands from interest groups, including users, conservationists, and on-site managers. Thus policies are mostly statements about the type of zones, which in the eyes of various interest groups, should be allocated to various classes of spatial units. Under this approach, ecological and environmental considerations appear as "demands from conservationists" (Cocks, 1984, pp. 368–369). But, of course, it is not only the demands of conservationists that are taken into account.

Cocks (1984) and Cocks *et al.* (1983) have proposed a method, SIRO-PLAN, for zoning land masses such as marine reserves. This method was used as a comparative exercise with alternative methods such as LUPLAN in formulation of the draft zoning plan for the Cairns section of GBRMP. This procedure as applied to this problem and described by Cocks (1984) is not an optimization procedure but a search and trial-and-error approach, which aims for a satisfactory solution. It has an important quality in view of the GBRMP legislation of allowing for adjustments for demands by interest groups. However, danger exists of this method becoming a way of justifying the opinion of the client whether that opinion is well based or not.

Given the above issues, more research needs to be done to evaluate the effectiveness and value of zoning in the GBRMP and more work is required on the principles of zoning generally, especially on how best to allow for political pressures and demands on resource-use by different groups. In this respect the two-zone coastal and marine area management scheme proposed for the Galapagos Islands may be worthy of attention for it combines simplicity and economy (Silva and Desilvestre, 1986; Broadus *et al.,* 1984, pp. 62–74).

Role of Natural Science Compared to Social Science in the Management of Marine Reserves

The majority of staff employed in organizations managing marine reserves have a training in natural science and the major portion of the research programs of marine reserves appear to be directed to natural science, e.g., physical oceanography and marine ecology. In comparison, social sciences seem to have been given a small role. For instance, if the staff of the GBRMP in the sections Park Management, Planning and Research, and Monitoring are considered, 18 out of the 26 staff members (70 percent) have their training (higher education qualifications) in natural science or engineering (S. Driml, GBRMPA, pers. comm. February 20, 1987).

The management of marine reserves involves not only the management of natural resources but in addition the management of people by people. Social scientists have a role to explore ways and suggest methods so that humans using reserves obtain a more worthwhile experience and conform with rules. Given that political factors influence the fortunes of bodies managing marine reserves and that conflict between different users of reserves have to be settled, social scientists may, for instance predict likely changes in the relative power of pressure groups, which, in turn, may have implications for the nature of development of a reserve. All management policies that use resources involve a social science dimension if for no other reason than the fact that the use of resources involves opportunity costs. The cost of opportunities foregone depend on valuation by people. The importance of evaluating economic factors and opportunity costs in reserve management and establishment is well recognized by administrators (Harvey, 1983, p. 188; Laist *et al.,* 1986). Legal aspects also have to be taken into account in the management of reserves as, for example, has been illustrated by reference to the Great Barrier Reef Marine Park Act.

Natural science can play a useful role in satisfying natural curiosity, in providing informative and educational material, and in supplying *one* of the ingredients required for the management of reserves. However, natural science (or social science alone) cannot supply all of the ingredients needed for effective management of marine reserves.

This can be illustrated in relation to the Crown-of-Thorns starfish *Ancanthaster planci,* a coral predator, noted earlier. Considerable concern has been expressed about the risk of its destroying a substantial portion of the Great Barrier Reef. In this case the role of natural scientists is mainly to predict the likelihood of such an event, spread of the starfish and other natural factors, and to determine steps that might be taken to control the pest. The role of the social scientist is principally to evaluate the social benefit of control and compare this with the cost of control. Economists in particular usually obtain considerable training in social cost-benefit evaluation. For example, an economist may be required to evaluate loss in tourist income if reefs in a particular area are destroyed. The general economics of pest control are also relevant. The GBRMPA is funding research into both the natural science and social aspect of the problem and its social science aspects, and this seems to be a wise decision.

There is sometimes conflict between social and natural scientists. Many do not accept an anthropocentric approach (which is commonly but not universally adopted by social scientists) to the planning of marine reserves. The possible conflict of philosophy between social scientists and natural scientists is highlighted by the following ecocentrism principle expounded by Ray (1976, p. 34):

> Strong arguments for socio-economic (i.e., homocentric) decisions on land use persist. There should be no man versus nature dichotomy in resource decisions. On the other hand, socio-economic issues should be secondary to ecocentric ones in the decision-making process. The nature of ecosystems is our paramount concern, not to be diluted by overriding concern for monetary value, non-conforming social custom, or "needs" and desires which may result in deleterious environmental impact. The education of social scientists, lawyers and businessmen, engineers, politicians and economists in the essence of ecosystem dynamics is a goal worthy of pursuit.

Nevertheless even if one does not accept anthropocentrism, but accepts naturalistic ethics to some extent, it is difficult to see how a strong case can be made for ignoring in the planning of marine reserves the needs and desires, habits, and aspirations of human beings.

Conclusions

As shown, a wide and complex range of issues need to be considered in establishing marine reserves, managing them, and determining their optimal size and configuration. The difficulties involved, although not insuperable, are more substantial than in the case of terrestrial biosphere reserves and are highlighted by multiple-use problems and the determination of optimal zoning of reserves. No simple perfect formula exists for determining the optimal establishment and management of marine reserves, but this paper provides a social science/economics perspective on the subject that differs in a number of respects from those perspectives commonly given by natural scientists. Hopefully, the consideration of this subject from a number of angles will lead to a better appreciation of it.

Acknowledgments

The first draft of this paper was completed while Clem Tisdell was guest investigator, Marine Policy Center, Woods Hole Oceanographic Institution. Research funding in part was provided by the Johnston Endowment Fund, and the J.N. Pew, Jr. Charitable Trust at Woods Hole Oceanographic Institution's Marine Policy and Ocean Management Center. We wish to thank Chris Joyner, Frank Gable, Porter Hoagland, Alan Poole, and K. Ramakrishna, and especially David Fulharty for their helpful suggestions on the first draft. Also we would like to thank several reviewers for their useful comments on the second draft. The usual caveat applies.

References

Anon. (1985). "Torres Strait Treaty in Force." *Australian Fisheries,* February, p. 22.

Arrow, K.J., and A.C. Fisher. (1974). "Environmental Preservation, Uncertainty and Irreversibility." *Quarterly Journal of Economics* 88:313–319.

Bishop, R.C. (1982). "Option Value: An Exposition and Extension." *Land Economics* 58:1–15.

Bjorklund, M.I. (1974). " Achievements in Marine Conservation: I Marine Parks." *Environmental Conservation* 3:205–223.

Broadus, J., I. Pires, A. Gaines, C. Baily, R. Knecht, and B. Cicin-Sain. (1984). *Coastal and Marine Resources Management for the Galapagos Islands,* Woods Hole Oceanographic Institution Tech. Report, WHOI-84-43.

Cocks, K.D., J.R. Ive, and I.A. Baird. (1983). "SIRO-PLAN and LUPLAN: An Australian Approach to Land Use Planning." *Environment and Planning B* 10:331–345.

Cocks, K.D. (1984). "A Systematic Method of Public Use Zoning of the Great Barrier Reef Marine Park, Australia." *Coastal Zone Management Journal* 12(4):359–383.

Harvey, S. (1983). "Title III of the Marine Protection, Research and Sanctuaries Act: Issues in Program Implementation." *Coastal Zone Management Journal* 11(3):169–197.

Hoagland III, P. (1983). "Federal Ocean Resource Conflict: Interagency Conflict and the Need for a Balanced Approach to Resource Management." *Virginia Journal of Natural Resources Law* 3:1–33.

Hopkins, L.D. (1977). "Methods for Generating Land Suitability Maps: A Comparative Evaluation." *Journal of the American Institute of Planners* 43(1):388–398.

Hufschmidt, M.M., D.E. James, A.D. Meister, B.T. Bower, and J.A. Dixon (1983). *Environment, Natural Systems and Development: An Economic Valuation Guide*. Baltimore: Johns Hopkins University Press.

Kelleher, G. (1986). "Managing the Great Barrier Reef." *Oceanus* 29:13–19.

Krutilla, J.V., and A. Fisher. (1975). *The Economics of Natural Environments*, Baltimore: Johns Hopkins University Press.

Laist, D.W., T.E. Bigford, G.W. Robertson, and D.R. Gordon. (1986). "Management of Coral and Coral Ecosystems In the United States." *Coastal Zone Management Journal*, 13(3/4): 203–239.

Lien, J., and R. Graham. (1986). *Marine Parks and Conservation: Challenge and Promise*, Ottawa: National and Provincial Parks Association.

McConnel, K.E. (1983). "Existence and Bequest Value." In *Managing Air Quality and Scenic Resources at National Parks and Wilderness Areas*, R.D. Rowe and L.G. Chestnut (eds.). Boulder, CO: Westview Press, pp. 254–273.

Olewole, E., and D. Sedu. (1980). "Momora (the dugong) in the Western Province," In *Traditional Conservation in Papua New Guinea: Implications for Today*, L. Morautu, J. Pernetta, and W. Heaney (eds.). Boroko, P.N.G.: Institute of Applied Social and Economic Research, pp. 251–255.

Ray, G.C. (1976). "Critical Marine Habitats: Definition, Description, Criteria and Guidelines for Identification and Management." In *Proceedings of an International Conference on Marine Parks and Reserves*, International Union for the Conservation of Nature and Natural Resources, Morges, Switzerland, pp. 15–19.

Salm, R.V., and J.R. Clark. (1984). *Marine and Coastal Protected Areas: A Guide for Planners and Managers*, Glands, Switzerland: IUCN.

Silva, E.M., and I. Desilvestre. (1986). "Marine Coastal Protected Areas in Latin America: A Preliminary Assessment." *Coastal Zone Management Journal*, 14(4):311–347.

Silva, E.M., E.M. Gately, and I. Desilvestre. (1986). *A Bibliographical Listing of Coastal and Marine Protected Areas: A Global Survey*. Woods Hole Oceanographic Institution Tech. Rept. WHOI-86-11, pp. 1–2.

Soulé, M.E., and B.A. Wilcox. (1980). "Conservation Biology: Its Scope and Its Challenge." In *Conservation Biology: An Evolutionary-Ecological Perspective*, M.E. Soulé and B.A. Wilcox (eds.). Sunderland, MA: Sinauer Associates.

Tietenberg, T. (1988). *Environmental and Natural Resource Economics*, 2nd ed. Glenview, IL: Scott, Foresman.

Tisdell, C.A. (1972). "Provision of Parks and the Preservation of Nature: Some Economic Factors." *Australian Economic Papers*, 11(19):154–162.

Tisdell, C.A. (1983). "An Economist's Critique of the World Conservation Strategy, with Examples from the Australian Experience." *Environmental Conservation*, 10:43–52.

Tisdell, C.A. (1986). "Conflicts about Living Marine Resources in Southeast Asian and Australian Waters: Turtles and Dugong as Cases." *Marine Resource Economics*, 3:89–100.

Tisdell, C.A. (1988a) "Sustainable Development: Differing Perspectives of Ecologists and Economists and Relevance to LDCs." *World Development*, 16(3):373–384.

Tisdell, C.A. (1988b) "Economics of Weed Control on Public Conservation and Recreation Land: Assessing Costs and Benefits." *Weeds on Public Land,* Proceedings of a Symposium presented by Weed Science Society of Victoria and the School of Environmental Science, Monash University, pp. 36–41.
United Nations Educational, Scientific and Cultural Organization (UNESCO), Program of Man and the Biosphere. (1985). *Action Plan for Biosphere Reserves.* Paris: UNESCO.
Weisbrod, B.A. (1964). "Collective Consumption Services of Individual Consumption Goods." *Quarterly Journal of Economics,* 78:471–477.
Wright, J. (1977). *The Coral Battleground.* West Melbourne: Nelson.
World Resources Institute and International Institute for Environment and Development. (1986). *World Resources 1986.* New York: Basic Books.

DEFORESTATION AND CAPITAL ACCUMULATION: LESSONS FROM THE KERINCI-SEBLAT NATIONAL PARK, INDONESIA

Dradjad H. Wibowo, Clement A. Tisdell, R. Neil Byron

This study outlines a case where the behaviour of farmers in accumulating capital, rather than their poverty, as commonly assumed, results in deforestation. Field-work was undertaken in the Upper Kerinci region of the island of Sumatra, Indonesia. A financial analysis of the "net income" streams received by farmers from deforestation is performed. Because forest lands can be "captured" and privatised through clearing, forest clearing and the subsequent agriculture have the capacity to produce high financial returns for farmers as well as to provide adequate capital to finance the next forest clearing. Such a capacity enables landless farmers to become land owners. Forest clearing also enables farmers to own a "long-term maturity bond" in the form of a cinnamon plantation. Poverty precludes poorer farmers from deforestation, and decisions to clear a forest rest mostly with more established farmers. Financial surpluses from outside the forestry and agricultural sectors are also used to finance forest clearing.

INTRODUCTION

Tropical forests are being deforested at a disturbing rate. According to most recent estimates of the Food and Agricultural Organisation (FAO), deforestation occurred at a rate of 15.4 million hectares/year, or about 1.2%/year between 1981-1990 (FAO, 1993). Worse still, forest extinction by early next century appears to be not unlikely for countries like the Ivory Coast, Paraguay, and Nepal where forests disappear by 5.9, 4.6 and 3.9%/year, respectively (Repetto, 1988). Whilst many recognise that deforestation has multiple causes (Myers, 1991, 1993; Vanclay, 1993), and some causes or mix of causes are regional specific (Rudel and Roper, 1996), a significant portion of deforestation may be associated with the action of farmers. In Indonesia, for example, smallholders are said to be responsible for 55% of the nation's deforestation rate (World Bank, 1990).

Dradjad H. Wibowo is currently with the Department of Economics at The University of Queensland. He previously worked as a senior researcher at the Centre for Policy and Implementation Studies (CPIS), Jakarta, Indonesia.

Clement A. Tisdell is Professor and Head, Department of Economics, The University of Queensland. He has written widely on Environmental and Resources Economics.

R. Neil Byron is Assistant Director-General at the Centre for International Forestry Research (CIFOR), Jakarta, Indonesia. He previously taught Environmental and Development Economics at the Australian National University.

It is often assumed that farmers clear a forest because of their poverty. While such an argument may be valid for certain cases, e.g. in the case of shifting cultivation and fuelwood collection in Zaire (Barbier *et al.*, 1991), our report shows that deforestation can depend on the capital accumulation behaviour of richer farmers and holders of capital. Poverty is usually a deterrent to deforestation because the poorest farmers have inadequate capital to finance forest clearing and other associated costs.

METHODS

The study was conducted in the Kerinci-Seblat National Park (KSNP), the province of Jambi, Indonesia in 1995. Located on the island of Sumatra, the KSNP covers an area of about 1.56 million hectares. Despite being declared as a national park since 1982, the KSNP remains under constant threat of forest intrusion by nearby farmers. It relates to poor policing, improperly determined national park boundaries, and population pressure.

The district of Kerinci was selected as the research site because almost 60% of its administrative territory falls within the KSNP area (Figure 1), creating an "enclave" of farming and residential settlement inside the KSNP. Given Kerinci's reputation as the production capital of cinnamon in Indonesia, the "enclave", which is occupied by about 16,500 households, becomes a major source of forest intrusion into the KSNP. Three villages in the Kerinci Upper Region were selected because they have severer deforestation problems than do the other villages[1]. The villages are located in the mountainous range of Mount Kerinci, with an altitude varying from 1200 to 1500 metres above sea level.

Primary data were collected from interviews with a randomly-selected sample of 55 farmers. The questionnaire includes questions about household characteristics, history of forest clearing and land ownership, ownership of other agricultural capital, and farm production and consumption expenditure. Price and trading volume data were collected from farmers' transaction records kept by a major village trader who also happens to be the head of one of the villages surveyed. The records contain information on actual selling price received by each farmer, number of delivery times, the quantity of output sold per delivery, purchase of farm inputs, and the amount of each farmer's outstanding loan for the period of October 1994-July 1995. Yield of the main tree crop in the KSNP region, i.e. cinnamon, was estimated by actual measurement of yield obtained from cinnamon trees of 4, 5, 6, 8, 12 and 15 years of age. Estimates for each age group were obtained by taking 2-5 samples of trees. Throughout the fieldwork, a series of observations on *ladangs* (dry-land farming) at the forest frontier were undertaken. These *ladangs* are located about 1800 to 2000 metres above sea level and can only be reached by walking for about 3-4 hours from the villages.

The main tenet of the report is that deforestation occurs because it is financially beneficial for farmers to clear a forest[2]. Thus, emphasis will be given to the

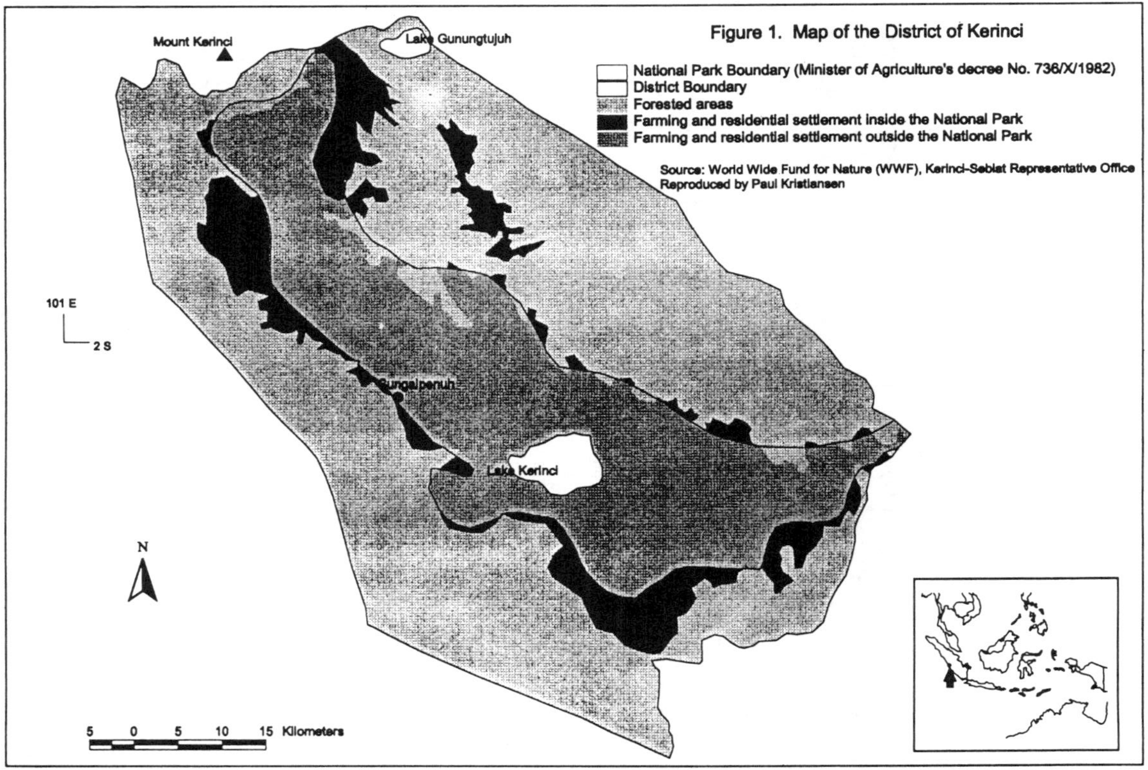

Figure 1. Map of the District of Kerinci, with its location within Indonesia indicated. Source: The World Wide Fund for Nature's representative office in Kerinci. Reproduced by Paul Kristiansen.

financial analysis of "net income" streams received by farmers from conversion of forest land into a *ladang*. The term "net income" refers to the surplus or deficit after investment and operational costs are deducted from revenues. In the financial analysis, no wages are paid to family labour employed in the farm, while the financial cost of land is equal to the total costs of converting a forest land into a *ladang*. For comparative purposes, a simple economic analysis is undertaken. In this case, the shadow price of family labourers is set equal to the prevailing market wages, while that of land to the actual market price of a *ladang*. The Net Present Value (NPV) at a social discount rate of 16%[3] and the Internal Rate of Return (IRR) are computed. The NPV refers to the value today of future net income when discounted at a given discount rate, while the IRR is the discount rate that equates the NPV to zero.

RESULTS AND DISCUSSION

Ladangs and Farmers at the Forest Frontier

The most common farming system found in *ladangs* is multicropping involving cinnamon *(Cinnamomum burmanni)* and annual crops. Cinnamon represents a long-term investment for the farmers while annual crops provide the short term, regular production. Cinnamon trees are generally planted in rows about 4 metres apart, and spaced about 1-2 metres apart along each row. Potato is the most popular type of annual crop planted, with a relatively small amount of scallion and maize. This system of multicropping is practiced until cinnamon trees reach an age of about 6 years. Afterwards, the system will become a monoculture of cinnamon, with a negligible amount of annual crops or bananas grown on the edge.

On the basis of their relation to a *ladang*, farmers can be grouped into: (a) *anak ladang* (tenants), (b) *anak ladang*/land owner, (c) land owner, and (d) *induk semang* (land owner and capital provider). *Anak ladangs* are operators of a *ladang*. They are usually landless, young (i.e. below 30 years of age) and have limited household capital. With the exception of a few unsuccessful farmers, after several years working as an *anak ladang*, older farmers are usually capable of accumulating adequate capital to own a *ladang*, by way of purchasing an existing *ladang* and/or clearing a nearby forest. In this case the farmers become land owners. They may opt to operate all of the *ladang*(s) if they have adequate family labour, or to let new *anak ladangs* operate some of the *ladang*(s). In the latter case, the farmers become *anak ladangs* and land owners at the same time. Alternatively, they may opt to let new *anak ladangs* operate all of the *ladang*(s), thus becoming purely land owners. *Induk semangs* are on the highest rung of the ladder. They are usually land owners and cash capital providers who often hold a respected position in the village, e.g. as head of the village.

Establishment of a *Ladang* and Property Right Arrangement

According to the Indonesian constitution, forests within the Indonesian jurisdiction belong to the state. In practice, however, traditional tribes consider forests as free, communal assets. Those who clear a forest are entitled to claim ownership of the cleared land.

In the villages surveyed, after clearing a forest the owner usually leaves the land idle for about 1 to 12 months to let the fallen trees dry out. During this "drying period" regrowth of *Imperata cylindrica* or "alang-alang" occurs and covers the land. The length of the drying period, however, depends not only on rainfall intensity but also on the availability of potential *anak ladangs*. This is because the owner is often not endowed with sufficient family labour to cultivate all the land. Thus, the land is not utilised until an *anak ladang* asks for a contract to sharecrop the land.

Depending on the owner's judgment, the sharecropping contract can be set for a period of as short as one year to about 12-15 years. The contracts usually take on the following forms:

a. **The 1:1 system.** This is the most popular system in the villages surveyed. The system entitles *anak ladangs* to keep the income from their annual crops. The owner is to provide cinnamon seedlings, but not a living allowance nor cash for the purchase of farm inputs. Income from cinnamon is divided equally. If however *anak ladangs* have inadequate cash to support themselves and/or to bear the costs of potato farming, they can borrow cash from an *induk semang*. Normally no interest payment is imposed on the borrowing, but *anak ladangs* are obliged to sell their potatoes to the *induk semang*. Loan repayment is directly deducted from the value of output upon delivery.

b. **The 1:2 system.** Under this system, in the first three years of the contract the owner supplies *anak ladangs* with about 50 kgs of rice per month, or about 200 kgs per planting season. Income from annual crops is divided equally, while that from cinnamon is distributed as follows: one-third for *anak ladang* and two-thirds for the owner. The system is rarely adopted because it is financially less attractive for *anak ladang*. The average size of *ladang* operated is about 0.2 hectare, with an average yield of 1867 kgs. Given that potato prices are usually comparable to or higher than those of rice, it is very uneconomical to trade off half of potato production (i.e. 933.5 kgs) and one-sixth of cinnamon output for 200 kgs of rice[4].

After a contract is agreed upon by both parties, the land is cleared of regrowth. Land owners usually hire *anak ladang*(s) to do this job. Once land clearing is completed, *anak ladangs* may start cultivating the land. They are free to plant any annual crops, but potato is the most popular one because of its agro-climatic suitability, attractive price and relatively high yields. *Anak ladangs* are also obliged to grow cinnamon during the period of the contract.

For the first 6 years of the contract, *anak ladangs* rely mostly on income from annual crops to support themselves. Between year 4 and 6 about half of the total number of cinnamon trees are cut down to thin the crop. This practice provides additional income for *anak ladangs*. Some *anak ladangs* may also earn income from wet-paddy farming and/or from working as paid labourers. After six years, due to shading, no annual crops can be grown in the *ladang*. In this case *anak ladangs* may, subject to owner's approval, harvest some of cinnamon trees to allow enough space to grow annual crops. However, the owner usually opts not to harvest a 6-year-old plantation because it produces bark of low quality. If such is the case, *anak ladangs* need to have another contract to operate another *ladang*. As for the land owner, he or she receives no income before cinnamon is harvested. Stages in the establishment of a *ladang* are illustrated by Figures 2a-2d.

The Modes of Capital Accumulation

We observe three different modes of capital accumulation in the villages surveyed. The first two relate to the accumulation of land capital by successful anak *ladangs* and land owners, while the third to the accumulation of capital in the form of cinnamon plantations. To illustrate the first two modes, land ownership history of individuals A and B is presented. Land owner A is an *induk semang* and a potato trader. He began clearing an area of 2 hectares in 1971, but then gradually added another 11 hectares over a period of 21 years (1971-1992). Initially he financed his forest clearing from a financial surplus generated from his trading activity, but in the 1980s and 1990s his cinnamon plantation provided adequate surplus to clear other forests. Land owner B has a different history of forest clearing. He began as an *anak ladang* in the mid-1970s and had since accumulated adequate capital from a cinnamon plantation to clear a three-hectare forest in 1986. He cleared another 5 hectares between 1990 and 1993. Both farmers A and B never purchased a *ladang*.

These stories indicate that forest clearing and the subsequent agriculture, i.e. cinnamon and potato farming, have the capacity to generate capital to finance for further forest clearing. This is the first mode of capital accumulation. Using this mode an *anak ladang* is able to move to a higher social status, that is, to become a land owner.

The second mode of capital accumulation is by the use of financial surpluses generated from other sectors, e.g. the trading sector. There are a number of reasons for this. First, the social values held in the region result in greater land ownership giving a higher social status. This motivates farmers to increase their land ownership. Secondly, farmers are attracted by the high financial returns obtained from forest clearing and the subsequent agriculture (See Table 2 for details). Such high returns are in stark contrast to the limited availability of other financially attractive investments at the village level. Thirdly, farmers feel more at ease with the technical details of forest clearing and the subsequent agriculture than those of other investments.

Figure 2a. A new ladang at the forest frontier, with damaged forests shown in the background. The farmer is a new, young, anak ladang of 18 years of age. Photographer: D.H. Wibowo.

Figure 2b. Regrowth during the drying period. Photographer: D.H. Wibowo.

Figure 2c. A ladang after 5 years of plantation, with potato and cinnamon as the main crops. The ladang is on sloping land. Photographer: D.H. Wibowo.

Figure 2d. A ladang after cinnamon trees reach an age of 12 years or more. This could be called a monospice agroforest, with a negligible number of banana and cassava planted on the edge. Photographer: D.H. Wibowo.

By clearing a forest, farmers acquire a parcel of land which enables them to invest their time and cash-capital in cinnamon plantation. It takes 4 years before the investment starts producing a financial return, but farmers normally opt not to harvest the plantation for at least another 8 years. Thus, cinnamon serves as a "long-term maturity bond" which will be liquidated after 12 years. The choice of liquidation (or harvesting) timing depends not only on the prevailing prices of cinnamon bark and the age of the plantation, but also on whether or not the farmer is in need of immediate cash for large expenses. The most cited reasons for liquidation are for expenses of land purchase, children's education (e.g. college entry costs), pilgrimage to Mecca and the building of a house.

Who Makes the Decision to Clear a Forest?

Our study indicates that instead of being a cause of deforestation, poverty (or more precisely lack of adequate capital) precludes poor farmers from clearing a forest. Young and poor *anak ladang*s have in fact very limited role in the decision making that leads to forest clearing. The reason is that, first, unless they have adequate family labourers to clear a forest, *anak ladang*s cannot afford the minimum capital required for forest clearing. To clear a hectare of forest costs about Rp 300,000, while the subsequent land clearing adds another Rp 450,000[5]. These costs are far beyond the financial capacity of an *anak ladang*. Secondly, even if they have adequate capital to finance forest clearing[6], *anak ladang*s cannot gain adequate cash to support themselves during the period between forest clearing and annual crop harvests, termed as the idle-period, which normally takes more than a year.

For these reasons, the decision to clear a forest rests mostly with *induk semang*s, land owners and more established (and older) *anak ladang*s. They are most likely to have adequate capital to finance forest clearing <u>and</u> to support themselves during the idle-period. As Table 1 shows, while <u>all</u> land owners and *induk semang*s had in the past cleared a forest, only a tiny 3% of *anak ladang*s (1 respondent) did so[7]. The fact that 83% of farmers in the *anak ladang*/land owner group had in the past cleared a forest indicates that while as a young farmer an *anak ladang* is precluded from deforestation, in the later years, after accumulating adequate capital he or she is likely to clear forest land.

Financial Returns from Deforestation

Table 2 presents estimated returns from forest clearing and the subsequent agriculture. Inputs, output and data of prices used here are summarised in the Appendix. Because the average length of the drying period is 9.6 months, while land clearing takes about 2 to 4 weeks, the land is not cultivated until 11 or 12 months after forest clearing is completed. For simplicity, we assume that the agriculture commences the following year. Thus, if forest clearing occurs at year 0, potato farming and cinnamon plantation will begin at year 1[8].

In general, the results presented in Table 2 explain why farmers are able to accumulate adequate surplus to finance the next forest clearing. First let us look at the 2nd and 3rd columns of Table 2 which show returns from a hectare of *ladang* if the distribution of income and costs between land owner and *anak ladang* is not taken into account. In financial terms, forest clearing and the subsequent agriculture produce a high NPV of Rp 14.6 million hectare^{-1} (=US$ 6970 ha^{-1}) over 13 years. However, if land price is set at the prevailing market price of Rp 4.63 million ha^{-1} (US$ 2205 ha^{-1}) and family labourers are paid wages at the current wage rate, the NPV declines sharply to Rp 5.8 million ha^{-1} (US$ 2773 ha^{-1}). This is the economic return of forest clearing and the subsequent agriculture. Despite such a decline, the economic IRR remains very high at 47.4%. These figures indicate that forest clearing and the subsequent agriculture are capable of producing very high financial and economic returns for both the land owner and the *anak ladang*.

A clearer picture emerges if the financial returns to land owners and *anak ladang*s are computed separately. Without getting involved directly in cinnamon plantation, a land owner receives a financial return (IRR) of 24.5% or an NPV of Rp 846, 191 ha^{-1} (US$ 403 ha^{-1}). More importantly, the land owner receives a lump sum of Rp 9.2 million at year 12, which in today's value is equal to Rp 1.3 million. It means that 13 years after the first forest clearing, if the land owner wishes to add his/her land ownership, he or she will have sufficient cash to finance another forest clearing.

As for *anak ladang*s, the picture is more interesting. From year 1 to 5 the *anak ladang* obtains an annual net income of Rp 4.0 to 4.3 million ha^{-1}. Because the average size of a *ladang* operated by an *anak ladang* is 0.2 ha, this means the *anak ladang* receives a monthly net income of Rp 67, 488 to Rp 71, 595 (US$ 32-34 month^{-1}). By rural Indonesian standards, such a level of monthly income is adequate to support a family of 2-3 persons. It explains why *anak ladang*s can rely on potato farming to support themselves. More importantly, as does the land owner, the *anak ladang* receives a lump sum equivalent to Rp 1.3 million in today's value in year 12. It explains why older *anak ladang*s are able to gain adequate capital to finance future forest clearing, and thus, to become land owners.

One possible explanation why forest clearing and the subsequent agriculture produce such high returns is that forest lands are virtually an "open-access resource" and are significantly undervalued. Farmers are able to clear a forest and to claim ownership over the land underneath by investing Rp 750,000 ha^{-1} (US$ 357 ha^{-1}), much less than the prevailing price of a *ladang.* Had forest lands been valued properly, forest clearing could have been made financially unattractive for farmers. For example, if land cost is set at Rp 1,731,582 ha^{-1} (US$ 825 ha^{-1}) land owners would have received a zero financial NPV at a discounting rate of 16%. It would significantly reduce the incentive for deforestation because land owners are the major decision makers in this process.

CONCLUSION

While in some cases deforestation can be associated with poverty, our study reveals that deforestation can very well be caused, and in the case under study, is being caused, by those with capital and the desire of wealthier members of the society to accumulate capital. Poverty is a deterrent to deforestation because poorer farmers have inadequate capital to finance forest clearing and to support themselves during the idle-period. The decision to clear a forest rests mostly with more established farmers such as land owners.

Because forest lands are available at a fraction of their true economic worth, forest clearing and the subsequent agriculture are capable of producing high financial returns for farmers. In the early years, the net income generated from these activities enables poorer farmers (i.e. *anak ladangs*) to support themselves. Later, i.e. at the time of cinnamon harvest, a large cash capital is generated. This enables both poorer farmers and land owners to finance the next round of forest clearing. The social values held by the society, which result in greater land ownership giving a higher social status, motivate farmers to own a land and to increase their land ownership. In addition to financial surplus from the forestry and agricultural sectors, surpluses generated from other sectors, e.g. the trading sector, are also used to finance forest clearing. For farmers, forest clearing enables them to own a "long-term maturity bond" in the form of a cinnamon plantation.

The policy implication of this study is straightforward. If deforestation is caused by capital accumulation behaviour of villagers, to ease the pressure on forest lands the government may need to, in addition to other measures, stimulate the creation of other financially attractive investments at the village level. This policy should be incorporated into a broader, and integrated, village development program to ensure economic and budgetary efficiency. The government may also increase the financial costs and risks of illegal deforestation in order to make the activity less beneficial for farmers. Increased fees and/or fines for forest intruders may be considered provided that the government is not plagued by widespread corruption. Revenues generated from these fees and fines may then be used to finance any programs designed to protect a national park, such as improved policing.

Table 1

Proportion of farmers who in the past cleared a forest and the average size of forest cleared (... -1995)

Group of farmers a)	Proportion of farmers that cleared forest b)	Average size of forest cleared (hectare) c)	Average size of land owned (hectare) d)
anak ladang (n1= 31, age= 23.4)	3 %	0.01	0.01
anak ladang/land owner (n2= 12, age= 33.6)	83 %	1.27	3.38
Land Owner (n3= 5, age= 48.2)	100 %	5.93	7.96
Induk Semang (n4= 7, age= 45.4)	100 %	8.41	10.50

Notes:

a) Number of respondents = N = n1+n2+n3+n4= 55. The variable "age" represents the average age of the head of household in the group.

b) It represents the number of respondents in each group who cleared a forest at least once during his/her life divided by the total number of respondents in each group.

c) The average size of forest cleared by each group of farmers.

d) Only includes ownership of *ladang*s (dry lands).

Table 2

Estimated returns from forest clearing and the subsequent agriculture (Rp hectare^{-1})

	Total Net Returns		Financial Net Returns To	
Year	Financial	Economic	Land Owner	*Anak Ladang*
0	-750 000	-4 630 000	-750 000	0
1	3 843 885	2 643 231	-205 400	4 049 285
2	4 049 285	2 107 978	0	4 049 285
3	4 049 285	2 107 978	0	4 049 285
4	4 360 859	2 403 552	155 787	4 205 072
5	4 542 160	2 584 853	246 438	4 295 722
6	2 817 085	1 740 432	396 221	2 420 864
7	0	-104 000	0	0
8	0	-104 000	0	0
9	0	-104 000	0	0
10	0	-104 000	0	0
11	0	-104 000	0	0
12	18 314 458	18 150 458	9 157 229	9 157 229
NPV at 16%	14 637 740	5 824 234	846 191	13 791 549
IRR	n.a.	47.4%	24.5%	n.a.

Note: n.a. = not applicable.

ACKNOWLEDGMENT

We wish to acknowledge the financial support provided by the Australian Government's ADCOS scheme. Also, we thank the Centre for International Forestry Research (CIFOR) for funding the fieldwork. We thank Djoko Suroso of the Indonesian Ministry of State for Environment and staff members of the KSNP authority and the World Wide Fund for Nature (WWF) representative office in Kerinci for their help and assistance. We are very grateful to Paul Kristiansen who helped us in reproducing the Kerinci Map.

NOTES

1. Based on a qualitative assessment by the World Wide Fund for Nature (WWF) which established a research station and a representative office in the Kerinci region in the early 1980s. However, no estimates of deforestation rate, by village, are available.
2. This premise, however, specifically excludes externalities associated with forest clearing and conservation. Negative externalities such as flood and landslides are likely to be overlooked by farmers as long as they pose no threat to the farmers' daily life. So are environmental bads of regional and global relevance such as biodiversity losses and increased levels of atmospheric carbon dioxide.
3. Wibowo (1993) argues that the "best guess" for the social opportunity cost of capital in Indonesia is in the order of 24%. Given the annual rate of inflation of about 8%, a social discount rate of 16% (in real terms) is then adopted.
4. If the 1:1 system is adopted, the *anak ladang* would have received one-half of income from cinnamon. By adopting the 1:2 system, the *anak ladang* would only be entitled to one-third of the income. This means a foregone earning of one-sixth of the income.
5. US$ 1.00 = 2100 Rupiahs (Rp).
6. For example, because they opt to clear a small parcel of forest (e.g. 0.1 hectare) which they can afford to finance.
7. The *anak ladang* used a "loan" from his father-in-law to finance the forest clearing. He considers the land as not his own until he repays the loan.
8. Potato is cultivated twice a year from year 1 to 5. In year 6, only a season of potato is available because of shading problem.

REFERENCES

Barbier, E., J. Burgess and A. Markandya (1991), "The Economics of Tropical Deforestation", *Ambio,* Vol. 20, pp. 55-58.

Food and Agriculture Organisation (FAO) (1993), *Forest Resources Assessment 1990,* FAO, Rome.

Myers, N. (1991), "Tropical Forests: Present Status and Future Outlook", *Climatic Change,* Vol. 19, pp. 3-32.

Myers, N. (1993), "Tropical Forests: the Main Deforestation Fronts", *Environ. Conserv.,* Vol. 20, pp. 9-16.

Repetto, R. (1988), "Overview", in Repetto, R. and M. Gillis (eds.), *Public Policies and the Misuse of Forest Resources,* Cambridge University Press, pp. 1-42.

Rudel, T. and J. Roper (1996), "Regional Patterns and Historical Trends in Tropical Deforestation, 1976-1990: A Qualitative Comparative Analysis", *Ambio,* Vol. 25, pp. 160-166.

Vanclay, J.K. (1993), "Saving the Tropical Forest: Needs and Prognosis", *Ambio,* Vol. 22, pp. 225-231.

World Bank (1990), *Indonesia: Sustainable Development of Forest, Land and Water,* a World Bank country study, The World Bank, Washington, DC.

Wibowo (1993), *A Microeconomic Analysis of Health, Safe Water and Sanitation,* unpublished Master's (Economics) thesis presented at the University of Queensland, Brisbane, Australia, (pp. xv + 281).

Appendix : Inputs, output and data of prices

A. Potato Farming (season^{-1} hectare^{-1})	
Seeds (kgs)	874
Fertilisers (kgs)	
Urea (nitrogen)	257
Phosphate	514
Mix of pesticides and insecticides (unit)	57
Number of delivery times for:	
Fertilisers	15
Output (potato)	129
Family labourers used (days)	221
Hired labourers (days)	62
Output (kgs)	
Large size	7540
Medium size	1594
Small size	468

B. Cinnamon Plantation 1)	
Number of initial plants	1956
Survival rate	
Year 1	89%
Year 2	94%
Year 3	96%
Years 4-12	100%
Replanting (number of plants)	
Year 1	98
Thinning (number of plants)	
Year 4	249
Year 5	249
Year 6	332
Harvest (number of plants)	
Year 12	830
Family labourers used (days)	26-79
Hired labourers (days)	0
Output (kgs plant^{-1})	
Year 4 (wet bark)	1.07
Year 5 (wet bark)	1.65
Year 6 (wet bark)	1.99
Year 12 (wet bark)	18.40

C. Prices and Wages	
Potato seed (Rp kg^{-1})	670
Cinnamon seedling (Rp plant^{-1})	100
Urea (Rp kg^{-1})	290
Phosphate (Rp kg^{-1})	450
Mix of pesticides and insecticides (Rp unit^{-1})	17 000
Delivery costs (Rp delivery^{-1})	
Fertilisers	2250
Output (potato)	5000
Wages (Rp day^{-1})	4000
Potato prices 2)	
Large size (Rp kg^{-1})	546
Medium size (Rp kg^{-1})	375
Small size (Rp kg^{-1})	188
Price of cinnamon bark (Rp kg wet bark^{-1})	1200
Land acquisition costs	
Forest clearing (Rp ha^{-1})	300 000
Land clearing (Rp ha^{-1})	450 000
Market price of a *ladang* (Rp ha^{-1})	4 630 000

Exchange rate US$ 1.00 = Rp 2100

Notes: 1) No fertilisers, insecticides and pesticides are used in cinnamon plantation.
2) Weighted average of prices over the period October 1994 - July 1995 with each farmer's sales volume used as the weighing factor.

[23]

Community-based forestry in Yunnan: dictates of environment and socio-economics[1]

Zhuge Ren[2] and Clem Tisdell

Abstract

Yunnan is a mountainous region of South-west China and six large rivers flow through it – the Mekong, Salween, Irrawaddy, Yangtze, Song Hong and the Pearl. This means that the environmental conditions of upland Yunnan have significant environmental consequences, not only in China, but also in Indo-China. Silt loads, water quality and variability of waterflows in these major rivers are greatly influenced by conditions in rural Yunnan. The natural, rural environment in Yunnan is being degraded by cultivation on steep slopes, shifting agriculture and deforestation. Only 2.8 million hectares of Yunnan's land is suitable for cropping, but it has a population of 40 million. Furthermore, 67 per cent of its arable land is on slopes. In addition, 70 per cent of its forest resources are located in mountainous areas. Consequently, Yunnan's hilly areas are under pressure both from agriculture and logging.

Yunnan contains 25 minorities and some, such as the Dai, have traditionally adopted forestry practices that conserve its natural, rural environment, reduce soil erosion and biodiversity loss and promote sustainable livelihoods. However, this is not true of all minorities. Some minorities practise slash-and-burn agriculture and engage in cultivation of crops on steepland, such as maize, with no attention to soil conservation. In practice, Yunnan' s environment is deteriorating as cultivation of its land intensifies and extends, and as its forests are destroyed or overexploited. About 25 million people live on mountainous land in this province.

The possibility of using community forestry to solve the present environmental problems of upland Yunnan is explored. Community forestry may reduce shifting agriculture, cropping on steep slopes, desertification of river valleys, soil erosion, biodiversity loss and rural poverty. It may, for example, provide a more effective approach to establishing shelter-belt forests in Yunnan for the Yangtze River than is the present practice. The present one involves forcibly trying to prevent local people from cultivating steeplands and the mass planting of steeplands with trees by a central agency. Without decentralisation and community support, this shelter-type reforestation project may fail, or be less economic and environmentally effective than would be community-based forestry.

Introduction

This chapter stresses the importance of community-based forestry for the conservation of natural resources and alleviation of poverty in upland Yunnan. In contrast with state-managed forests, which account for the bulk of forested land in many countries, including China, community-based forestry is a decentralised form of forestry that empowers local people to manage and establish forests. Forestry based in local communities can take many forms. It can involve forestry, including agroforestry, on the private land of individual villagers, or it can entail communal or social forestry, for example the communal establishment and management of forests on wasteland or on degraded land.

Communal forestry has been practiced in parts of India for more than 20 years and was first adopted in West Bengal. It has been observed that in villages where community forests have been established, biodiversity has increased and the extent of poverty appears to have been reduced. While China has less experience with community-based forestry than India, some minorities in China, such as the Dais, have engaged in silviculture for centuries. There is growing interest in community-based silviculture in China, particularly in Yunnan, the prime region of interest in this contribution.

Yunnan, a frontier province in South-west China, has a long history of upland cultivation. Today, the inhabitants of its upland areas are demanding improvements in their environment and in their living standards. The simultaneous achievement of these objectives requires strategies to be found for environmentally sustainable development. There is worldwide interest in discovering strategies to achieve this and in particular China has adopted its *Agenda 21* (State Council, 1994) with a view to achieving such development.

Over the past decades, human exploitation has almost exhausted forests in upland Yunnan and its uplands have fallen into a vicious circle of poverty and environmental deterioration. Researchers in this province have been searching for a way to reverse this trend and have now concluded that the expansion of community-based forestry might be the most effective way to develop the area's rural economy and improve its environment. This can be seen as a new policy in China, where it is hoped that the establishment of community forestry will accelerate forest rehabilitation and foster environmental improvements.

In implementing this program, the benefits to the local area and its population are of prime concern, and local customs and beliefs will receive full consideration. Community forestry has been extremely successful in the developing countries of South and South-east Asia where these factors have been given priority. In view of this, it is felt that the advantages of community forestry far outweigh its disadvantages and that community forestry has great potential to help solve the development problems of upland Yunnan.

A feature of this chapter is its emphasis in its discussion of community-based forestry on: (i) the state of the environment, and (ii) the significance of institutional structures for appropriate economic decision-making and for the optimal use and conservation of resources. Decentralised governance structures linked with appropriate economic incentives to local communities can be a powerful force for improvements in decision-making about resource use and conservation. Nevertheless, they should not be regarded as a panacea for effective governance. The situation is more complicated than some advocates for the empowerment of local communities realise.

Background

Yunnan is a mountainous province. Of the province's total land area of 394 000 km^2, 94 per cent is categorised as mountainous. Elevations in the province range from 6740 m above sea level in the north-west down to 76.4 m above sea level in the south-east. Six famous rivers – the Lancangjiang (Mekong), Nujiang (Salween), Dayingjiang (Irrawaddy), Jinshajiang (Yangtze), Yuanjiang (Song Hong) and Nanpanjiang (Pearl) – and over one hundred of their tributaries, flow through Yunnan to the mainland of South-east Asia and the coastal provinces of China.

Yunnan has distinctive climatic conditions: the climate in its west is controlled by the plateau climate from Tibet and in the east is subject to the wet monsoon from East Asia; the central region is influenced by South Asian tropical monsoons. The pattern of mixing of the west winds with monsoonal air currents causes considerable oscillation of its climatic conditions. A dry season occurs in the winter and spring and the wet season is in the summer and autumn.

The diverse topography of high mountains, deep river valleys and steeply sloping land in Yunnan produces varied climatic patterns throughout the province such that almost every type of climate in China can be found within Yunnan. Consequently, the province contains a very wide range of vegetation types with over 17 000 higher plant species being found in the upland region.

Yunnan has a population of 40 million people but has only an area of 2.8 million hectares suitable for crop cultivation and 67 per cent of this arable land lies on mountain slopes. In addition, 70 per cent of its forest resources are confined to the north-western highlands and southern remote areas of Yunnan (Xue, 1984). Consequently, Yunnan's shortage of arable land and its lack of accessible forest resources greatly intensifies conflicts between the demands of the human population on its natural resources and the conservation of those natural resources.

Traditional practices involving rural land use and community forestry in Yunnan

During several thousand years of agricultural production in Yunnan, local people have developed many effective methods of cultivation. The following are the major types:

Trees for commercial non-timber products

Originally, the indigenous people of Yunnan traditionally planted trees for fruits, spices, oils and fibres near their houses or on the corners of their fields for self-consumption. Through selective breeding of varieties that adapted most successfully, some areas gradually became known for particular local products. For example, Funing county is today one of the major anise-producing areas of China. Although the county's yield of anise ranks second in China, its quality is ranked first. However, it was not until 1675 that a refugee introduced the first anise tree into Funing from Guangxi province. It thrived in this county and the scattered plantings developed into mass production. The county is also renowned for its anise by-products. Similarly successful local products in Yunnan include Baozhu pear, Mixiang pear, Hongxie pear, Dapao walnut, early maturing chestnut, Fengdong orange, Zhongpai orange, seedless persimmon, Diao plum, sweet pomegranate, sour pomegranate, Yanshui pomegranate, Nuomi pomegranate, three-year mango, fingered citron, prickly ash, tung oil, lac, natural silk, palm fibre and lacquer.

Home gardening

Home gardening is a traditional activity in the villages of Yunnan. Fruit trees, bamboos, spice trees, vegetable trees (for example, the sprouts of Chinese mahogany *Toona sinensis* from which a delicious dish is made from a traditional recipe) and other trees are commonly cultivated in the gardens. Dai people are particularly successful in managing their own gardens. They often plant trees, shrubs, vegetables, vines and epiphytes together in one patch of ground, each plant positioned to make the most efficient use of the sunlight. It is possible for home gardens to meet all the needs of the local people for fruit, wood, vegetables, spices, flowers and medicinal herbs (Yu et al., 1985).

Fuelwood

Dai people have traditionally cultivated the senna tree *Cassia siamea* for the production of fuelwood. When five years old, a tree can be coppiced with a stump of 0.5–1.5 m remaining and it will sprout two to three new shoots the following year. Then shoots can be cut from the tree for fuelwood at three-yearly intervals. One stump at between 30 and 50 years of age has over 20 shoots. Dai people usually divide a block of senna trees into three sectors so that they can rotate the collection of fuelwood each year. Some Dai people initially cultivate senna trees for timber and then switch to their use for fuelwood.

Many other minority groups are experienced in managing natural fuelwood resources. They identify the trees that provide good fuelwood and ensure that these remain dominant in their woodlands.

Village woodlands

In rural areas of China, it is widely believed that forests guarantee favourable weather and bumper harvests, and that trees ensure the prosperity of a village or community. Tree-covered hills around a village are often called 'dragon hills' or 'holy hills'. In Chinese folklore, 'dragon' is a monster that takes charge of rainfall. Another kind of protected woodland near villages is called 'water-source forest'. These woodlands help to maintain a continuous supply of water flowing into the villages and farmlands. Therefore, villagers always ensure that great care is taken of their local woodlands. Their indigenous knowledge of trees and the traditional management of woodlands have ensured that woodlands have flourished near villages for thousands of years. Unfortunately, a lot of protected woodlands were destroyed during the 'Cultural Revolution' when beliefs associated with them were seen as a kind of feudal superstition.

Agroforestry

Agroforestry is an ancient practice that has existed in China for thousands of years. In China, there are well-known examples of the intercropping of both *Paulownia* trees and Chinese wood oil trees with crops. A less well-known example is that of the intercropping of alder trees *Ainus nepaiensis* and upland rice, which has been practised in the south-western part of Yunnan for several centuries. In this system, upland rice and alder trees are intercropped in the first year. After the rice harvest, the alder trees are left to grow for fuelwood and for supply of green manure. Usually the alder trees can provide 1.5–2.5 tons per hectare of green manure by the fifth year. After seven to ten years, the alder trees can be felled for timber and fuelwood and the next rotation of crops and trees can commence (Xue, 1984). Besides providing timber and fuelwood, the nitrogen-fixing capabilities of alder trees add to soil fertility. This system is very similar to the 'Taungya System' first practised in Burma.

In central Yunnan, soybean, maize, wheat, buckwheat and radish are traditionally intercropped between rows of pine trees *Pinus armandi* for the first two or three years, after which the pine trees continue to be managed alone for timber. The edible seeds of the pine trees are sold for food. In addition, space and sunlight are used effectively in orchards, where various winter crops are planted under deciduous fruit trees.

In southern Yunnan, the local people cultivate tea bushes under natural forest. Ethnic minorities such as Jino, Rani and Dai people have practised this kind of agroforestry for at least 400 years. In Menghai county, there are plantations of camphor intercropped with tea (*Cinnamomum porrectum* + *Camellia sinensis* var. *assamica*). It is believed that the oldest tea bush in this area is over 800 years old. In earlier times, the Dai people occasionally planted tea seedlings under the natural camphor forests. Then they found that the most successful method was to create artificial mixed forests by intercropping camphor seedlings in the tea plantations. To date, more than 1 200 hectares of camphor-tea plantations have been established. Farmers can get 0.8–0.9 tons of tea and 0.2–0.3 tons of camphor from one hectare of camphor-tea plantation. In addition, the chemicals secreted by the camphor trees protect the tea trees from pests, resulting in higher quality leaves and shoots (Zou, 1995).

In south and south-east Yunnan, a shade-loving spice and medicinal plant, Tsao-ko (*Amomum tsao-ko*), is widely cultivated in the forests near streams at an altitude of 1 000–1 500 m. The Tsao-ko fruit is harvested in the third year and provides a good income. It is thought that this type of cultivation has been practised for over 300 years (Zou, 1991).

Non-timber products of forests

A rich knowledge of the non-timber products of forests, such as edible mushrooms, wild fruits, wild vegetables, bamboo shoots, spice and medicinal herbs, is held by almost all nationalities living in the forest areas of Yunnan. Other non-timber forest products include raw materials such as tannin, lac, aromatic oil, resin, cork, gum, fibre, dyes, starch, forage and green manure. In the spring of 1995, a research team led by Zhuge Ren conducted an investigation at the local vegetable markets in Dehong Prefecture of south-west Yunnan and collected 56 kinds of wild vegetables in this single season, including trees, shrubs, vines and herbs. Some of these wild vegetables have been introduced into home gardens, for example, *Erynigium foetidum*, *Solanum indicum*, *Oenanthe javanica*, *Gynura crepidioides*, *Acacia intsia* var. *caesia*, *Houttuynia cordata*, and *Solanum nigrum* var. *photeinocarpum*.

Another interesting aspect is the extent of indigenous knowledge of natural food additives and dyes. Dai people in south Yunnan mix the pulverised dried flowers of *Gmelina arborea* with glutinous rice to steam yellow-coloured 'Baba cake' for their New Year Festival. The flowers of *Buddleja officinalis* are widely used by the minorities in Yunnan as a food colouring. One plant used for food colouring, *Peristrophe baphica*, changes its colour from red to purple or black depending on the ash content of the plant. Yao people in south and south-east Yunnan use dye from this plant to colour rice for the celebration of their grand 'Panwang Festival' (Tao et al., 1993).

Handicrafts based on forest products

People from twenty-six different nationalities live in upland Yunnan and over thousands of years the various cultures have developed a variety of arts and crafts based on the rich resources of their land. Handicrafts based on forest products are commonly found in the countryside. The best known of these are Jianchuang wood carvings, Tengchong rattan wares, Dali wood-marble furniture, Heqing white tissue paper and Dali knot-dyed cloth (APCYP, 1990).

As far back as the Ming Dynasty (A.D. 1368–1644), Jianchuang wood carving was renowned throughout the country. The artisans from Jianchuang county were selected to build the Beijing Imperial Palace. In the Qing Dynasty (A.D. 1644–1911), the famous Yuanming Palace (destroyed by the Eight-Power Allied Expedition in 1900) was an outstanding example of the exquisite craftsmanship of Jianchuang artisans. Many ancient temples in Yunnan still preserve the consummate artistic handicraft in classical Chinese style of the Jianchuang carpenters who participated in their construction.

Tengchong county was renowned for its rattan wares during the Song Dynasty (A.D. 960–1279). 'Teng' in Chinese means 'rattan' and 'chong' means 'strategic pass'. The hand-made rattan wares of Tengchong are both beautiful and durable. The high quality raw materials come from the native rattan plants, *Clamus spp.* and *Daemonorops margaritae*.

Dali wood-marble furniture is made by hand using local timber and marble. Tables, chairs and beds are decorated with wood carvings of flowers and birds and embellished with the natural patterns of the marble. Natural Chinese paint is used on the surface of the furniture.

Tissue paper of Heqing county was in common use during the period of the Dali Kingdom (A.D. 937–1253). This white, soft and durable paper, made from the strong-fibred bark of the daphne tree, was one of the earliest artificial papers.

Dali knot-dyed cloth uses dye from the cultivated 'blue-dye plant'. White cloth is tied and sewn according to the pattern desired, then dyed in a vat and finally rinsed well to achieve the special print effect.

The abundance of natural bamboos in most parts of Yunnan has led to the development of crafts utilising the bamboo for hand-made wares, for example, Eshan bamboo work. In addition, a market has been developed in processed bamboo shoots – dried, slivered, pickled and so on. Zhaotong Qiongzhuea bamboo shoots, Xishuangbanna sweet bamboo shoots and pickled bamboo shoots are well known in the province.

Community-based forestry, a solution for the present problems of Yunnan

An area of about 346 000 km^2 of the province is mountainous and contains a population of some 25 million people. Over the past decade, the increasing pressures from harmful agricultural practices, such as shifting cultivation based on short and shortening cycles of cultivation, cropping on steep slopes and so on, have led to a significant worsening of the ecological environment in Yunnan's mountainous areas. Introduction of community forestry to such areas could well alleviate these problems. Furthermore, the development of community forests in Yunnan is essential if the urgent problems of desertification of dry-hot river valleys, reduction of biodiversity, and other forms of environmental deterioration and rural poverty are to be solved.

Diversion of shifting cultivation

Shifting cultivation, or slash-and-burn agriculture produces food by simple techniques and minimum use of labour. It has been practised effectively by the upland local people for over ten centuries under conditions involving low population density and rich forest resources, and is still practised in some remote areas of south Yunnan. However, with the current increase in population and decrease in forest areas, shifting cultivation has become a problem that is threatening the limited natural resources of Yunnan. Shifting agriculture has become an environmental problem because the length of cultivation cycles has become very short, and an increasing proportion of land is under cultivation at any one time. Consequently, more land is exposed to erosion and biodiversity is reduced. Furthermore, with shortening cultivation cycles the productivity of the soil declines and cultivation becomes less economic (cf. Ramakrishnan, 1992). Government attempts to control the practice by legislation have generally been unsuccessful. Since forests provide local people with items to meet their basic needs, an alternative means of providing support must be found before the inhabitants can be persuaded to change their way of life. Community-based forestry encourages local people to depend on permanent forest land for their livelihood and conserves forest resources. The most successful way to achieve this is to replace the simple agricultural system with a more diversified economic system involving trees of commercial value as a complement to food production. For example, the local people living in a mountainous Aini village have practised shifting cultivation for many generations. In 1976, they were given help to establish a tea garden and as a result, their tradition of shifting cultivation has gradually changed. For nearly twenty years now they have lived on the same land in order to manage the tea garden and their living conditions have quickly improved (Long et al., 1985).

Restriction on steep slope cropping

The cultivation of grain crops on steep slopes is a major problem in upland Yunnan. In Nujiang prefecture of west Yunnan, 42.2 per cent of ploughed land is on slopes in excess of 25 degrees (Gao et al., 1992); the Yangtze River valley of north Yunnan also has about 40 per cent of its ploughed land on slopes exceeding 25 degrees (He, 1991). In some places, people even cultivate grain crops on slopes of 50 degrees. Today, the pressure of the increasing population on the land is leading to slope cultivation in most areas of the province. In addition, the lower productivity of steep slopes compared to flatter land requires the utilisation of a larger area of such land to yield the same quantity of production from grain crops. Soil erosion, mountain torrents, mud-rock flows, landslides and collapse of embankments frequently result from steep slope cultivation.

In the Yangtze River area of Yunnan, an ongoing project to establish protected forests is now addressing the reforestation of steep slopes. The main problem is to continue to satisfy the population's requirement for arable land when such a plan is put into practice in a densely populated area. A successful technique for slope cultivation that can be considered is agroforestry. This technique involves the planting of multipurpose trees along the terrace ridges with crops being planted in the 'alley'. By this means, not only can people obtain food, fuelwood, fodder and other living materials, but the tree lines help prevent soil erosion. In addition, if nitrogen-fixing trees are cultivated, this will improve the fertility of the soil. Where such an alternative is offered, it will be much more effective in convincing villagers to reforest the steep slopes, than mere prohibition of the cultivation of steep slopes by people.

Reforestation in the dry-hot river valleys

Over 800 000 hectares of dry-hot river valleys are scattered along the Yangtze, Mekong, Salween and Song Hong rivers. The primary forest vegetation of these areas has been destroyed and today it has been replaced by savanna-like woodland. The dry-hot climate of the dry season causes water shortages for living things and for farming, yet the heavy rain of the wet season frequently washes the soil from the bare land. From the 1950s through to the end of the 1970s, local governments implemented programs for the mass afforestation of these areas using both pine trees and broad-leaved trees, but all failed (Du, 1994).

Actually, there are many plants, both native and domesticated, which adapt well to the unique ecological conditions of the area. Coffee, mango, pear, orange, pomegranate and tamarind *Tamarindus indica* are commonly planted in the dry-hot habitat. Furthermore, *Phyllanthus emblica*, *Ziziphus mauritiana*, *Jatropha curcas*, *Calotropis gigantea* and *Dodonea viscosa* can be grown and used as industrial raw materials. Also, *Acaciafarnesiana*, *Bombax malabarica*, *Bischofia javanica* and *Ficus lacor* grow quickly in these areas. *Toona cilicata*, *Schima wallichii* and *Pistacia chinensis* can be grown to produce high quality timber. Exotic multipurpose trees, such as *Leucaena leucocephala* and *Eucalyptus spp.* are cultivated widely and are well received by the local people. In addition, the introduction of tropical crops into these areas has proved very beneficial and many spring or summer vegetables can be grown in winter due to the high winter temperatures. It would also be advantageous to develop agroforestry systems by intercropping trees and crops or vegetables in the lower valley and to plant native trees or shrubs for reforestation of the slopes above the valley.

Conservation of biodiversity

Yunnan is famous for the diversity of its species of animals and plants. A total of 1 638 species of vertebrates, 261 species of mammals, 779 species of birds and 13 000 species of insects has been identified. Of these, 164 species of wild animals are regarded as rare and endangered and are under protection. There are about 14 000 seed plants, of which 5 300 are trees. The first edition of the State Red Data Book lists 145 of its plants as rare and endangered. Since 1981, Yunnan has established 105 nature reserves covering over 2 million hectares. However, shifting cultivation, the use of woodlands for crops and felling of trees for fuelwood have been threatening the conservation of biodiversity in its protected areas. Moreover, only about 70 per cent of those rare and endangered botanical species have been included in nature reserves. According to an inventory of forest resources in the province, the area of Yunnan's woodland decreased at the rate of 50 000 hectares per year during the period 1985–1992. Inevitably, if this rate of decrease continues, many living species will eventually disappear. Possibly the best method for conserving biodiversity is to develop rural industries and handicrafts to release people from the land and, at the same time, increase production of forest resources in order to meet the demands of local people for these. The development of community forests fulfils these requirements.

Improving the agricultural environment

According to official statistics, during the period 1950–1990, there were 297 disasters involving mud-rock flows, landslides and other types of geological destruction in Yunnan. As a result, 14 000 hectares of farmland were destroyed resulting in a reduction of 14.51 million kg in grain supplies (Liu et al., 1993). This decade has seen an increased frequency of major droughts and floods. Serious soil erosion now extends over an area of 140 000 km^2 (Kang, 1991). Deforestation is the link between increased soil erosion, desertification, reduced water supplies, mud-rock flows, landslides, drought and flood. Forests are the basis of mountain agriculture. It is clear that any measures other than reforestation will only alleviate the symptoms of the 'diseases'. Reforestation can no longer be undertaken by the simple government initiative of mass plantings. The traditional method of reforestation is centred on the establishment of large tracts of forestland, usually including few tree species. The essence of the modern community forestry is that it considers the needs of each individual and community in reforesting a region, and in that it differs from traditional state forestry. The current state project establishing the Yangtze River Shelter Forests in Yunnan has involved a massive labour force, considerable material resources and the expenditure of large sums of money. Little attention has been given to arousing the enthusiasm of the local people and to utilising their initiative. If the ideas of community forestry are to be incorporated into this project, the prime consideration in plans for reforestation and selection of trees must be the needs and aspirations of the local people.

Poverty alleviation

In Yunnan today, nearly seven million people, or one-sixth of the total population, are classified as living in poverty. Serious poverty occurs in mountainous regions in 73 counties containing over 3 500 administrative villages. In poor areas, the traditional agricultural economy usually involves food production depending solely on cropping systems with simple techniques, and extended areas of cultivation giving low yields. It is exactly as described by Dr Nancy Peluso (1988) in her famous PhD dissertation: 'Rich Forests, Poor People . . .'. Forestry policy also has a critical influence on the economy of rural areas. In China, all large forests belong to the state and local people are regarded as outsiders to be excluded. Even in the 1990s, many reports can still be found in official documents regarding the hostilities between government and local people concerning the use of forest resources.

Rural poverty has complicated roots some of which are linked with local conditions and customs and hence, any solution requires integrated measures. Community forestry focuses on the coordination of government forest resource management and use in conjunction with local people, thereby diminishing conflict between the government and the local people. Furthermore, community forestry is designed to take account of the cultural and economic activities of local people and help them to select the best options for the development of diversified land-use systems.

Perspectives on community forestry in upland Yunnan

Upland Yunnan has similar natural and social conditions to those of the countries of South and South-east Asia. Therefore, concepts and methods of community forestry being applied in these countries can also be introduced and developed in upland Yunnan. In fact, initial results from the practice of community forestry in Yunnan have been very encouraging.

Adjustment of development policies

The provincial government of Yunnan has recently adopted a development plan for the economy. The tobacco industry, which is currently the cornerstone of the province's economy, will be gradually replaced by industries based on forestry, flowers and plants, tourism, sugar, tea, and processing industries. In China's ninth 'Five Year Plan' starting in 1996, the alleviation of poverty and the exploitation of biological resources is a prime focus. The Eighteen Exploitation Projects of Biological Resources mainly include the comprehensive utilization of forest products and economic plants as a basis for rural development.

Tourism is a new and an expanding 'smokeless industry' in Yunnan. At the end of 1992, the development of tourism became one of the most important items on the agenda of the provincial government and soon afterwards, special policies for promoting tourism were instigated. In October 1994, the provincial government convened a province-wide Tourism Program meeting in Lijiang, a city in north-west Yunnan. At the meeting, the governor of the province requested that the speed of construction should be increased for communication facilities, such as high-grade highways, new main line railways, new airports and other tourist infrastructures. Along with community forestry, tourism may provide a basis for conservation of natural resources. Tourism can contribute significantly to rural development and yet be environmentally friendly.

Education

Since the end of the 1980s, Yunnan has sent dozens of researchers abroad to study community forestry and other areas related to rural development. Most of them have now resumed work in these fields. In addition, several training courses for community forestry and agroforestry, sponsored respectively by the Ford Foundation (FF) and the Worldwide Fund for Nature (WWF), have been conducted at various academic institutes in Yunnan. The Southwest Forestry College offers a course in community forestry. One of the aims of the FF-supported project is to train government officials and foresters 'on-the-job'. As a result of the training of policy-makers and forestry technicians in community forestry, it will be much easier to introduce concepts and methods of community forestry into traditional forestry activities. The 1995 academic year saw the introduction of a three-year course in community forestry at the Southwest Forestry College in Kunming. All students accepted for enrolment have at least two years experience in the forestry branch of the Ministry of Forestry and will return there after completing their studies. Subjects from the community forestry course are also available to students completing other specialisations at the Southwest Forestry College.

Plans for technical training for farmers are going ahead. The provincial government is sending scientists and technicians to poor areas to help educate local farmers in improved agriculture and forestry techniques. It is hoped that this will help to alleviate the poverty of Yunnan's seven million rural poor people.

Potential of natural resources for new uses

To date, only a few hundred species of plants have been cultivated in upland Yunnan, but thousands of wild plants, from which fruits, oils, tannin, fibre, starch, gum, resin, lac, dyes and drugs can be obtained, remain to be exploited. For example, according to recent research, there are 28 genera and 215 species of bamboo widely distributed in Yunnan, but only a few have traditionally been utilised. Researchers at the Bamboo Research Institute at Southwest Forestry College have developed processing techniques for local factories to enable them to produce plywood and plywood flooring from a variety of bamboos. They also developed a new technique for preserving bamboo shoot products. This has improved the economics of large-scale production of bamboo shoot products and has brought profound changes to some mountain regions. Another example is the production of soft drink from the wild plant, *Phyllanthus emblica*, which is found as a small tree in most parts of the province. During the 1980s, scientists discovered that the fruit of *Ph. emblica* is rich in vitamins and also contains a beneficial amount of selenium, which may help to protect the human body against carcinogens. Since then, large investments have been made in rural areas in the production of *Ph. emblica* and soft drink products based on it. It has become an important source of income for some rural communities.

The province of Yunnan has six state nature reserves, 99 local nature reserves, 17 national forest parks and over one hundred local forest parks. These reserves and parks represent diverse patterns of forests, ecological systems, climates and geographical conditions. Most of these are located in rural areas remote from cities and have been opened, or are to be opened, for forest recreation. Tourism in rural areas can bring many benefits. First of all, economic prosperity from tourism can bring improvements to local communications and to the rural economy. Second, the varied commercial demands of tourists can propel minority groups into a commercial world and make them less dependent on subsistence activities. Nevertheless, negative social and other impacts from tourism development are possible and these need to be guarded against. Tourism and rural development will be closely connected in the future of upland Yunnan.

Exploration of indigenous knowledge

It has been found that the traditional practices of community forestry that have been developed in local areas by local people are most successful. In addition to providing local people with supplementary incomes, as does cash-crop tree planting and home gardening, community forestry provides a basis for cottage industries and handicrafts, and leads to increased food production thereby assisting rural development. Traditional local products, especially handiworks of minorities, such as Dali knot-dyed cloth and Banna Tongpa (a small satchel made by the Dai people), are very popular purchases by tourists. In order to achieve sustainable local development it is important to find and develop products with local characteristics and in demand locally. Fuelwood from village woodland management will relieve the threat of insufficient energy for cooking and community forests can also help meet the demands of local people for wood for the building of houses and the production of furniture. The successful Taungya system in upland Yunnan is particularly practicable for the upland cultivation systems. Multi-purpose trees not only retard soil erosion and improve soil fertility, but also supply fodder, fuelwood, timber of short length and other forest by-products for local people. In developing community forestry and village silviculture, it is of great importance to tap indigenous knowledge about traditional production practices involving trees.

Extensive international cooperation

The natural advantages and special geographical position of Yunnan province have attracted much attention from international organisations in the past decade. The FF, WWF, World Bank, FTPP, UNFAO, UNESCO, IDRCC, RECOFTC, VSO, ICRAF, CARE, WINROCK and many universities in the developed countries, such as the United States, Canada, Australia, Germany, Britain and Holland, have all been involved directly or indirectly in projects concerning rural development of upland Yunnan. Government departments, research institutes and universities of Yunnan have worked with these international organisations towards the goal of poverty alleviation.

Concluding comments

Community-based forestry has the potential to remedy unsustainable land-use practices in much of upland Yunnan and can help alleviate poverty in many areas. In fostering community forestry, it is important to take account of indigenous knowledge about land use involving trees and create ecologically balanced land-use systems incorporating a variety of species. The development of these systems should draw on the traditional practice of community forestry in parts of Yunnan. Unlike in the case of traditional state-based forestry where local communities have mostly been ignored, consultation with and responsiveness to the needs of the local community are paramount in community-based forestry. Because of their lack of attention to local communities, many state-sponsored reforestation schemes are in danger of failing and are creating much rural hostility.

Community-based forestry can have favourable environmental and social effects: it can divert farmers from practising shifting cultivation, reduce environmental problems arising from the cropping of steep slopes, help the afforestation of dry-hot river valleys, conserve biodiversity, and generally improve environmental conditions for the practise of agriculture, and can also alleviate much poverty. Community-based forestry together with rural-oriented tourism can provide a basis for sustainable development in upland Yunnan. Programs for educating the rural people in Yunnan about new sustainable land-use practices are increasing the likelihood of such developments. Furthermore, international co-operation and recent progress in providing courses on community forestry and ecotourism at Southwest Forestry College are bringing these goals closer to fruition.

Acknowledgments

We would like to thank Professor Xue Jiru of Southwest Forestry College for his suggestions, and Dr Liu Dachang, Faculty of Arts, Deakin University, Australia, for his constructive comments.

Notes

1. This article originally appeared in C.A. Tisdell and J.C.H. Chai (eds), *China's Economic Growth and Transition: Macroeconomic, Environmental and Social/Regional Dimensions*, Nova Science Publishers, New York, 1997, pp. 333–54. The content of this article is the same as in the original (except for minor changes) but its presentation has been improved. Consequently, pagination is no longer the same as in the original.
2. Department of Forestry, Southwest Forestry College, Kunming, China.

References

Agriculture Program Committee of Yunnan Province (APCYP) (1990), *Yunnan Special Local Products*, Kunming: Yunnan People's Press.

Du, Tianli (1994), 'The orientation of exploitation and utilization of dry-hot river valley in Southwest China', *Natural Resources*, (1), 41–5.

Gao, Yingxin et al. (1992), 'An opinion on the ecologically based development of the economy in Nujiang Prefecture of Yunnan Province', *Ecological Economics*, (1), 44–9.

He, Yinwu (1991), 'On soil erosion and sloping fields returned to forest in shelter forest region of middle-upper reaches of the Yangtze River', *Ecological Economics*, (4), 18–20.

Kang, Yunhai (1991), 'On the methods of integrated irrigation in farmland', *Ecological Economics*, (4), 46–9.

Liu, Xiaohai et al. (1993), 'The calamity forecast about destruction of the ecological environment of Yunnan', *Yunnan Environment Sciences*, (1), 42–5.

Long, Yiming et al. (1985), 'The significance of expanding the rubber-tea community in the border villages', *Ecological Economics*, (2), 26–8.

Peluso, Nancy Lee (1988), *Rich Forests, Poor People, and Development: Access Control and Resistance in the Forests of Java*, PhD. dissertation, Cornell University.

Ramakrishnan, P.S. (1992), *Shifting Agriculture and Sustainable Development: An Interdisciplinary Study for North-Eastern India*, UNESCO, Paris and Parthenon, Carnforth, UK.

State Council (1994), *China's Agenda 21 – White Paper on China's Population, Environmental Development in the 21st Century*, Beijing: Environmental Science Press.

Tao, Guoda et al. (1993), 'Ethnic food pigments', *Botanical Magazine*, (2), 13.

Xue, Jiru (1984), *Yunnan Forests*, Kunming: Yunnan Science and Technology Press.

Yu, Pinghua et al. (1985), 'The study on traditional cultivated plants in Dai villages of Xishuangbanna', *Acta Bot. Yunnanica*, **7** (2), 169–86.

Zou, Shouqing (1991), 'Amomum cultivation in tropical forests', *Chinese Journal of Ecology*, **10** (1), 37–9.

Zou, Shouqing (1995), 'The patterns and the assessment of some traditional and newly developed agroforestry systems in Southern Yunnan', Prepared for the 'Workshop on Ethnobotany and the Cultural Context of Natural Resource Use and Agroforestry Management', held 16 March – 3 April 1995, at Chiang Mai, Thailand and at Xishuangbanna, China.

[24]

Joint forest management: villagers and the use and conservation of Indian forests[1]

C.A. Tisdell, K.C. Roy and A. Ghose[2]

Abstract

Provides a brief account of the development of the Joint Forest Management Scheme in India, especially in West Bengal, the state where joint forest management has been most widely adopted and which provided the genesis of the scheme that was adopted as part of India's Forest Policy 1988. The development, nature of and rationale for the scheme are discussed. Results of a survey of household heads in villages in the neighbourhood of state forests in the Midnapore region of West Bengal are reported. The survey provides information about the dependence of villagers on forest resources, the sustainability of current forest use as perceived by villagers, and reports their views about forest management issues, including the Joint Forest Management Scheme. The concerns of villagers about joint forest management are identified and analysed. It is suggested that some writers have been too ready to promote the sustainability and social welfare benefits of joint forest management as now practised. Some of its important limitations are identified. While joint forest management is preferable to open-access, the system in India is as yet deficient in terms of genuine communal and social management.

Introduction

Joint forestry management as practised in India is a form of partial co-management of state-owned forests, forests that probably were communally owned in the distant past. Although Indian joint forest management involves some management input from villagers, it is not a form of social or community-based forestry.[3] The latter is a form of forestry involving communal ownership by the village and is solely under the control of the village.

This article outlines the development of joint forest management in India, suggests the reasons for this evolution, giving particular consideration to the development of this system in West Bengal, the state where the joint forest management system is most widely used. It also reports results from a survey of three tribal Santal villages in the north Midnapore region of West Bengal. This survey was designed to obtain data from villagers about the degree and nature of their dependence on forest resources, the sustainability of current forest uses and practices as perceived by the villagers, and to provide an assessment of forest management issues, including the effectiveness of the Joint Forest Management Scheme. The outline and consideration of results from the survey are followed by analysis and discussion of issues raised in relation to joint forest management.

Development of the Joint Forest Management Scheme in India, especially in West Bengal

Origin of the scheme

The traditional bias of Indian forestry has been to concentrate on raising revenue from timber production (Mishra, 1998, p. 262). Within India, a government forest bureaucracy was created whose management of forests alienated local communities from their own ecosystems. However, policy directions began to change in 1998. India's 1988 Forest Policy emphasised a participatory approach to take greater account of community objectives and environmental concerns. Without providing specific directives, the Union Government advised the state governments to share the responsibilities and benefits of forest management with communities in and around the state forests.

West Bengal has been a pioneer of the joint forestry management (JFM) movement in India (Hobley, 1996, p. 60). JFM (a form of participatory forest management) has been widely adopted in West Bengal, especially in degraded lateritic areas of South West Bengal. In 1972 (long before India's 1988 Forest Policy), an Indian forester, A.K. Banerjee of Midnapore, undertook a pilot project in West Bengal known as the Arabari Socio-Economic Project in which 618 families from 11 villages participated (Harrison and Ghose, 2000; Harrison et al., 2001). In 1972, this Divisional Forest Officer in Midnapore, West Bengal, took over a block of 1 272 hectares of denuded forest for rehabilitation. Until then, the stumps left in the area had thrown up vegetative shoots every year that the local poor people cut and sold in the nearby market for subsistence. The value of the forest in terms of commercial timber production in 1972 was nil. In this period, there was no legal support in forest policies or laws for involving villagers in forest management. In addition to the lack of legal backing, the project was neither sponsored by the government nor by any agency. This forest officer divided 3 607 villagers into various groups and met these individually to explain that regeneration of degraded forest and their sustainable management could support livelihood of many villagers in the long run, and that both the villagers and the West Bengal Forest Department foresters needed to cooperate in these endeavours.

The Arabari Socio-Economic Project was widely adopted in several parts of West Bengal and its apparent success contributed largely to the development of the 1988 Indian Forest Policy. With the introduction of the 1988 Forest Policy, informal participation of indigenous communities in forest management was converted to JFM. Under this system, the West Bengal Forest Department in conjunction with the village-based Forest Protection Committees (FPCs) started managing forests.

Nature and rationale of the scheme

A major policy shift occurred during the 1970s and the 1980s in India's forest sector towards a more decentralised and people-oriented forestry. Until 1988, the planned and scientific forestry practices of India mostly involved top-down management aimed at meeting 'national timber needs'. However, India's national forestry policies now recognise the symbiotic relationship between villagers and forests. One of the new institutional arrangements created to take account of this new focus is the JFM program. Under this program, the state forest departments cooperate to some extent with local user-communities to protect and manage local forest resources.

As a result of centralised, state control of Indian forests in the past, user-communities became alienated from forest administration and management. Furthermore, restrictions on rights and access of villagers to forests adversely affected their lives and livelihoods. This alienation worked persistently against the forest conservation efforts of the administration, resulting in the forest management system being ill-equipped to cope with the enormous demands of the growing human and livestock population, industrialisation, urbanisation and overall economic development. It contributed to a perceived widening gap between demand for and supply of biomass for energy, fodder, timber and pulpable raw material from forest resources. This was instrumental in the formulation of the National Forest Policy of 1988, which was intended to assist tribals and other villagers living in and around forest areas in meeting their needs for fuelwood, fodder, forest food gathering, thatch and small timber.

Hobley (1996, Ch. 2) provides a systematic historical account of the development of forest policy in India and considers 1894, 1952 and 1988 as important milestones (Hobley, 1996, p. 62). The British policy, as formulated in 1894, was 'to restrict and regulate access of neighbouring villagers to the forests' and the main objective was 'to derive revenue for the state from the exploitation of valuable timbers' (Hobley, 1996, p. 62). After India's independence, the paramount interest of the state in India's forests was reinforced (cf. Tisdell and Roy, 1997). India's 1952 forest policy (post-independence) regarded the national interest in forests to be paramount compared to that of the local people and the state's emphasis on revenue generation continued (Hobley, 1996, p. 62). India's Forest Policy of 1988 indicated a new direction. This policy proposed that 'forest products as a right to be reserved for use of neighbouring communities' and that 'direct economic benefit be subordinated to the principal aim of ensuring environmental stability and ecological balance' (Hobley, 1996, p. 62). Although India's 1998 policy involves a change in principle, actual changes in practice seem to be slow in coming. While improved access of neighbouring villagers to forests has occurred and their legal use of its forest resources has been ratified, revenue generation still seems to be a major goal of state forest departments and their direct economic benefits appear only to have been subordinated to other objectives to a very limited extent.

The National Forestry Policy (1988) in India envisages involvement of villagers in the development and protection of forests – involvement of village communities and VO's in the regeneration of degraded forest lands (Circular No.: 6.21/89-F.P.). It stresses the need to determine how village communities, living close to forest land, could be given sufficient benefits to ensure their effective participation in the afforestation program.

The forest management guidelines issued by the Government of India arose from the reputed success of the pilot project (mentioned above) begun in 1972 in Arabari, in West Bengal. Vast areas of forests in the southern lateritic tracts of West Bengal had become virtually unproductive due to commercial overexploitation, illegal felling of trees for timber, unregulated fuelwood collection by poverty-stricken people, and overgrazing by village cattle. The main reason for introducing JFM appears to have been the hope that it would ameliorate such unsustainable use of forest resources by encouraging a participatory cooperative approach involving villagers and state forest departments.

In particular, it appears to have been aimed at reducing the illegal felling of trees in state forests by using members of the village-based FPCs as forest guards. The economic incentive provided for such cooperation was a quarter share for the villagers of net economic benefits for the sale of timber from the area of the forest adjoining the village, overseen by the village FPC to prevent theft of trees. Thus, it seemed possible that both villagers and state forest departments could benefit from this approach.

In practice, however, the JFM scheme is less successful than sometimes claimed (for example, by Mishra, 1998), as is indicated by our survey of villagers participating in this scheme in West Bengal. The results of this survey and its implications are discussed later. However, it can be mentioned now that the economic incentive provided to villagers by the scheme for protecting trees is low. Furthermore, the scheme only covers, in most instances, a portion of forest resources (namely timber and in a few cases cashews) and the participation of villagers in forest management itself, such as in logging decisions and replantation is extremely limited. The participation of villagers in forest management is mainly confined to the policing of their forests in areas near their village.

Although Mishra (1998, p. 262) suggests that villagers have become managers of forest in West Bengal because of JFM and that their indigenous knowledge is being integrated with the 'scientific' principles involved in modern forestry management, this was not supported by our fieldwork. In fact, tribal villagers complained that their forest management input was extremely limited.

Extent of adoption of the scheme in India, particularly in West Bengal

From Table 1, it can be seen that West Bengal has more than half of its forest area under joint forest management and that adjoining Bihar has over a quarter. However, most Indian states only have a small proportion of their forest area under JFM. Altogether, 16 Indian states have passed legislation to give effect to joint forest management (Hobley, 1996, p. 59).

In 1997, there were 3 289 FPCs in West Bengal. They had 371 700 members and protected 4 493 km^2 of forest land (http://www.iifm.org/ databank/jfm/progress.html). The number of all women FPCs is twenty. Since 1995, an area of 3 023 hectares of Sal Forests has been harvested in the state. In 164 FPC areas, a gross revenue of Rs 6.09 crores (10 million = 1 crore) was obtained after an expenditure of Rs 1.48 crores on extraction. The total one-fourth share from the final harvest distributed to the FPC members is Rs 11.5 million (Indian Institute of Forest Management website, http://www.iifm.org).

'Only degraded areas are to be covered under the JFM program. The net benefits accruing from the forest produce are to be shared between the government and the members of the committee in a ratio of 3:1' (Indian Forest Survey, 1999). This implies that a quarter of the net benefits are allocated to members of the FPCs. Because each family in a village participating in the JFM scheme usually has an equal number of members on the FPC, families in the village share village benefits from JFM equally.

Table 1 Actual forest cover and area under JFM in various states of India, 1997

State/UT	Forest Cover (km²)	Area Under JFM (km²)	JFM % of Forest Cover
Kerala	10334	20	0.19
Himachal Pradesh	12521	60	0.48
Jammu & Kashmir	20440	141	0.69
Karnataka	32403	339	1.05
Rajasthan	13353	244	1.83
Gujrat	12578	259	2.06
Madhya Pradesh	131195	3500	2.67
Orissa	46941	2960	6.31
Haryana	604	63	10.43
Andhra Pradesh	43290	6480	14.97
Bihar	26524	7103	26.78
West Bengal	**8349**	**4493**	**53.81**
Total	358532	25662	7.16

Primary Source: Society for Promotion of Wasteland Development (1998).
Secondary Source: The Planning Commission of India, http://www.planningcommission.nic.in.

While the introduction of JFM may well have reduced the illegal harvest of trees from state forests, in West Bengal, it has not been associated with sustained forest replanting. As can be seen from Table 2, the annual area planted with trees has fallen since 1991–92. In general, investment in replanting trees in state forests in West Bengal has declined. This was a source of complaint by many villagers interviewed for this study in West Bengal. It may be that JFM has increasingly been viewed by the state as a substitute for investment in forest resources, but it is at best, a partial substitute. Furthermore, it might be noted that the tree species selected for forest plantations by the West Bengal Forest Department (WBFD) are not always those of greatest economic value to villagers. For example, 25 per cent by area of its plantations in 1998 consists

Table 2 Flow of forest plantation by all public agencies in West Bengal, 1951–99

Period	Area planted in '000 ha.	Average per year in '000 ha.
1951–80	111.33	10.18
1980–85	155.90	31.18
1985–90	303.40	60.68
1990–91	62.15	62.15
1991–92	89.84	89.84
1992–97	387.37	77.47
1997–98	29.69	29.69
1998–99	18.05	18.05
Total	1157.73	24.12

Source: Based on NAEB, Ministry of Environment and Forestry, 1999, http://envfor.nic.in.

of exotic eucalypts. These are usually not favoured by villagers because of their adverse effect on non-timber forest resources, such as on grass cover and edible human food, and because they tend to lower the water table (cf. Harrison and Roy, 2000). Plantations consisting of native *Shorea robusta* (Sal) and *Tectona grandis* (Teak), which constituted in 1998, 30 per cent and 5 per cent respectively of the WBFD's plantations by area are more acceptable to villagers because they ensure greater amounts of non-timber forest resources for villagers.

Survey of household heads in three villages in West Bengal

In 2000, household heads of three villages located near or in forests in West Bengal were interviewed directly using a structured questionnaire. These three villages are located in the north Midnapore region north of Salbani, with Chandrakona Road being the nearest township. The general location of the survey area is indicated in Figure 1.

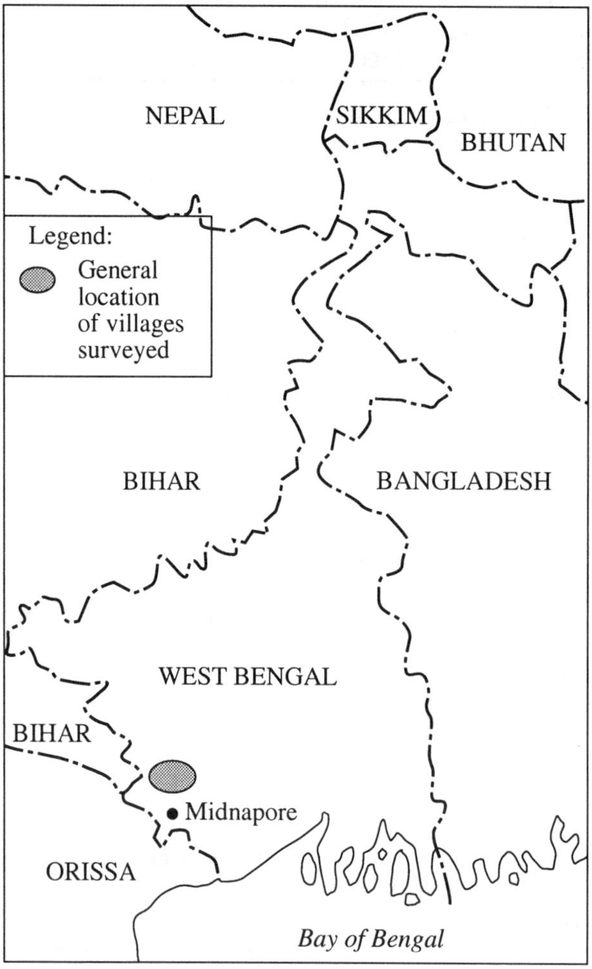

Figure 1 General location map for forest villages surveyed in West Bengal

The total sample consisted of 96 household heads, representing virtually all families in the villages of Atabanda (32 household heads), Barabugpichla (29) and Chandmura (35). The particular location of these villages is shown in Figure 2. Of these villages, Chandmura was most closely associated with the Arabari forest which, as mentioned earlier, was the scene of the earliest experiments with joint forest management in India.

The socio-economic conditions of the villages surveyed are rather similar. All villagers were Santals following the Sari religion and showed a high degree of economic dependence on nearby forests. Most of the villagers perceived that they belonged to the lowest economic group in relation to their community reference group. Table 3 summarises the sample and socio-economic characteristics for the villages surveyed.

Table 3 Sample and socio-economic characteristics for the Atabanda, Barabugpichla and Chandmura villages, West Bengal, 2000

Parameters	**Atabanda**	**Barabugpichla**	**Chandmura**
Name of the forest(s) used	Ghargra, Arabari	Barabugpichla, Moldangal, Birapatra, Bankumar	Maheshdubai, Backamati
Beat and Range[1]	Arabari	Kiyamacha, Nayabasat	Arabari
Scheduled tribe	Santal	Santal	Santal
Religion	Sari	Sari	Sari
No. in sample	32	29	35
Average family size	5.5	4.48	4.4
Average number of children	1.6	1.5	1.7
Families with dependent adults	13 (1 each)	7 (1 each)	7 (1 each), 1 (2 dependent adults)
Dependency ratio[2]	0.86	0.73	0.80
Upper economic status (perceived)	5	3	2
Middle economic status (perceived)	1	12	2
Lower economic status (perceived)	26	14	31

Notes: 1. Refers to section of forest used.
2. Dependents in relation to non-dependents.

Economic dependence of villagers surveyed on forest resources

Cash dependence

Where villagers are located in or near state forests in India, they are usually highly dependent on forest resources for their economic welfare. More than 80 per cent of households in the villages surveyed here obtained more than half their cash income

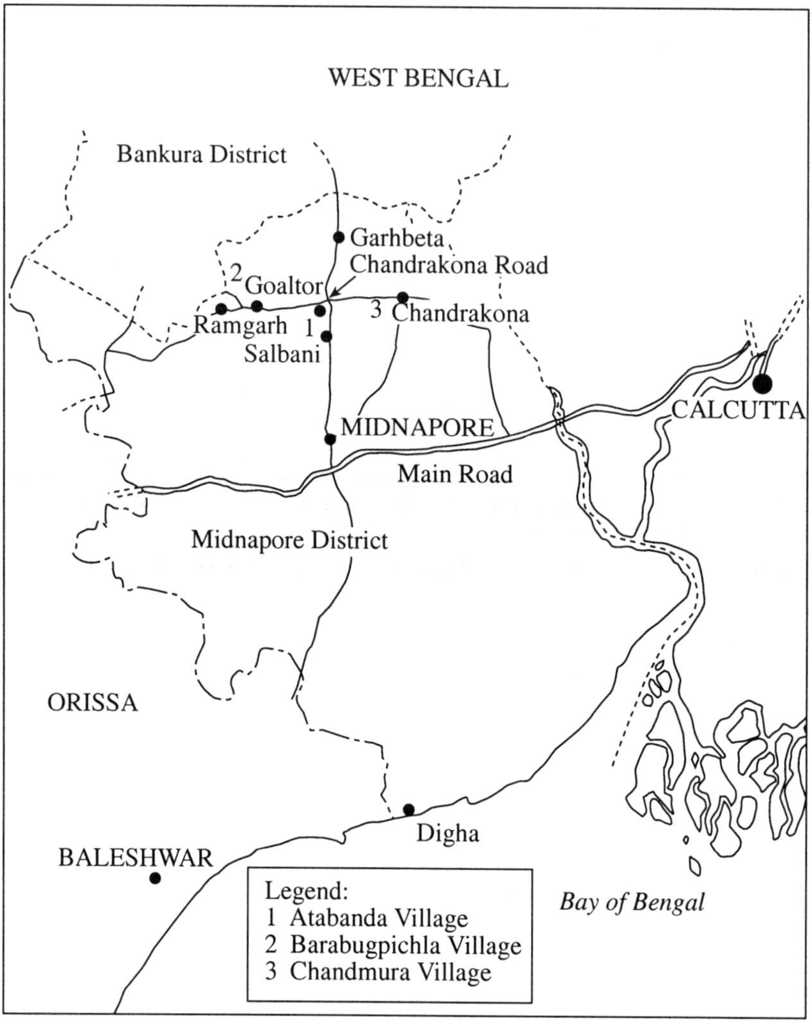

Figure 2 Specific location of the forest villages (Atabanda, Barabugpichla and Chandmura) surveyed

from forest resources, for example from products such as Sal leaves used for producing disposable plates for cash sales. The distribution of reported degrees of dependence of households in these villages on cash income from forest resources is shown in Figure 3. This distribution is based on 89 responses, since 9 household heads did not provide a response to the relevant question.

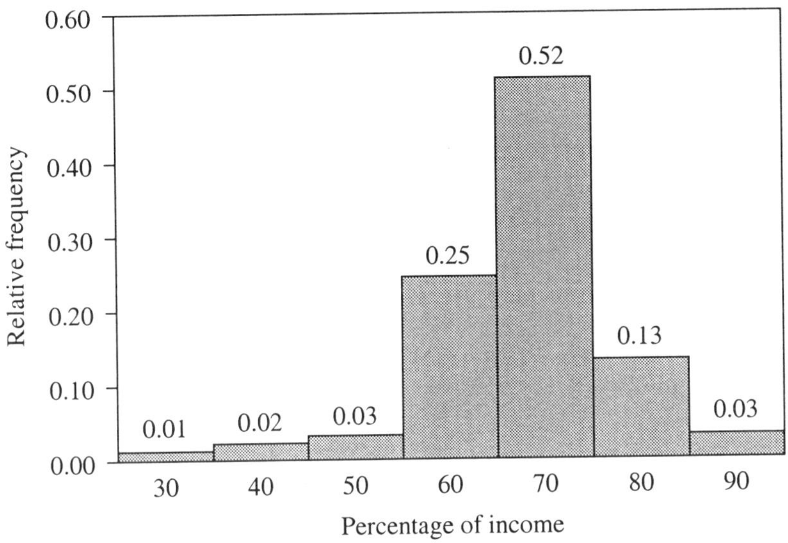

Figure 3 *Percentage of family household cash income from forest resources in villages surveyed in West Bengal. Relative frequency of responses, Atabanda, Barabugpichla and Chandmura combined, 2000*

Dependence on forests to meet basic family needs directly

There was also a high degree of dependence of the villagers on the forests to meet basic needs or economic requirements directly. Household heads were asked whether their household showed a high, medium or low degree of dependence on forests for various products for consumption. Overall, it was found that dependence was relatively high for building materials, for thatch material, for food, for fuel and for grazing livestock with dependence being somewhat less for herbs and medicine. Weighting a low response by 1, a medium one by 2, and high one by 3, the weighted average level of dependence is shown in Table 4.

Gender and the relative use of forest resources

Respondents were generally agreed that women made much more use of the forests than male villagers. Although 5.2 per cent of household heads did not answer this question, the 94.8 per cent who did stated that women made greater use of the forests than men. Furthermore, all those answering this question agreed that when women are able to use the forest and contribute more to the family's livelihood, they obtain more respect in their family. In declining levels of dependence, it was found that women were most dependent on the forest for collecting fuel, then food, then grazing

Table 4 Weighted average dependence on forest resources as reported by respondents in Atabanda, Barabugpichla, and Chandmura, 2000

Resources	Weighted average dependence
Building Material	2.88
Thatch Material	2.58
Food	2.46
Fuel	2.41
Grazing of Livestock	2.18
Herbs and Medicine	1.76

of livestock, collection of herbs and medicine, followed by collection of building material and then thatch material. The latter two activities tend to be male activities. The overall result is that village women are highly dependent for their family economic contribution on forest resources in these villages, and much more so than men.

Seasonal dependence on forest resources

All respondents agreed that they were very highly dependent on forests for their livelihood in some months of the year because of lack of availability of other economic opportunities. In order to see how important forest resources might be for 'insurance' purposes, respondents were asked: 'In terms of drought or a difficult season is your dependence for survival or livelihood on the forest high, medium or low?' 90 per cent of respondents said it was 'high', 9 per cent reported it as 'medium' whereas only 1 respondent, 1 per cent said it was 'low'. Thus, the forest plays an important role in the social security of these villagers. The importance of forests in providing social security for many villagers in developing countries has been previously pointed out by Chambers (1987, 1988) and Chambers and Leach (1989).

Sustainability of current forest use as perceived by village respondents

Respondents were asked whether they believe that their forests will contribute less to the income of their family in the future. 81 per cent said 'yes'. They mainly thought so because of declining forest cover and expected a rise in local population leading to greater competition for forest resources. The 19 per cent who said 'no' were mainly of the view that their future income could be maintained by better forest management and by the planting of cashew trees in the forest.

Specific threats of identified forest practices to livelihood

Nevertheless, all respondents stated that there were significant threats to their family's livelihood from a number of forest practices. Logging (which may be interpreted as excessive cutting of trees from the perspective of villagers) was ranked as the most serious threat, followed by reduction in forest size, overgrazing and others. Respondents were asked to indicate whether they regarded each of these forest practices as serious, medium, low or no threat. The responses are summarised in Table 5. Weighting the responses depending on the perceived magnitude of the threat by 3, 2 and 1 respectively, the weighted average pattern shown in Figure 4 emerges. Note that it is possible that the size of forest may have been interpreted by respondents as the size of trees in the forest. In any case, logging practices, failure to replant trees, reduction in forest size and overgrazing were all considered serious threats to the livelihood of families in these villages.

Table 5 Threats posed by various forest practices to family livelihood in the three rural villages surveyed in West Bengal in 2000

Forest Activity	Ranking of Threats	Frequency of Response	Relative Frequency (%)
Logging	Serious	86	89.6
	Medium	10	10.4
	Low or None	0	0
	Total Response	96	100
Failure to replant trees	Serious	67	69.8
	Medium	29	30.2
	Low or None	0	0
	Total Response	96	100
Reduction in forest size	Serious	34	35
	Medium	61	64
	Low or None	1	1
	Total Response	96	100
Overgrazing	Serious	7	7.3
	Medium	82	85.4
	Low or None	7	7.3
	Total Response	96	100
Others[1]	Serious	5	12
	Medium	33	78
	Low or None	4	10
	Total Response	42	100

Note: 1. Observations for others are incomplete. Atabanda had only 7 observations for others and Barabugpichla had none. However, Chandmura had 35 (all) responding observations.

Trends in variety of products for consumption available from the forest

Those interviewed were asked whether or not the variety of products available to them had increased, decreased or had been constant in recent years. One person interviewed did not answer. Of the 95 respondents answering, the majority (63.16 per cent) said that it had declined, whereas the remainder believed that it had increased mainly due to replanting of timber trees and the planting of cashew trees.

Trends in the variety of wild animals and plants present in the forest – that is trends in biodiversity

All respondents said that biodiversity had declined in their forest. This they attributed to such factors as a decline in forest cover combined with illegal cutting of trees. They

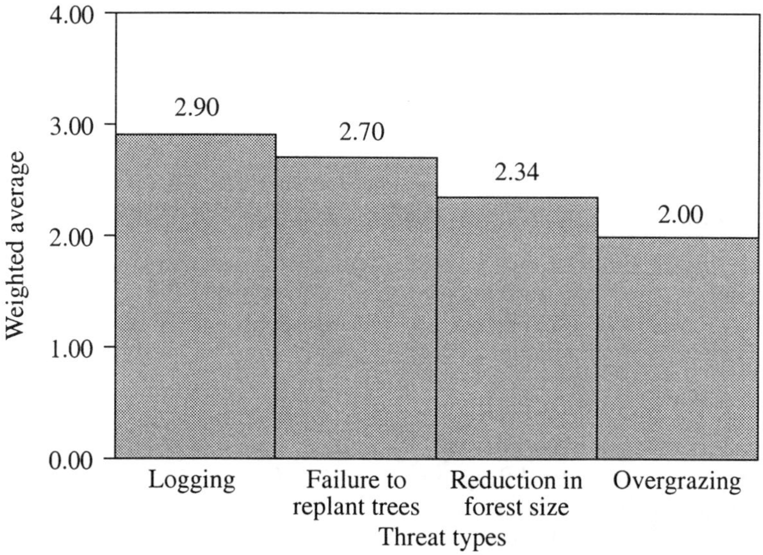

Figure 4 *Weighted threat to family livelihood of various forest uses in three rural villages in West Bengal, 2000*

suggested that this reduced available food for animals. An additional cause mentioned was the killing of animals. In this area, at least, it seems that the introduction of the JFM scheme is negatively associated with the preservation of biodiversity. While the relationship may not be a causal one, it seems that the JFM scheme has not stemmed a decline in forest biodiversity.

In particular, it might be noted that our survey results do not support the view of Mishra (1998, p. 263) that joint forest management has contributed positively to the preservation of biodiversity. Mishra (1998) specifically rejects the view of Robinson (1998) that collaborative or joint management of natural resources is likely to result in a loss of biodiversity in the long term. The fact of the matter seems to be that so far JFM has not stemmed a decline in biodiversity in the forests of West Bengal. A final assessment, however, requires more evidence.

Demand by villagers for forest-use value

It is probable that biodiversity *per se* is not a major goal for villagers. They appear to be most interested in changes in forest husbandry that increase the use-value of the forest to them. They suggested more planting of trees of greater use-value to them such as Sal, which provides valuable by-products for villagers and Amlaki, the fruit of which is eaten raw or pickled, consumed at home and also sold. More Neem trees were also favoured for purifying the air and these also produce valuable by-products that can be sold by villagers. In addition, the villagers believed that they would benefit by increased tree cover to improve conditions for the growing of wild mushrooms, potatoes and other vegetables as well as herbs and fruit trees. The assignment of more state forest land for social forestry was also favoured.

It is reasonable to conclude that current forest practices occurring under the JFM scheme are not maximising the value of forests from the perspective of villagers. Furthermore, the system seems inadequate to ensure sustainability of village economic benefits from the forests and it has failed to stem a decline in the variety of wild animals and plants available in the forests considered here as part of our survey in West Bengal.

Forest management issues and forest-dependent villages

Villagers were asked if they had any customary right to use their nearby forests and 95.87 per cent of respondents said 'yes' with the remainder answering in the negative. In fact, in West Bengal, because all the villagers interviewed belong to the scheduled Santal tribe, all have rights to traditional uses of the forests, such as the use of it for the type of economic activities listed in Table 4. However, none had the right to felling of trees for commercial timber sales. The WBFD reserved this right exclusively for itself.

Villagers were asked if the Joint Forestry Committee (Joint Forest Management Scheme) had improved the sustainable management of forests. The majority (96.8 per cent) of those responding (93) said 'yes' and 3.2 per cent said 'no'. Three household heads did not respond. Basically, joint forestry management was seen as a forward step, and the main reason given was that it reduced illegal felling of trees.

All except one family head said that families received 25 per cent of net revenue from the sale of timber in their forest beat (area). The one saying 'no' was from Barabugpichla and may have said 'no' because in that village the village council decided to use the last payment allocated to the village FPC for school building purposes. So, it was not assigned to individual families.

Nevertheless, when respondents were asked whether the income received as a result of the JFM scheme was sufficient to make them want to protect the forest from illegal timber felling, three did not answer, 83 said 'no' (89.25 per cent of those answering) and 10 (10.75 per cent of those answering) said 'yes'. It can be concluded that as far as these villages are concerned, the JFM scheme provides insufficient economic incentive to most villagers for them to want to prevent illegal taking of timber. In addition, all household heads who answered the question (93 out of 96) said that they did not get a fair share of the income from timber sold from their forest. They were concerned, for instance, that 'deals' were made involving forest officers where the price paid for the timber was below its market price.

It should be noted that income from harvesting timber is not continuous in all forested areas. This means that sometimes a village has no income from the JFM for several years. This has been the case for Chandmura village, which relies on a part of the Arabari Forest, because its relevant forest area is relatively degraded. The villagers of Chandmura are relatively poor with only one member having employment that brings a regular cash income. In these circumstances, the incentive to cooperate in illegal timber gathering is strong.

Despite the shortcomings of the JFM scheme, all respondents agreed that the scheme gives a higher return from logging and more benefits than non-protected forests, and that planted trees are more protected in state-controlled forests than in non-protected forests and that the former forests maintain greater capacity to assist poor families than the latter ones. All respondents believed, however, that forests would be better managed and provide greater returns to villagers under NGO management.

No evidence was found for the 'grassroots' village-based governance of the use and management of forest resources to which villagers had customary rights. There appears to be no effective mechanisms of governance for the allocation of use-rights between families within a village so *de facto* common-access to non-commercial timber resources seems to exist.

No strong governance mechanisms are present for regulating the management of forest resources used by the villages surveyed here in West Bengal. Furthermore, the villagers have a very limited input into management of the WBFD of forests for timber production. Their role is virtually restricted to helping protect forests against illegal harvesting of timber for commercial use. They have virtually no say in the extent of replanting of trees and the species planted. Furthermore, little silviculture seems to be practised by the WBFD. In informal interviews, the tribal groups interviewed complained of lack of consultation by the WBFD in relation to forestry management decisions. In contrast to claims by Mishra (1998), there was little evidence that indigenous knowledge was utilised in such decisions.

Most villagers interviewed believed that there is inadequate investment in tree planting. They agreed that, in principle, a fraction of the net returns from commercial timber harvesting should be invested in replanting and some suggested they would be prepared to forego a fraction of the village share of FPC funds to contribute. Declining levels of investment in tree planting in West Bengal in recent years are suggested by the figures in Table 2.

Discussion of concerns about Joint Forest Management

While the virtues of India's Joint Forest Management scheme have been widely acclaimed (for example, Mishra, 1998), our survey and interviews in West Bengal indicate that there are several issues of concern. Its shortcomings can be summarised as follows: While the JFM system reduces, to some extent, illegal cutting of forest trees, it does not eliminate it. Partly this is because the economic benefits obtained by villagers are low and shared by a number of villagers in the same village and by several villages in the same forest beat. In fact, as a forest becomes less productive, the incentive of villagers to illegally cut trees may increase. It seems that officers of WBFD are occasionally clandestine accomplices in such activities.

Replanting of trees (and investment in silviculture) is entirely dependent on funds available to the WBFD and its willingness to allocate funds for investment purposes. Villagers have little control of such activities. Most villagers interviewed in south West Bengal were of the view that the rate of harvesting of forest trees exceeds the rate of replanting, so forest cover is declining and the level of income from use of trees for timber is unsustainable. There was wide support from villagers for the suggestion that a proportion of net income from timber sales in their forest area be used for forest replanting and investment.

The management goals of WBFD are unclear but it seems that in the forest area surveyed, its goal is to 'maximise' the value of its timber sales. Its main emphasis in its management is on commercial timber yields with the value of non-timber products being an unimportant policy consideration.[4] This is a reflection of the fact that in this particular area, WBFD only receives income from sales of trees for commercial purposes and obtains no income from non-timber products. However, the latter products are very important contributors to the economic welfare of villagers. This can lead to conflicts in forest management between forest-dependent villagers and the WBFD. This is illustrated by Figure 5.

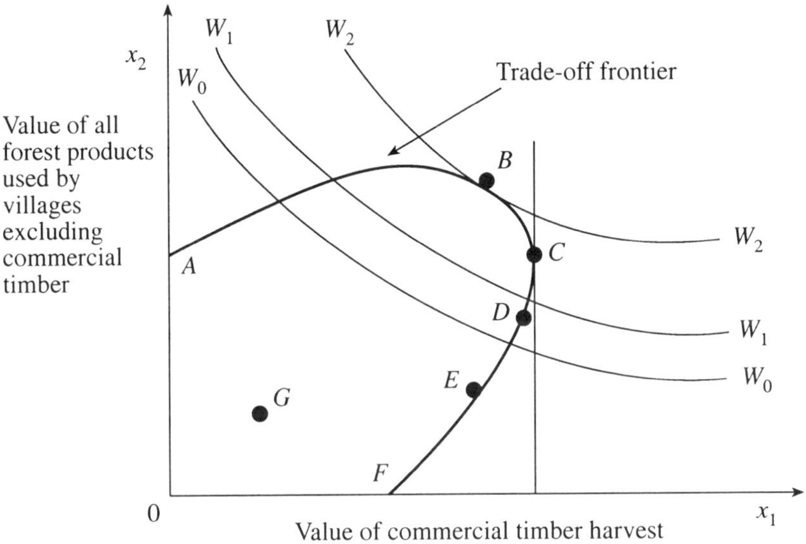

Figure 5 *Scope for conflict and cooperation in forest-use between villagers and WBFD, the state forest department*

In Figure 5, the curve *ABCDE* represents the trade-off frontier between commercial timber supply and all other products utilised by villagers and the indifference curves marked W_0W_0, W_1W_1 and W_2W_2 represent the collective preferences of the villagers. The ideal combination of products from the villagers' point of view corresponds to *B* but given that WBFD preference it to maximise the value of commercial timber production, its preferences is for the combination at *C*. If the WBFD is able to achieve point *C*, then welfare of villagers is below its maximum attainable level.

There is, however, no guarantee that the WBFD will be able to achieve point *C*. Even with the help of the JFM scheme, the best it may be able to do is to achieve the combination at point *D*. This, however, is superior both from its point of view and from the point of villagers to the combination at *E*, which might be the point achieved by the management strategies of WBFD in the absence of JFM. Open-access might result in a combination at point *G*, which is worse from the point of view of villagers than all the other alternative possibilities. The conceptual implications of this analysis accord with the survey responses obtained.

Furthermore, Figure 4 helps to emphasise the point that WBFD is not involved in total joint forest management with villagers. The WBFD only manages one type of resource in the forest and villagers the others, but there is no coordinated management of all the resources and village mechanisms of governance of those resources not managed by the WBFD are weak or non-existent.

The concept of total economic value (TEV) of forest use and management (see, for example, Harrison, 2000) can be used to raise a further issue: joint forest management by state forestry departments and villagers, even if holistic, is unlikely to maximise the TEV of forest use and management. In such cases, only two sets of stakeholders have an influence on forest-use decisions, namely the relevant forestry department and forest-dependent villages; the general public and other interest groups are not represented.

In such cases, direct use of forest resources is likely to be favoured both by forestry departments and villagers. Off-site economic values are likely to be ignored. Perhaps this issue can be illustrated by Figure 6. There the TEV of the management of a forest for producing commercial timber is considered as the independent variable. Possibly a state forest department would wish solely to maximise the value of commercial timber supply. Villagers will obtain greater TEV by less emphasis on this goal, notionally an emphasis of x_1 per cent in Figure 6. However, when all parties, including the general public are considered, the TEV for use of the forest for commercial timber production might be like the curve *GHJ*. This indicates that the maximum TEV of the forest under consideration for commercial timber is achieved when the degree of emphasis on commercial production of timber is only x_0 per cent, that is less than the villagers' emphasis on this aspect, and much less than the likely emphasis of a state forest department on commercial timber production.

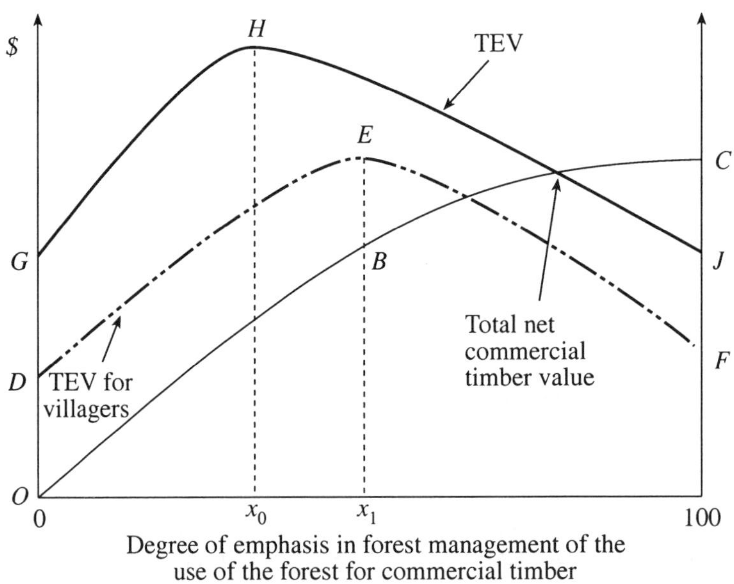

Figure 6 Joint forest management is unlikely to maximise the total economic value of a forest

Concluding Observations

In some parts of India, villagers, particularly tribals, remain heavily dependent on forests for their cash income, basic needs and survival. While in the distant past, most of these forests were communal property, they were assigned to the state following Britain's colonisation of India, and after India's independence the state still continued to 'own' these forests (cf. Tisdell and Roy, 1997). In practice, state forest departments have tried to manage these forests to maximise income from commercial timber production.

As time progressed, it became increasingly evident that this goal could not be achieved without the cooperation of villagers in and near state forests. The JFM scheme recommended by the Union Government was intended to help rectify this situation and possibly was designed mainly to reduce the illegal harvesting of trees for commercial purposes.

As outlined above, India's system of JFM is a very incomplete participatory scheme, and India's state forest system still seems biased in the main to the harvest of trees that can be sold for cash by India's forest departments.

Nevertheless, India's JFM is generally agreed to result in socially superior resource outcomes compared to *de facto* open-access. At the same time, corruption threatens the system. Ironically, the temptation for corruption and illegal logging seems highest in the most degraded or least productive forest areas. In addition, in West Bengal, the seemingly low level of investment in forest replanting and silviculture is of concern. It could be partly a result of state dominance of forestry and the possible siphoning off of funds by the state for other uses.

This study also found (in the villages surveyed) an absence of grassroots communal mechanisms for the management of those forest resources over which the villagers had effective control. Possibly such mechanisms existed in the distant past but they do not seem to be present now.[5] Thus, in this case, beneficial communal management of those natural forest resources shared by villages is lacking. It seems that the type of beneficial communal governance envisaged by Ostrom (1990) has yet to emerge or re-emerge in many Indian villages heavily dependent on forest resources. Village institutional mechanisms for the governance of the commons remain inadequate, both from a village as well as a wider community point of view.

Notes

1. A slightly revised version of a paper presented at the 'Ecosystem Conservation and Management' session of the 76th Annual WEA International Conference held in San Francisco, 4–8 July, 2001, chaired by Edward Barbier. Preparation of this paper has benefited from a small ARC Research Grant and the revision benefited from comments by Duane Chapman and other session participants. The usual caveat applies.
2. School of Economics, The University of Queensland, Brisbane 4072 Australia.
3. For a useful distinction between social forestry and joint forest management, see Hobley (1996, p. 63).
4. This may appear to be inconsistent with India's Forest Policy 1998. However, this policy is merely a recommendation of the Union Government. West Bengal has complied partly with this policy. Access of villagers in the neighbourhood of state forest to their forests has been legalised along with their direct use of forest resources, except trees intended for commercial sales, and in some cases, cashews to be sold commercially. These remain the property of the WBFD but under JFM, villagers receive a quarter share of the net income from sales of this produce by the WBFD.
5. It would, however, be a mistake to believe that all early societies had effective social mechanisms for the governance of common property. See, for example, Malm (1999).

References

Chambers, R. (1987), *Sustainable Livelihoods, Environment and Development: Putting Poor Rural People First*, IDS Discussion Paper No. 241, Institute of Development Studies, University of Sussex, Brighton.

Chambers, R. (1988), *Poverty in India: Concepts, Research and Reality*, IDS Discussion Paper No. 241, Institute of Development Studies, University of Sussex, Brighton.

Chambers, R. and M. Leach (1989), 'Trees as Savings and Security for the Rural Poor', *World Development*, **17**(3), 329–42.

Harrison, S.F. (2000), 'Total Economic Value of Multiple-use Farm Forestry and Non-market Valuation Techniques', in S.R. Harrison, J.L. Herbohn and K.F. Herbohn (eds), *Sustainable Small-scale Forestry: Socioeconomic Analysis and Policy*, Cheltenham, UK and Northampton, US: Edward Elgar, pp. 50–64.

Harrison, S. and A. Ghose (2000), 'Small-scale Forestry Systems in India', in S.R. Harrison, J.L. Herbohn and K.F. Herbohn (eds), *Sustainable Small-scale Forestry: Socioeconomic Analysis and Policy*, Cheltenham, UK and Northampton, US: Edward Elgar, pp. 165–89.

Harrison, S.R. and K. Roy (2000), 'Perceived Problems and Potential Role for Eucalypts in Farm Forestry Observations from East India', in S. Harrison and J. Herbohn (eds), *Socioeconomic Evaluation of the Potential of Australian Tree Species in the Philippines*, Canberra: Australian Centre for International Agricultural Economics, pp. 157–65.

Harrison, S.R, A.S. Ghose and J.L. Herbohn (2001), 'Lessons from Social and Community Forestry in the Tropics, with Particular Reference to India and the Philippines', in S.R. Harrison and J.L. Herbohn (eds), *Sustainable Farm Forestry in the Tropics*, Cheltenham, UK and Northampton, US: Edward Elgar, pp. 227–40.

Hobley, M. (1996), *Participatory Forestry: The Process of Change in India and Nepal*, London: Overseas Development Institute.

Malm, T. (1999), *Shell Age Economics: Marine Gathering in the Kingdom of Tonga, Polynesia*, Lund Monographs in Social Anthropology No. 8, Department of Sociology, Lund, Sweden.

Mishra, T.K. (1998), 'Users Become Managers: Indigenous Knowledge and Modern Forestry', *Economic and Political Weekly*, **33**(6), 262–3.

Ostrom, O. (1990), *Governing the Commons: The Evolution of Institutions for Collective Action*, Cambridge: Cambridge University Press.

Robinson, G.J. (1993), 'The Limits to Caring Sustainable Living and the Loss of Biodiversity', *Conservation Biology*, **7**, 20–28.

Tisdell, C. and K. Roy (1997), 'Good Governance, Property Rights and Sustainable Resource Use: Pacific Ocean Rim Examples', *The South African Journal of Economics*, **65**, 28–43.

Name index